The Psychology of
Social Interaction

INTERPERSONAL BEHAVIOUR
The Psychology of Social Interaction

Joseph P. Forgas
University of New South Wales

illustrations by
Richard Jones

PERGAMON PRESS
SYDNEY • OXFORD • NEW YORK • TORONTO • FRANKFURT

AUSTRALIA   Pergamon Press Australia, 19a Boundary Street,
                     Rushcutters Bay, N.S.W. 2011, Australia

U.K.   Pergamon Books Limited, Headington Hill Hall,
                     Oxford OX3 OBW, England

U.S.A.   Pergamon Books Inc., Maxwell House, Fairview Park,
                     Elmsford, New York 10523, U.S.A.

PEOPLE'S REPUBLIC   Pergamon Press, Quianmen Hotel, Beijing,
OF CHINA   People's Republic of China

FEDERAL REPUBLIC   Pergamon Press, Hammerweg 6,
OF GERMANY   D-6242 Kronberg, Federal Republic of Germany

BRAZIL   Pergamon Editora, Rua Eça de Querios, 346,
                     CEP 04011, São Paulo, Brazil

JAPAN   Pergamon Press, 8th Floor, Matsuoka Central Building
                     1-7-1 Nishishinjuku, Shinjuku-ku, Tokyo 160, Japan

CANADA   Pergamon Press Canada, Suite 104,
                     150 Consumers Road, Willowdale, Ontario M2J IP9, Canada

First Published 1985
Reprinted 1986, 1989

Copyright © 1985 Joseph P. Forgas

Cover design by Ingrid Padina

Typeset in Australia by Rochester Photosetting
Printed in Australia by Globe Press Pty Ltd

National Library of Australia Cataloguing in
Publication Data

Forgas, Joseph P.
    Interpersonal behaviour.

    Bibliography.
    Includes index.
    ISBN 0 08 029868 0.
    ISBN 0 08 029854 0. (pbk.)

    1. Interpersonal relations—Psychological aspects.
    I. Title.

158'.2

To Teeshie, Pono and Peti

CONTENTS

FOREWORD

We constantly need new textbooks in social psychology, to keep up with the rapidly changing state of research, and the emergence of new theoretical points of view. Authors of textbooks can provide a great service by presenting a fresh view of the subject, based on their particular knowledge and research experience.

This textbook provides a fresh view in more ways than one. It reflects the author's great expertise and extensive research in cognitive social psychology, it draws on Australian, British and European research as well as American, and it includes a number of 'new' topics not normally covered by previous books. Reference is made to a well-chosen selection of researches, including both classical studies, and many of the most recent investigations, including some by the author. They are well linked to some of the most important theoretical models. Theories and experiments are presented so lucidly as to make them sound easy. Indeed, the book is very well written and most enjoyable to read. A lot of interesting 'activities' are provided for the reader to complete which further enhance comprehension. At a number of points the book provides a novel and interesting integration of the literature. For example, Chapter 6 dealing with self-attribution brings together such topics as learned helplessness, research on the way people experience emotion, and the use of self-handicapping strategies, among others.

Joseph Forgas has a distinguished record of research in social psychology, and is now one of the best-known psychologists in Australia. He is the author of a large number of scientific papers, and has written or edited four other books. He is an enthusiastic researcher, and clearly enjoys his work as an investigator and a writer. He is expert at various forms of advanced statistics, and is one of the pioneers in the use of multidimensional scaling analysis in social psychology. He is a well-known figure not only among Australian social psychologists, but also in Britain (where he obtained his doctorate at the University of Oxford), in Germany (where he worked as a professor at the University of Giessen), and in the USA (where he has worked for prolonged periods at Stanford University while on study leave).

Social psychology is at an interesting stage in its development. The initial period of artificial laboratory experiments was severely criticised during the various 'crises' of the 1970s. The main outcome was a move towards field studies, an emphasis on cognitive processes, and the use of new and more ingenious research designs and statistical techniques. New areas of interest have continued to appear, and these are well represented in the book. For example, the study of attribution processes and lay explanations, research on non-verbal communication, and the study of social relationships are major new areas discussed here. A number of important practical applications have also emerged, such as the use of social skills training to help people with deficits in interpersonal skills, discussed in Chapter 16.

This excellent book should give a good start in social psychology to students from a variety of backgrounds, and should also be of practical benefit to the general reader interested in the social psychology of interpersonal behaviour.

Michael Argyle
Oxford, May 1985

PREFACE

Both in private life, and in our working lives, the ability to effectively engage in interactions with others is of crucial importance. This book is about the social psychology of the skills involved in everyday interactions between people. Although most interpersonal behaviours are performed automatically, without conscious reflection, the psychological processes involved can be extremely complex. The topics covered here include the way we perceive and interpret other people's behaviour, the way we form impressions about our partners, the use of verbal and nonverbal communication skills and impression management strategies, the development and management of rewarding personal relationships, processes of social influence, and the way we behave in groups.

There has been widespread general interest in these issues in recent times. Why is interpersonal behaviour so fascinating to a growing number of people? The unprecedented social, economic and political changes which have occurred in the last two or three centuries undoubtedly have had a lot to do with the fact that social interaction has become increasingly problematic for many people in industrialised mass societies. Our relationships with other people have become much more complex, diffuse and specialised than was the case in earlier times. A growing number of people suffer from isolation and loneliness, and find rewarding interaction and the establishment of supportive personal relationships increasingly problematic. The disproportionate growth of tertiary 'service' industries in all developed countries also means that 'people skills' have gained in importance relative to other skills in our working lives. For a great many individuals, skills in interacting with others now constitute an essential part of their professional working careers. This tendency is likely to accelerate in the near future, as technological advances free increasing numbers of people for employment in service-related jobs where face-to-face interaction is the major skill required.

Despite the obvious importance of interaction competence in contemporary life, reliable knowledge about the intricacies of social interaction processes is still in short supply. Many professional courses in fields such as management, law, nursing, medicine, social work, sales and education now also include material dealing with the psychology of social interaction. This book aims to provide a readable and concise (albeit selective) survey of current social psychological knowledge about interpersonal behaviour. It has been written for students and professionals in fields where understanding interpersonal behaviour is important. Apart from its use as a textbook, the volume should also appeal to laypersons with an interest in social interaction. No previous experience of psychology is assumed, and numerous exercises, activities, figures and illustrations are used to make the material easily comprehenisble to readers from a variety of backgrounds. The relevance of the material to everyday problems of social living is emphasised throughout.

The discussion follows a simple and logical sequence. Following a brief historical introduction (Chapter 1), in the first half of the book the two basic components of the interaction process are considered, person perception (Chapters 2-6), and interpersonal communication (Chapters 7-10). In the second half of the book we will turn to more complex issues, such as the nature and development of personal relationships (Chapters 11-13), social influence processes (Chapter 14) and interaction in groups (Chapter 15). The final chapter draws these various strands together, discussing the ecological, methodological and clinical aspects of interpersonal behaviour. Social interaction often involves complicated impression management, attribution and communication strategies, and these essentially cognitive skills are given particular attention throughout the book.

The important role of the surrounding culture in regulating interaction processes has also been strongly emphasised. We perceive, evaluate and form impressions about others on the basis of culturally shared stereotypes and person prototypes; the meaning of most of our verbal, as well as nonverbal messages depends on the conventions of our relevant culture; and close relationships are initiated, maintained and terminated in accordance with cultural requirements. It is in the course of everyday interaction that human beings, who have the unique ability to abstract and symbolise their experiences, cooperatively create a shared sense of social reality. Such shared representations of interaction episodes in turn guide our behaviour in similar encounters. Even such deep-seated personal qualities as our self-concept and self-esteem are social in origin, a reflection of how other people see us and react to us in our daily interactions.

Of course, most people are by definition already quite expert at social psychology. We all must possess a rich repertoire of social knowledge simply to function effectively in everyday situations. However, much of this knowledge is unsystematic, and most of it is implicit. A great deal of the fascination of the psychological research described here lies in the fact that it throws new light on something we see around us all the time: the way people get on with each other in day-to-day living.

I am grateful to many people and organisations who helped in the preparation of this book. I did much of the writing while occupying the Chair of Social Psychology at the University of Giessen, West Germany, and during a visit to Stanford University in 1984. I am grateful for the facilities and help I received at both institutions. Klaus Fiedler, Renate Muenzig, Stephanie Moylan and Gill Hewitt helped in various ways with the preparation of the manuscript, and several others read and commented on different sections of the book. Some of the research presented here has been financially supported by the Australian Research Grants Commission, and the Deutsche Forschungsgemeinschaft (DFG, German Research Society). But most of all, I am grateful to my wife, Letitia, who amidst all her other commitments found the time to read and correct every chapter several times over. And finally, thanks are due to my four-year old son, Paul, who provided many delightful moments of comic relief and diversion to interrupt the long hours of writing. Needless to say, none of the above mentioned persons or organisations bear any responsibility for this book, except perhaps Paul.

Joseph P. Forgas
Sydney, May 1985

1. Introduction: the psychology of interacting with people

1.

INTRODUCTION: THE PSYCHOLOGY OF INTERACTING WITH PEOPLE

This book is about the way individuals interact with each other in their daily lives, a topic which is of central interest to most people. We spend most of our waking hours in the company of others. It is of great importance to all of us that our interactions and personal relationships should be rewarding and successful. Interpersonal behaviour is not only an important aspect of our private lives. Increasing numbers of people work in fields where interacting with others is perhaps the main working skill required. With the growing economic significance of the various tertiary service industries, the ability to interact with people — the possession of 'people skills' — will become increasingly important in our working lives as well.

The study of how people solve the exceedingly complicated task of sharing their social lives with each other falls largely within the domain of social psychology. We will survey in this volume some of the knowledge accumulated to date by social psychologists on the processes and skills which make social interaction possible. We shall deal with issues such as person perception and attributions about people; the use of verbal and nonverbal communication; impression management strategies; the development and characteristics of human social relationships; and interpersonal influence and behaviour in groups. We will begin by taking a brief look at the discipline most directly concerned with the study of interpersonal behaviour: social psychology.

What is social psychology?
Human social behaviour has been one of the main preoccupations of philosophers, artists and laymen since time immemorial. In ancient times, classical philosophers such as Plato and Aristotle devoted much attention to questions such as: How is social life possible? How do many individuals, each unique, manage to live together successfully in a society? What is the form of government which best reflects the 'true nature' of people, and is best suited to harmonious social coexistence?

1

Questions such as these are still with us today, but we no longer seek answers to them in philosophy, and few believe that there is a single ideal view of human nature, which, once understood, will provide the key to understanding all social life.

Today, we attempt to apply scientific methods to the investigation of such problems. A whole branch of psychology — social psychology — is devoted to studying social behaviour. We may define social psychology as the study of how people interact with each other, and how their thoughts, feelings, behaviours or intentions are influenced by the actual, or implied presence of others (Allport, 1924). In this book we shall mainly focus on those findings of social psychological research which help to explain how people interact with each other.

Social psychology is not the only branch of science that deals with interactions between people. Sociologists have studied related problems for many decades, in an attempt to understand the way large-scale social systems work. Others, such as social anthropologists, typically study the social structure, customs and culture of small-scale societies. They have provided us with many interesting insights into the links between culture and interaction processes, something that is also of interest to cross-cultural psychologists (cf. Bochner, 1981). However, social psychology differs from these neighbouring disciplines in at least two respects.

'What are you trying to achieve, Humphrey?' Skilled interpersonal behaviour in sometimes difficult situations is one part of the working skills of increasing numbers of people, such as managers, salesmen, personnel officers, doctors and people in the helping professions.

Firstly, the methodology of social psychology places far more emphasis on quantified description and experimentation under controlled circumstances than is customary in either sociology or social anthropology. Secondly, social psychological research on human interaction has a psychological, rather than social or cultural orientation. We are interested in the role of psychological processes and variables in the way people interact with each other, and not in the explanation and understanding of the larger culture in which they live. But a hard and fast separation of social psychology from its neighbouring disciplines is probably impossible. There are many similarities as well as differences, and a greater awareness of sociological and anthropological research is regarded as highly desirable by many social psychologists. In this book we shall pay particular attention to the role of cultural and social influences in the way people interact with each other.

Social psychology and common sense
You may ask the obvious question: "Since most of us are already quite good at interacting with other people, what can social psychology possibly tell us that we do not already know?" In order to engage in successful social interaction, we must be able to accurately perceive, interpret and predict other people's behaviour, and to be good at communicating our thoughts, feelings and intentions to others. We must know a lot about the regularities of social life in order to adequately function as members of a society. This leads us to the first important characteristic of social psychology as a science. More than perhaps any other science, social psychology deals with human behaviour at the common, everyday, observable level, behaviour that we are all, by definition, 'experts' on (see Activity 1.1).

We all have certain theories, and perhaps even some data, on problems such as why people fall in love, under what circumstances they are likely to help each other, how they are affected by various nonverbal messages, under what conditions they will obey, conform to or resist others, and how their relationships develop and change. These are not only topics for social psychologists, but are also the everyday concerns of all of us. Since social psychology is so intricately tied to everyday problems of social living, the charge is sometimes made that social psychological findings and concerns are simply restating the obvious, or alternatively, that the results of social psychological studies sometimes manifestly contradict commonsense knowledge. What is the relationship between commonsense, 'naive' psychology and scientific social psychology?

First of all, we need to understand that commonsense and science are by no means mutually exclusive or contradictory avenues to understanding. Quite the opposite is the case: scientific hypotheses are often rooted in commonsense knowledge, and commonsense knowledge in turn is shaped and changed by scientific results. Examples of this

ACTIVITY 1.1
Commonsense and Science:
Looking with 'New Eyes' at Social Behaviour

In this activity you are asked to do something very simple. Try to observe a social interaction between two people in a public setting, for example on the street, in a shop, in a pub, etc., for about five minutes. While making this observation, (a) try to record every single move that these people make as if you were seeing it for the first time in your life, and (b) after the observation, ask yourself why each move was performed. In other words, try to look with 'new eyes' at something you have seen many times before. While doing this apparently simple task, you should experience the major difference between commonsense knowledge and scientific knowledge.

The people you are watching are using their commonsense knowledge to engage in an interaction. Minute by minute, they are sending and receiving verbal and nonverbal messages, often without thinking about them, or even becoming aware of what they are doing. Their knowledge is implicit and automatic. You as an observer have a very different perspective. The interaction for you is an object of study. By placing yourself outside this episode, and by using the empirical method of systematic observation, you should be able to notice many nuances and regularities which will remain hidden from the people you are observing. For example, you may discover the way your subjects use nonverbal signals such as distance, orientation, posture or gaze to communicate status, interest or attitudes towards their partner. You may notice how they automatically coordinate their turn-taking in speaking, their visual orientation and major shifts of posture. Even the simplest and most banal interaction between people is full of regularities which are readily discernible once the scientific stance of an observer is adopted, instead of the commonsense approach of the participant!

interdependence abound in social psychology. Most of us have an implicit knowledge and understanding of the way nonverbal communication is used in everyday interaction. We can interpret signals such as eye gaze, gestures, facial expression or tone of voice without the need to first consult lengthy scientific manuals. We can 'read' these cues, and understand their message as communicating interest, anxiety or happiness without thinking, almost automatically.

But we do not know everything about such nonverbal messages, and not everything that we do know is correct. The task of social psychology is to make such 'implicit' knowledge 'explicit'; to describe under controlled circumstances exactly what each nonverbal signal communicates under various circumstances. When does eye gaze signal intimacy, and when does it signal competition and aggression? Are there differences between different cultural groups in the use of facial expression to communicate emotions? What is it about a person's tone of voice that tells us that he is anxious or upset?

These questions go beyond the knowledge necessary for engaging in everyday interaction. To answer them, we must use sophisticated methods such as systematic observation, interviews, questionnaires, field studies and other specific techniques such as laboratory experiments (see Chapter 16 for a description of psychological methods). The results of such investigations in turn influence 'commonsense' knowledge. After you read Chapters 8 and 9 dealing with the results of nonverbal communication research, you will probably think differently about these signals: your commonsense understanding about these phenomena will be changed. Scientific research and commonsense knowledge are thus mutually dependent on each other.

Another example of the links between social psychology and commonsense is provided by research on conformity. Studies have shown that when confronted by a majority, most people can be pressured into uttering apparently unreasonable views or judgments (you may read more about this in Chapter 14). A well-known study by Solomon Asch showed that many people are even prepared to make obviously wrong judgments about something as simple as the length of different lines, when several people in front of them (in fact collaborators of the experimenter) confidently make the same clearly incorrect judgments. This research has become so well known over the years that it is now almost part of our popular thinking. Our everyday theories about group pressure and conformity are profoundly affected by it. Nowadays, it would be difficult to repeat some of these early studies in a first-year course of psychology, as most students would have already heard about them. Their commonsense knowledge now incorporates an understanding of conformity based on laboratory research.

Despite the complementary nature of science and everyday knowledge, social psychology is often criticised as being 'obvious' or 'just commonsense'. What is the reason for this? I think the main problem is that our commonsense knowledge is both very rich and very unsystematic at the same time. We have commonsense explanations for almost everything, and also for the opposite of almost everything. In that sense, there is not much that can be described in the domain of social life by social psychologists that would strike us as entirely unexpected. And when such non-obvious phenomena are indeed discovered, the commonsense reaction is usually disbelief. There is good reason to question our commonsense knowledge when it comes to generalisations about social behaviour. Commonsense rarely tells us the specific conditions under which certain behaviours occur and when it does, it is often mistaken. You may get some feeling for this conflict by completing Activity 1.2.

As we have seen, scientific research is not only stimulated by, but also helps to shape our 'naive' theories about social behaviour. Keep these examples in mind as you read this book. Often, you will be reading about phenomena which are part of your direct experience in interacting with people. But the theories and explanations offered by researchers go beyond our everyday theories, trying to provide more general and valid explanations.

ACTIVITY 1.2
Is It Just Commonsense?

We all have a great deal of commonsense knowledge about everyday social life. In this Activity, your commonsense knowledge will be put to the test. Please read each of the questions about various aspects of social interaction below carefully, and answer them as accurately as you can.

1. First-born siblings tend to seek the company of other people MORE/LESS than do later-born siblings.

2. People prefer to be ALONE/WITH OTHERS when they feel anxious about something.

3. Europeans use very DIFFERENT/SIMILAR facial expressions in communicating emotions to those used by New Guinea tribesmen.

4. Verbal messages are MORE/LESS effective in communicating attitudes towards another person than are nonverbal signals.

5. Accuracy in judging others IS/IS NOT a personal ability of certain people.

6. The way a person looks DOES/DOES NOT influence whether he/she is held responsible for a crime or transgression.

7. Committing a mistake makes a highly competent person LESS/MORE attractive.

8. Most people think that a person expressing unusual opinions is LESS/MORE likely to really believe in them.

9. If you pay a person for doing something he/she enjoys doing, he will engage in this activity MORE/LESS frequently in the future.

10. People WOULD/WOULD NOT refuse the orders of an experimenter to give dangerous electric shocks to another person.

11. Groups tend to take MORE/LESS extreme decisions than do individuals.

12. To detect deception, it is best to pay most attention to a person's FACE/ARMS AND LEGS.

The items listed above are just a small sample of the kind of issues both social psychology and commonsense knowledge deal with. If commonsense was indeed a good guide, you should have been able to give correct answers to most of these questions. On the basis of existing social psychological research, which you will read about in more detail as you progress through this book, the right answers should have been: 1 more; 2 with others; 3 similar; 4 less; 5 is not; 6 does; 7 more; 8 more; 9 less; 10 would not; 11 more; and 12 arms and legs. The problem is that in most cases, commonsense makes one alternative to these questions almost as plausible as the opposite: both answers could be the 'obvious' ones under some circumstances. As these examples show, something is indeed wrong with the entire argument of 'obviousness'. Since every kind of human reaction is conceivable, it is of great importance to know which reactions occur most frequently and under what conditions. This is precisely how social psychology differs from commonsense understanding.

Social interaction past and present: an historical digression

It is perhaps a curious historical fact that the scientific study of social interaction as such is only a very recent phenomenon. Of course philosophers, writers, poets and painters have always devoted a great deal of their time to the recording and expression of the many thoughts and feelings which are generated when people interact with each other. But the actual process of how such interactions occur was not considered a topic worthy of systematic study until recently. It may well be that our age is unique in that what was a natural process in the past, namely interacting with people, has itself become a problem — an object of study and scrutiny. Why this growing interest in how people interact with each other? How does our age differ from previous periods in the interaction possibilities it provides us with? Let us step back in history and compare our own social environment with those of earlier ages.

For most of human history, people existed in social environments such as the family, the clan, the tribe, the medieval village or even the small town where they knew personally almost everybody around them. Social interaction was the very essence of everyday life in such small face-to-face communities. Just imagine for a moment the kind of existence which was natural for human beings for most of our evolutionary history. Life from birth to death was almost entirely lived within the confines of the same small, familiar group. It was an environment populated by family, friends and acquaintances. Every person whom you would meet in the course of your daily activities would be familiar and well known — practically never a 'new face', a stranger.

Compare this kind of interaction milieu with the kind of social life we experience in large scale, Western industrialised societies. We are surrounded by strangers, and seeing a known face on the street or in a public place is very much the exception rather than the rule. Many sociologists have speculated about the implications of this drastic transformation from small-scale communities to large-scale societies for the way we interact with others. In a small community, or 'primary group' (see Chapter 15), where everybody knows everybody else, and where people meet each other on a regular daily basis, the life of the community and the life of the individual are practically indistinguishable. Social interaction is the very focus of existence, and every person has innumerable occasions to build up relationships with everybody else. Nobody can remain anonymous or separate himself from others. Under these conditions, interacting with others is probably as natural as eating or breathing — it is certainly not in any way problematic for the majority of the individuals.

Continuous interaction with a few others in a primary group was, of course, not as idyllic as it might appear. The price of social cohesion and adjustment was social bondage and loss of individual freedom. Although living in communes or communities may sound nostalgically desirable to some people nowadays, those who have tried it can testify that such small primary groups are often much more tyrannical than anything one is likely to experience in our society of strangers.

The demise of small communities and the emergence of large-scale societies is a very recent process, only a few hundred years old. Historians point to the French Revolution as the turning point in this development. Until the eighteenth century, the small group, the family, clan or village reigned supreme as the primary social unit for most people. The French Revolution and the philosophy of the Enlightenment prepared the ground for a dramatic change. The rationalist philosophy of the Enlightenment asserted that individuals, if freed from the bondage of communal life, can be independent, rational and happy without the support (and restrictions) of 'primary groups'.

Compared to the tens of thousands of years it presumably took for human beings to adapt to the requirements of living in small, familiar groups, these last few hundred years have perhaps been too short a period to enable us to adjust to the gigantic transformation which has taken place in our social relationships. It would be futile to argue here whether the philosophy of rationalism, the bourgeois political ideals of the French Revolution, or the demands of the industrial revolution were primarily responsible for the demise of simple face-to-face communities. What matters is that this age-old framework of social life has largely disappeared in industrialised societies during the last two centuries. We are now all faced with the task of leading our social lives under conditions to which we, as a species, have had little time to adapt.

What are the characteristics of social life in the kinds of large-scale societies which have appeared in the last couple of centuries? Our world is populated with strangers, by the faces of the thousands whom we encounter on the street and forget immediately, people with whom we shall never exchange a single word or gesture. Those people whom we do know, such as friends, relatives or acquaintances, are scattered both geographically and socially; we only see them intermittently, and our lives intersect only to a small degree. We may participate in work, entertainments, domestic life or hobbies with other people, but rarely does one other person satisfy our requirements in all these various activities. We have highly specialised and differentiated social lives, meeting certain people for work, others for entertainment, and building a family and a home with yet others.

Most of the people we encounter in everyday life, such as shop assistants, bus conductors, nurses, clerks or policemen are total strangers to us. We have to interact with such people from time to time, but we rarely come to *know* them. Many of us — psychologists, doctors, nurses, salesmen, teachers, receptionists or lawyers — also spend most of our working lives interacting with near strangers. One might almost say a new class of 'professional interactors' has emerged to satisfy the many human needs of an increasingly mobile and impersonal society.

Social skills and shyness
Social interaction under these circumstances is indeed a bewildering task requiring considerable skill. If you reflect for a moment on the subtlety and complexity that is involved in behaving correctly when talking to a friend, chatting with a shop assistant, having a discussion with your romantic partner or buying a car from a salesman, it should become clear what an enormous task, and sometimes burden, social interaction has really become. If you are not convinced, perhaps you might try the little experiment in Activity 1.3 yourself.

The number and complexity of the rules we must know to interact with people is enormous, and we must apply them instantaneously, unhesitatingly and correctly all the time if we are to engage in social interaction successfully. The vast diversification and specialisation of our many social relationships require interactive skills which are many times more complex than those necessary in a 'primary group'. So it is perhaps not so surprising, after all, that social interaction as a 'problem', a topic for research, emerged only relatively recently. That interacting with others is increasingly problematic is also suggested by the growing number of people who have difficulties in this field, many experiencing fear of social encounters, and shyness.

Undoubtedly interacting with people can at times be a difficult task for most of us. Almost everybody finds encounters such as a job interview, an argument with a boss, or the first few minutes of meeting a new person more stressful than usual. However, for many people, simple and common encounters may be just as difficult or stressful. Shyness, a common label for such reactions, was defined by Zimbardo (1982) as the "code word for all the forces within each of us, as well as those pressures from society, that combine to isolate us from one another. In this sense, shyness includes fear of (and prejudice toward) people who are different, and social situations that are novel" (p. 466). Nor is the experience of

---

ACTIVITY 1.3
The Rules of Interaction

As a first step, try to observe yourself in the same objective manner as you observed others in Activity 1.1, while engaging in an interaction with (a) your romantic partner, (b) your best friend, (c) a shop assistant, and (d) a member of your family. Note down all the important features of your behaviour in each of these interaction situations (for example, looking deeply into the eyes of your romantic partner, looking confident and disinterested to the shop assistant, keeping on nodding while your friend is talking, and so on). Then mix up these rules arbitrarily, and try to perform the interactions according to such new, arbitrary rules (for example, look deeply into the eyes of the shop assistant, look confident and disinterested to your friend, etc.).

The discomfort that you (and your partners) feel while engaging in these performances should tell you that some very important rules and conventions of social life are being violated. The point is that these rigid rules of interaction were always there, and you must have learnt to use them well without even thinking about your actions. By interfering with the usual routine governing these encounters, you may become aware of just how complex and subtle your performance must be to satisfy all of the numerous requirements and conventions which regulate social life.

shyness itself a recent phenomenon. Darwin (1890) noted almost a hundred years ago that "Shyness seems to depend on sensitiveness to the opinion, whether good or bad, of others....Some persons...are so sensitive that the mere act of speaking to almost any one is sufficient to rouse their self-consciousness .... almost every one is extremely nervous when first addressing a public assembly, and most men remain so through their lives" (pp. 330-2).

In an extensive research project on shyness, Zimbardo (1982) found that about 40 per cent of adult Americans described themselves as shy. The proportion of shy people was highest in Japan (60 per cent) and lowest in Israel (30 per cent). Shyness is a negative experience for those afflicted by it, even though outsiders sometimes find shyness endearing, particularly in females. The most common situations provoking shyness involve interactions with strangers, members of the opposite sex, novel or highly structured situations, and interactions with people of higher status. Most of these interactions are, of course, typical of the social routine of impersonal, large-scale societies.

One way of thinking about shyness is as the absence of certain interactive skills that other people possess. These skills can be perceptual (the correct perception of other people and situations), cognitive (the ability to form correct and sensitive judgments), behavioural (knowing what to say and do in a situation), and affective (reacting with appropriate rather than inappropriate emotions). People are not born shy, or socially skilled. We acquire the necessary skills in childhood and continue to refine our interactive strategies in adulthood. The social psychological research we shall survey in this book will be largely concerned with strategies which make up a skilled social performance. By making these usually implicit skills explicit (see Activity 1.1), researchers provide us with a welcome opportunity to reflect on our own particular interactive skills.

Approaches to studying social interaction
What is really going on when two or more people interact? What are the possible ways of studying and explaining interaction processes? We may seek explanations of interactions between people on at least three levels.

(1) We may look at the larger, all-encompassing social, economic and political systems which, to a considerable extent, influence our attitudes and personal behaviours. We may call this the macro-sociological approach. The underlying idea is one of social determinism: that social systems and their norms causally determine how individuals behave. Factors such as social class, race, income or the ruling political system all influence our interactive behaviours. Middle-class people interact differently from working-class people, and many forms of spontaneous interaction common in Western

societies are totally absent from the interactive repertoire of people living in traditional societies or in totalitarian countries.

(2) The second alternative is to study social interaction processes from the perspective of the individual. We may call this the psychological approach. Factors such as upbringing, intelligence, physical appearance, individual attitudes or communication skills all play a major role in how people interact with each other. We react very differently to good-looking rather than plain-looking people (see Chapter 12), and most of us have our private theories about people, their characteristics and motivations (see Chapter 3 on such implicit theories of personality) which determine how we behave towards them.

(3) The third possibility is to study interaction processes at their own level, as not reducible to either social or individual explanations. Rather than assuming that interactions between people are the *product* of either social (approach 1) or individual (approach 2) variables, we may turn the argument around and suggest that larger social systems and individual personalities are in fact *created* in the course of social interaction. It is important that we appreciate the originality of this idea, most clearly represented in the writings of symbolic interactionists such as George Herbert Mead (1934), Cooley (1902) and others (Stone and Farbermann, 1970; etc.). According to this view, when people interact with each other, several things happen. Because we are intelligent beings who are able to symbolise and abstract our experiences, the result of every new interaction is that we build up some general knowledge and expectations about proper ways of behaving in that situation.

Just think about your first university lecture, first group seminar, or first day at a new workplace: interactions such as these establish in our minds ideas of regulated, predictable interaction routines. All large-scale social systems ultimately depend on such shared expectations in the minds of their members for their order, regularity and predictability. It is in the course of daily interactions that social systems come to be established, affirmed or changed. But our interactions with others are also a major source of our view of ourselves, our enduring personalities. We have to establish, defend or, if necessary, revise our notions of self as a result of interacting with others (see also Chapter 10). It is in these two senses, then, that symbolic interactionist theorists believed that interaction is the source of both social and personal realities.

In the rest of this book we shall discuss many aspects of how people interact with each other, in couples or in larger groups. The majority of the research we shall consider comes from the psychological tradition, described as approach 2 above. Social psychologists perhaps more than other researchers have contributed to our knowledge of how various individual characteristics influence interactions between people, but you will find frequent examples of both sociological and symbolic interactionist explanations as well. The role of status, class and demographic variables in the development of friendships is an example of a sociological explanation (Chapter 12). As a theoretical approach, however, the third alternative, symbolic interactionism, is perhaps the most promising. It is the only approach which treats interactions between people as not reducible to other processes. Most recent developments in social psychology are moving in that direction as well (cf. Farr, 1981). Recent research on people's ability to perceive, represent and think about the social world around them paves the way towards understanding exactly how such knowledge is acquired in the course of interacting with others (Forgas, 1981).

Models of human nature and social interaction
As we have seen above, systematic research on how people interact with each other is a fairly recent development, but interest in the nature of human social behaviour is, of course, much older. From antiquity to this day, many people have sought to understand the riddle of human sociability by creating general theories of human nature. The most obvious (and perhaps the least helpful) way of explaining human behaviour is simply to suggest that it is the expression of some deep-seated need or drive, or better still, that it reflects universal 'human nature'. Allport (1968) in his review of the history of social psychology called such explanations 'simple and sovereign' theories, since they seek to explain all human behaviour in terms of one single principle. Since many of these theories survive to this day, even in psychology, it may be instructive to mention some of them briefly (see Activity 1.4).

Hedonism, or the assumed tendency of human beings to seek pleasure and avoid pain, has been an influential explanation of human social behaviour ever since Epicurus. Of course, people do not simply seek to maximise pleasure and minimise pain in the immediate situation — otherwise nobody would ever go to a dentist, or listen to possibly boring lectures at university. Philosophers such as John Stuart Mill, Jeremy Bentham and Herbert Spencer developed this idea further, suggesting a complex 'calculus' on which people rely to work out the actual and expected costs and benefits of each action in each relevant present and future situation. Going to the dentist may thus also be seen as an act of hedonism, since it reduces the likelihood of suffering from toothache in the long run!

This idea has found its way into psychological thinking. Behaviourists who use concepts such as reward, reinforcement or punishment to explain social behaviour are essentially followers of the simple and sovereign theory of hedonism. Many theories of social interaction

ACTIVITY 1.4
Simple and Sovereign Theories

Read the two brief stories below, and try to decide the possible reasons why the person acted in the way described.

1. During the lunchbreak, John made an effort to sit at a table with other people he did not know very well.

2. When doing her shopping the other day, Ann struck up a conversation with a woman in the supermarket who was pushing a small child in her shopping trolley.

Please tick the explanation(s) you think are most likely to apply to John's and Ann's behaviour

Why did he/she do this?	John	Ann
In order to derive enjoyment	—	—
In order to feel more independent and strong	—	—
In order to be kind to others	—	—
Because it seemed reasonable to do so	—	—

These explanations illustrate the way simple and sovereign theories often may be used to explain otherwise incomprehensible or unclear social behaviours. The list above offers you the simple and sovereign theories of hedonism, power, altruism and rationality as alternative explanations for actions which in themselves are quite meaningless. By assuming that a person has a 'hedonistic', 'egotistic', 'altruistic' or 'rational' motivation, or a combination of these, we can account for social behaviours in terms of these general theories of human nature. Just as you probably found it quite easy to use such explanatory devices to make sense of John's and Ann's actions, social philosophers, until the first quarter of this century, often relied on similar kinds of explanations.

processes also capitalise on the same idea. According to such views, people engage in social interaction with each other only as long as the actual and potential benefits of doing so outweigh the costs.

Apart from pleasure-seeking, the search for *power*, control and authority may also be used as a simple and sovereign explanation of social interaction. Nietzsche was a well-known exponent of this philosophy. Machiavelli, the Italian Renaissance writer, became well known on the basis of his detailed advice to rulers in his book *The Prince* describing the best (and most cynical) way of acquiring and maintaining power.

A third possibility is to account for human behaviour in terms of the universal tendency to *altruism*: are people perhaps guided by a desire to do good, and to help each other as much as possible? Altruism as a simple and sovereign theory of social behaviour has much to recommend it. Explaining why people cooperate, help each other or even make sacrifices for others can be more difficult than explaining aggression and violence. Unfortunately, a combination of altruism with evolutionary notions takes much of the gloss away from this idea of apparently selfless human sociability. Evolutionary theorists suggest that by helping those nearest to us (family, friends, relatives) we are in fact helping the survival of genetic characteristics similar to ours. Even self-sacrificial behaviour may thus be selfish in the biological sense, since it ultimately helps the survival of those to whom we are related (Dawkins, 1976).

At least since the French Revolution, another simple and sovereign theory, *rationalism*, has been gaining increasing acceptance. It suggests that human beings are essentially intelligent and reasonable decisionmakers who regulate their social behaviours by rationally considering and weighing the alternatives available to them. Many influential theories relevant to interaction processes are based on this

'*Do you think life is a vale of tears, Reverend?*' The search for simple and sovereign theories to explain all human behaviour is as old as humanity itself — such explanations as hedonism, egoism, altruism or rationalism in their various guises are still with us today, often implicit in the theories of psychologists!

implicit assumption. Attribution theory (Chapters 4 and 5) assumes that people behave like 'naive scientists', trying to infer the causal antecedents of other people's behaviours as a means of creating order and predictability in their social lives. This model of human behaviour also has found many adherents in cognitive science, who believe that by programming computers to make decisions similar to human beings we may come to understand the bases of human behaviour as well.

Perhaps as a reaction to the dominance of rationalism, the first few decades of this century saw a resurrection of explanations of human behaviour emphasising emotions and irrationality rather than rational thinking. Foremost among them was Freud's *psychoanalytic* theory, seeking to explain all human behaviour in terms of the unconscious ebb and flow of emotional and motivational energies. Although most of Freud's propositions turned out to be unamenable to empirical evaluation, and are thus not part of scientific psychology, many of his ideas and concepts continue to play a crucial role. His idea of ego defences to describe the dynamic, motivated character of dealing with threatening information has many relevant applications in the study of interaction processes. Many biases in the way we perceive and explain other people may be due to such ego-defensive distortions (Chapter 5).

Scientific theories of human interaction
The dominance of such simple and sovereign theories was broken by the emergence of scientific psychology in the second half of the nineteenth century. In 1908, two textbooks of social psychology appeared which foreshadowed much of the later development of the discipline. William McDougall's book took an individualistic, psychological perspective, arguing that a variety of drives, such as curiosity, self-assertion and repulsion, lie at the root of social behaviour. The other textbook, by Ross, was more sociological in orientation: he proposed that social processes such as imitation, suggestion and conformity are the forces which shape our interactive behaviours. By 1924, social psychology clearly emerged as an experimental, scientific discipline which approached social behaviour from the perspective of the individual (Allport, 1924). It is not particularly surprising then that most of the evidence relevant to interaction processes comes from this psychological tradition.

The following decades were a period of rapid expansion in social psychological research. *Behaviourism*, emphasising the role of external rewards and punishments in the regulation of behaviour, was a dominant theoretical orientation until fairly recently. Indeed, many simple and relatively inconsequential behaviours can be readily manipulated by offering rewards and punishments. Verplanck (1955) showed, for example, that simply by systematically giving reinforcements such as "I agree" or "You are right" in a conversation whenever a person expresses an opinion, a dramatic increase in 'opinion-giving behaviour' can be achieved. However, behaviourists tended to ignore the active, creative inner processes influencing social behaviour.

Another school, *Gestalt psychology*, sought to restore balance by paying particular attention to the way internal processes and representations determine the way we perceive and interpret the world. Solomon Asch (see Chapter 3) applied this idea to person perception, suggesting that we automatically create meaningful, whole images when forming impressions about others. Lewin used similar principles in his *field theory*, suggesting that the way we subjectively perceive and experience our environment and behaviour possibilities at a given time (our 'life space') is the major determinant of social behaviour.

In recent decades the *cognitive* orientation has been increasingly dominant. The basic assumption of this model is that to understand social behaviour, we must be able to accurately analyse the perceptions, cognitions and information processing strategies of people as social actors. Current research on person perception and attributions is a good illustration of this theoretical background. According to this view, person perception is basically a process of information integration which can even be modelled using simple arithmetical principles (Chapter 4). In the last few years, research on how we remember people ('person memory') has also had a major influence on this field.

There are, of course, many other theories and approaches we could have listed here. The point is that social psychology is a multi-theory science: no single view of human behaviour has an absolute monopoly. Theories have the function of helping us to organise the empirical observations already collected, thereby guiding researchers in asking the right questions next time. As we come to look in more detail at some of the processes briefly mentioned here, this organising function of theories should also become clearer. We shall have more to say, in the last chapter, about the methods used by social psychologists, by which time you will be better able to appreciate some of the problems involved.

Some suggestions for using this book
There are many books on the market which profess to tell you about interacting with people. Most of these will offer you some simple and readily comprehensible recipe as the universal explanation of all interpersonal problems. Such books can be both entertaining and insightful, and you are likely to get plenty of opportunity to reflect on your own interpersonal strategies while reading them. Unfortunately, few of these books really have a sound empirical basis for their simplistic analyses of human behaviour. This does not matter too much, of course, if you treat them as literature — entertaining but not necessarily true.

The present volume is based on an entirely different approach. It seeks to describe and summarise existing scientific knowledge on matters relating to human social interaction. The aim is to summarise and discuss the results of relevant empirical investigations. There is, as yet, no single comprehensive model or theory, no unique model that would explain all interaction phenomena. Social psychology is indeed a fairly young science, and its achievements do not, as yet, include the development of general theories. Its findings are more in the nature of collected observations and regularities, not always consistent with each other.

For all that, I believe that the studies you will read about in this book, and what they say about aspects of social interaction, are no less fascinating than are literary works. And they have the advantage of scientific testability: it is always possible to determine whether the predictions of these studies are correct or not by simply repeating them. Many of the results you will read about are fascinating, and some, no doubt, will strike you as less surprising. Not everything that is relevant could be included here — this would require several volumes of this size. The selection is by definition personal.

If you are interested in any of the studies mentioned in the book, or would like to follow up a particular area in more depth, the best idea is to look at some of the original papers and books listed in the References at the back of the book. Any university library should be able to help you locate these source materials.

The text also includes numerous Activities. These are usually small, easily done practical tasks which should give you a sense of personal experience and involvement in the material you are reading. They may be in the form of a brief questionnaire, some thought-provoking questions, or instructions for a minor experiment or observational project which you can carry out without too much investment of time or energy. It is unlikely that you will immediately rush off to carry out each Activity as you come across it in reading the book. But do try to read the instructions, and attempt to do the practical work when you get a chance.

The content of the book is organised according to a clearcut logical scheme. We begin with person perception and attributions, progress through verbal and nonverbal communication and impression management strategies to the study of social relationships and interaction in groups. The first three chapters (2, 3 and 4) deal with processes of person perception, a necessary preliminary skill to engaging in social interaction. The next two chapters summarise research on how we make attributions about other people (Chapter 5) as well as ourselves (Chapter 6). We then turn to the problem of interpersonal communication, the major component of interacting with people. Verbal communication (Chapter 7) and nonverbal communication (Chapters 8 and 9) are discussed, before turning to the strategies regulating such communications: impression management (Chapter 10).

The next three chapters deal with the nature and development of social relationships, an inevitable consequence of all social interaction (Chapters 11 and 12), with special attention given to intimate relationships (Chapter 13). Finally, in the next two chapters we survey social influence processes (Chapter 14) and group behaviour (Chapter 15). The last chapter (Chapter 16) deals with three important issues: the ecology of social interaction, the methods of social psychological research, and finally, the applications of research on interpersonal behaviour to social skills training and therapy.

2. Perceiving other people: the problem of accuracy

2.

PERCEIVING OTHER PEOPLE: THE PROBLEM OF ACCURACY

In order to engage in successful social interaction, we must first be able to correctly perceive the people we are dealing with. Person perception is one of the most important and at the same time most complex tasks we all face in everyday life. How can we tell whether a person is genuinely friendly or simply ingratiating, arrogant or just proud, honest or deceitful, irresponsible or enterprising? Almost everything that human beings do or say can be interpreted in a variety of ways. Yet if we want to be successful in our interactions with others, we must be able to correctly interpret, understand and predict other people's behaviour.

Just imagine what would happen if a person was wrong in his/her judgments about others most of the time. His expectations about people would often be mistaken, and his communications misdirected. Interaction with such an individual would become painfully embarrassing, even impossible. Such a person would almost certainly end up being socially isolated, unable to establish meaningful personal contacts with others. The ability to see others and ourselves as we really are, which requires considerable practice and skill, is thus very important for all of us. How do we accomplish this task? This is the central question that person perception research has tried to answer.

Person perception may also be seen as the first, crucial stage in any interaction between people. We must first perceive and interpret other people before we can meaningfully relate to them. In addition, during an interaction we are also engaged in the continuous monitoring of the persons we are dealing with. This monitoring is another important aspect of person perception. Finally, every social encounter results in the formation of certain impressions, expectations and predictions about the people we have just met. Person perception thus always plays an important role in the initiation, maintenance and termination of social interactions. It is for this reason that we shall start our discussion of social interaction processes in this book with the problem of person perception.

Physical versus social perception

Social perception, such as the perception of people, differs from the perception of physical objects in important ways. For one thing, while the perception of objects in the physical world (physical perception) is mainly directed at immediately observable 'surface' characteristics (size, colour, weight, taste, and so on), the perception of social objects, such as people, is predominantly concerned with characteristics which are not immediately observable, but must be inferred (for example, intelligence, attitudes, character, and so on). This means that social perception judgments are much more complex and difficult to make than judgments about the physical world. It also follows that we are likely to make mistakes far more often in perceiving people than in perceiving objects.

This would not matter too much, if we could at least readily improve on our judgments of people when they prove false. However, because of the 'hidden' nature of personal characteristics, a mistake in person perception (such as believing a person to be self-confident when in fact he is not) is much more difficult to detect, let alone to correct, than a mistake in physical perception. After all, if we make a mistake in assessing the size of a stone or a piece of furniture, the mistake will become quite obvious when we take a second look, and can be readily corrected by more careful observation. This is not the case when it comes to most judgments about people. Social perception is largely based on inferences about hidden qualities, while physical perception is not.

Apart from the inherent difficulty of judging internal characteristics in person perception, there is another much more serious problem. When it comes to judgments about people, we are rarely unbiased observers. Typically, we have pre-existing feelings, attitudes and motivations which

The differences between physical and social perception. Mistakes in perceiving physical objects usually concern readily observable characteristics, which can be corrected by repeated observation. Mistakes in social perception are much harder to detect and correct, since they concern internal, unobservable qualities of people.

influence our judgments from the beginning. For example, the perceived similarities and differences between ourselves and the people we judge can be important sources of biases. We are more likely to see good characteristics in people who are similar to us, and bad characteristics in people who are very different.

We often have a vested interest in seeing certain classes of people in a biased way. Few people manage to have a completely objective view of their bosses, their parents, their lovers, or even their subordinates, for that matter. Psychologists call such distortions 'motivational biases', and we will discuss them in more detail in subsequent chapters. With the added difficulty of detecting and correcting our mistakes, such personal biases in person perception are a serious threat to the accuracy of our judgments. Sometimes, such personal biases can even become a source of self-fulfilling prophecies: seeing our boss as an authoritarian could make us behave towards him in a way that will really turn him into one! Despite these difficulties, most of us manage to do a reasonable job of perceiving most people most of the time. How do we achieve this remarkable feat? We shall devote the first few chapters of this book to discussing the processes underlying person perception judgments.

Areas of person perception research

Social psychologists have looked at a number of aspects of person perception judgments over the years. The first obvious question which was addressed is: exactly how accurate are we in judging others? For the reasons outlined above, as well as on the basis of everyday experience, it seems that person perception judgments are quite often inaccurate. Yet there are many situations in which it is very important indeed that we perceive people accurately. Very many important decisions in our society are made on the basis of how we perceive people, ranging from the election of a political leader to the selection of an applicant for a particular job. Can we improve the accuracy of such person perception judgments? Is it possible to find people who are particularly good judges of others? If yes, what are the characteristics of the 'good judge'? Questions such as these were among the reasons why social psychologists first began to study person perception problems.

Apart from problems of accuracy, psychologists also looked at a number of other problems of person perception, which we shall discuss in later chapters. One such question concerns the influence of our pre-existing ideas about people, so-called *'implicit theories of personality'*, on the person perception process. The study of such implicit theories has given us some interesting insights into the fixed categories people use to judge each other. Another much studied problem is the way we form *impressions* about others. What sorts of techniques do we use to organise the many different kinds of information we have about a person into a coherent total impression? A further important area of research is how we make inferences and attributions about characteristics of people which are not immediately assessable on the basis of the observed information. How do we decide, for example, why a person behaves in a particular way? How do we decide when a person is personally responsible for an action? The study of such inference processes, *attribution research*, has been a most active field of research for the past few decades. However, before progressing to these areas, let us first look at the problem of accuracy in person perception judgments.

The accuracy of person perception judgments
During our everyday interactions, we tend to take it for granted that the assessments we make of other people are by and large correct. Is it really the case that most of us are reasonably accurate in perceiving people? Are there individuals who have the gift of being more accurate in judging others than most of us? Can one train people to be better judges of each other? For understable reasons, questions such as these were amongst the first problems investigated in person perception research. Because judgments about people are so important in everyday life, the issue of accuracy is clearly of the foremost practical relevance. There are many examples in modern society where we rely on person perception judgments in making crucial decisions. Just think of the faith we tend to place in eyewitness testimony, or the judgements jury members,

---

ACTIVITY 2.1
Who is a Good Judge?

Please give your answers to each of the questions below, with a short outline of why you believe your answers to be correct:

1. Do you believe that some people are better judges of persons than others?

2. If yes, what are the characteristics of 'good judges' in your opinion?

3. How can we decide whether a person perception judgment is in fact accurate? For example, if we judge a person to be 'friendly', 'self-confident' and 'warm', how can we determine whether our judgments are correct?

When you have written down your answers, keep your piece of paper in front of you while you are reading the rest of this chapter, to see how far your ideas have in fact been confirmed by research.

policemen, or interviewing panels make of other people. Just how reliable are such perceptions? You may be confronted with some of these issues more directly as you complete Activity 2.1.

In order to objectively study the accuracy of judgments about people, three things are necessary: (1) a way of presenting a person, usually called the 'target' or the 'stimulus', to the judges, (2) the collection of the responses from the judges indicating their perception of that person, (the target) and (3) a reliable yardstick, or 'criterion measure' against which the accuracy of the judgments can be established. There are many different ways of accomplishing each of these tasks, as the summary table below shows.

TABLE 2.1
A SUMMARY OF THE TECHNIQUES USED IN PERSON
PERCEPTION ACCURACY RESEARCH

1. Techniques for presenting a stimulus person for judgment:
   — in person (direct face-to-face meeting or interview)
   — in person (observation from behind a one-way screen)
   — on videotape
   — on motion picture
   — on photograph(s)
   — on tape recordings
   — using test scores or attitude scores on standardised instruments
   — using personal documents (letters, drawings, autobiography)
   — relying on the past personal experiences of the judges

2. Techniques for collecting person perception judgments:
   — ratings on bipolar scales
   — predictions of the target's future behaviour
   — prediction of judgments of the target by experts, e.g. psychiatrists
   — predictions of the target's performance on standardised tests
   — ratings of the target on adjective checklists
   — ranking the target person against other people
   — open-ended descriptions of the target
   — decisions made about the target (e.g. employment, grades given, etc.)

3. Criteria used for evaluating the accuracy of judgments:
   — scores of the target on objective psychological tests
   — information provided by the target (e.g. self-ratings)
   — assessment of the target by familiar others (e.g. friends)
   — judgments by work colleagues or superiors
   — demographic or other factual information
   — directly observed traits or behaviours

Adapted from Cline, 1964, p. 224

What is an 'accurate' judgment?
One of the major difficulties in studying accuracy is to decide what the *real* characteristics of the person judged are, against which the correctness of our perception may be assessed. In other words, what is the truly 'accurate' description of a person? This turns out to be a much more difficult question to answer than most of us suspected. Because most judgments about people concern features which are not directly observable (traits such as friendliness, selfishness, extroversion, and so on), how can we determine with absolute certainty the real characteristics of a person? Should we use objective psychological tests? Should we ask the target himself? Should we ask his/her best friends? Each of these possibilities has been used, and each has its serious shortcomings. Tests are not perfectly reliable and valid, people are nor unbiased in judging themselves, and friends may know just as little about certain characteristics of a person as a perfect stranger. We are faced with the problem that there may not be an absolutely correct and accurate way of describing people to use as a reliable yardstick. On most characteristics, we can describe people only in approximate terms. This means that in measuring person perception accuracy, we are often forced to use a yardstick which we know is also inaccurate.

Accuracy in perceiving emotions
While judging people in terms of enduring personality traits is quite difficult, it is often sufficient if we accurately perceive our partner's current, short-term emotional reactions. Knowing whether our conversation partner is interested or bored, happy or sad, tense or relaxed at this moment may at times be more important than knowing whether he is generally an extroverted, supportive, shy or dominating person. Trying to infer the current emotional state of a person is a special case of person perception judgment. How good are people in general in performing this more limited person perception task?

Facial expression is perhaps the most important information source we have about a person's emotions. Darwin was among the first to use empirical methods to study the expression of emotions in man and animals (see also Chapter 8). Several researchers following in his footsteps asked two interrelated questions: (a) How far is it possible to accurately perceive a person's emotional state from facial expressions? and (b) Are these facial cues the same across different cultures? Early studies used a simple method: subjects had to judge the emotional state of a person from photographs, which were taken while that person participated in an emotion-arousing situation. In a study by Landis (1924) for example, the target people were photographed while engaging in such emotion-arousing situations as looking at pornographic pictures, receiving an electric shock, listening to music, feeling around for frogs in a bucket of water, or sawing off the head of a live rat (!). Landis (1924) found that judges were generally not very good in detecting the emotions expressed by the photographed targets, and targets themselves reacted with a variety of different expressions to the same situation.

In a similar study, Sherman (1927) asked his subjects to judge the emotion expressed by babies photographed while hungry, surprised, angry or in pain. Again, most judges were quite inaccurate. The problem with both of these studies is that we really do not know what emotion the targets were really *experiencing* — so how can we tell whether the judges rating their facial expressions were accurate in detecting it or not? After all, the same situations (for example, listening to music, receiving an electric shock, being hungry or sawing off the head of a rat) may lead to very different emotional reactions in different people (for example, fear, depression, arousal, anger, and so on). The first lesson from these investigations is that people rarely react with a single, pure emotion to a complex situation. Rather, several or even mixed emotions may be experienced and communicated. It is not very surprising then, that subjects could not detect these complex emotional messages without knowing more about the situation in which they occurred.

In more recent research, Izard (1971) and Ekman, Sorenson and Friesen (1969) selected photos of faces expressing very basic emotions in a pure form (joy, sorrow, anger, fear, disgust, surprise, and so on), and found that most subjects could now indentify the facial expression signalling the emotion with high accuracy. In addition, Ekman also found that subjects from very different cultures (such as New Guinea tribesmen) were also able to accurately perceive the emotions communicated by these photographs of Caucasian faces. The results of the earlier and more recent studies together indicate that people are quite good at identifying basic, pure emotions from facial cues. But in realistic situations, our facial reactions are often too individual, mixed and complex to make the same degree of accuracy possible as can be achieved when judging 'pure' emotional expression.

However, in real-life interactions we do not rely on facial expression alone to judge a person's emotional state. The surrounding situation, our past encounters and the previous sequence of communications all provide us with useful additional cues to help to interpret mixed and fleeting facial expressions. It seems likely that our accuracy in deciphering emotional messages in real-life encounters is generally better than the early studies by Sherman and Landis suggest, simply because we usually know much more about the surrounding situation than their subjects did. We will return to the issue of how nonverbal messages are used in social interaction in Chapter 9. Detecting emotions from facial expressions is thus a relatively simple person perception task. Frequently, however, we have to make much more difficult judgments about a person's intentions, character traits and likely future behaviour.

Accuracy in the perception of personality traits
A common purpose of person perception judgments is not just to identify a short-term emotion in somebody's face, but also to correctly perceive the long-term, enduring personal characteristics of people. We have already seen that a major problem in research on accuracy is to decide what is the 'real' characteristic, relative to which the correctness of judgments may be measured. An even greater problem is that people do not behave consistently from one situation to another. A person who is friendly in some situations (for example at work, at parties) may still be very unfriendly in others (for example with in-laws, with neighbours).

ACTIVITY 2.2
Studying Person Perception Accuracy

By completing this activity, you may get some feeling for the problems involved in studying person perception accuracy. In the table below, you are asked to make a number of person perception judgments. In the first column, labelled 'Friend', rate one of your friends or acquaintances on each of the scales shown on the left-hand side. In the next column, labelled 'Self', rate yourself on exactly the same scales without showing him your judgements. In the third column, labelled 'Friend's self rating', ask your friend to rate him/herself on the same scales without showing him your judgements. Having collected this information you can now analyse your data in a number of ways.

RATING SCALES (1=very much true 5=definitely untrue)	1 FRIEND	2 SELF	3 FRIEND'S SELF RATING	(1)-(3) ACCURACY	(2)-(3) ACTUAL DIFF.	(1)-(2) PERCEIVED DIFF.
1. Reads a lot	—	—	—	—	—	—
2. Is dominant	—	—	—	—	—	—
3. Often talks about politics	—	—	—	—	—	—
4. Is friendly	—	—	—	—	—	—
5. Dresses well	—	—	—	—	—	—
6. Is honest	—	—	—	—	—	—
7. Likes dancing	—	—	—	—	—	—
8. Is competent	—	—	—	—	—	—
TOTAL SCORES				☐	☐	☐

TAKE LOWER SCORE FROM HIGHER SCORE IN EACH CASE

1. Using your friend's self rating as the criterion, as is often done in person perception research, you may calculate the accuracy of your perception of him/her, by adding the differences between each of the two sets of judgments in columns 1 and 3 (take lower score from higher score, and add the differences). This will be your *accuracy* score.

2. You can also take a separate look at how accurate you were in judging behavioural characteristics (scales 1,3,5,7) as against personality characteristics (scales 2,4,6,8), by working out the accuracy scores for these two groups of scales separately. Usually, people are better at perceiving concrete behavioural details than personality characteristics which require inferences.

3. Next, you should look at the *actual* differences between you and your friend, by calculating the differences between your self rating and his/her self ratings (columns 2 and 3).

4. Finally, you can also analyse the *perceived* differences between your friend and yourself, by calculating the differences between your rating of yourself, and your rating of your friend (columns 1 and 2).

There are quite a few things you should consider after completing this activity. How satisfied are you with using your friend's self ratings as your criteria of accuracy? Can you think of other criteria measures you could have used for each of the scales? Can you see how your rating of yourself and ratings of your friend are related? Were you more accurate in judging behavioural as against personality characteristics? What sort of things were likely to influence the accuracy of your judgments? As you can see, the problem of studying person perception accuracy is more complicated than it first appears!

Whose perception is accurate — the workmates who think he is friendly, or the in-laws who think he is not?

Psychologists studying personality characteristics are increasingly aware of the fact that our 'personality' is not a permanent and unchanging entity, but partly depends on the situation we find ourselves in. Even people we know very well can be judged to have very different characteristics depending on whether we encounter them at a party, at somebody's house, or in an academic colloquium (Forgas, Argyle and Ginsburg, 1979). Further, our perceptions of others also frequently depend on how those people are similar to or different from ourselves. Activity 2.2 will give you some idea about the links between judgments of ourselves and judgments of others.

What can we say about the accuracy of person perception judgments given the various problems outlined above? The extensive research effort on person perception accuracy yielded mainly contradictory findings. Vernon (1933) found, for example, that while some people were accurate in rating their friends, others did a better job of judging strangers, and different people again were the best judges of themselves. Other studies reported that the empathic ability of a person was related to person perception accuracy. In a review of most previous research, Taft (1955) found little evidence for a general trait of person perception accuracy. In different studies, good judges were variously found to be more artistic, more intelligent, with better academic performance, better emotional adjustment and integration, some interest or knowledge of drama and art, and working or studying in fields other than the behavioural sciences (Taft, 1955).

This last finding is not as surprising as it may at first seem. People trained in psychology, for example, have a tendency to pay too much attention to individual differences. As a result, they often over-differentiate between target persons, and tend to exaggerate observed differences. This accounts for their poorer accuracy scores. Other factors which were found to influence accuracy include the degree of acquaintance between the target and the judge, the amount of extrapolation (inference) required for the particular judgment, and the complexity of the specific target to be judged (Cline, 1964). Accuracy improves if the person to be judged is well-known to us, the characteristics are directly observable and not based on inference, and the target is simple rather than complex.

These are hardly surprising conclusions. The generally disappointing results of the search for the 'accurate judge' are at least partly due to the inadequate definition of the problem. What exactly is involved in making an 'accurate' judgment? According to Cronbach (1955), accuracy in judging others is not a single, unitary characteristic of people, but is composed of several, often unrelated skills and factors. People who are good in perceiving the *general* features which characterise a group of persons (stereotype accuracy) are often not very good in differentiating between single individuals within such a group (differential accuracy). The same applies the other way around.

Judges also differ in the way they use various rating scales. For example, some people tend to use only the middle range, others prefer extremes in their judgments. These differences also influence the accuracy score a person obtains in an experiment. Which group do you belong to, on the basis of your ratings in Activity 2.2? Can you see how simply using more or less extreme ratings in this Activity could have made your judgments seem more or less accurate? How far did you rely on typical group characteristics (stereotype accuracy), and how far on individual characteristics (differential accuracy) in judging your friend? As you can see, person perception accuracy is thus not a simple skill, but a process dependent on complex, multi-component variables.

It is for that reason that training people to be accurate observers of others often has a counterproductive effect. Such training usually concentrates on differential accuracy, emphasising individual differences. As a result, trainees (just like psychologists) will tend to exaggerate differences between people, seeing greater extremes than in fact do exist. This helps to explain the curious results of some studies suggesting that specialised training and more detailed information decreases rather than increases the accuracy of person perception judgments. Crow (1957) found that judgments of people by medical students who received special training were less accurate than judgments made by completely untrained students. The first group tended to over-emphasise individual differences (overdifferentiation). Gage (1952) reported that judgments made of people on the basis of only very general information were more accurate than judgments made following a period of direct contact with the person in question. The reason for this decrease in accuracy is again that individual features were exaggerated after a personal encounter.

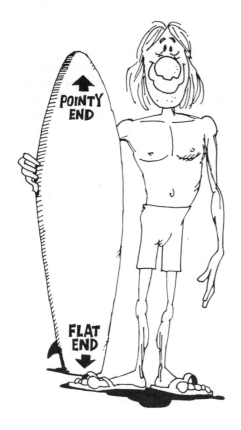

This is Bruce, the surfie. Look at him carefully — do you know the kind of person he is? Many of our person perception judgments are based on the stereotypes we have about people. You may know nothing about Bruce, but know quite a lot about surfies, so it should not be too difficult to guess Bruce's other characteristics. Such stereotypes can both help and hinder the accuracy of our judgments, depending on how biased our stereotypes are.

On the basis of later research specifically analysing each of Cronbach's (1955) components of accuracy (Cline and Richards, 1960), it appears now that any generality in accuracy across targets is mainly due to stereotype accuracy (the ability to identify the general features of 'types' of people). This seems quite surprising, since we often associate accuracy with a fine-grained understanding of the unique, personal characteristics of the people we perceive. Quite the opposite is apparently the case: our judgments will be more accurate more often if we concentrate on correctly identifying the general, typical characteristics of the group a target person belongs to, without worrying too much about the special, singular features of a particular individual. Other factors have also been found to influence the accuracy of our person perception judgments. These will be discussed in the following section.

The effects of mood on person perception judgments
The accuracy of judgments of people is also influenced by the temporary reactions of the judge. Surprising as it may sound, the way a person feels at the time of making a judgment has a noticeable effect on his/her accuracy. It seems that a person in a good mood is far more likely to identify positive, desirable characteristics in others than is a person in a bad mood. People experiencing a positive feeling state were found to rate ambiguous facial expressions as more positive, while people in a bad mood judged similar expressions as more negative (Schiffenbauer, 1974). Recently, Clark et al. (1984) found that people who were themselves experiencing emotional arousal were more likely to identify 'aroused' emotions in others. This effect is not specific for judgments of people, either. Ratings of material possessions (such as consumer durables), or pictures of neutral scenes can be just as much affected by the way a person feels at the time (Clark and Isen, 1981).

In an intriguing series of studies, Schwarz (1984) found that such superficial influences on mood such as nice weather, unexpectedly finding a coin, being in a pleasant, relaxing room, or knowing that your favourite soccer team has done well are sufficient to change how people judge their happiness, and their satisfaction with their work, housing or even life in general!

What happens when people have objective evidence, such as a videorecording of the target's social behaviour, to base their judgments on? Would they still distort their judgments depending on their emotional state? Forgas, Bower and Krantz (1984) videotaped a number of subject pairs while they were engaged in easy or difficult interviews. One day later, the same people were put into a happy, positive, or a sad, negative state using hypnosis, and they were asked to look at the videotape and judge their own, as well as their partner's behaviour in terms of the social skill displayed. Those subjects who experienced a positive mood at the time saw far more positive and fewer negative behaviours both in themselves and in their partner. Those subjects who were feeling badly, however, saw many more negative acts in their own behaviours, but not in their partner's (see Figure 2.1).

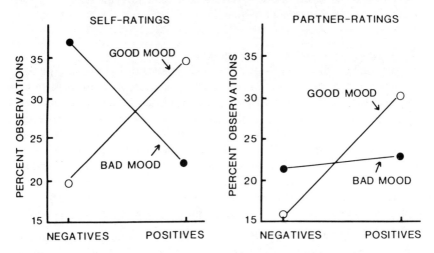

FIGURE 2.1 The effects of mood on person perception judgments. Subjects in a good mood perceived more positive acts and fewer negative acts in both their own and in their partner's interactions than did subjects in a bad mood (After Forgas, Bower and Krantz, 1984).

How can we explain such mood-induced distortions in person perception judgments? Social perception is both selective and inferential: we can only concentrate on a small part of the total information, and what we see will partly depend on the concepts, ideas, or interpretive categories that we have available in our minds at the time. (See also the next chapter on implicit personality theory, and Kelly's personal constructs.) According to the network model of Gordon Bower (1983), the mood state we are in will influence the constructs available to us to interpret social behaviours, by selectively activating those categories which were previously associated with a mood.

When you feel happy, more positive, happy thoughts, constructs and personal characteristics are activated, and consequently you tend to use these constructs to interpret the inherently ambiguous social behaviours of others. As a result, you will perceive positive, happy instances in the behaviours of others and yourself. The opposite would be the case in a bad mood state. In Figure 2.1, people probably judged others less negatively than themselves out of politeness. It is not 'done' to see bad behaviours in others, whereas there are no such restrictions on judging ourselves when we are in a bad mood.

It is for similar reasons that ambiguous or neutral non-social stimuli, such as pictures or scenes, are also perceived in a mood-consistent manner. Clark and Isen (1981) reported such a mood-bias effect in judgments of scenes. To the extent that person perception is both more complex and more ambiguous, mood-dependent biases in judging people are likely to be even more severe, and a considerable threat to the accuracy of our judgments of people.

Stereotyping as a source of inaccuracy

We saw earlier that identifying the characteristics of the group a person belongs to can be an important aid in accurate person perception judgments. We all need, and use, such simplified images of groups of people to help us with the task of classifying our environment. However, our ideas about the typical characteristics of a group can often themselves be distorted. Even in the unlikely case that we have a very accurate notion about what groups such as 'Italians', 'blacks', 'football players', 'surfers' or 'Hungarians' are *really* like, these characteristics do not necessarily apply to all the unique individuals we encounter. Stereotyping not only helps, but also hinders our person perception judgments.

Walter Lippmann, the famous columnist, was one of the first to use the term 'stereotype' to refer to the categorisation of people. The most common, and most insidious stereotypes have to do with ethnic, racial and national characteristics, and are particularly evident in multi-ethnic societies, such as the US, Australia and Canada. In a well-known study, Katz and Braly (1933) found that Americans had clear and rather negative stereotypes of Turks, Negroes and Jews. In Australia, attitudes towards Aborigines and certain migrant groups may similarly be affected by stereotyping (Taft, 1959). Stereotyping may also influence our ability to discriminate between members of a stereotyped group. Do you find it more difficult to differentiate between members of other races, than between members of your own race? To the extent that the group stereotype is a strong one, it may be difficult to perceive individual differences in looks, physiognomy, and so on in members of other groups. Eyewitnesses often remember the race or ethnic group of a person, but not his/her individual characteristics (Loftus, 1979). Brigham and Barkowitz (1978) also report that white subjects found it easier to recognise photos of whites than blacks, while blacks had the opposite problem: to them, all whites seemed to look alike.

Ethnic and racial stereotyping is often associated with strong feelings of prejudice. Needless to say, such prejudices make objective person perception judgments exceedingly difficult. There is some evidence that in divided societies, such as in Northern Ireland, children acquire their biased stereotypes at home at a very early age. It is in the nature of stereotyping that prejudiced perceptions are extremely hard to change: in the rich variety of human behaviours, it is almost always possible to find some evidence that will confirm our steotypes, if we search hard enough. And as we shall see, person perception has almost as much to do with what we are looking for in another person, as with the real characteristics of our target (Chapter 3).

A prejudice to accuracy. Stereotyping and prejudice often go hand in hand. People with a prejudiced view of a group of people (or indeed, feathered birds!) are unlikely to be accurate in their judgments of the object of their prejudice.

Some practical implications

Given the relatively disappointing results of research on person perception accuracy looking for the 'accurate judge', how much faith can we place in the validity of person perception judgments made in situations such as courtrooms, interviews, identity parades and the like? Eyewitness accounts are a particularly intensively studied example of such judgments (Loftus, 1979). Eyewitnesses of naturally occurring incidents often give very different accounts of what they saw. Of the many bystanders who witnessed Robert Kennedy's assassination, most gave widely divergent descriptions of what happened (Langman and Cockburn, 1975). In an experimental study, Buckhout, Figueroa and Hoff (1974) staged an assault on a professor in front of a large class, and asked the eyewitnesses to identify the attacker several weeks later. The majority, including the victim (!), picked the wrong man. All too frequently, people are distracted by irrelevant factors. Kassin (1983) found that jurors' judgments of an absentee witness were significantly affected by the behaviour of the person who happened to read out their testimony!

There are two conclusions which may be drawn from research on person perception accuracy. Firstly, it seems that the whole problem has been looked at from a somewhat mistaken perspective. Researchers, like most laymen, assumed that being accurate in perceiving others is a single, identifiable characteristic of people. It turns out that the ability to accurately judge others is not a single, universal skill. Rather, everybody may be an accurate judge of certain others in selected situations. Looking at it this way, we can say that there is no such thing as a generally accurate (or inaccurate) judge of people. The issue of accuracy is dependent on the characteristics of the judge, his mood at the time, the target and the situation. This is perhaps the reason why interest in person perception research has shifted towards other issues in recent years. Instead of looking for the 'accurate' judge, there is much more interest today in studying the exact process of how impressions and judgments are built up from the many separate information inputs we receive (see Chapter 4).

The second conclusion one can make on the basis of research on person perception accuracy is a cautionary one. It is important to remember both in our personal lives, and in areas of public decisionmaking, that judgments about people are much more difficult, and much more fraught with problems than we commonly believe. We should be more cautious about our own, and others' judgments of people than we usually are. This is the first, and necessary step towards improving our own person perception skills. Once we realise that our ideas about people are often mistaken or biased, it will be that much easier to improve our judgmental processes. One of the most common sources of bias is the preconceived notions we have about types of people, and the links we expect between their various personal characteristics. We shall look at this problem in the next chapter.

3. Seeing people as we expect them to be: implicit personality theories

3.

SEEING PEOPLE AS WE EXPECT THEM TO BE: IMPLICIT PERSONALITY THEORIES

We have seen in the previous chapter that the accuracy of our judgments of people is often questionable. The same person can be described very differently by different observers, and the same judge often describes many different people in terms of the same few characteristics. Why should this be so? The most likely explanation is that we all use our own unique storehouse of knowledge about people when judging others. In other words, we rely on our accumulated experiences and ideas about how personal characteristics are organised in perceiving people. It is not very surprising then that we often come up with the same characteristics, which are important to us, even when judging very different individuals. In this chapter we shall look at some of the reasons why such personal knowledge and expectations influence the way we perceive people.

Implicit theories of personality
The perception of other people is very much an active, constructive process, in which the perceiver's knowledge and past experience are sometimes more important than the actual characteristics of the person to be judged (the target). As Jones and Nisbett (1971, p. 11) observed, 'traits exist more in the eye of the beholder than in the psyche of the actor'. As a result of our accumulated knowledge about people, we all have an 'implicit theory of personality', which may be defined as the sum total of our accumulated hypotheses and expectations about the way other people's attributes and traits are organised.

We may illustrate this idea quite easily. Do you think that a person who is intelligent is also likely to be generous? In your opinion, are submissive people also usually polite? Your answers to questions such as these reflect your *implicit theory of personality*, your unique assumptions about the expected relationship between personal characteristics, based on your unique history and experiences with people. A totally objective observer, or a new-born baby (assuming he could talk) would not be able to answer such questions. Logically, whether two traits are *in fact* associated in a target person cannot be established on the basis of the past experiences of the observer!

Personal constructs and the role repertory test

George Kelly (1955) was among the first psychologists to study such implicit theories about people. He suggested that each of us behaves as if we were 'naive scientists' trying to understand and predict people and the events around us. According to Kelly, we systematise our experiences by creating cognitive 'constructs' through which we perceive the world. "Man looks at his world through transparent patterns or templates which he creates and then attempts to fit over the realities of which the world is composed. . . . Let us give the name of constructs to these patterns that are tried on for size. They are ways of construing the world.'' (Kelly, 1955, pp. 8-9). Constructs are highly personal: some people may look at others in terms of a personal construct such as 'likes me — dislikes me', others may rely on features such as 'useful to my career — harmful to my career', 'self-confident — shy', or 'assertive — gutless'.

Once we develop a personal construct system (and we all do), we seek to confirm it and to integrate new experiences into the pre-existing construct pattern. The number of constructs a person uses may indicate his/her cognitive complexity, or the fineness with which he/she discriminates between people. Kelly also developed an empirical technique, the role repertory test, to elicit and measure people's construct systems. The test elicits constructs by asking subjects to describe ways in which two well-known other people (e.g. your father and your mother) are similar to each other, and at the same time different from a third person (e.g. your sister or brother). A long list of such questions may be used to elicit a number of 'constructs' or characteristics which a person uses to discriminate between important other people.

Several statistical techniques also exist for the analysis of such construct matrices. These allow an investigator to study the quality, complexity and elaboration of a person's construct system, that is, his/her view of other people. Kelly's theory and the repertory grid technique have important applications not only in social psychology but also in clinical practice. The analysis of a client's views of the world, and significant others in it, is of obvious importance both in the diagnosis, and the treatment of a variety of psychological problems. You may get a better idea of the usefulness of Kelly's role repertory grid by completing Activity 3.1 on the facing page.

Following the work of George Kelly, there have been many studies looking at implicit personality theories. To illustrate how important such pre-conceived ideas about people can be in person perception judgments, we may look at one interesting study by Dornbusch, Hastorf, Richardson and Muzzy (1965). These investigators simply asked a group of children in a camp to describe every other child in their own words. If such judgments genuinely reflect the characteristics of the child being

Before completing this grid, please read the instruction overleaf carefully!

ACTIVITY 3.1
The Repertory Grid Technique

Write actual names below each of the person categories:

Myself	Spouse/ partner	Father	Mother	Best friend	A casual acquaintance	An old teacher	A recent enemy	CONSTRUCTS
X		X		X				
	X	X	X		X			
X			X	X	X	X	X	
X		X	X		X	X		
X					X		X	

To complete the repertory grid overleaf, follow these steps:

1. First, write the actual names of the people described on the top of each column in the space provided. From now on, think about them as distinct individuals rather than as abstract categories.

2. In each row there are three crosses. Your task is to think carefully about the three people so marked, and decide in which way two of them are similar to each other, and at the same time, different from the third one. Write the name of that characteristic in the column on the right-hand side labelled 'Constructs'.

3. Next, rate each person on that particular construct using a seven-point scale, indicating how much in your opinion, each person has that particular characteristic. For example, if they don't have it at all, you may give them a score of '1', and if they have it very strongly, you should give them a score of '6' or '7'.

Now that your role repertory grid is complete, you could analyse your judgments in a variety of ways. A simple inspection of the constructs on the right-hand side gives some idea of the characteristics you typically use in judging people. Of course this is a very 'small' grid, and will reflect only a small part of your personal construct system.

Next, you may want to look at your implicit theory of personality, that is, the way any two of your constructs are related to each other as indicated by your judgments. You can calculate an overall 'similarity score' between each possible pair of constructs by summing the differences in your ratings of each target person on these two constructs.

This grid also allows us to analyse how you perceive the people listed relative to each other. You can calculate a 'similarity score' between any two target individuals by adding up the absolute differences between your ratings of any two target persons on each construct. On the basis of this information, it is possible to create a model of your 'people space', showing how you see these individuals relative to each other.

Of course, much finer analyses could be made using statistical techniques. But even this small demonstration should give you a feeling for the method. Often, quite surprising insights into your own implicit personality theories, and perceptions of familiar people, can be achieved by this relatively simple technique.

described, we would expect that many different observers would describe the same target child in a similar fashion, and each judge's description of different others would be different. In fact, exactly the opposite happened. Most children used the same few characteristics in describing almost everyone else, and there was little agreement between various children in how they described the very same target person. Apparently, children used their pre-existing ideas about 'important' characteristics (their 'implicit personality theory') in judging others, instead of focusing on real differences. Adults tend to do the same, according to the evidence of many studies (see also Activity 3.2).

ACTIVITY 3.2
What Sort of a Person is Joe?

You will see a brief description of a person, Joe, below. Please read this description carefully, and then decide what sort of a person Joe is on the following scales.

"Joe opened the door to the restaurant, and waited until a couple passed through before entering. Inside, he politely asked a waiter for a table. Soon after he had sat down, his partner arrived. He immediately got up, and helped her to take her coat off and hung it up on a hanger. He held his partner's chair until she had sat down."

What sort of a person is Joe, in your opinion? Please indicate your perception of Joe on each of the adjectives below, using the following 5-point scale:

1 = Joe is not at all like this

2 = Joe is not very much like this

3 = I can't tell

4 = Joe is somewhat like this

5 = Joe is very much like this

intelligent	—	extroverted	—
kind	—	competent	—
warmhearted	—	goodlooking	—
polite	—	assertive	—
dominant	—	impulsive	—
charming	—	popular	—

Now read the text further before looking at your judgments again.

Research on implicit personality theory

We have already seen that in person perception judgments we are almost always faced with the problem of forming complete impressions on the basis of fairly sketchy information. We usually rely on our 'implicit personality theory' to decide which characteristics are important, and to assess to what extent the few observable characteristics of a person are likely to be associated with other, unobservable features. If we see someone being polite, for example, as in the above story about Joe, we might expect that such a person would also be kind, warmhearted, charming, popular, and so on — although we have absolutely no direct knowledge about these latter characteristics in the case of Joe. In the brief description of Joe above, we really are not told anything else about this character except that he behaved in a superficially polite way in a public place. Yet most people feel quite competent in judging Joe on characteristics such as kindness, warmheartedness and even perhaps intelligence, about which we have been given absolutely no information. You can try to ask others to complete Activity 3.2 — you will find that very few people refuse on the grounds of insufficient information!

Now have a look at your judgments above. If you could rate Joe on any characteristic other than politeness, you must have done it on the basis of your implicit theory about people. The more extreme your judgment of Joe on any of the other traits, the stronger the association in your implicit personality theory between politeness and that other characteristic. You may believe that persons who are polite are also kind, or alternatively, you could believe that polite people are usually unkind. Your judgments in fact say much more about *you* and your view of people, than about Joe, about whom, after all, we know nothing more than that he is polite!

Bruner and Tagiuri (1954) were among the first social psychologists to realise the importance of studying how we associate known characteristics of people with other, unknown ones. Such associations are a reflection of our particular implicit personality theories. How can we analyse such implicit theories of people? The small activity you just completed illustrates one method. The way you used particular constructs to describe different people (Activity 3.1) also revealed how close or distant these constructs are to each other in your private view of people. There are other, more complex methods as well, capitalising on the same principle.

An interesting example for studying implicit personality theory is a study by Rosenberg and Jones (1972). These authors wanted to investigate how Theodor Dreiser, an American writer, thought about people. They decided to analyse his implicit theory of personality on the basis of his descriptions of characters in one of his books, 'A Gallery of Women'. Rosenberg and Jones argued that the more often two adjectives occurred together in the description of a character in the book, the stronger those two adjectives were associated with each other in Dreiser's private view of people. They simply calculated an index of co-occurrence for every possible pair of adjectives in the book, and analysed these data using a procedure called multidimensional scaling (MDS). This technique represents the adjectives in a spatial model, where the distance between every adjective indicates the frequency of their co-occurrence in the book.

The result is very much like a psychological map of the adjectives used by Dreiser, his 'implicit theory of personality'. This map showed that the writer discriminated between people in terms of two major dimensions: male (hard) — female (soft), and conforms — doesn't conform. These implicit personality dimensions seem to make a lot of sense considering Dreiser's life history. His relationship to women was of central importance to him both in his private and in his professional life, and his fight against conformity and conventionalism was a central theme in his life as well as in his writings. It is not surprising then, that the characteristics which we know were important to Dreiser during his life are also at the root of his view of people, as revealed by this analysis.

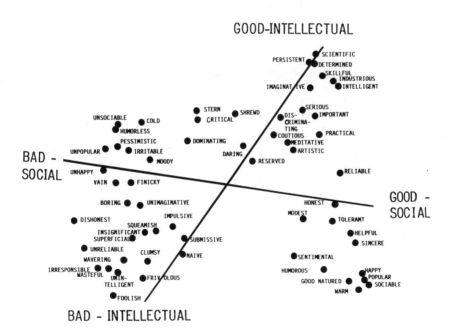

FIGURE 3.1 The relative positions of personality traits in the implicit personality theory of students; these traits are organised in terms of two underlying dimensions: intellectual good-bad and social good-bad characteristics. (After Rosenberg, Nelson and Vivekananthan, 1968).

Of course, the same methods may also be used to study the implicit personality theories of any other person or persons. Rosenberg et al. (1968) analysed the implicit theories of personality of university students and found that this group differentiated between people in terms of two major dimensions: intellectual good-bad and social good-bad (Figure 3.1). For such analyses, the data need not even be written documents — our pronounciations, judgments or descriptions of others provide a rich source of information about our implicit personality theories, waiting to be analysed!

Rosenberg and Sedlak (1972) used similar techniques to study how single individuals see others. Such analyses can be based simply on the descriptions subjects give of a large number of others they know. Looking at the frequency of association between adjectives, unique individual personality theories may be discovered. Particular trait clusters, for example 'good-looking, lazy, homosexual' or 'red-haired, unintelligent, promiscuous' are highly characteristic of particular individual judges. What is important to remember is that we all use such theories in our perceptions of others. The quality of person perception judgments often depends as much on the perceiver as on the perceived, as each of us brings a slightly different set of expectations and hypotheses to our judgments.

Could this man be a great lover? Our implicit personality theories allow us to make judgments about unknown characteristics on the basis of known ones; being a street vendor is unlikely to be associated with 'being a great lover' in most people's minds, although, of course, there is no reason why it couldn't be.

Cultural theories of personality

Implicit personality theories need not be entirely individual and idiosyncratic. To a greater or lesser extent, persons living in a shared culture also share their implicit theories about people (e.g. Figure 3.1). What would we find if we compared the implicit personality theories of many different individuals? Norman (1963) studied the ratings a large number of people, some well acquainted with each other and some almost strangers, made about each other on 20 attributes. It seemed to matter very little how well the judges knew the targets they were rating — pretty much the same characteristics were used in all the judgments. In a later study (Passini and Norman, 1966), judgments of complete strangers again revealed the same structure as in the earlier study. Since the judgments were independent of how well the raters knew the target persons, it seems that Norman's judgmental dimensions were implicit in the perceivers, revealing their underlying, common and shared view of personality.

The dimensions found by Norman reflected characteristics such as extroversion, agreeableness, conscientiousness and emotional stability. How universal are these dimensions in judgments of people? Later studies went one step further by asking judges to make general judgments about the links between all possible pairs of the 20 attributes used by Norman, without rating anyone in particular. Once again, the same dimensions emerged, suggesting the universal role characteristics such as extroversion, agreeableness, conscientiousness and emotional stability play in our theories of people.

However, all these studies were carried out in Western cultures. Surely different cultures have different implicit theories of personality? Would the Chinese, for example, still rely on the same basic dimensions in judging each other as was found by Norman? We know that their culture values community spirit and conformity much more than our own competitive, individualistic culture. Shouldn't this be reflected in the implicit view of personality the Chinese have? Bond and Forgas (1984) in a recent study looked at that possibility, comparing the person perception judgments of Australian and Chinese (Hong Kong) subjects. Results showed that the predicted important cultural differences in fact existed. Conscientiousness, for example, was far more important in the Chinese group, and extroversion was a more important determinant of reactions to people in Australia.

Implicit personality theories are one of the most important influences on our judgments of people. It is perhaps not surprising that our accumulated experience and knowledge of what people are like constantly affects the characteristics we attribute to people about whom we may know little. However, our expectations about others are not always formulated in terms of isolated, individual traits. Sometimes, we use 'typologies' to classify others. Such person typologies have also been shown to have quite important influences on person perception judgments, as we shall see below (see also Activity 3.3).

Perception and classification
Many years ago, Bruner (1958) noted that "the most self-evident point . . . . is that perceiving or registering an object or an event in the environment involves an act of categorisation" (p.92). We see our environment not as it is, but in terms of the categories we possess for its description. This is the same idea that George Kelly proposed in his personal construct theory. Constructs are simply categories for classifying the world. In cognitive psychology, Bartlett's (1932) pioneering work on memory also showed that people are actively engaged in the continuous creation and modification of a system of cognitive representations, which are often called schemata, about their environment. We use such schemata for classifying and interpreting new information. Classification is thus an integral part of perception.

Person perception and person types
Our implicit knowledge about people is thus not restricted to expectations about trait co-occurrence. An alternative source of information is provided by what we know about the *types* of persons we have come across. Simply describing a person as 'a student activist type', 'a female executive type' or 'a typical young lecturer' conveys a very rich image in a very few words. By categorising people into 'types' we are able to systematise our accumulated knowledge about people and greatly simplify the task of person perception. Such 'typologies' make it possible to describe basically unknown individuals in terms of the characteristics of a well-known, familiar 'type'. When the 'types' are defined in terms

---

ACTIVITY 3.3
Typologies of People

On a piece of paper, write down the various 'types' of people you are familiar with in your work environment, amongst your friends, acquaintances, etc. For each 'type', try to give (a) a summary label, as well as (b) a more detailed description of the most important characteristics of this type. Try to describe at least five to eight such 'types' of people known to you. Next, try to think of an individual you actually know who would be a good representative of each of the types you noted. Now read on, and refer back to your list as you find out more about the way we use such person prototypes.

of highly visible ethnic or racial characteristics, and are widely shared by others, we may speak of a stereotype (see Chapter 2 also).

The most frequent problems we face in everyday person perception are problems of classification. In order to be able to form a quick and reasonably accurate impression about a person we have just met, the best strategy is usually to try to decide to which particular group or category the newly encountered target person belongs. You may remember that the correct identification of types of people was found to be an important component of person perception accuracy (c.f. stereotype accuracy). By correctly classifying people into 'types', such as the 'extrovert', the 'student radical', the 'feminist', the 'surfie' or the 'trendy', we greatly simplify our job of judging them. Next we shall consider the consequences of such classification into person types.

How 'typical' is that person?

Perceiving people is no exception to the universal rule of classification. We all acquire an extensive repertoire of 'person types' throughout our lifetime, and these 'types' are later used to classify new persons we come across. The person categories which influence our judgments of people are frequently called person *prototypes*. Person prototypes are mental schemata about the types of people we are familiar with in our social environment. A prototype is the idealised combination of characteristics, the 'perfect' example of the group of people in question. Of course, not everyone fits into a prototype equally well: prototypicality is a matter of degree. Some persons are 'good' examples of such familiar prototypes as a 'workaholic', an 'extrovert' or a 'practical joker', while others may only possess some of the required qualities and not others. Such people are less 'good' examples of the prototype: they are less prototypical. We all know examples of people who are 'typical' or 'atypical' of a class of persons. (You may want to go back to the list of person types you prepared in Activity 3.3, and decide for each of the persons you listed how 'typical' he/she is of that class of people.)

Whereas research on implicit personality theory is concerned with how expected links between traits or constructs influence our judgments of others, research on person prototypes shows that our thinking about people is also influenced by the prototypicality of the people we judge. To take an example, if you come across a person in the supermarket who has all the obvious characteristics of a typical 'housewife' or a typical 'punk', you will probably find it easy to form an impression about, and remember that person. In contrast, if you meet a person who does not remind you of any particular group of people, or has a mixed bag of characteristics (is not prototypical) you will find impression formation a more difficult task.

A person may thus be more or less 'prototypical' depending on the number of defining features of a prototype he/she possesses. In other words, there are varying degrees of 'housewifeyness' or 'punkiness'; some people are better examples of a 'typical' housewife or a 'typical' punk than are others. The greater the prototypicality, the easier it is to form impressions about, and remember a person. This can also be demonstrated experimentally. Cantor and Mischel (1979) created descriptions of people which were either consistent or inconsistent with person prototypes such as the typical 'extrovert' or the typical 'introvert'. Subjects had to form impressions of, and later remember these people. Results indicated that prototype-consistent person descriptions were generally better remembered than inconsistent ones.

Are 'typical' people always easier to judge?

However, the matter is somewhat more complicated. Is it really the case that typical people are *always* easier to remember and form impressions about? Just think of our example of the typical housewife you just met in the supermarket. As you enter the next aisle where breakfast cereals are sold, you come across another woman who is very non-prototypical. In fact, she reminds you of several conflicting prototypes; she acts like a housewife, but wears unusual clothes, has a pair of rollerskates on, and has expensive jewellery. Is it really going to be so much more difficult to remember and form impressions about this unusual, non-prototypical woman? Quite the opposite. As we all know, sometimes it may be much easier to form judgments when a person deviates from our expectations.

One problem with the prototype idea is that it focuses on the rational, cognitive aspects of person perception. Judging and categorising people is seen as essentially a problem of information processing and memory. Yet there is much more to person perception judgments. We almost always have some feelings, emotions, attitudes or expectations about the people we come across which interfere with simple information processing. The prototype model as put forward by Cantor and Mischel ignores the non-cognitive, sometimes value-loaded, emotional character of person perception judgments (for example the effects of mood on accuracy discussed in Chapter 2). Contrary to Cantor and Mischel's (1979) results, some other research has shown that judges sometimes remember inconsistent, non-prototypical people — people who display unusual, novel characteristics which do not fit into our expectations — better than prototypical people (Hastie and Kumar, 1979). To return to our previous example, most of us would probably find it quite easy to form an impression about the non-prototypical rollerskating housewife mentioned above.

Is it possible to somehow make sense of these conflicting findings? When is it easier to form impressions about prototypical people, and when is it easier to judge deviant, non-prototypical characters? The affective reactions people have to a prototype may be of central importance in guiding these two impression formation strategies. In other words, the way we feel about a particular person type could determine whether prototypical, or non-prototypical people are easier to perceive and remember.

In a recent study, we attempted to separate these two influences on impression formation: the prototypicality of a target, and how we feel about that prototype (Forgas, 1983). We expected that very different strategies would be used in judging person types about whom people have strong or weak feelings. We began by collecting a representative list

ENGINEER

STUDIOUS STUDENT

COLLEGE TYPE

An artist's impression of three different 'student types'. If you are a full-time university student, you may yourself be familiar with these student 'types', reported to be common by our student subjects at a Sydney campus!

of person prototypes actually used in a student environment. You may be interested to see what sort of 'types' we found most common amongst students. These are shown in Table 3.1. We also analysed how students differentiated between these different prototypes. As Figure 3.2 shows, academic performance, extroversion, social status and political radicalism were the major determinants of how students perceived these various types.

TABLE 3.1
LIST AND DESCRIPTION OF THE 16 STUDENT 'TYPES' MOST
COMMONLY MENTIONED BY A GROUP OF UNIVERSITY STUDENTS

1. RADICALS Scruffy appearance, often protesting, wear overalls or Indian clothes, hand out leaflets on library lawn, wear badges, organise marches, outspoken, noisy, usually leftist, live in communal accommodation, aggressive.
2. CHRISTIANS Fairly innocuous, keen, thrifty, studious, clean, caring, narrow-minded, have "Jesus loves you" stickers all over briefcase, fish signs over books, try to convince others about religion, go to Bible readings.
3. MATURE AGE STUDENTS Anxious, conscientious, housewifey females, sensibly dressed, orderly habits, keen, often talk at tutorials, stable, motherly, well-off, middle-aged, conservative.
4. STUDIOUS STUDENTS Hard working, pale, dogged expression, conscientious, neat dress, work consistently throughout session and during holidays, spend much time in library, submit assignments on time, do extra reading for classes, take down everything in lectures, never miss classes, get good marks, not much social life.
5. LAZY BLUDGERS Messy, untidy, just here to pass time, bored, apathetic, sit around lawn sunbaking, do minimum amount of work, miss lectures, repeat subjects, no idea why attending uni, try to bludge using other people's work, uncaring.
6. COLLEGE TYPES Healthy country looks, clean cut, good natured, a bit dazed by it all, wear college sweaters, often get drunk, have a good time, go to college for lunch, spend holidays in the country, have college friends.
7. MEDICAL STUDENTS Conservatively dressed, very middle class, cliqueish, snobbish, elitist, self-centred, wear lab coats, act cool, congregate around Golf House Cafeteria, talk about medical topics, rarely mix outside faculty, materialistic, rich.
8. SPORTY TYPES Wear shorts all the time, dumb in tutorials, go around in ADIDAS shoes and track suits, join clubs, participate in sports competitions, spend much time in gymnasium, often carry squash or tennis racquets, go jogging during lunchtime, look healthy.
9. GAY LIBBERS Have pierced ears and wear earrings, wear gay lib badges, have own discos and parties, involved in protests and demonstrations, well-spoken, affected accent, intense emotional life, unstable, sociable.

10. TRENDIES Rich, middle-class, very fashionably dressed, Eastern suburbs background, never wear thongs, talk properly, women wear makeup, tight designer jeans, drive sports cars, go on overseas trips, frequently go to discos and restaurants, go skiing, ambitious, elitist, frequent the cafeteria.
11. ASIAN STUDENTS Neat, conscientious, wear glasses, ambitious, competitive, lonely, work hard, they stick together, unfriendly, never speak English when in groups, bright, conservative.
12. ENGINEERS Often in groups among themselves, chauvinistic, wear checkered shirts and jeans, short hair, glasses, like beer, live at home with parents, poor social skills, arrogant, little concern for culture, carry calculators, uncouth behaviour, interested in football, go to pub frequently, play cards.
13. RADICAL FEMINISTS Left-wing views, outspoken, often lesbian, usually unattractive looking, no bra, wear women's lib badges, sell feminist literature, aggressive, chip on the shoulder, wear overalls.
14. QUIET LONERS Shy, never interacting with people, spend lunchtime alone, contribute little to tutorials, inconspicuous, hard to get acquainted with, don't go to parties.
15. SURFIES Bleached blond hair, wear thongs and shorts, drive panel vans, go up the coast for holidays, have suntan all year round, dumb, very fit, sexist, use drugs.
16. INTELLECTUALS Straight, introverted, academic types, old fashioned clothes, carry many books, hands in work early, often debating obscure subjects in likeminded company, involved in work, know about literature and culture, go to theatre and opera, wear glasses, neatly dressed.

After Forgas, 1983, pp. 158-9

The study confirmed our expectations: the affective character of a prototype determined whether prototypical or non-prototypical person descriptions were easier to process. These results suggest that consistency with a single 'person type' is only an advantage in impression formation when that type has strong positive or negative emotional reactions associated with it. Otherwise, more complex persons incorporating features from multiple 'types' may be both more memorable and may result in stronger impressions.

The biasing effects of person classification
The categorisation of people may even have retrospective consequences, as an interesting study by Snyder and Uranowitz (1978) demonstrated. Subjects in this experiment were asked to read an extensive and detailed description of a woman, Betty K, including many details about her childhood, education, friendships, career choice, and so on. After reading this biography, some subjects were told that Betty K. lived a

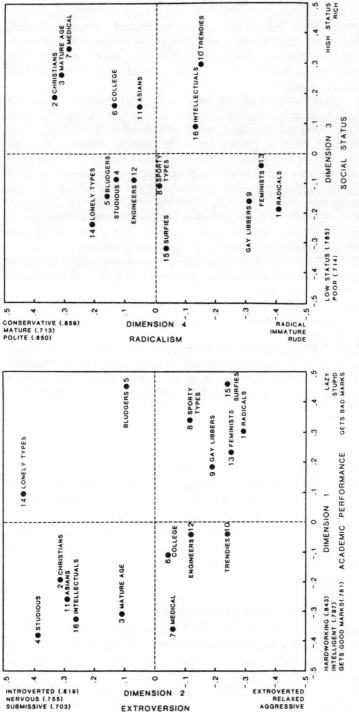

FIGURE 3.2 The perception of person prototypes. This is the way a group of Australian university students differentiated between 16 'prototypical' student categories. (After Forgas, 1983, p. 160).

lesbian lifestyle, others were told that she was heterosexual, and yet another group received no additional information. This information was provided so that subjects should 'classify' Betty K. as a normal heterosexual, or a lesbian 'type'. Subjects were asked to recall as many details about Betty K. as they could one week later. Those who were told that Betty was a lesbian reinterpreted her life and 'recalled' more events suggesting homosexuality than the other two groups. Snyder and Uranowitz (1978) suggest that these biases indicate a retrospective interference with memory through the effects of powerful activated person categories.

The problem with this interpretation, as Bellezza and Bower (1982) point out, is that there is no known memory process which would explain how information is modified once it is committed to memory (that is, after subjects read the initial biographies). Once we have 'stored' the information about Betty K., later information could not really interfere with that memory trace. Instead, the better 'recall' of category-consistent, 'lesbian' or 'heterosexual' incidents can be best explained as due to guessing by the subjects, who were guided by the prototype label they later received. It is remarkable that subjects can thus 'make up'

Are non-typical people with inconsistent characteristics harder to form impressions about? It largely depends on how you feel about the people concerned; we know more about the characteristics of 'typical' housewives, but 'untypical' housewives, say on rollerskates, can be particularly memorable and informative stimuli!

characteristics of a person to fit a prototype, without realising that they have no real evidence to substantiate their judgments.

As social psychologists, the nature of the underlying memory mechanisms is of less interest to us than the fact that category labels such as 'lesbian' or 'heterosexual', 'extrovert' or 'introvert', 'trendy' or 'engineer' have such powerful effects on impression formation, even when they are communicated well after all other relevant material has already been digested. Classifying people can have even more insidious effects. Once we have classified a person as belonging to a particular category, we often tend to selectively look for information that confirms our classification, and disregard information that contradicts it.

This was demonstrated, for example, in several studies by Snyder and Campbell (1980) and Snyder and Whyte (1981). They gave their subjects the task of selecting 12 questions which they would like to ask from a future partner in order to find out whether that person was an extrovert or an introvert. People tended to select predominantly those questions which would confirm their expectations, even though they had no actual reliable information about their partners. In other words, they seemed to intentionally exclude the possibility that their questions might elicit unexpected disconfirming information.

Some practical implications

In practice, these results have important implications in everyday person perception situations. Particularly people who come into contact with a large number of superficially known others, such as sales clerks, nurses, doctors and the like, often rely on the categorisation of their partners into 'types' as the basis of their impression formation strategies. Ask any nurse about the types of people she deals with in a hospital, and she will be able to give you a fairly exhaustive classification. John Menyhart conducted a study which addressed this very question in a Sydney repatriation hospital, and found that even trainee nurses very quickly developed a clearcut classification scheme of people in the hospital milieu.

While such shortcuts are necessary in order to reduce the information processing load which would be involved if we made an independent assessment of each new person we encounter, it can also often result in mistaken impressions. If you are somebody who meets many other people in the course of your daily routine, it helps to remember that instantaneous categorisation has its definite dangers. It tends to make you blind towards existing characteristics which do not fit the prototype, and makes you stick to your first impressions despite contrary evidence. While categorisation of people is an inevitable consequence of our limited information processing ability (just imagine if we had to treat each bit of information about people separately, without recourse to simplifying categories!), we must learn to modify our categories in the light of subsequent experience.

If you are on the receiving end, being assessed by somebody in a situation such as an interview or a first encounter, you may also turn the universal tendency for categorisation to your advantage. If you can elicit a positively evaluated person prototype in the observer right at the beginning, this prototype may well come to dominate future impressions.

Conclusion

To summarise, it appears that classification of people is an essential part of the person perception process, which helps us greatly to form impressions of people. However, classification may also have serious biasing effects. People tend to remember and rely more on category-consistent information, to retrospectively distort what they see to make it fit into a category, and to selectively search for information that confirms rather than disconfirms the classifications they have made. Since the kind of cognitive theories focusing on memory processes and categorisation described above have only appeared in social psychology fairly recently, it is too early to draw final conclusions at this stage. However, one thing is certain: person perception processes are not reducible to simple rational information processing, as some recent theorists claim (e.g. Hastie et al. 1980). The social, motivated and value-loaded character of such judgments is what gives them their special interest and importance (Tajfel and Forgas, 1981). There is every reason to believe that we have several information processing strategies at our disposal, and deal with different kinds of person categories differently.

We have seen in this chapter how important pre-conceived notions about people are in how we form impressions of others. Both expectations about trait-patterns (implicit personality theory) and person classification schemes influence our judgments. However, our theories and expectations are only one source of influence on person perception judgments. Impression formation involves the combination of many different sources of information, some observed and some inferred, to make up a single picture. Exactly how do we go about accomplishing this task? This will be the topic of the next chapter.

4. Impression formation

4.

IMPRESSION FORMATION

In the previous chapters we have seen that person perception is a much more problematic process than we commonly believe. Not only are we often mistaken and inaccurate in our judgments of people (Chapter 2), but frequently our own expectations and ideas are more important in forming impressions than the real characteristics of the people we have to judge (Chapter 3). Because of such problems, social psychologists have increasingly turned in recent years to studying exactly *how* we form impressions about people. In contrast to the previous chapters which looked at *what* we see when judging others (the content of person perception), in this chapter we shall turn to the related problem of *how* we form judgments of others (the process of person perception).

The question underlying all impression formation research is a simple one. How can we form a complete, well-rounded impression of another person, when the information we have to base it on is usually fragmented and piecemeal? What sorts of mental processes are involved in putting together the isolated bits of knowledge we usually have about people? Let's take an example. You may know about your acquaintance, Anne, that 'she is tall ', 'she has brown hair', 'she is friendly', 'she has big brown eyes', 'she has a good figure', 'she is hardworking' and 'she is a receptionist'. How do you construct a global impression of Anne as a pretty, pleasant and desirable companion? There are several alternative models which may account for such impression formation. It could be that we rely on a few really important and informative 'central' traits to build up an impression, assimilating other characteristics into the central trait. Alternatively, we may use something like an arithmetic process, adding up or averaging the various pieces of information we receive about people. We shall look at the evidence supporting both models below.

The Gestalt approach and the central trait hypothesis
Gestalt theory (Gestalt means in German 'form, shape, figure') arose in the first half of this century as a reaction against the fragmented,

atomistic approaches to psychology represented by behaviourist and structuralist theories. The early Gestalt theorists (Wertheimer, Koffka and Koehler) were mainly concerned with perception, and as the name of the theory suggests, believed that people are 'programmed' to perceive unitary, indivisible forms rather than fragmented isolated bits of information. A central problem in perceptual psychology in those days was how to explain the 'apparent motion' phenomenon: why do we perceive motion when several stationary images are presented in quick succession, as in motion pictures? The Gestalt theorist's answer was as simple as it was radical: there is nothing to explain, since it is simply an inherent feature of human beings that they perceive and react to meaningful, whole structures and forms, or 'Gestalten', which cannot be reduced to their constituent elements.

Solomon Asch is perhaps the most important representative of the Gestalt movement in social perception. Like the other Gestalt theorists, he was interested in how whole, complete impressions about people arise from the numerous bits and pieces of information available to a perceiver, a question which lies at the heart of research on impression formation to this day. Asch suggested that impression formation is not simply the result of the mental averaging of the various traits of a target person. Rather, it is a holistic process in which certain 'central' traits have a disproportionate influence on impressions, and serve as the anchor points around which all other information about a person is crystallised: "the subject tries to reach the core of the person through the trait or traits" (Asch, 1946, p. 284).

To test this hypothesis, Asch gave his subjects a set of adjectives which described a target person. Subjects were asked to indicate their impression of the target on a second set of personality traits. To some subjects, the target person was described as 'intelligent, skilful, industrious, warm, determined, practical and cautious'. Other subjects read the same description, but 'warm' was replaced by 'cold'. According to arithmetic theories of impression formation, the replacement of one adjective out of seven should only have a small proportional effect on the quality of the final impression.

Asch found that the substitution of a single, central trait such as warm for cold in fact had a major effect on impressions. The target person in the 'warm' condition was judged to be a very different kind of individual from in the 'cold' condition (see Table 4.1). In a control experiment, Asch used the same procedure, but instead of the central warm-cold adjectives, two peripheral traits (polite-blunt) were manipulated. This time, the replacement of these non-central traits had only very minor effects on impressions (Table 4.1).

As Table 4.1 shows, when 'warm' was part of the description, the person was more often judged to be generous, wise, happy, good-natured, popular, sociable and humorous than in the 'cold' condition.

TABLE 4.1
THE EFFECTS OF CHANGING A CENTRAL TRAIT (LIST 1 vs LIST 2) AND A
PERIPHERAL TRAIT (LIST 3 vs LIST 4) ON IMPRESSION FORMATION.

	Central traits		Peripheral traits	
	Stimulus list 1	Stimulus list 2	Stimulus list 3	Stimulus list 4
	intelligent	intelligent	intelligent	intelligent
	skilful	skilful	skilful	skilful
	industrious	industrious	industrious	industrious
	WARM	COLD	POLITE	BLUNT
	determined	determined	determined	determined
	practical	practical	practical	practical
	cautious	cautious	cautious	cautious

Percentage of subjects who judged the target person to
have each of the characteristics listed:

generous	91	8	56	58
wise	65	25	30	50
happy	90	34	75	65
good-natured	94	17	87	56
humorous	77	13	71	48
sociable	91	38	83	68
popular	84	28	94	56
humane	86	31	59	77
altruistic	69	18	29	46
imaginative	51	19	33	31

After Asch, 1946, p. 263

On the whole, the replacement of a peripheral trait, polite with blunt, had no such effects. As Asch suggested, whether a trait is 'central' or 'peripheral' also depends on what sort of other information is available to us. In the company of another set of traits, warm-cold may have had a much smaller effect on impressions.

Asch's findings aroused a fair bit of interest, as well as criticism. To what extent can we generalise from judgments made about seven adjectives to perceptions of real people? A common criticism of the Asch study is that it used extremely unrealistic stimuli and judgments. Kelley (1950) repeated the Asch experiment under more realistic conditions. Psychology students were given an advance description of a guest lecturer containing the same kind of adjective manipulations Asch used. Half of the subjects had 'warm' in their description, and half had 'cold'. After a real lecturer was presented to the class and talked for about twenty minutes, students were asked to rate him on a number of scales. Results showed that the substitution of a single adjective had significant effects on judgments even in this highly realistic and complex situation

(Table 4.2). Students who received the 'warm' advance description not only rated the guest lecturer more positively, but were also found to interact with the lecturer more readily than the 'cold' group.

TABLE 4.2
THE EFFECTS OF CHANGING ONE ADJECTIVE IN A PRIOR DESCRIPTION ON JUDGMENTS OF A PERSON ACTUALLY ENCOUNTERED*

Responses	'Warm' description	'Cold' description
self-centred	6.3	9.6
unsociable	5.6	10.4
unpopular	4.0	7.4
formal	6.3	9.6
irritable	9.4	12.0
humourless	8.3	11.7
ruthless	8.6	11.0

*The higher the number, the more the person was judged to have that characteristic.
After Kelley, 1950, p. 434

Arithmetic models of impression formation
The holistic, Gestalt orientation of Asch represents only one approach to the study of impression formation processes. Other theorists took a different orientation, seeking to construct mathematical models representing the process of how we integrate information when forming impressions about others. This approach, often labelled 'cognitive algebra', has resulted in the development of two alternative models of impression formation, the *summation* and the *averaging* models.

According to the summation model, the overall impression we form of a person is simply the sum total of the value of the characteristics he possesses (Fishbein and Hunter, 1964). If, for example, you believe that a target person, Dick, is honest and helpful, and these characteristics have values 7 and 6 on your subjective scale of favourableness which runs from -7 to $+7$, then your final impression of Dick would have a favourableness value of $7 + 6$, or 13. According to this model, any characteristic which is even marginally favourable will enhance the final impression. For example, if you now discover that Dick is also a collector of matchbox labels (a trait with a favourableness value of $+1$), your positive impression would be further improved by that information (to $+14$). If you accept the summation model, you will believe that however marginal, every little bit of positive (or negative) information counts. Consequently, one should display even the most marginal 'good' characteristics to make the best possible impression on people.

The averaging model of impression formation, developed by Anderson (1965; 1974) has different implications. The final impression, according to this model, is simply the arithmetic average of the input characteristics. Taking our previous example, the overall impression formed of Dick would be more favourable when only the first two highly positive traits (honest and helpful) are communicated (7 + 6/2 = 6.5). The addition of the third, marginally positive trait (collects matchbox labels) would result in a decline in the average favourableness of the final impression (7 + 6 + 1/3 = 4.33). The averaging model implies that only information which is more favourable than the existing average will improve impressions. In practical terms, according to this model we should mention only highly positive traits in job interviews, for example, and keep quiet about marginally positive characteristics (such as collecting matchbox labels)!

Research on information integration
In practice, research on arithmetic models of impression formation relies on a pool of personality trait adjectives which are already scaled for 'likeability'. Anderson (1968) constructed likeableness norms for 555 personality trait adjectives, based on subjects' judgments of them (see Table 4.3 for an extract from his list).

In a typical experiment, subjects are provided with lists of words with known likeableness values allegedly describing a person. They are then asked to rate how much they would themselves like such an individual. Using pre-rated word lists such as the one shown in Table 4.3, researchers have tried to decide which of the two models, the summation or the averaging model, is a better predictor of final impressions. Several studies showed that the addition of new characteristics (increasing the size of the set) further influences impressions (the so-called 'set size effect'), thus apparently supporting the summation model (Fishbein and Hunter, 1964). However, Anderson (1967) argued that such set size effects may also be explained by an averaging model, if one makes the reasonable assumption that the judge starts from an initially neutral impression, corresponding to a 0 likeableness value on a -7 to + 7 scale. Thus, both models can explain the change in impressions due to increasing the 'set size'.

Ultimately, the two models may be contrasted in how well they explain what happens to impressions when marginally positive or negative information is added to a set. Anderson (1965) performed an experiment in which initially highly positive (PP) and highly negative (NN) descriptions were supplemented by either highly positive or negative (PPPP or NNNN), or marginally positive or negative (PPpp; NNnn) further items. The results of the study are summarised in Table 4.4.

The averaging model was supported by this study, since the addition of marginally positive items resulted in a decrease in positive impressions, and not an increase as predicted by the summation model (columns 1 vs 3 in Table 4.4). The averaging model has been further

TABLE 4.3
RATINGS OF LIKEABLENESS AND MEANINGFULNESS OF PERSONALITY
TRAITS: SOME EXAMPLES OF HIGH, MEDIUM AND LOW LIKEABLE
TRAITS

	Rank order (out of 555)	Word	Likeableness (7-point scale)	Meaningfulness (7-point scale)
HIGHLY	1	sincere	5.73	3.70
POSITIVE	2	honest	5.55	3.84
WORDS	3	understanding	5.49	3.68
	4	loyal	5.47	3.66
	7	intelligent	5.37	3.68
	8	dependable	5.36	3.86
	12	considerate	5.27	3.72
	16	warm	5.22	3.56
	18	kind	5.20	3.68
HIGHLY	531	loud-mouthed	.83	3.76
NEGATIVE	532	selfish	.82	3.64
WORDS	533	narrow-minded	.80	3.74
	538	rude	.76	3.76
	539	conceited	.74	3.78
	540	greedy	.72	3.38
	543	insincere	.66	3.64
	544	unkind	.66	3.78
	545	untrustworthy	.65	3.76
	548	malicious	.52	3.46
	549	obnoxious	.48	3.76
	552	cruel	.40	3.76
	555	liar	.36	3.92

After Anderson, 1968

modified by Anderson to take account of the fact that all traits are not equally important in influencing impressions (a point which, of course, was first made by Asch in his 'central trait' hypothesis). This revised *weighted averaging* model has received some support in laboratory investigations. A particularly interesting question is what determines the weight, or relative importance given to various sorts of information. We shall look at some of the variables which influence the weights assigned to personality characteristics in the second half of this chapter.

Some problems with arithmetic models
To what extent can real-life impression formation processes be reduced to such simple and elegant arithmetic formulas? At first sight, there is something appealing about these formulations. However, on closer inspection, a number of problems become apparent. All the research is

TABLE 4.4

SUMMATION vs AVERAGING MODELS IN IMPRESSIONS FORMATION:
THE EFFECTS OF ADDING HIGHLY OR MODERATELY POSITIVE OR
NEGATIVE TRAITS ON JUDGMENTS OF A TARGET PERSON

| | Likeability ratings* | | |
| | Initial set | Add highly positive or negative items | Add moderately positive or negative items |
	(1)	(2)	(4)
Positive lists	(PP)72.85	(PPPP)79.39	(PPpp)71.11
Negative lists	(NN)23.70	(NNNN)17.64	(NNnn)25.67

*Higher values indicate greater liking
After Anderson, 1965, p. 396

based on the twin assumptions that (a) personality traits have permanent and unchanging 'likeableness values', and (b) impression formation is essentially a simple, rational cognitive process. Both of these assumptions may be incorrect. While some traits may be judged positive and likeable in one context (e.g. 'proud' is a positive characteristic when seen in the context of a person being independent or confident), the same traits may have negative values in another context (e.g. proud in the context of arrogant or aggressive) (cf. Hamilton and Zanna, 1974).

As Asch suggested, "as soon as two or more traits are understood to belong to the same person, they cease to exist as isolated traits ... traits lead an intensely social life, striving to join each other in a closely organized system" (1946, p. 284). Nor do we normally function as unbiased arithmetic machines averaging input cues. A few highly negative pieces of information about a person may completely override all previous positive cues, irrespective of the arithmetic average (cf. Riskey and Birnbaum, 1974).

The research on impression formation also provides a nice illustration of some of the most common problems of laboratory research in social psychology. We all know that everyday impression formation judgments are influenced by thousands of factors, including such 'uncontrollable' variables as the weather that day (see Schwarz, Chapter 2), and how our judge slept the previous night. It is customary in science to try to eliminate or control all such influences in order to study a few variables at a time in their pure, undiluted form. This is exactly what research on cognitive algebra attempted to do. By using word-lists rather than real people, we can manipulate 'likeability' exactly and without interference from other variables. However, the resulting judgmental problem is so far removed from the typical complexity of impression formation judgments that some critics suggest that the findings may no longer apply to more realistic situations. You may want to spend a few minutes at this stage considering whether you agree with this criticism, and whether you can think of better ways of studying impression formation processes. We shall have more to say about research methods in Chapter 16.

Anderson's weighted averaging formulation thus leads us to ask perhaps the most important question in impression formation research: what determines the weights people assign to various cues they perceive about a person? Why do we sometimes weight one cue heavily, while on a subsequent occasion we might ignore it entirely in forming an impression? Impression formation may often be influenced by irrational, emotional biases such as strong likes and dislikes, interference from our implicit personality theories, personal convictions, and so on. We shall now turn to a brief discussion of the various common biases which influence impression formation judgments.

The influence of the background and the context
Information we receive about people is always interpreted within specific contexts. The meaning of a perceived trait or characteristic is not permanent, but will partly depend on the background, situation, setting and other information we already have about a person. Even apparently irrelevant information, such as the physical background of an observed interaction, may influence the way we interpret people's behaviours. In one study, we (Forgas and Brown, 1978) simply photographed several young couples engaged in conversations of varying intimacy. We then used photographic procedures to superimpose images of these people on images of various physical backgrounds (such as a theatre lobby or a street scene). Results showed that exactly the same people in exactly the same conversation were judged differently, depending on the physical background of the encounter. The information the couple communicated about themselves carried more weight in a warm, intimate setting than in a cold, non-intimate environment.

Halo effects
Halo effects are a special case of impression formation biases. They refer to the tendency of judges to assume that once people possess some good (or bad) characteristics, their other, unrelated characteristics are also likely to be consistent, that is, good or bad. If you have a positive evaluation of your colleague Steve who once helped you to sell your car, and somebody asks you whether Steve would be the right person to run the office party, you are more likely to answer yes, not because you have any knowledge about his relevant skills, but because you generally think positively of him. An interesting example of halo effects is when external, physical appearance serves as the basis for inferring internal, personal characteristics (see Activity 4.1).

ACTIVITY 4.1
What Shall We Do About Rachel?

Below you will find a brief description of an episode involving a small child. After reading the story, please answer the questions below.

"Rachel is a sweet little three-year-old girl. She has beautiful blonde hair and lovely blue eyes. The other day when she was playing with the neighbour's little four-year-old boy, she threw a stone at him which hurt his arm so badly that he had to be taken to a hospital."

Imagine for a moment that you have just witnessed this incident. Do you think that in the circumstances

Rachel intended to hurt
the little boy?   yes 1 — 2 — 3 — 4 — 5 no

She should be punished?   yes 1 — 2 — 3 — 4 — 5 no

She is likely to do it again?   yes 1 — 2 — 3 — 4 — 5 no

She is likely to be an
intelligent child?   yes 1 — 2 — 3 — 4 — 5 no

You would allow your child
to play with her?   yes 1 — 2 — 3 — 4 — 5 no

Now read the text further before returning to consider your judgments again.

Dion, Berscheid and Walster (1972) asked subjects to rate pictures of people who were physically attractive, unattractive or average looking on a number of scales which measured attributes quite unrelated to looks (for example, personality, occupational status, intelligence, etc.). Good-looking people were consistently rated more positively than plain-looking targets. It seems as if judges expected attractive people to be superior even on completely unrelated traits, such as intelligence. Other studies have also shown that good-looking people (or even children) are judged less severely when committing an offence than are unattractive looking persons.

Now have a look at your judgments of Rachel in the previous activity. Do you think that you might have been less hard on her simply because she was described as a physically very attractive child? You may be interested to learn that many studies have demonstrated exactly such a bias in person perception judgments (see Chapter 12 for details!).

It is quite interesting that not only physical attractiveness, which is at least a permanent feature of people, but even short, temporary displays such as a smile may lead to similar halo effects (Mueser et al. 1984). In a recent study, Forgas, O'Connor and Morris (1983) asked people some questions very similar to the ones you answered about Rachel. Subjects had to decide about the guilt, and the most appropriate punishment for a student who allegedly cheated in an exam. Apart from a detailed description of the incident, judges also received a photo of the person in question, which showed him/her either with a smiling, or a non-smiling, neutral expression. Those judges who saw the smiling photo thought that the student was less responsible for the offence, and suggested less severe punishments than subjects who saw the non-smiling picture!

Even more surprising are the findings of Harari and McDavid (1973), who asked some school teachers to grade compositions allegedly written by fourth and fifth grade children. The children were identified only by their first names, for example 'David' and 'Michael' (regular, positively evaluated names), or 'Hubert' and 'Elmer' (unusual, negatively evaluated names). Although the essays were exactly the same, 'Elmer' and 'Hubert' averaged almost one whole grade less than 'Michael' and 'David' on their essays.

Halo effects. We often tend to assume that people who have positive characteristics in one area, say physical appearance, are also better in other, unrelated areas such as motivation or competence.

Another example of halo effects was demonstrated by Wilson (1968), who told his subjects, Australian students, that a guest lecturer they were about to hear worked as a professor, senior lecturer, lecturer, tutor, or student at another university. After the lecture, students were asked among other things to estimate the height of the guest, as well as the height of their usual lecturer. Students who thought the visitor was a professor estimated his height to be almost 6 cm greater than judges who believed he was only a student. There were no such biases in estimating the height of the usual lecturer. In this case, it appears that positive characteristics on a status dimension, such as academic rank, exerted a halo effect on judgments of a physical trait, height. Such halo effects may also be thought of as reflecting a universal 'implicit personality theory' we all share — namely, the belief that good characteristics are generally more likely to be associated with other good characteristics than bad ones.

Primacy and recency effects

Are first or last impressions more important in influencing our judgments of people? Apart from halo effects, the order in which we receive information about another person has a major influence on its relative 'weight' in impression formation. Most of us tend to behave as if first impressions were far more important than later ones. We tend to take special care of our appearance, and go out of our way to appear good-looking, friendly and intelligent when we meet somebody for the first time, be it a date, a potential friend or a future colleague.

Solomon Asch was among the first to investigate such order effects. In one study, he gave subjects two alternative descriptions of a hypothetical person. The first one read: 'intelligent, industrious, impulsive, critical, stubborn and envious'. The second list contained exactly the same adjectives, but in a reverse order: 'envious, stubborn, critical, impulsive, industrious, intelligent'. Did you get a different impression of such a person while reading the two lists? Asch's subjects certainly did. They rated the person in the first condition (intelligent, etc.) far more positively than the person described by the second list (stubborn, etc.). This study provides clear evidence that the information received first may have a disproportionately large effect on judgments, a so-called primacy effect.

Asch believed that this phenomenon was caused by a shift in the meaning of the later adjectives in a direction to be more consistent with the first few adjectives. This *assimilation of meaning* hypothesis is of course entirely consistent with the Gestalt view, according to which the meaning of personality traits is not constant, but depends on the other traits which make up the whole person.

Asch's study was once again criticised on the grounds that rating a few adjectives is very different from judging more complex stimuli. Luchins

(1957) created a more realistic stimulus by providing subjects with two detailed paragraphs describing the activities of a person called 'Jim'. In the first paragraph, Jim was described as a friendly, extroverted and gregarious person, while in the second paragraph Jim behaved as if he was shy, introverted and generally unfriendly. Subjects read these two paragraphs either in the extroverted-introverted, or the introverted-extroverted order. Once again, strong primacy effects were found: impressions were largely determined by which paragraph subjects read first.

Even more realistic conditions were created in a study by Jones et al. (1968). Here, subjects observed a person taking a test consisting of 30 items. In one condition, the person started off very well, answering correctly almost all questions, but his performance decreased in the second half of the test. In the other condition, exactly the opposite occurred: the person started off very badly, but improved dramatically in the second half of the test. In reality, both persons performed equally well, each answering 15 of the 30 questions correctly. Yet subjects observing these performances thought that the person who started off well was more intelligent, and would do better in a later test, than the person who started off slowly.

Surprisingly, these strong primacy effects are quite easy to eliminate if subjects are warned not to make up their minds until they have read all the relevant information, or if the presentation of the first and second information sets is interrupted by a pause or some other activity. Under such circumstances, a recency effect is found — that is, the information

The power of first impressions. First impressions can often have a major impact on our impressions of people, unless special care is taken to avoid such bias.

presented last will dominate impressions. The most obvious explanation of recency effects has to do with memory. If a judge has not yet made up his/her mind about a person on the basis of early information, the last few items will have the greatest influence simply because these are most likely to be well remembered. Recency effects also occur when people are warned, or instructed to pay equal attention to all items of information.

One explanation of primacy effects is simply that people pay less attention to later information than the first few items. When subjects are interrupted in the middle of the task, or are told to pay equal attention to all information, the primacy effect disappears. Hendrick and Costantini (1970) created such a situation simply by asking subjects to read out aloud each item describing a person. Under these circumstances, people concentrate as much on the last as on the first item. As predicted, a slight recency effect was found instead of a primacy effect. In conclusion, it seems fair to say that in most everyday situations first impressions are indeed extremely important. However, it is quite easy to eliminate such biases by interrupting the presentation, or getting judges to pay equal attention to later information by some other means. If you have no control over your judges, it is still best to concentrate on creating the best possible first impression in critical encounters!

Stereotyping and categorisation biases

You may remember that earlier we discussed the role of person prototypes and stereotypes in influencing the accuracy of person perception judgments. The ability to correctly recognise the characteristics of the group a person belongs to can greatly facilitate the impression formation process. Indeed, social perception always involves such categorisation. When we see another person, what often comes to mind is an image of the typical member, or 'prototype' of the group he belongs to (see Chapter 3). Once a person is associated with such a type or category, he is automatically assumed to have many of the same characteristics as the typical group member. This may lead to serious distortions in person perception judgments.

Razran (1950) reported a study which illustrates such distortions very clearly. He asked subjects to rate 30 female university students, whose pictures were projected on a screen, for likeability, intelligence, ambition, character and beauty. Two months later, the same subjects were once again asked to rate the same pictures, mixed in among several others. This time, however, they were also told the girls' names, which were manipulated so that some girls had obviously Irish, Jewish, Italian or Anglo-Saxon names. The influence of these group stereotypes on judgments was quite startling. When compared with the earlier judgments of the same girls, Jewish girls for example were now thought to be much more intelligent and ambitious, but less likeable than before.

Clearly, the characteristics which were thought to be typical of Jews at the time became part of the impressions formed of these individuals.

Stereotyping usually occurs on the basis of highly visible characteristics, such as skin colour, looks, accent or name, as in the Razran study. Often, the way a person is dressed is enough to elicit a stereotype. In one British study (Sissons, 1978), an actor asked for directions at a railway station while dressed in middle-class (bowler hat, etc.) or working-class clothes. The reactions were dramatically different, and the middle-class person received far more help. Even unusual, 'hip' clothes may confer an advantage on their wearer in certain settings. At a demonstration, people wearing 'hip' clothes were more successful in collecting signatures than people wearing traditional attire (Suedfeld, Bochner and Matas, 1971).

The categorisation of people into known 'types' does not necessarily imply prejudice or intentional bias on the part of the observer. Given the immense variety of information confronting us, it is necessary to simplify and organise the world around us into familiar categories. You may remember that this idea was the basis not only of George Kelley's theory of personal constructs, but also of much contemporary research on person perception (Chapter 3). But such categorisation may also be a source of significant bias in judging others. By becoming aware of the way categorisation operates to influence judgments, we may be able to control the distortions which follow much better. We shall have more to say about such processes later.

Other biases due to expectations
Our knowledge of the world is organised not only in terms of typologies of people, but also in terms of typologies of events (Forgas, 1979). Representations about typical, expected event sequences, or 'scripts' may also influence person perception judgments. An experiment by Owens, Bower and Black (1979) illustrates this effect quite well. Bower gave his subjects five simple paragraphs to read about a character, Nancy, describing her daily activities such as shopping, making coffee, attending a lecture, visiting a doctor, or going to a party. However, half the subjects were also given an additional three sentences to read before the paragraphs: 'Nancy woke up feeling sick again, and she wondered if she really were pregnant. How would she tell the professor she had been seeing? And the money was another problem.'

The next day, all subjects were asked to recall as much as they could about the daily routine of Nancy. Those who read the brief introduction suggesting that Nancy was pregnant tended to 'remember' details which were consistent with a 'typical' unwanted pregnancy script. It appears that the existence of strong views and expectations about situations involving unwanted pregnancies (a 'script') influenced the way information about Nancy was interpreted and recalled. This effect is very similar to the distortions demonstrated by Snyder and Uranowitz in a study we discussed in the previous chapter, where subjects' impressions strongly depended on the information they were given about the sexual preferences (homosexual versus heterosexual) of a girl they read about.

Negativity biases

When we form an impression of a person, do we treat positive and negative information the same way? Would it have an equally positive or negative influence on you to find out that a person is hardworking or lazy, intelligent or stupid, pleasant or unpleasant? Research has shown that negative information tends to have a disproportionately large weight in determining impressions, and negative first impressions are also much more resistant to change than positive first impressions. This bias can be best explained in terms of the relative informational value of positive and negative cues about a person. Positive deeds and characteristics are generally in accordance with social expectations, and thus say relatively little about an individual: he is simply as he is supposed to be. We are all generally expected to perform positive acts and say positive things about each other.

Negative deeds, however, usually go against socially accepted standards, and thus are likely to reveal genuine and informative individual characteristics. As such, negative information about a person is often treated as a particularly reliable indicator of 'true' character, and has a disproportionate effect on impressions.

Is this a nice person? Leniency versus negativity bias. Because of the force of cultural norms, we generally assume positive rather than negative characteristics about others. When direct evidence of negative characteristics is obtained, however, it tends to have a disproportionately large impact on impressions.

Leniency biases

These biases refer to the fact that in the absence of clearly negative information we generally expect people to have positive rather than negative qualities. Just as negative behaviour has a disproportionate effect on impressions as it cannot be explained by adherence to cultural conventions, in the absence of any negative information people tend to follow the same conventions in assuming positive characteristics. It is for this reason that more than 75 per cent of all public figures rated on Gallup polls are judged positively rather than the 50 per cent one would expect by chance. We prefer not to judge others negatively unless clear evidence of negative characteristics is available.

This general leniency effect also explains, for example, why students are quite prepared to be extremely critical of the courses they are offered, without extending the same criticism to the professors who after all produced those courses. Not having direct information about stupidity or neglect, it is usual to assume the best intentions! Nor are social psychologists exempt from such leniency biases. To take an example, in the voluminous research on physical attractiveness, unattractive targets are never described as 'ugly'. Other, less extreme words, such as 'plain' or 'homely' (!) are preferred in most textbooks, including this one. In the absence of any reason for negative evaluations, we prefer not to use loaded or critical terms.

Conclusions

The list of the various factors influencing impression formation is by no means exhaustive. The general point is that in judging others, we always simplify and categorise the incoming information in accordance with our 'implicit theories of personality', our past experience and knowledge about person types and event scripts, and the expectations and norms of our culture. We can now link what we learnt in the previous chapter to the problem of impression formation by suggesting that these various biases function as *weighting factors*, increasing or reducing the weight of particular information units that we receive about people. Such a weighted averaging model of impression formation is sufficiently general to explain both Asch's central trait hypothesis and Anderson's information integration model. The most important question is: what determines the weight we give to a particular piece of information about a person? We saw that factors internal to the perceiver, such as his expectations, feelings and knowledge, play a crucial role here.

The effects of such expectations on impression formation can sometimes have quite disturbing implications, leading to a self-fulfilling prophecy where the target in fact ends up conforming to our expectations. There are some interesting studies demonstrating such effects. Rosenthal and Jacobson (1968) told elementary school teachers that some children in their class (randomly selected) could be expected to improve their performance significantly during the school year, on the basis of their scores in a test. At the end of the school year, the children's IQs were assessed in a real test. Those randomly selected children who were expected to do well by their teachers showed a marked real gain of over 10 IQ points more than did other children. Apparently, the good impressions and expectations of improvement by the teachers were translated into real improvement, probably because the teachers paid particular attention to those children whom they expected to perform well.

Such self-fulfilling prophecies may be even more important when the characteristic in question is not as easily measured as is intelligence. When we expect a person to be unfriendly or aggressive, information about the validity of this expectation is hard to obtain. Such people may often end up reacting as we expected, not because they are really unfriendly or aggressive people, but because we behaved in an unfriendly and defensive way towards them. Similarly, expectations of positive behaviour may often be confirmed by subsequent experience simply because our own behaviour was more positive to begin with. Perhaps this is also a reason for the 'leniency bias' we discussed above. It makes sense to assume that other people have positive characteristics until we are convinced of the opposite, since this belief will make our own behaviour easier to plan and more productive.

In considering the various processes and biases which operate in impression formation, we have come very close to discussing the problem of how we make inferences and attributions about other people. Many of the same variables which affect impression formation also influence how we attribute intentions to people, a question which has received much attention in recent years. In the next chapter we shall turn to research on inferences about people, the topic of attribution theory.

5. Inferences about people: attribution theory

5.
INFERENCES ABOUT PEOPLE: ATTRIBUTION THEORY

We have seen throughout the previous chapters that social perception is essentially inferential. It involves the reconstruction of a person's invisible traits and characteristics from directly observable actions and behaviours. A special category of such inferences seeks an answer to the question: *why* does a person behave in a particular way? Inferences of this kind are addressed by attribution theorists. Attribution theory is not a clearly formulated theory as its name would suggest. Rather, it consists of a broad set of ideas, rules and hypotheses concerned with how we make inferences about the causes of our own and other people's behaviour (see Activity 5.1).

The correct identification of why people behave as they do is perhaps the most important and complex issue in person perception. Almost any example of human behaviour can be interpreted in a multiplicity of equally plausible ways. A colleague may be friendly (a) because he likes you, (b) because he wants to borrow some money from you, (c) because he is always friendly to everybody, or (d) because his boss told him to be, and so on. How do we know which of these several conflicting interpretations is correct? Attribution researchers believe that in deciding why people behave the way they do, we are dealing with problems such as (a) determining the causal antecedents of an action, and (b) establishing the intentionality of the actor. The relevant causal antecedents of an act may be found inside a person (for example, 'he really likes me'), or external to him ('his boss asked him to be friendly to me'). If the causation is internal, we must further decide whether the act was intentional or not. Attribution research deals with how, and under what circumstances we make such decisions (for example, Nesdale, 1983).

Heider and the logic of attribution
Perhaps the first psychologist explicitly interested in such attributions was Fritz Heider (1958). He argued that in order to successfully engage

ACTIVITY 5.1
Why Did He Do It?

You will find below descriptions of several everyday occurrences. Read each of these episodes carefully, then answer the questions below them in writing on a separate piece of paper.

1. A policeman directing the traffic at a busy intersection noticed that a driver crossed the street after the traffic lights changed to orange. He stopped him, and gave him a ticket.

   Why did he do it?

2. Dr Smith, your local doctor, has been bitterly complaining about the introduction of a new health care scheme. He maintains that it will interfere with the doctor-patient relationship and result in worse service. It is also well known that doctors will make somewhat less money under the new scheme.

   Why is Dr Smith complaining?

3. Your friend Evan has just returned from an overseas trip and has brought you a beautiful present which is much nicer that his presents to other people. He always seems to be much nicer to you than to other people.

   Why did he bring you the present?

4. In the face of considerable opposition from his parents, who wanted him to study accountancy, Bob decided to study psychology at university, even though he knows that the job opportunities in that field are very limited.

   Why did he do it?

These examples will give you some idea of the kinds of problems attribution theory addresses. For each of the answers you gave to the above questions, decide (a) whether you explained the behaviour in terms of internal, or external causes, and (b) whether the causes you used were stable and enduring, or short term. As you read on in the text, keep referring back to the answers you gave to these questions, to see how far your attributional strategies match the various models you will read about.

in social interaction, we must be able to understand, predict and control our social environment effectively. We accomplish this, according to Heider, by assuming that behaviour is caused, and we look for the sources of causation either in the person or in the environment. For Heider, people in everyday life function as 'naive scientists', using the same principles of causation and logic to understand each other that scientists use to understand the physical world.

Heider thought that our belief that people are causal agents is a basic and universal human characteristic. Since we know that our own intentional actions can causally influence our social or physical environment, we seem to look for similar causal powers in others to explain events in the outside world. In an interesting experiment, Heider and Simmel (1944) showed that even objects as far removed from human beings as geometric figures moving on a screen were frequently perceived by judges 'as if' they were human agents, 'causing' other geometric figures to behave as if they were also humans (to fight, escape, chase, and so on).

Heider attempted to use logic to describe how the principles of causation are used in everyday attributions. In predicting other people's behaviour, we first try to discriminate between external, environmental influences, and internal, individual influences. Internal causation can only be inferred if there are no plausible external pressures explaining a person's actions. In the previous example, if you know that your colleague is friendly because his boss told him to be (external causation), you cannot tell whether he really likes you or not (internal causation). Similarly, in Activity 5.1, the actions of the policeman are fully consistent with the requirements of his role, so we have no real basis for making judgments about his internal qualities and intentions. When a person does something *against* considerable odds, such as Bob in Activity 5.1 who decides to study psychology despite parental pressure and bad job prospects, we know that strong internal intentions and effort best explain that action.

The causal agency residing inside a person in turn can be subdivided into two components: the power or *ability* people possess to carry out an action, and the *effort* they exert. Heider suggested that environmental and internal (dispositional) forces are in an additive or subtractive relationship: they can supplement, reduce or even eliminate each other. The two internal components of personal causation, ability and effort, are in a multiplicative relationship, implying that if either is absent the sum total of their joint effects would also be zero. Ability without effort, or effort without ability will not result in any action.

Our perception of the relationship between the internal factor of ability, and the external factor of environmental difficulty, Heider called the perception of *can*. When the external difficulty is greater than the ability the action becomes impossible, and if it is minimal no great ability is required to perform it. It is in moderately difficult situations that we are most likely to obtain useful information about an actor's ability. Another basis of our naive analysis of action is the perception of *trying*, which is determined by two things: the actor's intention, and his/her effort in achieving an act. Underlying Heider's ideas is the concern with the two basic attributional questions: (a) is an action caused by internal dispositions or by external pressures? (b) if caused internally, was it intentional or unintentional?

We must continuously make such judgments on short notice in everyday life. Is the shop assistant who has been studiously ignoring you for the past five minutes a rude, incompetent person (internal attribution), or is she under great pressure to complete the paperwork in front of her (external attribution)? Did your colleague show dislike by not returning your greeting this morning (disposition), or was he distracted by a family row at home? Is your doctor friendly to you because he genuinely likes you (disposition), or because it is part of his job and you pay him for it (external)? The answers we give to such questions will guide our behaviour (for example, whether to complain about the shop assistant, whether to repeat our greeting to our colleague more loudly, or whether to change our doctor), and it is essential that we make the correct attribution if our behaviour is to be appropriate. How we accomplish such tasks is what attribution research tries to discover.

As you saw above, Heider thought of social actors as 'naive scientists', who use the cold rules of logic to infer whether an action was internally caused or not. Whenever an action is consistent with external pressures and expectations (as the doctor's behaviour above), we have little reason to attribute internal causation. When behaviour is not externally

Why is he ignoring me? Attribution theory deals with the way people explain the behaviour of others. Whether intentionality is attributed in a case like this will determine the person's reactions.

constrained, we must use logic to decide whether the action was intentional or not. In trying to describe the phenomenology of naive actors, Heider's model remained rather non-specific, a shortcoming which later attribution theorists tried to remedy.

Jones and Davis' theory of correspondent inferences

Once we have decided that a particular action had internal causes, how do we go about working out exactly what the motivation for the action was? Jones and Davis (1965) suggest that we have to work backwards from the multiple effects associated with every action, to decide which of several effects was *intended*. We can do this by assessing whether the actor had prior knowledge of such an effect, and whether he believed that he had the ability to produce the effect. Actions which are (a) socially undesirable and (b) produce few effects which are (c) uniquely associated with that action are easier to attribute to dispositions than socially desirable actions which can be produced by a great many non-unique causes. The observer is thus engaged in a process of discounting: "The role of a given cause in producing a given effect is discounted if other plausible causes are also present" (Kelley, 1971, p.8).

Several studies illustrate this principle. Jones, Davis and Gergen (1961) asked subjects to make judgments about individuals who behaved in accordance with, or contrary to, the requirements of a job for which they were applying. Some applicants appeared introverted and self-sufficient when interviewed for a job requiring introversion; others appeared introverted for an extrovert job and extroverted for an introvert job. People who behaved according to the job requirements were rated near the neutral point of the scale. In contrast, the behaviour of persons which conflicted with role requirements was judged to reflect genuine personal characteristics. In another study, US students were asked to attribute political dispositions to the writer of an anti-Castro or pro-Castro essay, which they believed was written either by free choice, or under coercion. Judges were most certain in their judgments when (a) the essays were done freely (no external cause), and (b) they reflected non-conformist, deviant attitudes (pro-Castro) (Jones and Harris, 1967).

Acting against outside pressures and, occasionally, against one's own apparent interests results in more confident attributions of intentionality, as well as the greater credibility of the behaviour. Experiments also show this effect: a low-status communicator, such as a convicted criminal, may be more persuasive and credible than a high-status communicator, such as a lawyer, if he argues that courts should be given more power, since this is against external expectations as well as against his best self-interests (Walster, Aronson and Abrahams, 1966). And conversely, when medical practitioners criticise a health scheme under which they make less money as 'unworkable'(see Activity 5.1), we tend to discount the possibility that they have *our* best interests at heart.

Kelley's multidimensional model of attribution

So far we have dealt with a number of more or less intuitive principles which help us to make reliable internal attributions: low social desirability, unique effects and systematic covariation between cause and effect. Harold Kelley (1967; 1971) developed a more sophisticated theory in which three sets of variables are considered simultaneously: hence the term 'cube theory' or 'three-dimensional theory' to describe his model. The three dimensions are (1) the situation or context in which a behaviour occurs, (2) the target or object of the action, and (3) the actors who perform it. We may attribute an action to either of these three categories: the actor, the target or the situation. The idea of covariation is at the heart of Kelley's system: we attribute causality when causes and effects occur or disappear simultaneously over time. We can do this by looking for covariation across each of these three dimensions.

First, an observer would want to know whether an observed action is *consistent* over time and across different situations. Does the person react the same way to a similar situation over time, and across different modalities? When consistency is low, it is difficult to make either an internal, or an external attribution — we can at best explain the actor's behaviour in terms of chance or variable circumstances. High consistency is necessary for either external or internal attributions to be made. Returning to our previous example, your colleague's friendly behaviour would be difficult or impossible to explain unless you first observe a consistent pattern of friendliness across time and situations.

Second, our observer would need to know whether the action is *distinctive*. Does the observed behaviour occur only in reaction to this particular person, situation or stimulus (high distinctiveness), or does the actor display this behaviour indiscriminately, in reaction to all kinds of other stimuli, persons or situations (low distinctiveness)? Is your colleague friendly to everybody, or just you? High distinctiveness leads to external, situational attributions.

Thirdly, an observer would seek information about how other people behave in reaction to the same stimulus, the extent of *consensus* in the observed behaviour. When other people behave the same way in reaction to a similar situation we may speak of high consensus; if it is only the actor who behaves in this way, the consensus is low. If all your colleagues are always friendly to you (high consensus), you are not only a very fortunate person, but you would also be able to reliably attribute their behaviour to a cause which is external to them: yourself!

The various combinations of these three modalities (consistency, distinctiveness and consensus) lead to different attribution strategies. A test of Kelley's theory requires that each of these three variables, distinctiveness, consensus and consistency be varied independently. Such a study was carried out by McArthur (1972), who asked subjects to make attributions about a hypothetical simple event (why did Mary laugh at the nightclub comedian last night?). The manipulations introduced into the story, and the resulting attributions are summarised in Table 5.1. We can see from this table that, by and large, the findings confirm Kelley's expectations: high distinctiveness and consensus lead to external, and low distinctiveness and consensus to internal attributions, but only if consistency is high. Of course, in real life we do not always have precise information about each of these three modalities. Often, we have to make an attribution on the basis of very limited information, as you had to do in Activity 5.1. In such situations, Kelley suggests that we rely on general causal models which we build up over time to explain occurrences. This is what you must have done in completing Activity 5.1.

TABLE 5.1
WHY DID MARY LAUGH AT THE COMEDIAN? AN ILLUSTRATION OF KELLEY'S THREE-DIMENSIONAL MODEL: THE EFFECTS OF CONSISTENCY, DISTINCTIVENESS AND CONSENSUS ON ATTRIBUTIONS

Information available to judges			
Consistency	Distinctiveness	Consensus	Typical attribution
1. High: she always laughs at him	High: she didn't laugh at anyone else	High: everyone else laughed as well	To the stimulus: the comedian
2. High: she always laughs at him	Low: she always laughs at comedians	Low: hardly anyone else laughed	To the person: Mary
3. Low: she almost never laughs at him	High: she didn't laugh at anyone else	Low: hardly anyone else laughed	To the situation/ circumstances

After McArthur, 1972

Some assumptions of attribution models
The models of attribution we have looked at so far all make certain assumptions about the way human beings think and behave. It is implicit in these formulations that (a) attribution is essentially a *rational, logical* and therefore predictable process, in which (b) the perceiver's main concern is to identify necessary *prior causes* in order to explain an action. As Shaver (1975) argued, "Heider's ideal perceiver can be thought of as a *philosopher*, using nothing but the rules of logic. . . . the ideal perceiver for Jones and Davis can be thought of as a highly disciplined *information processor*. . . . in contrast, Kelley's ideal perceiver is a *social scientist* whose task is to locate the source of an event by considering, among other things, the judgments of other persons" (pp.58-59).

The notion of the scientific, detached perceiver embodied in all these theories may be something of an oversimplification. Our attributions about others are often influenced by irrational, motivational biases as well as our inability to deal with the available information effectively. Research on the various sources of bias in attributions has revealed a fascinating variety of judgmental shortcomings which we shall discuss in a later section.

The methods of Sherlock Holmes. All attribution theorists assume that people use the rules of science and logic, just like a good detective, to infer the causes of events. This view of human nature may perhaps apply to Sherlock Holmes, but not always to others.

Research on attributions

The main attraction of attribution theory for researchers is that it offers a model for the explanation of many everyday judgmental phenomena. What are the real attitudes of people we meet? How can we explain unexpected behaviours? Why do some people succeed and others fail? Questions such as these illustrate the breadth of attribution research.

We have already mentioned the problem of *attributing attitudes*. The more socially undesirable an action, and the fewer the external restrictions that apply to an actor, the more confident we are that the observed behaviour reflects genuine attitudes. The study by Jones and Harris (1967) showing that pro-Castro essays (undesirable attitude) written under free choice conditions resulted in the strongest attributions about the writer's real attitudes illustrates this point. (Table 5.2).

An interesting aspect of this experiment is that even when the actor had no choice in what kind of essay to write, subjects still felt able to

TABLE 5.2
THE EFFECTS OF FREE CHOICE OR LACK OF CHOICE, AND THE
DESIRABILITY OF THE ATTITUDE EXPRESSED ON ATTRIBUTIONS
ABOUT UNDERLYING ATTITUDES

Attitude expressed	Choice condition*	
	Free choice	No free choice
Desirable attitude (anti-Castro essay)	17.38	22.87
Undesirable attitude (pro-Castro)	59.62	44.10

*The larger the number the stronger the attributed pro-Castro attitude

After Jones and Harris, 1967

make attributions about his real, underlying attitudes. We shall have more to say about this tendency later.

A person's *status* may also influence attributions, since high status people are often thought to have more power and freedom to act as they wish than low-status persons. In a study by Thibaut and Riecken (1955), subjects had to persuade a high and a low-status partner to comply with a request to donate blood. Both complied, but subjects thought that the high-status person did so because he wanted to (internal causation), while the low status person complied because he was forced to (external causation).

The same principles apply when the freedom of action of the person we judge is restricted due to our own actions. Strickland (1958) asked his

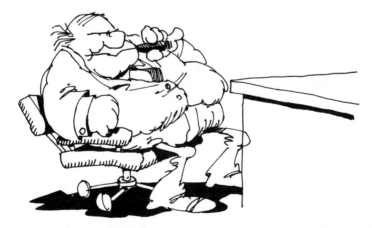

Attributions and the boss. People usually assume that persons in positions of status and influence have much more freedom to act as they wish than those people themselves believe is the case. Supervisors and leaders, in turn, attribute less internal motivation and trustworthiness to those subordinates who are most controlled by them.

subjects to act as 'supervisors', checking either frequently (nine times) or rarely (twice only) on a 'worker' who performed ten trials of a boring task. Although both workers performed equally well, supervisors trusted the frequently controlled person less, and thought that his performance was due to outside pressure (i.e. their supervision). Such findings have important implications in real life, where those in power (such as team leaders, teachers, and so on) may make more negative attributions about those subordinates whose performance they most directly control.

Attributions of success and failure
Explaining why people succeed or fail in the tasks they undertake is a particularly interesting problem not only in everyday life, but also in attribution research. Was your colleague promoted because (a) he worked very hard recently, (b) he has the ability and intelligence, (c) the boss favoured him, or (d) he simply had good luck? How you answer questions such as these will influence your attitudes and behaviour at work. These four alternative explanations are examples of a scheme of attributed causes for success and failure constructed by Weiner (1974). He argued that apart from deciding whether an action was internally or externally caused as Heider and Kelley suggested, a further question in attributions of success is whether the cause is stable or unstable over time. By combining these two dimensions (external-internal and stable-unstable) he constructed four attributional categories for success or failure (see Table 5.3).

Considerable research on attributions of success and failure has been carried out using Weiner's categories. Despite the usefulness of such a system for classifying attributed causes, it is not certain that people in real life necessarily also use the same sort of causes to explain success and failure. Analyses of open-ended explanations of achievement do not always yield the same categories (Falbo and Beck, 1979).

TABLE 5.3
WEINER'S CATEGORISATION OF ATTRIBUTED CAUSES FOR SUCCESS
AND FAILURE

	Internal	External
Stable	e.g. ability	e.g. the situation
Unstable	e.g. effort	e.g. luck

Explanations of wealth and poverty
The way success or failure is explained may also have considerable social and political consequences. Do you believe that people who are wealthy reached their status by hard work, intelligence and ability, or through luck and the inequalities of our economic system? Are poor people

themselves responsible for their fate, or is the 'system' to blame? Do the unemployed share in the responsibility for not working, or is it all caused by external forces we cannot do anything about? Answers to these questions have profound ideological and political consequences. Recent research has shown that attributions for wealth and poverty, for example, do not exactly follow Weiner's fourfold classification (Furnham, 1983).

In a recent study we found that the four variables most commonly used to explain wealth were external/social, internal/individual, family background and luck/risk taking (Forgas, Morris and Furnham, 1982). Such everyday attributions for achievement were also strongly dependent on the sex, income and political affiliation of the judges, and the ethnic background and social class of the targets. In this Australian study, immigrants were more commonly seen as acquiring their wealth through individual effort than native-born people, and people of immigrant background were more likely to believe that anybody who gets rich does so in this way.

This study also illustrates the point that attribution is not always an individual activity (Semin, 1980). Often, the explanations we have for common occurrences are derived from social and political groups. Political parties, churches and other institutions, among other things, also provide their members with a scheme of attributions for common and problematic occurrences. In the above study, left wing voters were more likely to attribute wealth to family background or luck, while immigrants and conservative voters thought individual ability and effort were the main causes of personal wealth.

Another influence on attributions of success and failure may be the target's sex. Women are often given less credit for occupational success than men, and blamed more if they fail. Feather and Simon (1975) found that when women succeeded on a task, it was more likely to be attributed to luck and the ease of the task than a similar male success. Conversely, lack of ability is more often given as the cause of a female's than a male's failure. It is also quite remarkable that the status and prestige of an occupation tends to be directly related to the proportion of males in that occupation (Feather, 1975). This could be because there is more discrimination against women in high-prestige occupations. But it is also possible that a high concentration of women leads to decreased attribution of ability, and lower occupational status. An interesting example is the high proportion of females amongst general practitioners in the Soviet Union (Hendrick-Smith, 1977). Apparently, this group has a much lower occupational prestige there than in the West.

These various studies indicate that everyday attributions are not always guided by an impartial, logical search for causes as Heider and most attribution theorists assumed. Our attributional strategies are apparently also influenced by such factors as our background, political affiliation, status, sex, attitudes, personality and motivations. We shall return to some of these non-rational influences on attributions judgments in a later section.

Attribution of responsibility

A related problem is how we allocate responsibility to people in everyday life. When is a person to blame, and when is a person innocent of committing a transgression? How do we make such essentially moral judgments? The issue is of great importance in our daily lives, and many individuals and agencies (teachers, lawyers, judges, policemen, parents) must routinely make such decisions about the responsibility of others. Piaget (1965), together with most attribution theorists, believed that responsibility attribution is essentially a rational process, which is learnt as an individual develops.

In his studies of children, Piaget found that under the age of seven, most children attribute responsibility solely on the basis of the objective consequences of an act. They believe that a child who accidentally broke several cups should be punished more severely than another child who broke one cup as result of intentionally disobeying a command. After the age of nine, however, most children take into account subjective intentions in their judgments. Intentional misdeeds are now punished more severely, even if the consequences are less serious, than unintended accidents.

From a scientific point of view, an important problem is exactly what we mean when we say somebody is responsible. Does it mean simply that the action was caused by that person? Does it also have to be intentional? Is the severity of consequences a factor? Does it involve moral, or legal accountability? The written and unwritten laws of most societies essentially consist of a pragmatic combination of such considerations. Despite such a codified guide to responsibility attribution as written laws provide, decisions about culpability are rarely simple even within the legal system. The specific interpretations given to written laws by judges, juries and lawyers play a crucial role in deciding responsibility. How do individuals cope with such attributions about responsibility in their everyday lives?

Attribution research shows that everyday judgments of responsibility are often influenced by apparently irrational considerations. Walster (1966) found that a person was held more responsible for an unpredictable accident (a parked car's handbrake failed, and it rolled down a hill) when the resulting damage was serious rather than negligible. This seems to be the same strategy that Piaget found in young children. We seem often to hold innocent victims partly responsible for uncontrollable events (Lerner, 1965; see also section on the 'just world hypothesis' below). Shaver (1970) found that people who are similar to us are held less responsible for the same incident than dissimilar others. Attractive and good-looking people are often held less responsible for a transgression than plain looking people (Sigall and Ostrove, 1975; see also Activity 4.1), and even a passing nonverbal expression, such as a smile, can influence reponsibility attribution judgments as we saw in the previous chapter (for example, study by Forgas, O'Connor and Morris in Chapter 4).

As the above examples illustrate, research on real life attribution problems soon indicated that theoretical attribution models assuming unbiased information processors looking for causes only tell us part of the story. Various cognitive and motivational biases often play a very important role in attributions. We shall look at some of these biases next.

The bias towards causality in attributions

There is a very respectable philosophical view which maintains that causality is not a feature of the natural universe, but lies in the eye of the beholder. In other words, the idea of cause-effect relationships is a human invention. Certainly people have a strong tendency to think in causal terms, even when there is little reason to do so. Some experimental investigations led to similar conclusions. We tend to perceive causality, regularity and even intentionality where there could not possibly be any. In a study we have already touched on, Heider and Simmel (1944) showed subjects an animated film in which various geometric shapes moved about in various ways. Female subjects who were asked to interpret the film described the actions in causal and dispositional terms, as if the shapes were animated beings, 'chasing', 'fighting' or 'running away' from each other.

In a more recent study, Bassili (1976) used computer-generated films of moving abstract figures as stimuli, and manipulated the distance and the time between the actions. Subjects were most likely to infer causality when the shapes moved immediately after each other. The nature of the interaction reported (hitting, chasing, and so on) depended on how close the figures came to each other. These studies are consistent with the Gestalt model of social perception, according to which we tend to see the world in terms of coherent and meaningful patterns, even when the available information is very sketchy.

Since most of the information we deal with is about people, a tendency to look at things 'as if' they were people is a simple and common way of interpreting the world. As we 'know' that our own intentions and actions can have a causal effect on our environment, we prefer to explain the behaviour of other people, and even inanimate objects in similar ways. This bias towards causality can be a serious source of distortions in attributions, leading us to see causes and even intentions when there is little more than a spatial and temporal correlation between an action and its consequences.

The bias towards internal attributions

There is also a strong tendency in attribution judgments to see personal, internal causation even when environmental forces are clearly predominant. It seems as if saying that "a person is the origin of an event is the simplest and most satisfying explanation available. Indeed, the actor's behaviour is so overwhelming that it engulfs the field, often obscuring truly environmental causes" (Shaver, 1975, p.38). In the study by Jones and Harris (1967) mentioned earlier, judges who had to estimate the attitudes of a target who wrote an essay about Castro tended to attribute a genuine disposition to the writer even when they were told that the essay was written under pressure.

Other studies demonstrated a similar bias towards dispositional attributions even more forcefully. Schneider and Miller (1975) manipulated the enthusiasm communicated by speakers presenting forced opinions. Once again, even the forced opinions presented by an unenthusiastic, bland speaker were thought to some extent to reflect his genuine attitudes. When the speakers presented essays allegedly written by somebody else, judges still thought that the speakers agreed with the

---

ACTIVITY 5.2
Explaining Ourselves and Others

Please give brief written answers on a separate sheet of paper to each of the following questions:

1. Think about the last time you were late for an engagement. Why were you late, and how did you explain your lateness to your partner?

2. Now think of the last occasion when you were kept waiting by somebody. In your opinion, why was that person late?

3. Think of an occasion when a person of superior status criticised or punished you for something you did. In your opinion why did your superior behave in this way? Could he/she have acted otherwise?

4. Remember a situation when you had occasion to criticise or punish a person of subordinate status. Why did you do it?

Now try to classify these various attributions in terms of whether external or internal causes were given as explaining each of these actions. Refer back to your answers as you read the following sections.

opinions expressed. In many everyday situations, the behaviour of the actor tends to 'dominate the field' to such an extent that internal attributions are erroneously made. This tendency to explain events in terms of internal dispositions is so pervasive that it has been labelled the 'fundamental attribution error' by some psychologists (Ross, 1977).

Actor-observer bias
Just as there is a tendency to attribute the actions of an observed other to internal rather than external causes (the dispositional bias discussed above), there is a complementary tendency for people to attribute their own behaviours to external, situational factors (Jones and Nisbett, 1971). When male students were asked to write a brief paragraph explaining why their best friend (a) studied a particular subject, and (b) liked his romantic partner, attributions were mainly dispositional ('because he wanted to'; 'because he is insecure'). When they were asked to answer these questions for themselves, attributions were mainly situational ('because the lecturer is interesting'; 'because she is nice').

To put it simply: we tend to believe that *we* do things because the situation requires us to, but others act the way they do because they want to. In another study, West, Gunn and Chernicky (1975) approached some people, asking them to participate in an elaborate Watergate-style break-in (potential actors), but simply described the circumstances to others (observers). Actors later explained their behaviour in terms of external circumstances ('I was under pressure', 'it could be a useful learning experience'), while observers thought the actors' behaviour was caused by internal dispositions (they were perhaps immoral people). The same kind of processes could have influenced the way Nixon's men perceived their behaviour: they said there was an overwhelming external need for them to act as they did (see also Activity 5.2).

Even in less extreme circumstances, people rarely explain their own behaviours as caused by internal factors. Few of us say 'sorry for being late, but I am a disorganised person'. Rather, we blame external forces, such as our watch, the traffic, or a last-minute telephone call. Quite the opposite happens when making attributions about others. When we are kept waiting by somebody, we invariably blame the person: he or she is an impolite, disorganised or forgetful person. Did you use these strategies in the answers you gave to Activity 5.2?

Such attributional bias may be particularly important in unbalanced power relationships. Subordinates may attribute more internal power and freedom of action to superiors than the latter believe they possess. Conversely, supervisors may believe that their subordinates' performance is largely determined by internal factors (laziness, stupidity), while subordinates themselves blame external variables. In an experimental study of such a situation, Gurwitz and Panciera (1975) gave the roles of 'learner' and 'teacher' to randomly selected subjects.

Learners consistently believed that teachers had more power to punish or reward them than the teachers themselves thought they had. If you are like most people, your answers to questions 3 and 4 in Activity 5.2 probably demonstrate the same kind of bias!

Salience effects

How can we explain such overriding biases in the attribution process? One possibility is that actors and observers have *different perspectives* on the same event. While observers naturally focus on the actor, leading to the dispositional bias described above, actors themselves are engrossed in the situation they have to deal with. Information which is in the focus of attention in turn is often given causal status by judges. Storms (1973) found that when actors were provided with information about how an observer would see them, by being shown a videotape of themselves, they gave more internal attributions. In effect, their attributions became more like those of observers.

It seems then that attributions are guided by what is in the focus of our attention, what is 'salient' or highly visible in a situation. Taylor and Fiske (1975) tried to evaluate this theory in a rather interesting experiment. They hypothesised that in judging an interaction, more causal influence will be attributed by observers to the individual who is easier to see, and therefore more perceptually salient. The targets were two actors, seated opposite each other, who engaged in a brief conversation about topics such as family, work, and the like. Six observers were seated around them, so that two were facing actor A, two were facing actor B and two had equally good views of both actors (see Figure 5.1).

As Figure 5.1 shows, observers attributed more causal influence in the interaction to the person they happened to be facing. Judges who had an equally good view of both partners, attributed causality to both partners equally. In a somewhat similar study, McArthur and Post (1977) asked subjects to watch and make attributions about two males engaged in casual conversation. One of the targets was made more visually salient either by sitting in a well-illuminated spot, or by being seated in an unusual rocking chair. Again, more internal attributions were made to the 'salient' partner.

In the study by Kassin (Chapter 2), jurors' perceptions of an absentee witness were influenced by the behaviour of the person who happened to read out their evidence. It seems that the attention we give to salient targets is almost automatic, and we are rarely aware of the perceptual distortions that follow. Even the loudness of a person's voice can cause such attributional biases (Robinson and McArthur, 1982). The research on salience suggests that people who are for some reason visible, stand out, or have a 'high profile' are both more often held responsible, and are more often given credit for actions they do not in fact control.

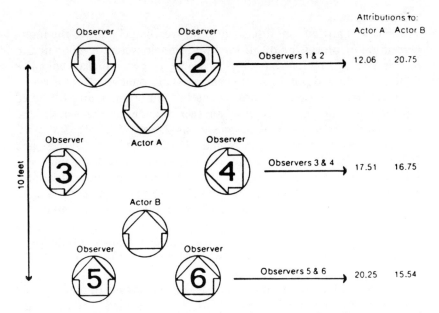

FIGURE 5.1 Visual salience and attributions. Observers attributed greater causal control in an interaction to the person they saw best, who sat opposite them. (After Taylor and Fiske, 1975, p. 441).

Bias against consensus information

You may remember that one of the three dimensions which Kelley considered important for attributions was consensus: do other people in general behave the same way in a similar situation as the target? If attribution was a purely rational process, we should give as much weight to this dimension as the others. Yet there is considerable evidence suggesting that information about how other people 'in general' behave (consensus information) is often ignored in attribution judgments. We seem to be captivated by the concrete details of the behaviour of the person in front of us, and forget the statistical base-rate information (Kahneman and Tversky, 1973). When students decide about which courses to take, the advice of one or two acquaintances usually outweighs the less captivating, but more reliable statistical information about course popularity in 'alternative' handbooks (Borgida and Nisbett, 1977).

However, consensus information is only ignored when more vivid specific information is available. When judges saw videotapes of several objects amongst which an actor had to choose, they tended to attribute the actor's choice to the objects, without considering how other people chose (in effect, ignored consensus information). Without the videotape of the objects (that is, without the 'captivating' details), consensus information had a significant effect on attributions (Feldman, Higgins, Karlovac and Ruble, 1976).

Self-serving bias

The biases in attributions discussed so far were largely due to the faulty perception or processing of information. People were not motivated to misperceive a situation, but did so because of perceptual or cognitive limitations. In addition to such *cognitive* shortcomings, the *motivation* to avoid blame and seek rewards is another important source of biased attributions (you may recognise another version of the simple and sovereign theory of hedonism discussed in Chapter 1 here!). Such self-serving biases are particularly common in explanations of success and failure. We tend to take credit (find internal causes) for our own successes, and blame others for their failures, but give situational explanations for our failures and others' successes. Common examples of such biases are explanations given by politicians after winning or losing an election, or sportsmen after winning or losing a game. Winners tend to take credit for their hard work and achievement, while losers invariably blame external circumstances such as the opponent, the procedure or the judges for their loss.

Self-serving biases may also influence our relations with others. In an experiment by Cialdini, Braver and Lewis (1974), subjects had the simple task of persuading a confederate of the experimenter, who appeared to be persuaded in some of the cases. 'Successful' persuaders rated the intelligence of their partner much more highly than 'unsuccessful' persuaders. Similarly, we like and esteem those who are rewarding or agree with us. Such self-serving biases may have important consequences in working relationships. Teachers often claim responsibility for the good performance of their pupils, but blame lack of improvement on the pupils themselves. Such selective attributions are no doubt very common in other settings as well.

The false consensus bias

Another variety of self-serving bias is the so-called false consensus effect observed by Ross (1977). This refers to the tendency of people to believe that their own attitudes, beliefs, values or behaviours are in fact widely shared by the population at large. We all like to think of ourselves as 'normal' people, and this entails believing that in important respects we are like 'most people' around us. Participants in various political movements are notorious for overestimating the support their particular cause enjoys, and numerous minorities, ranging from homosexuals to Esperantists, claim wider consensual support for their interests than is actually the case.

Experiments have also demonstrated this 'false consensus' bias. In one study, student subjects were asked to volunteer to walk around their university campus carrying a large billboard requesting the population at large to 'Eat at Joe's!'. Those who agreed thought that 62 per cent of all students would do likewise. Those who refused in turn thought that *they* were the majority, and 67 per cent of all students would also refuse to wear the sign. The principle seems to be: whatever I am doing, most people would do as well, therefore I am 'normal'!

The 'just world' hypothesis
The common tendency to believe that the failures and misfortunes of others are largely their own fault may also be explained as due to a self-serving, ego defensive bias. Lerner (1965) suggested that such attributions are at least partly a reflection of our desire to maintain a belief in a just world, where people get what they deserve. Lerner's studies showed that judges tended to blame even completely innocent victims randomly assigned to receive electric shocks. In everyday life, there are many examples of victims of rape, accidents or other uncontrollable events being held at least partly responsible for their misfortunes.

By blaming the victim, we are not only trying to 'balance the books' and maintain our belief in a 'just world'. By holding people responsible for their fate we also help to maintain a belief in the controllability of events. If we hold people personally responsible for their misadventures, we imply that they had some control over their misfortunes. By implication we can then avoid similar problems by behaving differently.

Summary and conclusions
As we have seen in this chapter, attribution research deals with a very broad range of issues which all have to do with how we explain everyday

Unemployment and the 'just world' effect. By blaming people for uncontrollable events, such as unemployment, we can maintain our belief in a 'just world', and at the same time assume that since the misfortune was due to internal causes, we can avoid it by acting differently.

behaviours. The original logical model of attributions developed by Heider has undergone numerous modifications. Most of the attribution models have continued with the assumption that people seek to uncover causes in understanding others, and that they do this by using rational, scientific principles. In reality, the task is much more complicated. Our attributions are influenced not only by the inherent limits of our perceptual and cognitive processes, but also by overriding normative and cultural factors. Nor do we seek explanations for all possible observed acts: only certain classes of unusual or unexpected events call for an attributional account (Hastie, 1984; Nesdale, 1983).

Explaining an action is not simply a scientific, but also a moral and an ethical process (Harre, 1981). The causes we identify have implications for the legitimacy and justifiability of the action to be explained. Sometimes, we do not seek past causes at all, but attribute an action to some future goal. You may be reading this book not because of some past cause, but because of a future goal, for example, to pass an exam, to become a psychologist, or simply a desire to understand people better. In recent years, attribution research has been reformulated in more general terms. It is the psychology of everyday explanations (Antaki, 1981; Lalljee, 1984) rather than causal explanations as such that we are dealing with.

In this context, attributional biases are a particularly important topic of study. Most of the attributional biases described here may be

Only unusual people or events call for attributions. We do not always search for causal explanations, as many attribution theorists assumed, but only when confronted by unusual or unexpected events.

explained both in terms of *cognitive*, and *motivational* factors. Cognitive sources of attributional bias refer to faulty or biased perceptions and interpretations of the available information. Even the 'blaming the victim' phenomenon may be explained in terms of such cognitive biases. We may (reasonably) tend to see past events affecting others as more controllable than future events about which we have less information. Ego-defensive biases, which help a person to maintain a positive and consistent self-image are qualitatively different from cognitively based distortions. Although there has been much discussion in attribution research about whether cognitive or motivational factors best explain everyday distortions in the attribution process (Zuckermann, 1979), in practice this question is of little direct interest, and may in fact be badly stated. There is no reason why both cognitive and motivational influences could not exist side-by-side, jointly influencing our judgments.

We have already seen that most attributional strategies involve making decisions about ourselves, as well as about others. In the next chapter we shall look at one of the most interesting problems addressed by attribution researchers: how do we use attributional strategies to explain our own behaviours?

6. Self-attribution: making sense of our own behaviour

6.

SELF-ATTRIBUTION: MAKING SENSE OF OUR OWN BEHAVIOUR

So far, we have assumed that the major purpose of attribution judgments is to accurately infer the underlying reasons for *other* people's behaviour. We tend to believe that our own actions and behaviour are not so problematic — we simply 'know' why we behave the way we do. Surprising as it may sound, there is a considerable body of evidence showing that we may not have such privileged access to the causes of our own behaviours. Indeed, we may use the same principles to infer our own attitudes, beliefs and intentions as we use to judge others.

This suggestion is quite a radical one. It contradicts one of our most cherished beliefs about ourselves, that we are absolutely in control when it comes to knowing our own minds. Theories of self-perception and self-attribution have provided a new perspective on social judgments in recent years. According to these theories, self-knowledge often comes not from 'inside', from direct access to our internal processes, but from 'outside', from the observation and interpretation of our actual behaviours. These theories are particularly important when it comes to understanding social interaction processes, as we shall see later.

Bem's self-perception theory
Bem was initially concerned with the problem of how people come to know their own attitudes. A well-known study by Festinger and Carlsmith (1959) showed that people will change their attitudes to match their behaviours, if they find themselves behaving in a way that is inconsistent with their earlier attitudes, and have no other plausible explanation for their behaviours. Bem's self-perception explanation is based on the assumption that "individuals come to know their own attitudes, emotions and internal states partially by inferring them from observations of their own overt behaviour and/or the circumstances in which this behaviour occurs" (Bem, 1972, p.2).

In other words, people may use the same process to infer their own attitudes as they use to make attributions about others. The process may go something like this: I just gave two dollars to an insistent collector for a charity which I don't usually support. Since I am not usually easily influenced, I must infer that I have a much more positive attitude towards that charity than I initially thought. Although self-perception theory proved to be an inadequate explanation of the kind of motivated attitude change studied in the dissonance experiments of Festinger and Carlsmith and others (cf. Wicklund and Frey, 1981), it has gained considerable acceptance in other areas.

Bem's position is also consistent with radical behaviourist theories. He believes, as do behaviourists such as Skinner, that external, observable behaviour is always primary, and internal states are secondary, to be inferred from observed behaviour. It is not internal states, such as attitudes that cause behaviour, but the other way around: behaviour causes attitudes! Of course, stated in this way the theory sounds rather extreme. We do have some knowledge about our attitudes even in the complete absence of behavioural information. After all, people do have attitudes which endure from one moment to another and are not entirely based on current behaviour. It is most likely that this self-perception affect holds best when the attitude issues involved are unimportant or inconsequential.

An interesting study by Taylor (1975) tends to support this conclusion. She varied the 'importance' of attributions female judges were asked to make about a male target by telling them that they would (or would not) meet him. While viewing the pictures of the males, the women were given false feedback about their alleged arousal reactions by listening to what they thought was their own heartrate through an earphone. Previous research has shown that subjects may sometimes use such false heart-rate

I guess I really must like that car! According to self-perception theory, we infer our own attitudes on the basis of our behaviours. Doing a lot of things to look after our car would thus be a sure sign on the basis of which to infer a positive attitude!

feedback to interpret their own reactions to something, as if reasoning 'If my heart beats faster, I must have a positive reaction' or 'Since my heart rate is unchanged, I must be unaffected'. In Taylor's study, such false feedback had little effect on judgments of the males when the attribution was important, i.e. the women expected to meet the person. But the false feedback did affect ratings of attractiveness when there was no likelihood of future meeting, and the judgments were therefore unimportant to the women.

Self-attribution processes

Bem's theory provides no specific guidelines as to *how* attitudes and beliefs are inferred from behaviour. We must look to theories of attribution, such as Kelley's three-dimensional model, for more detailed predictions. Kelley maintained that the search for distinctiveness, consensus and consistency is also the basis for attributing internal states to ourselves. You may get a better idea of how this model works when applied to self-attribution by completing Activity 6.1.

The principle of self-attribution has been applied to many different areas of human social behaviour, to explain the often surprising and unexpected interpretations people put on their behaviours. Next we shall look at some interesting examples of how self-attribution works in realistic situations.

The actor as observer: objective self-awareness

You will remember that in the last chapter we discussed the important differences in the attributional strategies used by actors and observers. Whereas an actor tends to concentrate his/her attention on the surrounding situation, tending to identify causal forces in the environment, observers focus on the actor, and usually see him/her as the causal agent. Self-attribution presents us with something of a problem, since in thinking about our own actions we are free to adopt the stance of either the actor, or the observer. Duval and Wicklund (1972) dealt with this problem elegantly by introducing the concept of objective as against subjective self-awareness. In our usual state we concentrate on the environment, and are only subjectively aware of ourselves. However, in some situations we are forced to look at ourselves as others see us. At such times we find ourselves in a state of objective self-awareness.

It seems quite easy to bring about such a state. Simply looking into the mirror, or being aware of the fact that others are watching us, photographing us or are in some way recording our behaviour is usually sufficient to turn us into something like an outside observer when thinking about ourselves. We see ourselves as others might do, objectively. Would attributional strategies be influenced by these different forms of self-awareness?

ACTIVITY 6.1
Why Am I Doing This?

Imagine that you are sitting at home watching the re-run of a *Monty Python* episode on television, and find yourself roaring with laughter. (For those of you who do not know *Monty Python*, it is a British TV comedy). Why are you laughing? Is the cause of your behaviour to be found in the show, yourself or some other factor? To find an answer, according to Kelley's model, you would proceed like this:

1. Is my behaviour consistent? Do I often laugh at *Monty Python*, or is this an isolated incident? Only highly consistent behaviour can lead to reliable internal or external attributions.

2. Is my behaviour distinctive? Do I laugh at all kinds of funny shows, or only at *Monty Python* episodes? If your behaviour is very distinctive (you only laugh at *Monty Python)*, you can make a reliable external attribution to the show. If the behaviour is not distinctive, the cause of your laughter is likely to be internal: your highly developed general sense of humour perhaps?

3. How do other people behave? If consensus is high (everyone else is laughing too), you can make an external attribution. If only you are laughing, the cause is likely to be internal: you may have seen something in the show that escaped others.

Compare this process with McArthur's (Table 5.1) illustration of how Kelley's model works for external attributions. Can you see the parallels between **self-attributions** and other attributions? Of course, you do not proceed in such a step-by-step fashion in everyday life, but the process may be quite similar to this illustration. We all find ourselves in situations at times when we ask 'Why am I doing this?' Kelley's model should help you to find an answer! Try to use this model to explain one of your actions that you find genuinely puzzling.

Several studies have shown that objectively self-aware people will tend to account for their own behaviours very much like outside observers do, by locating causality in themselves instead of the environment. Usually, a simple manipulation like placing a large mirror in front of the subject is sufficient to bring about this drastic change in attributions (Duval and Wicklund, 1973). This research supports the view that attributions, including self-attributions, have a lot to do with what is the focus of a person's attention at the time. Taylor and Fiske's research on salience effects in attributions, discussed in the last chapter, illustrates this same point: whatever is the focus of attention is more likely to be accorded causal status, even if 'it' happens to be ourselves!

The effects of self-attribution on motivation

Attribution theory is based on the assumption that human action is brought about by either internal, or external causes. When a behaviour can adequately be explained as caused by external reward or pressure, we need not look for internal causes, according to Heider. An interesting question suggests itself: when people receive a reward for performing a behaviour which they previously performed simply because they liked doing it (out of 'intrinsic motivation'), the actors may interpret the reward as indicating their lack of intrinsic motivation, and will subsequently only perform the behaviour when rewarded. The problem has considerable practical implications. It suggests that providing external rewards such as extra pay, good marks or bonuses for improved learning or work performance may sometimes have a counterproductive effect. Instead of increasing a person's intrinsic enjoyment and motivation to perform a task, they might reduce it.

Lepper, Greene and Nisbett (1973) demonstrated such an effect with young (three- to five-year-old) children, some of whom were offered a reward for drawing some pictures, while others engaged in this task without expectation of reward. A week or two later, the researchers found that children who previously expected and were given a reward for drawing now played much less with these materials than children who were not rewarded. Similarly, school children who were consistently rewarded for working on math problems for 12 days worked much less than other children when the rewards ceased (Greene, Sternberg and Lepper, 1976). These studies point to the disturbing possibility that tangible and expected rewards may become the sole reason for doing something that was previously done for its own sake, as an actor comes to attribute his motivation to entirely external causes. However, not all rewards reduce intrinsic motivation: intangible social reinforcement, such as verbal praise, may have positive effects (Deci, 1975).

There are many everyday examples of external rewards having a counterproductive effect. Some studies show that people who are induced to buy a particular line of grocery by the offer of an extra bonus are less likely to repeat their purchase once the bonus period ends. The external reward must be expected and salient for such effects to occur. You should remember that within an attributional framework, it is not the fact of being rewarded itself which influences motivation, but the symbolic interpretation we attach to that reward. If we can identify it as the sole cause of our behaviour, it could reduce intrinsic motivation. If, on the other hand, the reward cannot be seen as the sole cause of our behaviour, intrinsic motivation is less likely to be affected.

The practical implication is that whenever external rewards are offered for something that people previously did without rewards, we must ensure that the previous intrinsic motivation is maintained. This can be done for example by emphasising such things as the incidental nature of the reward, and the intrinsic value and enjoyment that can be derived from doing the task irrespective of the reward.

Self-handicapping strategies

There is one very important difference between self-attributions and other-attributions: being forced to make negative inferences about ourselves can be much more threatening and unpleasant than making such judgments about others. No wonder that we use highly specialised defensive strategies to avoid the need to blame ourselves for negative outcomes. Imagine a situation where you have to take an important test, and you have reason to believe that you may do badly. What would you do?

According to Berglas and Jones (1978; Jones and Berglas, 1978) people in similar situations often construct artificial handicaps for themselves, so that they can blame subsequent failure on external difficulties rather than their own shortcomings. In their study, subjects who were led to believe that they would do well, or might do badly in a coming test were given a choice of two drugs, one allegedly helping, the other retarding performance. Subjects who thought they might do badly preferred the second drug (see Figure 6.1). Taking the performance retarding drug made it possible for them to blame the drug if they did do badly, but to take double credit if they did well, despite the drug.

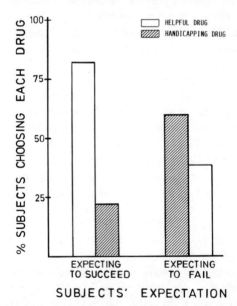

FIGURE 6.1 Self-handicapping strategies. When given a choice, subjects who expected to fail preferred a drug which interfered with their performance, so that they could later blame their failure on an outside cause. Subjects expecting to succeed preferred a drug which helped performance. (After Berglas and Jones, 1978).

Berglas and Jones (1978) called this a *self-handicapping strategy*. We may observe similar behaviours in everyday life. People often drink too much, sleep too little or take drugs before important events such as exams, job interviews or important negotiations. One of the reasons for such apparently irrational behaviour may be that it allows possible failure to be attributed to external causes (the drink, drugs or lack of sleep), thus enabling the individual to protect his/her self-image as a responsible intelligent person! The tendency to behave in this way is even stronger when others can also observe our performances (Kolditz and Arkin, 1982). In effect, self-handicapping can be used at times as an impression management strategy. More generally, the theory of self-attributions suggests that people will do their best to participate in, and create situations in which the necessity for negative self-attributions is minimised.

Learned helplessness
Of course, we are not always able to structure our behaviour in such a way that negative self-attributions can be avoided. Occasionally, we are exposed to completely uncontrollable or even random occurrences. When people (or for that matter, animals) are exposed to uncontrollable aversive events for long periods, they eventually give up trying to master the situation, or even to escape — a condition which has been labelled 'learned helplessness' by Seligman (1975). To put it simply, "When a person is faced with an outcome which is independent of his responses,

Doctor, could you make my plaster bigger? When faced with the probability of failure, people often do things which will make the failure more likely, so that they can blame their lack of success on outside forces. Such self-handicapping helps to preserve the person's self-image as a responsible and competent person!

he learns that the outcome is independent of his responses" (p. 46), and gives up any attempt to control that outcome.

There are some dramatic examples of 'learned helplessness' behaviour. Animals exposed to uncontrollable electric shocks may become totally passive. People experiencing natural disasters or prolonged hunger and other deprivation often react with similar passivity and resignation. You may often observe such reactions in people in news reports of earthquakes, famines or floods. In many more common and less dramatic contexts, individuals experiencing consistent failure in a field (for example, making friends, finding a job or finding a partner) may become passive and even clinically depressed as a result.

In its original form, learned helplessness was formulated in terms of a simple learning process. However, how a person subjectively explains and interprets the causes of negative events also has an important influence. The symbolic interpretation we put on our experiences can negate the learned helplessness phenomenon. When children who experienced consistent failure in solving math problems are repeatedly told that they failed because they did not try hard enough, they do not exhibit 'learned helplessness' (Dweck, 1975). The recent combination of the learned helplessness model with attribution theory offers a promising framework for analysing behavioural reactions to such uncontrollable outcomes as unemployment, poverty, marital breakdown and other stressful situations. Unemployed workers who (however unreasonably) blame themselves for their negative experiences may be less likely to give up the search for a job than people who attribute their problems to external, uncontrollable economic factors.

Helplessness can be learned! When people are exposed to uncontrollable influences over long periods of time, they become passive and stop trying to influence their fate — a state psychologists called 'learned helplessness'.

Psychological reactance

The initial reaction when confronted with uncontrollable outcomes is typically not learned helplessness, but an increased motivation to regain our lost control and freedom. Brehm (1972) coined the term 'psychological reactance' to describe the motivational state which is aroused when we feel that our freedom of action is in some way threatened. Reactance can take many forms, depending on the circumstances. Actions or objects which are restricted or limited appear more valuable and interesting the moment our access to them is threatened. Just think of the immediate increase in interest in materials threatened by censorship!

Psychological reactance may also occur if we are too strongly pressured towards accepting an attitude or an opinion. In such situations, we may re-assert our freedom by taking exactly the opposite view. This is a common danger in high-pressure advertising campaigns. Reactance is particularly easy to observe in children. They are especially fascinated by toys or activities which are prohibited to them, and teenagers often break parental rules for no better reason than to symbolically re-assert their freedom. The idea of psychological reactance has considerable appeal as an explanation of many puzzling real-life behaviours. In face-to-face interaction in particular, reactance is a common reaction to threats to personal freedom.

Self-attribution of emotion

An interesting and highly complex question within the field of self-attribution research is how we identify and interpret our own feelings and emotions. What sorts of processes are involved in deciding which particular emotion you are experiencing at a given time? The objectively measurable aspect of an emotion is usually just physiological arousal, noticeable by increased heartrate, sweating of the palms, faster breathing, and so on. But how do we know whether it means we are happy, sad, upset or anxious? Psychological research indicates that the arousal states associated with different emotions are practically indistinguishable from each other.

William James suggested over a hundred years ago (James, 1884) that emotions may consist of two components, affective arousal, and the subsequent cognitive labelling and interpretation of arousal. Thus emotions may not be the *cause*, but the consequence of physiological reactions. To take an everyday example: if you hear a sudden noise in the forest at night, you immediately experience arousal and might start to run, and may only later identify your physiological arousal as 'fear' by taking all the relevant circumstances into consideration.

Schachter and Singer (1962) performed a classical experiment illustrating this process. In their study, subjects were given an arousal-inducing drug (epinephrine) and were either told about its effects (palpitations, increased heartbeat, etc.), or were told that it was a harmless vitamin injection. Thus, some subjects were 'informed' about the reasons for their subsequent arousal symptoms, while others were 'ignorant' of it. Subjects were then joined by a trained confederate of the experimenter, who acted either in an extremely happy, euphoric fashion, or in an angry, irritable manner. When subjects were later asked to report on their own emotions, those in the 'ignorant' group, who had no plausible explanation for their arousal, were more likely to report an emotion consistent with the confederate's behaviour as anger or happiness than the 'informed' subjects. It seemed as if subjects who had no expectation or plausible explanation for being aroused used the most obvious cue in their environment, the behaviour of the confederate, to explain their emotion.

According to the Schachter and Singer model, different emotions are essentially different cognitive interpretations or attributions placed on the same basic arousal symptoms. The model goes beyond the self-attribution framework, by suggesting that not only our own behaviours, but almost any event in the environment may be influential in defining our emotional experiences. The implications are quite far-reaching: if human beings have no direct, privileged access to their own feelings and emotions, it may be quite easy to influence how people interpret their feelings by providing them with appropriate external information. We shall return to the many practical applications of this idea later.

The misattribution of arousal effect
Despite some recent criticisms of the methods and interpretations of Schachter and Singer's study (Maslach, 1979; Marshall and Zimbardo, 1979), considerable evidence has been accumulated over the years supporting such a view of emotions. The model was taken one step further by Valins (1966; 1972), who suggested that actual arousal may not even be necessary to experience an emotion. It may be sufficient for subjects to *believe* they are aroused for them to experience an emotion. In a somewhat bizarre experiment, male subjects were shown a number of centrefold nude pictures from Playboy magazine, while listening through earphones to what they believed was their own heartbeat. In fact, the heart-rate feedback was manipulated by the experimenter according to a prearranged schedule: some pictures were accompanied by faster heartbeats than others.

After the experiment, subjects were most attracted to those pictures during the viewing of which they had heard their 'own' heart-rates increase. Even when subjects were told at the end of the study that the heart-rate feedback they received was bogus, they still preferred the nudes previously associated with 'arousal'. We should remember, however, that such preferences are easiest to manipulate when the choice is of little importance to the subject. Choosing between various nude pictures is hardly a serious decision for most of us. When the decisions become more important, for example if we expect to meet the people we are asked to judge, the bogus heart-rate feedback procedure proves much less effective, as we have seen in the study by Taylor (1975) described earlier.

Some practical consequences of self-attributions

Schachter and Singer's (1962) two-factor model of emotions, together with Valins' (1972) self-attribution of arousal research, suggest that neither physiological arousal, nor directly accessible internal reactions are necessary for experiencing an emotion. This self-attribution model of emotions also has some intriguing practical implications. If the experience of emotions is a matter of inferences, can we perhaps control negative emotions, such as anxiety, by manipulating attributions?

Nisbett and Schachter (1966) attempted to do just this. They gave their subjects placebo pills (neutral pills with no chemical effects whatsoever), and told some of them to expect arousal, tremors, palpitations, and so on, while the others expected no physiological symptoms. Next, both groups were exposed to a series of electric shocks. The group which could at least partly attribute their arousal to the pill taken earlier reported less pain and showed greater tolerance to the shocks than the other group. The study suggests that the attributions we place on internal experiences, such as pain and arousal, may significantly influence how we react to them.

In another study, Storms and Nisbett (1970) attempted to use the same principle in a therapeutic way. They suggested that insomniacs may have trouble going to sleep because of their inability to reduce physiological arousal. They remain anxious and aroused, at least partly because they worry about their insomnia. If they could attribute their arousal to an outside cause, they would be less worried about it, and able to sleep more easily.

In the experiment, Storms and Nisbett gave insomniacs placebo pills, again telling some of them to expect arousal symptoms, while others expected an opposite, relaxing effect. Subjects expecting to be aroused went to sleep more easily, presumably because they could readily attribute their arousal to the expected effects of the pill. Although there remains some doubt about the reliability of these findings, clinical psychologists are increasingly interested in influencing the explanations and inferences used by clients as a means of therapy.

The self-attribution model provides us with many other interesting possibilities for changing the interpretations people put on their experiences. Whenever a behaviour is influenced by arousal states, it is possible to use similar procedures. Dienstbier and Munster (1971) suggested, for example, that unpleasant arousal is one of the consequences of dishonest behaviour such as cheating at an exam. If people can attribute their arousal to an external agent, such as a drug, they will be more prepared to cheat since arousal is no longer attributed to cheating per se. In their study subjects were given a placebo, and told that it would or would not produce arousal. They then had a chance to cheat by copying the answers to a difficult test. Those who expected to be aroused by the drug were more likely to cheat than the other group. The general conclusion from these studies is quite clear: arousal states tend to be interpreted in the light of circumstantial information, and the interpretation we use will largely determine how we react to the arousal state. Such self-attribution processes are particularly important in face-to-face interaction, where our emotional reactions to our partners may depend on such external influences.

The transfer of arousal research

Both the Schachter and Singer (1962) experiment, and the misattribution of arousal research have been criticised on methodological grounds (Cotton, 1981), since the arousal states underlying all emotions were only indirectly manipulated. Zillmann (1972, 1978) used a different and quite ingenious technique to study the self-attribution of emotions. Instead of receiving an adrenalin injection, subjects simply performed an arousing task (riding an exercycle) to influence their physiological state. They were subsequently insulted by a confederate of the experimenter. Subjects who were aroused at the time reacted more aggressively towards the offender than non-aroused subjects.

The finding can again be explained in terms of a self-attribution model. Subjects who were aroused and then insulted could easily attribute their arousal to the insult, and identify their reaction as anger, leading to more aggressive responses. Non-aroused subjects had no basis to attribute anger to themselves, and remained non-aggressive. Zillmann suggests that these findings indicate a transfer of arousal to a plausible external cause through attribution processes — hence the label 'excitation transfer' for the phenomena he describes. Once again, the everyday implications are obvious. If we find ourselves in an aroused state, we may easily attribute our arousal to a plausible external circumstance, and react inappropriately. For example, being upset about work, or having an argument at home creates an arousal state which may be readily transferred to whatever other irritant is most salient in our environment at the time.

Self-attribution of cognition

The idea that we have no direct access to our own emotions but have to infer them from the circumstances is controversial enough. But how much do we know about our cognitive and decisionmaking processes? Are we able to answer questions about our mental processes on the basis of introspection alone? When somebody asks us on what basis we chose one item of clothing instead of another one, why we like one person and dislike another one, how we decide which car to buy, do we really know how such decisions are made? Most of us would say that we simply *know* these things, since after all, we have made those decisions ourselves. But are we able to introspect about how we arrived at such judgments? Do we really know our own minds?

Nisbett and Wilson (1977) argued in a provocative paper that we may be just as unable to accurately describe our own judgmental processes as we are unable to label our emotions without external cues. In their typical experiment, the experimenter manipulates a variable which reliably influences subjects' choices, who are then asked to explain why they decided as they did. Typically, subjects cannot identify the variable controlling their behaviour.

For example, when asked to select one of several identical stockings in a row, people usually take the one on the right hand side. When asked to explain their choice, subjects talk about nonexistent quality differences or personal preferences, without realising that the position of the stocking was the determining variable in their choice. When the importance of position is suggested to them, subjects deny that it played any role in their choice. Nisbett and Wilson argue that such findings support the view that people have no direct private access to their own cognitive processes. Although right-hand position in the above example was clearly shown to determine subjects' choices, they were unable to report on this variable.

In another study, subjects were asked to judge the physical appearance of a person who behaved in a warm, friendly or a cold, hostile way. The usual halo effect (see Chapter 4) was found: the same person was judged as less atractive looking when behaving in a hostile, negative way. When subjects were asked what influenced their judgments, they failed to report that the target's behaviour had any effect on their perceptions. When this was put to them directly, they denied it. The implications are obvious: in many interpersonal situations, we may rationalise our behaviour or judgments in a similar way, without really knowing how or why we react in a particular manner.

If people really don't know their own mental processes in these studies, what are they reporting when questioned? Nisbett and Wilson (1977) suggest that most of us tend to give explanations which we think are appropriate to the circumstances. 'Rational' people are not supposed to be influenced by the mere position of an article in their choice, so subjects deny the influence of this variable. Instead, they give socially approved, if incorrect explanations (quality, preferences). Similarly, we are supposed to be able to separate behaviour from looks in our judgments about people, so this is what subjects will report. When asked 'Why did you think, choose or act that way?', we tend to give the expected, rather than the true, answer, according to these studies.

Despite this experimental evidence for the contention that people are indeed unable to report on the true causes of their decisions in situations where the experimenter manipulates those 'causes', the issue is far from resolved. Indeed, it is an interesting philosophical question as to what exactly accurate reporting on mental processes would entail. Since decisions are made up of a long chain of interrelated mental processes, how do we know which of these various instances in a causal chain is the 'true' explanation? You may remember how difficult it was to decide what constitutes an accurate interpersonal judgment. It is many times more complicated to determine what is an accurate report on the mental process of how we make such judgments (White, 1984).

However, the Nisbett and Wilson research certainly raised a very important and critical question, which challenges our concept of unlimited direct access to our own cognitive processes. At least in some circumstances, our cherished belief that we can simply 'tell' how we think is clearly mistaken. Instead of really knowing what goes on in our minds, we tend to give explanations which seem to be suitable to the situation. The self-attribution model thus provides a series of interesting and stimulating explanations of the way people account (or cannot account, as the case may be) for their everyday decisions.

Summary and conclusions

Research on inferences and attributions has been a major area of social psychological enquiry for the past several decades. Much has been discovered about the way people understand and predict each other, and the sorts of mistakes which may prejudice this process. The study of attributional biases is particularly important, since by becoming aware of these tendencies, we can all become more objective in our judgments of ourselves and others.

Attribution theory is based on two assumptions: that people are rational information processors, and that they seek to discover prior causes to predict each other, just as scientists do. We have already seen that the first assumption had to be drastically revised. Irrational, motivational biases in attributions may completely distort the model of the rational information processor advocated by Heider, Kelley and others.

The second assumption of attribution theories, that perceivers invariably search for prior causes, has also been criticised recently. Human action is not always explained in terms of prior causes. Indeed, the whole idea of one prior cause is suspect. Every human action represents the end result of a long chain of causal events. It is impossible and arbitrary to pick out one 'cause' as the true explanation from such a chain of events. The fact that I am sitting here typing this paragraph is 'caused' by multiple events, such as my background, education, work as an academic in which writing is rewarded, interest in social behaviour, the contract I have with Pergamon Press to write this book, and so on. No one of these causes has an absolute monopoly on explaining my behaviour — rather, they are parts of a long causal chain the end result of which is my writing these very words.

Past causes are also not the only kinds of explanations for human behaviour. Other classes of explanations, for example, reasons for actions carried out in order to achieve future goals, can be very important (Buss, 1978), particularly in self-attributions. People commonly explain their own, and others' actions by reference to aims, reasons or moral imperatives (for example, I did it because I thought it was right). In practice, accounting for our own and others' behaviours takes on a moral character, where the various social and cultural norms and conventions influence the kind of explanation which is 'acceptable' in the circumstances (see works by Antaki, Harre and Lalljee, referred to in the previous chapter).

Perhaps the most interesting area of attribution research is the question of self-attributions. The explanations we give to others (and to ourselves) about our own actions, emotions and thoughts constitute one of the core issues in psychology. Attribution research has provided us with a sobering insight into how such judgments are made. Instead of the rational information processor making pronouncements about directly accessible internal events, such as attitudes, feelings, and thoughts, we have come face-to-face with the fact that human beings may be at times incapable of doing any of these things. Research on attributions and self-attributions should help us make our social judgments both more realistic and more rational. Since attributions and inferences are also at the heart of interacting with people, the work surveyed here should also help us become more sensitive in our dealings with others.

7. Interpersonal communication: the uses of language

7.

INTERPERSONAL COMMUNICATION: THE USES OF LANGUAGE

Perceiving, understanding and even predicting our partner is the necessary first step in the social interaction process. In the chapters so far we have concentrated on the problems of person perception, impression formation and attributions as aspects of social interaction. However, person perception is only a necessary, but not a sufficient component of the interaction process. Just think of any common social encounter, such as having a discussion with a friend, or buying something in a shop. Perceiving other people in such encounters is in a sense a prerequisite for the actual process of interaction, but it is not the interaction itself. Interacting with people consists to a large extent of a regulated exchange of messages, or *communication*. In this chapter we shall begin to look at some of the most important features of interpersonal communication, and in particular, we shall discuss the role language plays in social interaction. In the next chapter we shall turn to a survey of how non-verbal messages are used in social interaction.

The process of communication
In the most general sense, communication may be defined as a process involving the transmission of information from a sender to a receiver. From this definition it follows that any communication involves the following important elements: (a) a *sender,* or source who *encodes* the (b) *message* to be transmitted through (c) a particular *channel,* to (d) a *receiver,* who *decodes* the message. The characteristics of the sender, the message, the channel and the receiver all have important influences on the communication process. For example, a telephone line as a communication channel has certain physical limitations (such as the absence of visual cues) which definitely modify our communication strategies when using that channel. Similarly, the characteristics of the sender and the receiver (such as status, power, intelligence, shared interests) also influence the communication strategies adopted. Finally, the nature of the message itself can be very important in determining how

we communicate: one uses very different language when asking about the weather from that used when asking for a raise in salary at work.

However, the above definition of communication is also limited in some ways. It suggests that communication is a simple, one-way process, and that messages are sent and received without reference to the surrounding world and the sequence of past and expected future events. Alternative theories of communication emphasise that communication is usually a dynamic, two-way process, in which sending messages and monitoring the partner take place simultaneously. Further, all interpersonal communication relies to some extent on the *shared social knowledge* between the sender and the receiver. In other words, messages usually only make sense within a given, well-defined social environment, be it a family, a school class or a cultural group. Sentences which are perfectly clear when spoken between two brain surgeons, bridge players or two schoolchildren may make no sense at all to others outside these groups. We take a lot of shared knowledge for granted when communicating with each other (see Activity 7.1).

In addition to our earlier definition, communication is thus also a dynamic, ongoing process which capitalises on past knowledge and the shared history of the partners. Despite the limitations of the above definition, it will be useful to keep in mind the four basic elements of communication it refers to (sender, message, channel and receiver) when

---

ACTIVITY 7.1
What's in a Sentence?

You may get a better idea of what we mean by 'shared social knowledge' by completing this activity. Get a record of three different short conversations between two people (you may use radio or television broadcasts, books or observed everyday interactions as your sources). Next, analyse each of these conversations, sentence by sentence, by asking the question: what does the listener already need to know in order to be able to make sense of this sentence? You will probably find that almost every statement made in a conversation contains only a very small part of the total knowledge which is necessary to understand that message. The list of already existing shared knowledge between the speaker and the listener which enables them to communicate is sometimes so extensive that it is impossible even to compile. The greater the 'shared knowledge' between the partners, the easier it is for them to communicate with each other, and the more difficult it is for outsiders to correctly understand the meaning of their sentences.

reading the following discussion of the specific characteristics of verbal and nonverbal communication channels in social interaction.

Is language unique?

Most of our interactions with others involve the use of language. No other communication system used by any other species even approximates the complexity and subtlety afforded by human language. When we compare the features of human language with features of other communication systems, we find that many characteristics of language are not unique, but can also be found in some other species. Hockett (1963) suggested that language may be characterised in terms of a number of such 'design features'. Examples of these design features are (a) *displacement*, or the ability to refer to things not immediately present; (b) *openness*, or the ability to create and communicate new meanings; (c) *tradition*, or the ability to learn and to pass on new symbols and messages; and (d) *duality of patterning*, or the ability to combine a finite number of words, symbols or components into an infinite number of possible messages.

Many communication systems have some of these features, but only language has all of them. Some well-known attempts to teach chimpanzees a language code which has tradition and duality of patterning appear to have been successful (Gardner and Gardner, 1969; Premack, 1971), although critics suggest that the animals' performance can also be explained as simple imitation. Honeybees can communicate about the existence and location of distant food sources by a 'dance' signal, a communication code which has displacement, since it communicates about things not immediately present. But language remains unique as a communication system which possesses all of Hockett's design features simultaneously.

Indeed, one of the very few things which is universal across *all* the many different human cultures we know of is that they all use language. The uniqueness of human language has lead theorists such as Lenneberg (1967) to propose that language is a species-specific ability which has evolved in man by natural selection. This view implies that there are genetic determinants which predestine humans, and only humans, to acquire and use language. Another well-known proponent of this so-called 'nativist' view is Chomsky. The second, alternative view of language is represented mainly by learning theorists such as Skinner, who maintain that language is acquired in exactly the same way as every other behaviour in humans and animals: through systematic reinforcement procedures. However, attempts to teach animals similar communication codes have failed to clearly establish that other species can use this tool. Language-like performance by chimpanzees may be explained as meaningless repetitions controlled by reinforcements, according to some critics of such studies.

How do we learn to use language?

A third model of language development, critical of both the nativist and the learning theoretical formulations, was recently proposed by Bruner (1983; Bruner and Sherwood, 1981). On the basis of several years of research with infants and children at Oxford, Bruner suggests that learning social interaction skills and learning a language are intricately related. Bruner and his co-workers found that contrary to commonly held beliefs, infants are actively exploring their physical and social environment from the very first day in their lives, and are capable of reacting to, and imitating social messages much sooner than previously thought. Infants engage cooperatively with their caretakers in developing interaction routines which are mutually understood, and use non-verbal signals such as smiling, crying, giggling, grasping and so on in a structured fashion. In other words, children know how to interact before they know how to speak (Bruner, 1985). It is because of this prior social knowledge that language acquisition, once it commences, proceeds as quickly as it does.

The cognitive performance of children in learning a language is truly astonishing. In less than twelve months they develop from no language at all to almost fluent speech. Probably no later performance in adult life is as impressive as this early accomplishment. How do children do it? Bruner's research suggests that what children learn is not so much a language, but how to interact and communicate with others. Once a pre-linguistic child knows how to take turns in a peek-a-boo game, how to use smiles, giggles and cries to communicate emotions, how to co-ordinate his gaze and attention with the caretaker, the substitution of words for such messages is less daunting than it may appear. Children also learn about shared interaction 'formats' such as the rules and sequence of behaviours involved in such episodes as feeding and playing well before they can speak (Bruner, 1985). The important contribution of Bruner's research is that it points to the close links between learning a language and learning social interaction. Not only do we use language as a means of social interaction throughout our lives, but apparently we can learn a language only because we first learn about how to interact.

The study of language

The study of language traditionally encompassed several related questions. The order and structure which regulates how words are put together is the subject matter of *syntax*, or grammar. *Phonology* is concerned with the study of the sound patterns and regularities in spoken language. But the essence of language is that it communicates meanings. Words, or morphemes are the smallest meaningful units in language, and *semantics* is the study of meaning in language. There is a fourth, additional level of language analysis which is perhaps most relevant to social psychology. Language is a communication system, and it cannot be separated from the actual practice of how messages are sent and received in real everyday situations. Charles Morris (1946) used the word '*pragmatics*' to describe this fourth level of studying language as it is used. Knowing a language perfectly involves not only knowing the words, the grammar and the pronunciation rules, but also knowing what to say, where, when, how, and to whom. A whole field, sociolinguistics, is devoted to the study of how such social variables influence the way we use language (Forgas, 1985).

Language, thought and culture
Another important feature of human language was pointed out by Vygotsky (1962). Language is not only the medium of external communication between people, but it is also the internal medium we use to think, and to represent, systematise and organise the world around us. The role of language as a link between the external and the internal world is crucial for both cultural, and individual evolution. It enables us as individuals to symbolise, accumulate and share our experiences, and it enables groups and societies to pass on their accumulated knowledge to future generations. Language as a system of symbols lies at the very heart of human social life (Mead, 1934), as well as social and cultural evolution.

In the previous section we discussed some of the features of human language which make it unique as a medium of communication. Although, as we have seen, the use of language is a universal human characteristic across all cultures, the differences in language use between cultures are just as important. Language and culture closely interact with each other. The way we name and categorise things reflects our way of seeing the world, and in turn we perceive and think about our environment in terms of the linguistic categories and terms available to us. This interdependence can be carried even further. As Vygotsky (1962) argued, inner speech (the medium of thought) and external speech (the medium of social communication) are mutually interdependent. As a result, cultural differences not only influence the use of language as a medium of communication but, through language, also determine differences in thinking.

The theory of linguistic relativity
The theory of linguistic relativity developed by Sapir and Whorf concentrates on this interdependence between language and thinking. According to the theory, different languages are not simply alternative vehicles for describing the same reality — rather, people speaking different tongues may also see the world differently. In its strongest form, this theory asserts that language determines thought. Since we can only comprehend the universe in terms of the concepts available to us, and since those concepts are provided by our language, people speaking

different languages must see the world differently from us: they must live in a different 'cognitive universe'. The much more widely accepted 'weak' form of this theory does not go that far. It only implies that differences in language tend to predispose people to see the world differently. The relationship between language and thought is neither direct, nor absolute.

Benjamin L. Whorf, perhaps the best-known representative of the linguistic relativity theory, started his career as a fire-insurance inspector, and became a very talented and influential amateur linguist. Whorf was deeply impressed by the different ways people explained and accounted for the causes of the fires he investigated. These observed differences in language use led him to study the languages of other cultures, such as various groups of American Indians. On the basis of his studies, Whorf came to the conclusion that these different cultural groups not only used different languages, but also lived in different cognitive universes.

He thought that "Formulation of ideas is not an independent process, strictly rational in the old sense, but is part of a particular grammar, and differs, from slightly to greatly, between different grammars. We dissect nature along lines laid down by our native languages ... We cut nature up, organise it into concepts and describe significances as we do, largely because we are parties to an agreement to organise it in this way — an agreement that holds throughout our speech community and is codified in the patterns of our language" (Whorf, 1956, pp. 212-213). Examples of such patterns abound. Although in English we differentiate between living and non-living flying things, the Hopi Indians use the same word for a bee and an aeroplane. Eskimos have many different terms to describe different kinds of snow. Personal pronouns in Japanese allow a much more subtle differentiation of interpersonal relationships than is the case in European languages. There are many words in German to describe complex inner states which are absent in English, but there is apparently greater scope for humour in English than in German.

Do we think the way we speak?
Everyday life provides many examples of the language-culture-thought connection described above. The study of the words used by various political movements offers an excellent illustration of the intended manipulation of culture and thought through language. Orwell, in his book *1984*, describes a new language, Newspeak, specifically developed by the rulers of this utopian, totalitarian society to manipulate people's thoughts and their ability to understand and describe the reality surrounding them. By eliminating verbal terms that could be threatening for the regime, people should be less able to even think such thoughts. Orwell's *1984* was modelled on the communist, totalitarian societies of

his day which have changed surprisingly little, as far as their use of language is concerned (see Activity 7.2).

Even today, the meanings of terms such as 'election', 'party', 'candidate', 'constitution' and 'voting' as used in the Soviet Union and Eastern Europe are entirely different from the meanings that they have in Western societies. Readers of *Pravda*, when they read in the paper about such universal concepts as 'democracy', 'freedom', 'peace' or even 'human rights' have a different understanding of these concepts to

---

ACTIVITY 7.2
The Politics of Meaning

Does it matter if the meanings of words do become a matter of political convenience? George F. Will, the well-known American columnist, thought so very much when commenting on the American decision to give notice of their withdrawal from an increasingly politicised United Nations agency, UNESCO. Read his comments below, and try to decide for yourself whether you agree with them.

'The damage done by UNESCO is less in enforcing pernicious rules than in making the world's few democracies collaborators in a terrible taxidermy. The categories of Western political thought are emptied and then stuffed with new meanings, as when, at a conference on education, Western delegates politely listened to the delegate from the Ukrainian Soviet Socialist Republic report that Soviet schools teach 'respect for human rights and fundamental freedoms'. A liberal society's most deeply rooted sentimentalism is faith in communication — dialogues, negotiations. Is it not always better to talk than not to talk with enemies? No, not when the mere act of meeting to talk about important things — freedom, justice, rights, trade unions, journalism — suggests, falsely and to the enemy's advantage, that all participants use those words to denote essentially the same things. Or, worse, when the mere observance of diplomatic niceties — the stately minuet of conferences — legitimizes the idea that there are two quite different but equally eligible meanings for those words. UNESCO is an instrument for the intellectual disarming of the West.' (George F. Will, in the *Washington Post*, extract published in the *International Herald Tribune*, Paris, Monday, 26 December 1983).

Is Will right? Does it matter if important words slowly lose their meanings? If it was no longer quite clear what was meant by an election, human rights, political parties or trade unions, would it really matter to us? Does having the same words describe different things make social interaction difficult? Do you think the U.S. and Soviet representatives in UNESCO had, and continue to have, difficulty interacting because of this?

Western readers. All of these terms have their special 'Soviet' uses which have to do with the legitimisation of the rule of the party hierarchy, and not with individuals' rights and choices. Terms with negative connotations such as 'price increase', 'secret police' or 'propaganda' are rarely used to refer to domestic issues in the USSR. They are replaced by more innocuous terms such as 'price adjustment', 'state protection authority' and 'public information' in the official jargon.

It is sometimes extremely difficult for observers brought up in Western cultures to truly understand the alternative Soviet meanings of these terms. For interesting and readable descriptions of the very different thought-worlds Soviet citizens still live in, you may like to look at a couple of excellent books by Western correspondents who worked in Moscow: Hedrick-Smith's *The Russians* (1977) and Shipler's *Russia: Broken Idols, Solemn Dreams* (1983). There are of course many other examples of the linguistic manipulation of culture and thought for political purposes. The propaganda machinery of Nazi Germany provided many classical illustrations of such manipulation, innovations which unfortunately are still with us today, as the rhetoric of present day totalitarian societies clearly indicates.

Some linguistic campaigns, such as the contemporary movement towards the use of non-sexist language, also illustrate the way language and thought are interrelated. The proponents of this campaign suggest

The politics of meaning or the meaning of politics? Political terms are particularly open to conscious manipulation by those who have an interest in influencing people's capacity to think about the matters they refer to.

that if we eliminate linguistic categories differentiating, for example, between married and unmarried women (by using 'Ms' instead of 'Mrs' or 'Miss'), and between men and women (by using 'person' instead of 'him' or 'her') this will eventually result in a changed way of thinking about such differences. (It is interesting to note that one of the unintended side-effects of such campaigns may be that they introduce new, and certainly unintended category discriminations. Women identifying themselves as 'Ms' rather than 'Mrs' or 'Miss', may now be categorised as feminists or women's-libbers by some people, possibly an even more discriminatory cognitive distinction than the original married/unmarried categories the campaign tried to eliminate.)

The theory of linguistic relativity also applies to differences in language use between groups of people within the same culture. You may have had the experience of communicating with somebody who comes from a very different background to yours: although you both speak the same language, you probably use it very differently. When patterns of language use are related to differences in social class, the results can be particularly important. Bernstein (1970), on the basis of his research in Britain, suggested that working-class people use a more concrete and restricted linguistic code than do middle-class individuals. As a result, argues Bernstein, working-class children could be automatically disadvantaged in an educational system in which teachers are middle-class and use a middle-class language code which places particular emphasis on the expression of elaborate abstract ideas. In other words, the language used by working-class children may lock them into a 'cognitive universe' which makes communication with their teacher difficult, and could therefore be an educational handicap.

Linguistic relativity assessed
Despite these interesting links between language, culture and thought, the extent of cognitive differences between cultural groups speaking different languages are not always as extreme as Whorf sometimes believed. He suggested that even "various grand generalisations of the Western world such as time, velocity and matter are not essential to the construction of a consistent picture of the universe" (1956, p. 216), but are simply linguistic conventions specific to our culture. It is unlikely that language imprisons us into quite such an impenetrable cognitive universe, a single unalterable way of seeing the world.

After all, we can translate meanings from one language to another without too much difficulty, politicians and businessmen can learn to understand the true meaning of the Soviet vocabulary, and Whorf himself seemed to be quite successful in understanding the Hopi way of seeing things. Thus, language does not impose impenetrable cognitive barriers on us, although it is still likely that the concepts and structures of our language focus our attention on certain things around us and blur others, influencing the way we categorise and remember things. Human beings are active, creative and not simply passive users of language, and attempts at thought manipulation through language may sometimes achieve exactly the opposite results from those intended.

The theory of linguistic relativity has implications not only for actual language use, but also for cognitive information processing. According to the Sapir-Whorf theory, those objects and concepts for which an explicit linguistic category exists (which have a name) should be more easily remembered, recognised, coded and processed than objects or concepts without a clear semantic label. Several experiments support this idea. Brown and Lenneberg (1954) showed, for example, that those colours for which an unambiguous semantic label or name existed could be remembered significantly better than colours which were not associated with such a name (see Activity 7.3).

How shall I call you? Addressing people in social interaction

The first step in any social encounter, and one of the most important uses of language in interaction, is to address our partner. The way we use such language forms as personal pronouns and forms of address in a

---

ACTIVITY 7.3
Naming and Remembering

Are things with a name really easier to remember than similar objects without a name? You can quite easily evaluate this prediction yourself by carrying out a simple experiment. Get two copies of a colour chart (which shows a large number of colours) from any paint shop. Some of these will be colours which have a name (such as blue or red) and others will be complex, mixed colours which have no commonly known name. Cut up the first paint chart into a number of little coloured squares, and cut off the colour names. Select say 10 colours of the first kind, with well-known names, and ten of the second kind, without commonly used names.

For a short time show your volunteer subjects the mixed-up sample of colours you have selected. After a few minutes, give them the second, intact colour chart (with the colour names again cut off or painted out!). Ask them to recognise and pick out those colours you showed them before. Did the colours' names influence their thinking and remembering? In terms of the Sapir-Whorf hypothesis, they should do better in recognising the ten colours which have a common name than in picking out the ten colours which have no well-known names.

conversation is also strongly influenced by cultural conventions. Different cultures at different times provide their members with very different language repertoires to use in their daily interactions. Roger Brown made an extensive study of how the use of address forms and personal pronouns changes across cultures and over time (Brown, 1965; Brown and Gilman, 1960). Forms of address, as do all other linguistic forms, follow explicit rules which are universally recognised within a particular society. Many European languages offer two alternatives in addressing a person, an informal familiar form, and a formal polite form; 'du' or 'Sie' in German, 'tu' or 'vous' in French, 'tu' or 'lei' in Italian, 'te' or 'Ön' in Hungarian. In many Asian languages, for example Japanese, the address forms are even more finely differentiated, as if reflecting the greater importance and elaboration of status differences in such cultures (Wetzel, 1985).

Roger Brown offered the hypothesis that the use of address forms universally follows two simple norms: the *status norm* and the *solidarity norm*. The status norm prescribes that the informal, familiar form should always be used when addressing all members of the lower class, irrespective of whether the speaker is from the same class or from the upper class. The polite formal address form should be used according to the status norm when addressing all members of the upper class by both upper and lower class persons. This pure form of the status norm existed in many feudalistic societies in Europe prior to the French Revolution, when even intimately related members of the upper class (for example, husband and wife) used the formal form to address each other. Members of the lower class, in turn, used the informal form to address even strangers in their own class.

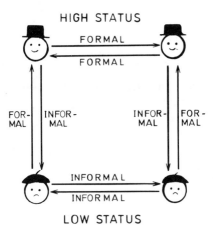

FIGURE 7.1 The status norm in address forms. According to the traditional status norm, all low-status people were addressed informally, and all high-status people were addressed formally, irrespective of the intimacy of the relationship between them. (After Brown, 1965).

The alternative *solidarity* norm regulates personal address on the basis of the partners' intimacy with each other, instead of their status. This norm prescribes the use of the polite address form with all persons with whom the speaker is not on intimate terms, and the use of the informal familiar form with all partners with whom the speaker is on intimate terms, irrespective of their class position. The superimposition of the solidarity norm on the status norm after the French Revolution resulted in conflicting expectations regarding the appropriate form to use. As Figure 7.1 illustrates, the two norms conflict in the address forms prescribed for upper-class intimate and lower-class non-intimate relationships.

This conflict eventually was resolved in Europe by the gradual elimination of the status norm, and the almost universal acceptance of the solidarity norm. This example illustrates very nicely how social and cultural changes come to determine appropriate patterns of language use. The status norm was characteristic of rigidly ordered hierarchical societies typical of the feudal age, while the solidarity norm is more in accord with the values and expectations of the liberal culture which traces its beginnings to the French Revolution.

For those not used to these address forms, for example English speakers (there are no similar distinctions in modern English), who have to communicate in German or French, deciding which form to use may present considerable difficulty even today. At the German university where I used to work, most professors address each other formally even after many years of working together, while students address each other informally even when they are strangers, suggesting a residual status norm. The transition from using the formal 'Sie' to the informal 'du' is marked by strictly regulated rituals in Germany. Initiating the familiar form is the prerogative of the elder partner or the partner with the more senior status, and the transition is usually marked by a drink or some other small celebration. A person's political ideology may also influence how he or she uses these different address forms. Brown and Gilman (1960) found, for example, that radical and conservative individuals differed in the use of address forms. Radical students in France tended to use the more informal 'tu' form more frequently than was the case with conservative people.

The language of social groups
We have seen above that language as a system of communication is shaped and influenced by the surrounding culture. As people interact with each other, they inevitably develop specific language codes. One of the reasons for this is that on the basis of their growing knowledge of each other, there is less and less need to spell out every detail in their verbal communications. In other words, their language becomes more and more indexical: much of the message to be communicated is not

actually expressed, but only indicated or implied (you may also have seen this in Activity 7.1). For example, a simple question 'Shall we have a dip?' is not in itself meaningful. In order to correctly interpret it, we must know many things which are only implied here, such as (a) dip is vernacular for swimming in this group, (b) the questioner refers to a nearby swimming pool familiar to his partner, (c) both of them can swim, (d) they have gone there together in the past for the purpose of swimming.

Language thus always relies on the shared knowledge of the interactants to make communication more economical. The closer the relationship between the sender and the receiver, the more specific their language use becomes. Lovers, good friends and families may develop language codes which are almost incomprehensible to outsiders. Less intimate groups, such as people in the same university, tutorial class or work team also tend to have their own specific 'lingo'.

The shared social environment of a group thus necessarily leads to the development of group 'lingo'. The reason is not simply to capitalise on shared knowledge, and thus economise communication. Having one's own 'language' in turn also helps to define a social group. Those who are familiar with the local language are by definition 'in', members of the group, while outsiders may find it difficult to understand the language, and thus to become members. Language use may thus serve to define and reinforce the separate social identity of a group.

Relatively few empirical studies have looked at this link between language and group identity. In one relevant study, Friendly and Glucksberg (1970) suggested that learning the local jargon was one of the

A case of linguistic relativity? The meanings of words largely depend on who is using them, where, when, with whom, and in which situation.

hallmarks of becoming a properly socialised member of the group of Princeton students they studied. These authors elicited a list of subculture-specific jargon terms, and then used multidimensional scaling to analyse how students understood the semantic meanings of these terms. They found that new students had a more simple understanding of these words than advanced students, who had a complex and elaborate knowledge of the shades of meaning expressed by these words. Table 7.1 shows some of the words which were part of this subcultural lexicon, and their meanings.

TABLE 7.1
LEXICON OF SOME COMMONLY-USED PRINCETON
JARGON TERMS

Word	Meaning
wonk	an introverted student who studies all the time; generally considered to be physically unattractive.
stud	a good-looking student who is successful with women; cool and detached.
star	1. centre of attention; 2. athletic ace.
lunch	a graceless, socially unattractive student.
meatball	same as lunch, only more physically and intellectually unattractive.
punter	student who studies little; devotes himself to unproductive activities (i.e. television).
grind	a student who studies diligently for long periods of time; a periodic wonk.
faceman	1. an attractive student who makes a good first impression; 2. always selling himself.
Cottage type	stereotype of person belonging to Cottage Club, a selective and prestigious eating club; generally considered conservative and superficial.
Ivy type	stereotype of person belonging to Ivy Club, a selective and prestigious eating club; generally considered aristocratic and snobbish.
Cannon type	stereotype of person belonging to Cannon Club; a selective and well-known (though not prestigious) eating club; generally considered to be a crude, unintelligent jock.

Word	Meaning
Colonial type	stereotype of person belonging to Colonial Club, a selective and somewhat prestigious eating club; generally considered to be a pseudointellectual, nonathletic culture buff.
Key and Seal type	stereotype of person belonging to Key and Seal Club, a selective but socially undesirable eating club, generally considered lunch.
Wilcox type	stereotype of person belonging to the Woodrow Wilson Society, a nonprestigious eating society with open membership; seen as bearded, long haired, nonathletic, radical and wonkish.
ceptsman	a person who gets through his courses knowing a few important ideas and having a fluid pen; a lazy scholar.
gut hopper	a "gut" is an easy course; hence, a student who takes only easy courses.
bull thrower	student who speaks often but says little; a blatherer.

After Friendly and Glucksberg, 1970 p. 557

In a somewhat similar study, we (Forgas, 1983) looked at the categories students at an Australian university used to describe other students. It is instructive to compare our list shown in Chapter 3 (see Table 3.1) with that of Friendly and Glucksberg (1970). Although

Is this person a wonk, a stud, a lunch or a gut hopper? He is none of them. He is most likely to be a grind, according to the lexicon of Princeton jargon terms collected by Friendly and Glucksberg (Table 7.1). The use of group-specific jargon eases communication and helps to establish a group's special identity.

Australian students had specific terms such as 'surfies', 'lazy bludgers' and 'Asian students' which were not used by the Princeton group, the overall similarities across the two lexicons are quite surprising. It appears that student subcultural milieus generate fairly similar linguistic expressions across cultures, apart from a few very localised terms.

Groups do not always adopt a special language code for ease of communication alone. We have seen above that having your own language has important secondary consequences, such as the establishment and reinforcement of the group's own social identity. Groups which are particularly uncertain of, or concerned about, their own status often adopt jargon words simply as a symbol of their status, rather than to help communication. Professional groups and academics are particularly prone to such practices. The archaic English terms used by lawyers in legal documents no longer serve the purpose of precise legal expression, but are there to signify the special knowledge and status of lawyers as the only people qualified to interpret them. If those documents were written in plain English (as many knowledgeable experts suggest), anyone could understand and act upon them, and the need for qualified lawyers to do this (expensive) job would be much less obvious.

Similarly, medical practitioners have long preferred to use obscure Latin terms to describe common illnesses for which perfectly adequate English names exist. Knowing the jargon once again symbolises the specialised knowledge and worth of this professional group. Unfortunately, psychologists are also often guilty of unnecessary indulgence in jargon (Harre, 1985). As Table 7.2 shows, the complex subject matter of psychology (and most other social sciences) gives its practitioners excellent scope to use almost meaningless jargon.

Language and social situations
We have seen that the language we have available to us for use in social interaction is in many ways determined by the wider culture we live in, and the norms, rules and shared history of our group or interaction unit. In addition, sociolinguistic research has indicated a whole range of other important situational influences on the way we use language. Language as a communication system is so rich that we can select from amongst a number of alternative verbal forms to express similar messages. The requirements of the particular social situation we are in have a major influence on what we say and how we say it. We shall take a brief look at some these situational influences below.

When more than one language or dialect is spoken in a particular community (polyglossia), the choice of one code over the other gives interesting insights into the social rules regulating verbal interaction. Fishman (1971) showed that bilingual Americans speaking Spanish and English used the two languages in very different situations. English was

TABLE 7.2
A GUIDE TO (ALMOST) MEANINGLESS JARGON

The 'creative' use of language often includes the generation of unnecessary and confusing jargon, which serves to establish a social group's identity rather than good communication. You will find a small sample of such phrases used by social scientists below: you may combine almost any word in column 1 with almost any word in column 2 and column 3 to generate what may be impressive-sounding but probably almost meaningless phrases!

1	2	3
ongoing	personal	construct
complementary	cultural	contexts
confirmatory	social	reactions
dissonant	individual	stimulus
future	natural	evaluations
rational	scientific	representations
successful	cognitive	judgments
intuitive	psychological	ratings
manipulative	conceptual	predictions
classic	descriptive	structure
present	functional	perceptions
complex	mental	situations

It is much easier to make up such a list than you would think — you can try it yourself!

---

the language of employment and education, and Spanish was used at home, in the neighbourhood and in religion. Sometimes code-switching may occur within the same sentence. For example, Rayfield (1970) describes conversations in which Yiddish words are used when referring to family matters in an otherwise English sentence by members of the Santa Monica Jewish community. Similarly, in the Norwegian community studied by Gumperz and Hymes (1972), a local dialect was used by townspeople in the community office when greeting and enquiring about the family of the official. The dialect was switched to the standard code as soon as the official part of the client's business was discussed. Studies such as these show that in social interaction people have a keen awareness of the requirements of the communication situation, and adapt their linguistic choices accordingly.

The particular situation influences not only what we say, but also how it is going to be interpreted. In a series of interesting experiments, Gallois and Callan (1985) found that people even react to a speaker's accent differently depending on the situation in which they hear it. It was found to be far more acceptable to have a Greek or an Aboriginal accent among Australians in informal, person-centred situations, than in formal, achievement-oriented situations. Situational influences on language are learnt very early in life: children use slightly different language patterns when engaged in a cooperative or a competitive game (Garton, 1983), and five- to seven-year old children are already quite competent in adapting their communication strategies to fit in with specific rules they have been given (Pratt, 1983).

Another interesting question is how we select from the numerous available semantic alternatives the one that best fits the situation. For example, I can tell my partner that I want him to shut the door in many different ways: 'I think there is a draught in here'; 'Do you want the door open ?'; 'I am cold'; 'Could you please shut the door?'; 'Shut the door!'; 'I wonder who left the door open'; 'Do you have automatic doors in your house?' and so on. Why do we choose one alternative over another in communicating our request? Sociolinguistic research showed that people

---

ACTIVITY 7.4
Communication in Conflict Situations

Imagine that you have just received a gift which is so bizarre and useless that you don't know whether it was intended seriously or as a joke. When you next meet the person who gave it, she asks you: "Well, how did you like the gift I gave you?" What would be your answer? Select one of the following alternatives:

1. Thank you for such a lovely present, I really love it. It was very nice of you to think of it.

2. Thank you, but I don't really like that sort of thing. How did you ever come to the idea of giving me something like this?

3. Thanks, I got your present. Is it true that a person gives what she would like to receive? I hope I can return the favour some day.

If you are like most people, you would probably choose the third alternative. Notice that this message says almost nothing about the gift, whether you liked it or not, or about you and the person who gave it. The situation described above is a conflict situation: if you enthuse over a gift which was meant to be a joke you will look foolish, and if you show displeasure over a present that was given with good intentions, you will upset the person's feelings. The best way out is to say something that could be interpreted either way — in effect, say something that says nothing! You can find out more about such messages in the next section.

have an extremely clear and finely tuned idea about the requirements of various situations, the status and relationship between themselves and their partners, and the reasonableness of their message in the circumstances (Forgas, 1985). Among the request alternatives listed above, each could be the 'conventional' form in making a request in some situations (Gibbs, 1985). In every conversation, each and every utterance is carefully selected from a very large number of alternative linguistic forms with similar meanings to best fit such social requirements.

Saying something that means nothing
One of the most important characteristics of social interaction is that the partners must act in accordance with certain rules. In verbal exchanges or conversations, we must say things which are relevant, say them in an appropriate sequence, be polite and considerate, try to avoid silences, and so on. Grice (1975) suggested that such so-called 'conversational postulates' are at the heart of verbal interaction. Yet sometimes we find ourselves in a situation where we would rather not say anything at all. When your best friend gives a terrible paper at a seminar, and afterwards asks you 'How did I do?' what do you say? You could be honest (and hurt his feelings), you could save his feelings (and lie), or you could say something like 'You did the best you could', or 'Many people would have done much worse'. Such statements satisfy the requirement of saying something that is relevant, without really expressing any particular opinion (see Activity 7.4).

Verbal utterances which are so indirect and uninformative may be called 'disqualified' messages according to Bavelas (1985). She studied such messages in some detail, and found that people produce them only when they find themselves in an avoidance-avoidance conflict: that is, they have to choose between two disliked communication alternatives, for example, hurting somebody's feelings, or lying, as in the past example and in Activity 7.4. Such disqualified messages are quite common in everyday life. When you want to sell your car which you know is a bomb, or try to console a friend who rightly failed an exam, you are likely to use disqualification.

Bavelas (1985) carried out a series of interesting experiments to study the conditions under which people use disqualification. In one study, subjects had to pretend that they were shopkeepers trying to sell off some meat which was either good, or of doubtful quality. They answered questions about the meat on the telephone, and their answers were recorded and later analysed. You will find a sample of typical responses in Table 7.3. The numbers indicate the extent to which each communication was ambiguous (disqualified). Positive numbers denote messages judged to be disqualified, and negative numbers denote messages rated to be direct and informative.

TABLE 7.3
HOW GOOD IS THAT MEAT? THE EFFECTS OF CONFLICT
ON THE QUALITY OF VERBAL MESSAGES*

	Messages	Scale values
Non-conflict condition (i.e. the meat is good)	It's good quality meat, yes.	-3.28
	It sure is, it's top grade A meat.	-2.34
	Yes it's very good quality.	-1.74
	We wouldn't be selling bad meat, you'd only bring it back.	-1.48
	Oh yes it's all very fresh we just put it on sale to reduce inventory.	- .85
	Um, I can be, be reasonably assured that it's good. I haven't had any fault with, with the meat there before. If you if you find something um has gone bad like the chicken, ah it can be exchanged.	- .54
Conflict condition (i.e. the meat is doubtful)	I think it's quite good, yes for the price.	.05
	Well it is on sale because it has been in the store for a while but that doesn't mean that it's bad.	.13
	I, well, yes it is good meat the ah I uh I'd like you to realise though that it ah is day old meat or older so that it may not have some of the colour that uh the meat that you would find cut freshly today . . . so and it's not top quality meat, it's . . . There's nothing wrong with the meat but it's not your um cross your standing rib roast or your sirloin steaks that are on sale but it's all um there's nothing at all wrong with it but the colour may have gone out of it.	.91
	Oh, it's fairly fine yes.	2.6
	Um . . . ah the reason why they're selling is because it's um it's a little bit old.	3.52
	It's the usual.	3.94

*Positive scale values indicate noncommunicative, ambiguous disqualified messages; negative scale value indicates unambiguous messages.

After Bavelas, 1985

Verbal communication — a conclusion

We could do little more in the limited space available than to give some general hints about the complexity of human language as a medium of interpersonal communication. As we have seen, theorists tend to emphasise either the uniquely human, universal features of language (cf. Lenneberg, Hockett, Vygotsky), or the specific cultural variations in language use (Brown, Whorf, Sapir, etc.). Language is undoubtedly one of the few characteristics which clearly differentiates human beings from other species. It is language which makes it possible to abstract and think about our daily experiences, to build up complex symbolic representations, and thus create larger cultural systems. Symbolic interactionist theorists in particular, such as George Herbert Mead, Cooley and Blumer emphasised the important function of language as the medium of social and cultural life.

The role of language in everyday social interaction deserves special attention. All kinds of social groups have a tendency to create more or less specialised language codes. Social and political changes also influence patterns of language use, as Brown's analysis of address forms showed. Knowing the specific local language code is a prerequisite for successful social interaction. Finally, numerous subtle social and situational factors play a role in influencing the actual message selected from the verbal repertoire of a speaker. However, language also has its limitations in face-to-face interaction. The auditory channel in which it is transmitted (for example in a conversation) has only very limited carrying capacity. In face-to-face interaction, a great deal more is communicated than is said by words, much of it visually. We shall look at some aspects of the various nonverbal channels of communication in the next chapter.

8. Nonverbal communication

8.

NONVERBAL COMMUNICATION

Verbal messages constitute only a small part of interpersonal communication. The messages sent using words and sentences are usually accompanied by a rich array of nonverbal signals, which support, modify or even completely replace the verbal message. Some quite complicated social encounters can be entirely made up of such nonverbal messages. In situations where explicit verbal communication is for some reason difficult or impossible (for example, in the presence of high background noise, across a distance, or between lovers in the presence of others) a complicated exchange of nonverbal signals may be substituted, consisting of eye gaze, smiles, gestures, postural changes, and so on. Many encounters between members of the opposite sex begin as elaborate exchanges of nonverbal signals, indicating interest and availability, before a single word is spoken.

As we shall see, the ability to effectively send and receive such nonverbal messages is essential for successful social interaction. Argyle (1969) suggested that this ability is a learned skill like any other. Some people are simply better at it than others. Consistent lack of skill in nonverbal communication often results in serious maladjustment, which may be remedied by adequate training in the necessary communication skills (see Chapter 16).

In this section we will look at the most important characteristics of nonverbal communication, and how it differs from language. The evolutionary roots of nonverbal messages will be considered, and finally, research on various kinds of nonverbal messages (such as gaze, facial expression, distance, posture) will be summarised. Most of this research is relatively recent. Although Darwin (1872) wrote a book on the nonverbal expression of emotions in man and animals over a hundred years ago, social psychologists have not returned to this topic until fairly recently. The process of nonverbal communication is much more complex than recent popular books on 'body language', 'silent messages'

The use of body language to indicate heterosexual interest. In many interpersonal situations, nonverbal messages can be more important than verbal messages in communicating attitudes and emotions; sometimes, whole intricate exchanges can be carried out using nonverbal messages alone. The cartoon above shows a rather more simple form of bodily communication!

and the like would suggest. The application of social psychological methods has resulted in a radical expansion of knowledge in this field, as we shall see below.

Similarities and differences between verbal and nonverbal communication

Nonverbal messages are not simply alternatives to using language. Nonverbal communication (NVC) as a communication system has very different characteristics from language. The decoding of, and reactions to, nonverbal messages tend to be much more immediate and automatic than reactions to verbal messages. When your interaction partner smiles at you, stares at you or winks at you, there is usually no delay in interpreting and reacting to these signals; we do not need to consciously analyse and decode what these messages mean. In contrast, verbal messages usually undergo a much more thorough encoding and decoding sequence: it takes much longer to understand, interpret and prepare a reply to a verbal statement.

It appears thus that nonverbal messages are often less subject to *conscious interpretation and monitoring* than is the case with language. As a result, nonverbal cues may often give a speaker away, revealing attitudes, feelings and emotions which we may not want to reveal. Such *nonverbal leakage* can also inform us about when a person tells the truth, and when he is lying. Ekman and Friesen (1974) investigated this phenomenon in some detail, and suggested that peripheral cues, such as movements of the body, arms and legs are under less conscious control, and therefore more likely to give a liar away than central cues such as facial expression and gaze. They carried out several studies of this effect, using, for example, films of psychiatric patients who were attempting to cover up how anxious and upset they really felt, "simulating optimism, control of affect and feelings of well-being" (Ekman and Friesen, 1969, p. 100).

Films of these patients, showing their head only, their body only, or both their head and body were shown to observers, who were asked to tick those words on a list of adjectives which in their opinion best described the patient's condition. The results, summarised in Table 8.1, clearly show that body messages were more effective in revealing the

TABLE 8.1
NONVERBAL LEAKAGE: OBSERVERS' PERCEPTIONS OF AN ANXIOUS
PATIENT TRYING TO SIMULATE NORMAL ADJUSTMENT AND
HAPPINESS BASED ON VISUAL NONVERBAL CUES COMMUNICATED
BY HEAD OR BODY

		% Head	% Body
Traits predominantly communicated by head cues	sensitive	83*	36*
	friendly	50	14
	cooperative	50	14
	self-punishing	50	02
Traits predominantly communicated by body cues	tense	44	82
	excitable	22	79
	highly strung	39	75
	fearful	33	68
	hurried	0	61
	changeable	39	61
	awkward	33	61
	complaining	11	54
	touchy	28	54
	affected	33	54
	restless	06	50
	impulsive	17	50
	impatient	0	50
	rigid	17	50
Information communicated by both head and body cues	anxious	89	100
	emotional	89	82
	confused	72	82
	defensive	72	71
	worrying	50	68
	dissatisfied	56	57
	despondent	56	50

*Percentage of judges identifying each emotion from each of the two cues.
After Ekman and Friesen, 1969, p. 101

patient's true condition (tension, excitement etc.) than were head messages. The latter were better controlled by the patients, and communicated a deceptively sensitive, friendly and cooperative attitude. In addition, there were some symptomatic messages which were revealed by both body and head cues. Later studies tended to support these findings, suggesting that peripheral nonverbal cues are indeed under less stringent conscious control than central nonverbal cues, which in turn are generally less well controlled than verbal messages.

Nonverbal communication differs from language in another way: nonverbal messages tend to be much more efficient in transmitting information about *attitudes and emotions* than is language. This may seem surprising at first, since it is commonly thought that nonverbal cues simply accompany and support language. To determine the relative effectiveness of the two communication systems in conveying information about attitudes and emotions, we must consider what happens when the verbal message is actually *contradicted* by nonverbal communication. Which of these two opposing messages will be more powerful in influencing an observer's judgments?

Two studies evaluating this issue were carried out by Argyle, Salter, Nicholson, Williams and Burgess (1970), and Argyle, Alkema and Gilmour, (1971). In both of these experiments, observers had the task of forming impressions of people who communicated consistent or contradictory messages in the verbal and nonverbal modalities. In the first study, subjects were shown a videotape of a woman lecturer who communicated highly superior attitudes verbally ('I doubt if you would understand this experiment', etc.), combined with nonverbal messages of inferiority, such as 'deferential, nervous smile, head lowered, nervous, eager-to-please speech' (Argyle et al. 1970, p. 224). In other conditions, the messages communicated in the two modalities were reversed, or were consistently superior or inferior in both channels. The results suggested that nonverbal messages were much more powerful in communicating attitudes of inferiority or superiority than were words: "It was found that nonverbal cues ... had 4.3 times the effect of verbal cues on shifts of ratings, and accounted for 10.3 times as much variance" (p. 222). Similar results were found in the second study, in which the attitudes communicated were friendliness or unfriendliness (see Activity 8.1).

One explanation of these intriguing findings is in terms of the cultural restrictions placed on what can be acceptably communicated using language. In most Western cultures, it is usually not acceptable to express interpersonal attitudes and emotions towards others directly. As a result, we habitually communicate such information nonverbally. If verbal and nonverbal messages contradict each other, we are perhaps culturally conditioned to look for the nonverbal cues as revealing the true message. Darwin suggested that there may also be another reason for the dominance of nonverbal signals over language when it comes to expressing emotions and attitudes: in evolutionary terms, the nonverbal signalling system is much older than language, and thus more adapted to the communication of basic messages dealing with emotions. We may sum up the differences between language and nonverbal communication by concluding that nonverbal messages are usually sent and received much more quickly, are under less conscious control and monitoring, and are more powerful in communicating attitudes and emotions than is language. One consequence of these differences is that while language is primarily suited to conveying information about the external world, tasks to be solved, and the like, nonverbal messages play a particularly important role in social life, communicating values, attitudes, liking, and other personal reactions. Nonverbal messages play a particularly important role in communicating emotional states to others.

ACTIVITY 8.1
Which is More Important:
What We Say or How We Say It?

You could try to replicate the findings reported by Argyle and his co-workers yourself. All you have to do is to practise in front of a mirror communicating contradictory information in the verbal and nonverbal modalities. You can then use contradictory communication with people and observe how they react. For example, you could say something very friendly while sending very unfriendly nonverbal messages, or you could say something suggesting inferiority while communicating superiority nonverbally. Do people pay more attention to what you say, or to how you say it? You should find, just as Argyle did, that how you say something is often much more important than what you are saying!

Darwin and the study of emotional expression
Darwin's extensive travels and observations of a large number of animal species formed the background to his theory of evolution. Darwin was also an avid student of comparative behaviour, and his book published in 1872, *The Expression of Emotions in Man and Animals* is the first empirical psychological work on this topic. He was impressed by the strong similarities he observed in the nonverbal expression of emotion by people in very different cultures, and further, the apparent similarities between some of these expressions and the emotional signals of certain

non-human species, particularly primates. In an extremely simplified form, Darwin's arguments ran something like this. Since the expression of emotions (smile, laughter, crying, fright, etc.) appears to be extremely similar in all human societies, this communication system must have some genetic basis shared by all humans. Furthermore, since some sub-human species, such as primates, apparently use some emotional expressions very similar to humans, the communication of emotions is not only genetically determined, but was probably shaped by the same evolutionary pressures as physical features.

Darwin collected an impressive amount of empirical material to support his theory. He carried out systematic cross-cultural observations of emotional signals, collected and studied photographs of emotional expression in man and animals, and devoted particular attention to observing the emotional communications of infants and the insane, whom he expected to display the genetically determined signals in their pure form, unbiased by cultural norms and expectations. Figure 8.1 illustrates some of the descriptive evidence which Darwin used to support his evolutionary theory of communication.

Darwin's book has stimulated considerable interest in the communication of emotions in recent years. Ekman and his co-workers (Ekman, 1973; Ekman and Friesen, 1975; Ekman, Friesen and Ellsworth, 1972) collected a great deal of evidence relevant to Darwin's theory. These data show that some facial expressions of emotion are indeed universal in the human species. New Guinea tribesmen who had

FIGURE 8.1 Facial expressions of emotion. These pictures, based on early photographs by Dr Duchenne, were used by Darwin to illustrate the facial expressions of terror (left) and horror and agony (right). (After Darwin, 1872).

had next to no contact with Western civilisation were able to correctly interpret the emotions shown on photos of white people, and in turn, their own facial expression in response to emotional cues matched those used in our culture. Similar results were obtained by Ekman in a number of other cultures. On the basis of this recent evidence, it may be concluded that at least some forms of emotional signals (for example, facial expression) appear to be universal.

It is much more difficult to obtain evidence for Darwin's second proposition, that these expressions evolved out of more primitive animal signals. The 'bared teeth' display of primates indicating submission may be superficially similar to a human smile — but the meaning of a smile is so dependent on complex cultural conventions, that any evolutionary continuity must remain doubtful. It is more likely that any similarities in facial expression between man and primates are due to the similar facial bone and muscle structures of the two species. Ekman also investigated the various muscles which are involved in facial expressions, and found that the number of expressions which may be generated are quite limited. It is not surprising then that human facial expressions sometimes resemble primate facial expressions. However, such similarities do not indicate that the *meaning* attached to an expression is also shared.

In more recent studies, Ekman, Levenson and Friesen (1983) went one step further. They asked their subjects to enact various facial expressions by instructing them to move the appropriate facial muscles. They found that "emotion-specific activity in the autonomic nervous system was generated by constructing facial prototypes of emotion muscle by muscle" (p.221). These findings suggest that emotional experience and facial expression may be linked by direct neural pathways, something that would be consistent with Darwin's original speculations. However, the evidence for such a link is far from conclusive at this stage.

We should also note that by far the majority of emotional signals are not as universal as facial expression. Most nonverbal messages are culture specific, and even the meanings of those signals which occur in several cultures are extensively modified and elaborated by the particular culture. Darwin's studies, and Ekman's more recent investigations were effective in directing attention to one of the most fundamental differences between language and nonverbal communication. Unlike language, nonverbal signalling systems can be found at many levels of development among animals. The social organisation, and thus, potential for survival, of many species is based on such efficient nonverbal communication systems. Since nonverbal messages represent a much older communication system than language, the particular effectiveness of some nonverbal signs in instantly eliciting and communicating emotions and attitudes may well have an evolutionary explanation.

The functions of nonverbal communication

As we have seen above, language and nonverbal messages as systems of communication have very different characteristics, which to some extent determine what their optimal role is in social interaction. In most everyday encounters we use both verbal and nonverbal messages simultaneously, but for differing purposes. These two communication modalities are usually coordinated and support each other, for example, our gestures, gaze and tone of voice emphasise and elaborate the information communicated using words. Indeed, it may be said that a person does not speak a language properly until he/she knows exactly how to supplement his speech with the appropriate accompanying nonverbal gestures.

Among linguists, it is increasingly recognised that one cannot study language as an abstract system of communication without also considering how language is actually used in everyday life (Forgas, 1985). One speaks a language by using not only words, but also one's whole body. The French, the Italians, the British and the Greeks use very different nonverbal signals to accompany their conversations (see Activity 8.2).

The two channels, verbal and nonverbal, may on occasion communicate contradictory messages, or even function independently of each other. A single wink may negate the most elaborate speech, by indicating that whatever is said verbally is not to be taken seriously. To take another example, a male giving a formal lecture in the verbal modality may simultaneously use nonverbal signals to express heterosexual interest in a female member of the audience. Between these

---

ACTIVITY 8.2

Cultural Differences in Nonverbal Communication

You may demonstrate that people of different nationalities use different nonverbal signals to accompany their speech quite easily, by asking your friends to guess what language people speak, when their voices cannot be heard. You may collect different samples of conversations by selecting and recording segments of foreign films from television as your stimulus materials. But you must be careful that the scenes chosen do not reveal the speakers' nationality through cues other than gestures, such as dress or background scenery. Languages where the nonverbal channel (for example, gestures and body movements) is extensively used, such as Italian and French, should be much easier to recognise than languages with few accompanying nonverbal signals.

extremes, there is a certain amount of specialisation between the verbal and nonverbal modalities: we tend predominantly to use nonverbal messages for purposes not easily handled by language. Nonverbal signals are mainly used to accomplish five functions: (1) to manage the social situation, (2) self-presentation, (3) the communication of emotional states, (4) the communication of attitudes, and (5) channel control (cf. Argyle, 1969; 1972).

Managing the social situation

We are not usually aware of it, but even the simplest social interaction requires careful and complex management by the participants. We need to continually indicate to our partner our positive or negative reactions to what he communicates, our increasing, decreasing or constant interest in the interaction, our desire to redefine or terminate the encounter, and many other messages which are essential for the smooth continuation of the encounter. When two people engage in a conversation, their verbal exchanges are managed, supported and continuously monitored in the nonverbal modality. Such cues are extremely important. Despite verbal expressions of interest, it is almost impossible to continue a conversation with somebody who nonverbally communicates boredom or lack of interest. We find it difficult to talk to people who do not look at us, do not nod at what we say every now and then, stand too far away from us, or adopt a body position which is non-reinforcing, oriented away from us. Whatever the topic of conversation — the neighbour's cat, politics or football — without the continuous flow of nonverbal messages supporting and managing the encounter the interaction would be impossible to maintain.

Such nonverbal messages are not only important in the regulation of already established interactions. The initiation and termination of encounters is an even more difficult task that is usually accomplished nonverbally. In settings where opportunities exist for initiating new encounters (at parties, meetings, seminars and the like where strangers may legitimately meet), a subtle sequence of nonverbal signals is normally used to establish such interactions. Usually the first signal is eye contact, which, once reciprocated, may lead to more complex signals, such as smiles and nods serving to acknowledge the existence of the potential partner. This is normally followed by moving towards each other, re-adjusting head and body orientation towards the partner, and finally culminating in the first exchange of words.

Breaking into a circle of people talking to each other at a party is a more complex example of such a nonverbal ritual. Moving from a public to a social distance (see section on distance behaviour in the next chapter) and establishing eye-contact with the group members appearing most accessible should lead to an 'incorporation' ritual, the approached member slightly turning towards you, moving somewhat to the side offering you a place in the circle, and some of the other group members finally acknowledging your arrival with brief eye contact and perhaps a smile.

The ability to skilfully terminate encounters is an even more crucial nonverbal skill. We all know the extremely awkward situations which may result when neither of the partners is able to skilfully finish an interaction which they both wish had ended a long time ago. Looking at your watch is a very unsubtle ploy here! The sequence to be used is roughly the reverse of the incorporation ritual. Reducing eye contact and looking away, slowly increasing the distance (if standing) or making preparatory moves to get up (when sitting) usually does the trick. The 'looking away and moving away' ritual at cocktail parties is again well established.

Nonverbal skills in joining a group. One of the important functions of nonverbal messages is the management of social situations, for example, when we wish to initiate or terminate an encounter, or join or depart from a group. Eye gaze, body orientation, or smile indicate an interest in joining a conversation — of course, one may use more direct cues, as the cartoon illustrates!

Self-presentation

It is an essential feature of all social interaction that our self-esteem and self-image are usually on trial. We must successfully establish (with new partners), and keep maintained (with established partners) our own view of ourselves. The task may be excruciatingly difficult and threatening when we are uprooted from our normal social milieu, and have to present ourselves to numerous strangers, often in large groups, without the benefit of support from people who already know who we are! Such situations arise, for example, at summer schools, residential conferences, package tours or when joining a new institution, company or university.

Verbal communication is of little help as a carrier of self-presentation messages in such situations. We rarely introduce ourselves to strangers by affirming 'I am a nice, intelligent, goodlooking person of immense charm, most people like me, and so should you'. Western cultures in general, and Anglo-Saxon cultures in particular, prohibit the explicit verbal communication of such messages, but signals communicating something like that nevertheless must exist. We do this nonverbally, using smiles, the odd headnod or wrinkled forehead to suggest friendliness, kindness, critical ability or intelligence, as the situation requires. More straightforward personal characteristics, such as status, sexual availability or wealth may be signalled more directly, using clothes, appearance or various insignia (jewellery, badges, etc.) as the carriers of the message.

Studies of British football fans by Marsh, Rosser and Harre (1978) show for example, that their apparently weird dress (ankle length pants, tartan scarves twisted around the waist, etc.) in fact subtly signal the status and position of a fan within this subculture. Football fans live in a hierarchical society just like everyone else, and their progress from novices to seniors is marked by their changing location on the football terraces, as well as the costumes they wear. It is extremely important for these fans, as for all of us, that our established status and image of ourselves should be accepted and confirmed by others. We request and receive such confirmation mostly by nonverbal means.

Is this person trying to communicate something? The wearing of badges, certain clothes, hairstyle or facial expression can all serve the purpose of non-verbal self-presentation, and the communication of attitudes, personality characteristics, and so on.

Communicating emotional states

We have seen above that some nonverbal signals, such as facial expression, function as highly specialised and culturally universal carriers of information about emotional states. Verbal messages about emotions are not only slower, but often also more ambiguous. A related and quite interesting problem is that in order to communicate emotions effectively by words, we must first clearly identify and label the emotion we are experiencing, a lengthy, and sometimes quite unreliable process, as we have seen earlier in the section on self-attribution of emotions (Chapter 6). There are no such problems with using facial expression to send emotional messages. Ekman et al. (1983) recently showed that the link between emotions and facial expression is so strong that people seem to experience the appropriate emotion simply by being instructed to move their facial muscles to a position normally associated with sending an emotional signal.

In addition, we have already seen that cultural norms in Western societies strictly limit the verbal communication of emotions. Who can talk about what emotions to whom and in what circumstances is strictly regulated. Most commonly, nonverbal messages have to fulfil this important function. Apart from facial expression, emotions such as anxiety, happiness, fear, joy or disgust may be communicated through a variety of other channels as well, including posture, gestures, distance, gaze and so on. The ability to send and interpret such emotional messages varies across individuals. There is some evidence that females are both better senders and better receivers of emotional communications than are males.

The communication of attitudes

Most enduring attitudes can usually be expressed verbally as well as nonverbally. Reactions to political leaders, washing powders or tinned pet food can be discussed, but the nonverbal signals accompanying such discourse usually significantly expand on the verbal content. Studies showed that even the most unbiased television newsreaders can inadvertently reveal quite a lot about their own political beliefs in *how* they read various political news items. In social encounters, many other attitudes, particularly those which are temporary and change by the minute, are exclusively communicated through nonverbal channels. Your attitude towards your partner's way of eating his dinner, his topic of conversation, the fly buzzing around your food, or your mother-in-law who has just been mentioned are rarely worth a verbal comment. Such attitudes are communicated nonverbally, by an instantaneous and continuous flow of smiles, nods, frowns and eye contact. These messages are not only carriers of attitudinal information, but are also part of 'managing the social situation' as we have seen above.

It is interesting to note that nonverbal channels differ in effectiveness in communicating attitudes. When vocal, facial and verbal cues communicating attitudes were combined into consistent or inconsistent messages, Mehrabian and his colleagues found that vocal cues were five times, and facial cues almost eight times as effective as verbal cues. The relationship can even be expressed in the following formula (Mehrabian and Weiner, 1967; Mehrabian and Ferris, 1967): PERCEIVED ATTITUDE = .07X VERBAL CUES + .38X VOCAL CUES + .55X FACIAL CUES. The accuracy suggested by such a formula is of course somewhat illusory. But taken together with the research we reviewed above by Argyle and his colleagues, there seems to be strong evidence suggesting that nonverbal cues play a major role, far outweighing that of language, in the communication of interpersonal attitudes.

Channel control

A very special aspect of managing the social situation is controlling who is speaking, for how long, and who is taking the floor next. Verbal interaction is usually highly organised and structured, since the auditory communication channel has only very limited carrying capacity. However large the group, only one person can speak at a time so as to be understood. To efficiently apportion this scarce resource, turn-taking has to be highly coordinated to minimise wastage. *Channel control* refers to the function of nonverbal communication signals, for example gaze, in controlling the use of the verbal channel.

Once a group is comprised of more than two or three people, the required coordination can be quite complex, yet it is usually achieved without verbal messages, without individuals explicitly asking for, or being given permission to speak. There are well-recognised nonverbal signals to accomplish this. The speaker indicates his preparedness to yield the floor by signals such as lowering the voice, looking up and scanning the audience for somebody to take over, relaxing muscle tone and posture, and so on. The coordination of such a subtle sequence of turn-taking and turn-yielding signals is far more complex than previously thought, as Michael Walker (1983) has demonstrated in several recent experiments.

Kendon (1967) has shown that the patterns of gaze employed at the beginning and at the end of an utterance are quite different. The person wishing to take over usually signals his intention by catching the speaker's eye, taking a (sometimes audible) deep breath, leaning forward and perhaps by performing some attention-seeking postural and gestural signs. If the ritual breaks down for any reason, and several speakers start speaking at once, a brief battle may ensue, in which loudness of voice, rate of speech and persistence of gaze or gestures may decide the winner after a few words have been uttered in unison. Since the underlying flow of nonverbal signals is far more sophisticated than previously suspected (Walker, 1983), it is quite a remarkable feat that most turn-taking in conversations takes place without a hitch or any noticeable disruption in the exchange.

Towards a classification of nonverbal messages

We never send and receive nonverbal messages in isolation: our communication always consists of the combination of multiple signals in a variety of modalities, such as eye gaze, gestures, vocal cues. How can we, then, characterise the total impression which is communicated by such complex message arrays? Mehrabrian (1969) empirically analysed a large number of nonverbal behaviours and suggested that the meaning of nonverbal messages may be described in terms of three separate dimensions: (1) *immediacy* or intimacy cues are used to communicate liking and evaluation; (2) *relaxation* cues are used to communicate status differences and differences in social control, and (3) *activity* cues are used to communicate alertness and responsiveness.

You will find some examples of typical nonverbal messages used to communicate in each of these dimensions in Table 8.2. For example, we may indicate liking by such immediacy cues as touching, eye contact and

TABLE 8.2
KINDS OF NONVERBAL MESSAGES USED TO COMMUNICATE LIKING, STATUS OR CONTROL, AND RESPONSIVENESS

---

1. Immediacy cues (communicating like or dislike)
   Eye contact
   Body orientation
   Body forward lean
   Interpersonal distance
   Touching

2. Relaxation cues (communicating status and social control)
   Body sideways lean
   Arms crossed vs not
   Torso relaxation/reclining angle
   Hand relaxation
   Legs crossed vs not

3. Activity cues (communicating responsiveness)
   Degree of gesticulation
   Leg and foot movements
   Head nods
   Facial activity and pleasantness
   Speech volume, rate and intonation

After Mehrabrian, 1969

close distance. Relaxation cues communicate status and power: the greater a person's status, the more relaxed and at ease he/she will be, while low status persons communicate attention and tension in this dimension. Responsiveness to our partner is communicated through activity cues: the greater the level of facial and bodily activity, the more responsive we seem to our partner.

It is interesting to note that the three dimensions of nonverbal messages proposed by Mehrabrian correspond fairly well to several previous methods for the classification of communication. Osgood, Suci and Tannenbaum (1957) found that most words and other semantic units may be described in terms of three dimensions: evaluation, potency and activity. Schlossberg (1954) suggested that expressions of emotion may be classified in terms of three characteristics, pleasantness, tension, and attention. Of course, these schemes, as well as Mehrabrian's (1969) model, are unlikely to fit every type of message. Nevertheless, considering the immense variety of nonverbal message combinations possible, it should help us to focus on the most common kinds of messages that can be sent. You should keep this classification in mind as you read about the various nonverbal communication channels in the next chapter.

Conclusions
We have looked at some of the general features of nonverbal communication above: how it differs from language, how it supplements or defeats what is communicated verbally, and what the major functions of nonverbal messages are. We have seen that our face, eyes, gestures and body are most important when it comes to communicating interpersonal messages about who we are, how we feel, and how we react to people and objects around us. Language has serious limitations when it comes to communicating about these matters. We use nonverbal messages for a variety of purposes, such as managing our interactions, expressing emotions or attitudes, and conveying information about ourselves. It is perhaps for this reason that nonverbal cues can be powerful enough to override even verbal messages, when it comes to communicating attitudes, for example. However, we have, as yet, said little about how each of the various nonverbal communication channels is actually used in interaction. We shall turn to this in the next chapter.

9. Varieties of nonverbal messages

9.

VARIETIES OF NONVERBAL MESSAGES

As the previous chapter suggests, in most real-life interactions nonverbal messages are sent and received in several channels simultaneously. We communicate with our gaze, facial expression, posture, gestures, vocal quality, dress and distancing behaviour simultaneously, and these messages are usually coordinated with each other as well as with our verbal messages. For example, the meaning of a signal sent in one channel, say a gesture, is qualified by another channel, say eye contact, which may indicate who it is meant for. Typically, however, research on nonverbal communication has looked at individual message types (communication channels) separately, and we shall follow this practice here in summarising the most important findings. But you should always remember that these signals are hardly ever used in isolation: the total message is always the sum of several parts.

Using the eyes: gaze and mutual gaze
Eye contact is one of the most common and powerful nonverbal signals we possess. The image of the eyes is among the most potent visual symbols even in modern Western cultures, to which people react with automatic attention. Advertisers know how to exploit this reaction, as even a brief inspection of billboards and magazine ads will show. It is interesting to note that ancient beliefs and superstitions connected with the eyes are still alive in many cultures. Traditional fears about the 'evil eye', and techniques for avoiding it are to this day common in many parts of southern Europe. Infants react to eye-like patterns before they can recognise most other stimuli. The eyes were commonly thought to be a window on the soul, and most people still give special significance to the eyes in revealing inner information. Teachers ask school children to 'look into their eyes' if suspected of cheating, in the belief that the eyes could not lie. (Research by Ekman and Friesen described earlier would tend to suggest that they would do better looking for peripheral signs in arm and leg movements to detect deception!)

Even philosophers give special attention to the meaning of eye contact. In a well-known passage, Jean Paul Sartre, the existential philosopher, described the essence of intersubjectivity and the alienation of personal freedom, using the example of eye contact to illustrate his point. His argument ran something like this. When the other person looks at me, I am forced to become aware that my individual subjectivity is not unique, that this other person has his/her own way of seeing the world which is inaccessible to me. Through his gaze, I realise that I am just an object in his universe, my unique individuality and subjectivity are nonexistent for him. His eye contact signals the alienation of my freedom. Phenomenological writers, such as Schutz also recognise the importance of eye contact in their analyses of social interaction: mutual awareness of the other's subjectivity, most powerfully communicated through eye contact, is the focus of such analyses.

Social psychologists are less concerned with such subjective beliefs about the eyes. They have been more interested in studying exactly how eye contact is used in communication. Gaze usually signals focussed interest, and results in increased arousal in the recipient, but the exact meaning of eye contact largely depends on the context. Eye contact may signal intimacy, involvement and attraction, or it may signal dominance, aggression and superiority. Just think about the very different meanings of prolonged eye contact between a couple of young lovers, and two enemies trying to stare each other down before a fight. In both cases, their gaze elicits arousal in their partners, but the meaning of the arousal is vastly different. (You may remember the research on self-attribution of emotions, discussed in Chapter 6, which could explain how the same arousal reaction may be interpreted as very different emotions, depending on the other cues which are present).

The eyes have it! Eyes play a central role in the nonverbal communication of many interpersonal attitudes and emotions.

ACTIVITY 9.1
Which One Do You Like More?

Have a look at the two pictures shown below, and quickly decide which of the two photos you find more attractive. Once you have made a decision, read on in the text to see whether your choice is the same as most other people's, and why! After you read the next section, you could also use these pictures to test other people and see whether their reactions are similar to yours.

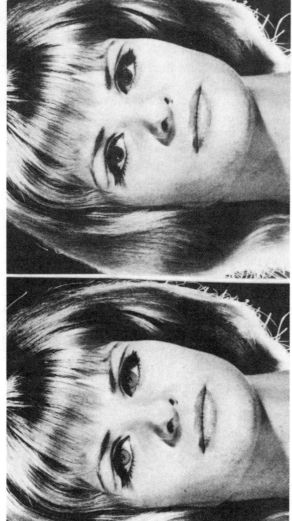

After Hess, 1975, p. 96-97

Pupils tell a story
Rather surprisingly, gaze not only produces arousal in the person we are looking at, but our eyes may also communicate our own state of arousal. In Activity 9.1 above, which of the two photos did you find more attractive? The two pictures were in fact identical, except for one small difference. The size of the pupils has been retouched to be somewhat larger in one of the pictures. If you are like most people, you would have chosen the picture with the larger pupils as somewhat more attractive. What is the reason for this? Researchers have shown that the size of our pupils changes not only in reaction to light intensity, but also depending on our state of arousal. One of the reasons why our arousal level changes from time to time is that we react with like or dislike to people and objects in our environment.

On the basis of considerable research on this issue, it appears that we learn to unconsciously notice the size of other people's pupils, and interpret the observable changes in pupil size as indications of positive or negative attitudes on the part of our partner(s). Hess (1965; 1975) coined the term *pupillometrics* to describe the experimental analysis of how pupil size is influenced by such psychological reactions. Studies showed that people react with enlarged pupils to pictures of objects or people they strongly like or dislike. Sexual arousal, among other things, may also be communicated through enlarged pupil size. Females react with enlarged pupil size when looking at pictures of interest to them, such as a baby or a nude male. Males in turn react with larger pupils when shown a picture of a nude female (see Table 9.1). Homosexual males show pupil enlargement to nude male rather than female images.

TABLE 9.1
CHANGES IN THE PUPIL SIZE OF MALES AND FEMALES IN REACTION
TO VARIOUS PICTURES

Nature of picture shown	% change in pupil size by	
	Males	Females
Baby	+ .2%	+17.0%
Mother and baby	+ 5.5%	+24.5%
Nude male	+ 7.0%	+20.0%
Nude female	+18.0%	+ 5.5%
Landscape	− 7.0%	+ 1.6%

After Hess, 1975, p. 15

How much should one look? Visual balance in interaction
Although we do not normally think consciously about the *amount* of eye contact we use, research has shown that in most everyday encounters the correct amount of looking is delicately regulated. The visual balance

(who looks, when, at whom, and how much) of most interactions is defined in terms of the sex, status, intimacy of relationship and the nature of the interaction. Even in one-sided interactions, such as a lecture, correct gaze patterns are essential if the interaction is to proceed smoothly. A lecturer is expected to distribute eye contact fairly evenly through the audience, scanning the listeners for non-verbal cues of interest, disapproval, boredom and the like. The audience, in turn, is expected to gaze at the speaker most of the time. When these very simple rules are violated, the interaction may break down.

An example may better illustrate the point. During an Open University summer school I taught in Britain, the students in a lecture audience were told to manipulate their eye gaze at their lecturer (one of my colleagues) so that in the first half of the lecture everybody on the left-hand side of the room would be looking at him, and nobody on the right-hand side, while in the second half of the lecture the roles would be reversed. My colleague was initially somewhat disturbed by the apparent complete lack of attention on the right-hand side of the room, but quickly adjusted to the situation by positioning himself on the left-hand side of the theatre, and gazing predominantly at the attentive part of the audience. When the switch-over occurred half way through, he reacted with considerable disturbance, lost the thread of his argument, and found it quite difficult to readjust to the situation. Of course, he was much relieved when the strange behaviour of the class was explained to him later. The point is that we always rely on such simple rules of visual communication to make interactions possible, and even minor deviations may lead to the breakdown of the encounter.

In more intense encounters, the amount of eye contact is very finely calibrated. The listener tends to look somewhat more than the speaker, and mutual eye contact is usually maintained only for a fixed proportion of the total interaction time (Exline, 1974). In a typical two-person conversation, people look at each other about 61 per cent of the time, and their gaze coincides (mutual gaze) about 31 per cent of the time (Argyle and Ingham, 1972). Mutual gaze lasts on the average only about one second, while each individual gaze is usually about three seconds long. The same person will look more when listening (75 per cent of the time), than when speaking (41 per cent of the time). There are some important cultural differences in these expected gaze patterns. Interestingly, black people have exactly the opposite pattern from whites: they tend to look more when speaking than while listening (LaFrance and Mayo, 1976).

Looking too much may be just as uncomfortable as looking too little or not looking at all (see Activity 9.2). Other variables, such as the person's need for affiliation, his/her sex and the competitiveness of the situation also influence eye gaze. Exline (1974) found that women on the

---

ACTIVITY 9.2
The Rules of Looking

You may carry out a small experiment along similar lines yourself. First, make sure that the subject you choose is a good friend of yours, and is unlikely to take offence at your strange behaviour towards him/her! Engage in a usual interaction with your chosen partner, and act as you would normally in every respect, except as regards your eye contact. After the interaction is established for about five or ten minutes, do one of two things: (a) either establish too much eye contact, by looking at your partner almost all the time, or (b) reduce the eye contact significantly, by almost never looking at your partner. Make sure that your other behaviours and verbal communication remain completely normal. It is likely that your partner will sooner or later react with signs of disturbance, and will eventually ask you about the cause of your unusual behaviour. His/her reactions illustrate just how important such subtle conventions as the rules of gaze are in making social interactions possible.

---

whole tend to look more than men, and that gaze is more common in cooperative than in competitive situations. In a competitive situation, prolonged eye contact sharpens tension, especially for women: "in a competitive situation, the intimacy inherent in the mutual glance could be interpreted as the intimacy of combat" (Exline, 1974, p. 75).

Gaze as an aggressive signal
Eye contact is thus not always a signal of attraction and intimacy, but may communicate aggression when accompanied by certain other cues. Uninterrupted stare is an ancient signal of challenge and dominance. Children sometimes play such 'staring down' games allowing them to experience the thrill and excitement which is still associated with prolonged eye contact. Exline and Yellin (1965) proposed that continued stare as an aggressive signal has evolutionary roots. Prolonged stare is a signal of dominance in many species of birds, and amongst dogs and primates. We may frequently observe members of these species engaging in lengthy eye contact as a preliminary to fighting, or to determine status hierarchies. Even a stare between members of two different species may be interpreted in a similar way. Exline and Yellin (1965) found that when human experimenters stared at rhesus macaque monkeys in a zoo, this behaviour was apparently also interpreted by the monkeys as aggressive,

leading to displays of arousal and threat. You may try this experiment yourself when you next find yourself at a zoo!

Inappropriate stare amongst human beings has similar effects, as Ellsworth, Carlsmith and Henson (1972) found. The typical reaction to a challenge signal amongst animals is either fight or flight. Ellsworth and her colleagues used an interesting unobtrusive experiment to demonstrate similar reactions among people. Some car drivers who were forced to stop at a red light at a traffic intersection were systematically stared at by the experimenter's confederates, while others were not. The dependent variable was the driver's speed of escape (flight response), defined as the amount of time it took for each driver to cover a pre-established distance across the intersection after the lights changed to green. Drivers exposed to the stare 'took off' significantly faster than drivers who received no stares, which Ellsworth et al. interpret as a modified form of the ancient 'flight' response found in many other species. This study has since been repeated using not only drivers, but pedestrians and cyclists as the unwitting subjects, with essentially identical results. Since inappropriate staring is clearly an aggressive signal, possibly leading to an aggressive response, I would not encourage you to repeat this experiment yourself without due precautions!

The intimacy-equilibrium theory
We have seen that the meaning of gaze as a signal of intimacy or aggression largely depends on the context and other nonverbal cues. Argyle and Dean (1965) proposed that for every interaction and relationship there exists a carefully regulated level of intimacy which the partners maintain by the continuous adjustment of their various nonverbal intimacy signals (gaze, smiles, distance, etc.). We communicate and maintain different levels of intimacy in different encounters, depending on whom we are talking to (friend, colleague,

Administering an aggressive stare. Inappropriate gaze at strangers often functions as an aggressive signal, leading to a 'fight or flight' response in the recipient. In one study, drivers stared at at an intersection 'took off' at much greater speed than other drivers who did not receive this manipulation.

spouse, etc.), about what (the weather, finances), and where (on the street, in a restaurant, in a lift, etc.).

This so-called *intimacy equilibrium theory* predicts that when intimacy signals are increased in one modality, for example by very close interpersonal distance, people will compensate for this by decreasing intimacy in another modality, for example eye contact. In Argyle and Dean's (1965) experiment, subjects engaged in a conversation with either same-sex or other-sex confederates of the experimenter, who adopted various interpersonal distances. Results showed (Figure 9.1) that as the confederates moved closer and conversational distance became smaller, subjects automatically decreased their eye contact to maintain the previous level of intimacy.

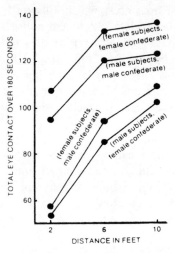

FIGURE 9.1 The intimacy equilibrium model. As interpersonal distance decreases, total eye contact is reduced. Note that level of eye contact also depends on the sexual composition of the dyad. (After Argyle and Dean, 1965, p. 300).

A similar phenomenon may be observed in everyday life as people enter into closed spaces, such as lifts. As people are forced to adopt unusually close interpersonal distances in such confined places, the usual reaction is to reduce or completely eliminate eye contact. Passengers in a lift tend not to look at each other directly, but perhaps glance fleetingly at each other just after entering or before leaving (Zuckerman et al. 1983). One consequence of this reduction in eye contact is that conversation becomes difficult or impossible: without being able to look at, and monitor our partner, it is difficult to continue talking. Hence the often observed phenomenon that people tend to stop conversing when entering a lift, and to take up the conversation immediately upon leaving it (see Activity 9.3).

ACTIVITY 9.3
The Intimacy Equilibrium Model

You may carry out a systematic observation of how the intimacy equilibrium theory operates in situations when people are forced to adopt close distances, such as in lifts, on public transport, etc. You should note the (a) presence or absence of conversation before people enter such a space, for example a lift, (b) the interpersonal space adopted in the lift (partly dependent on how crowded the lift is), (c) the amount of shared eye contact between the partners, (d) whether conversation is stopped or not, and (e) whether conversation is resumed after leaving the lift. You will probably find that eye contact is reduced or eliminated when close distances have to be adopted, and interruptions in the conversation should also be directly related to the elimination of eye contact.

(Non)-interaction in lifts. When people are forced to adopt unusually small interpersonal distances, for example in lifts, they usually compensate for this increase in intimacy by reducing eye contact, which in turn makes conversation difficult or impossible.

The hidden dimension: space

After eye gaze, the use of space and territory is perhaps the second most universal nonverbal signal we have at our disposal. Researchers have used two quite different approaches to study the role of distance and space in human interaction. The first possibility is to take a descriptive, social anthropological orientation. Hall (1966) took this approach in attempting to describe the various cultural rules and conventions which regulate the use of space, a field of study he named *proxemics*. Sommer (1959; 1969) in contrast used experimental, social psychological methods to investigate how various situational factors influence the use of space.

Hall suggested that we segment our social environment into quite distinct regions, which surround our bodies as if they were invisible 'bubbles' we carry with us. He identified four such surrounding personal spatial zones: the intimate zone (circ. 0-60 cm); the personal zone (circ. 60 cm-1.20 m); the social-consultative zone (circ. 1.20-3.30 m); and the public zone (circ. 3.30 + m). Each of these interactive zones is characterised by very different kinds of norms, expectations and behaviours (see Activity 9.4).

The transition from one distance zone to another is usually signalled by a distinct change in behaviours. A common example is that we feel no constraint in looking at an approaching stranger on the street as long as he is in the public zone, but once he crosses the boundary of our social zone (comes closer than about 3 m), eye contact is usually abandoned. Unless we avert our gaze at that point, some form of ritualistic recognition (such as a smile or a mumbled greeting) is necessary, to signal that minimal social contact occurred within this more intimate region.

The distance we adopt when interacting with people also depends on such things as whether we like them, as well as their status relative to

---

ACTIVITY 9.4
Crossing a Personal Boundary

Hall's suggestions about the existence of such personal boundaries can be easily put to the test. Using the above example, all you have to do is to violate the norm of gaze aversion inside the social boundary, and observe what happens. While walking on the street, randomly select every third or fourth person walking towards you as a subject. Choose about ten males and ten females in all. Stare directly at your subject until he/she is about three metres away, then avert your gaze. With the same number of subjects, repeat the procedure but continue looking until the person passes you. It is likely that your subjects in this second condition will in some way attempt to establish contact once they cross into your 'social' zone, and may even ask you "Do I know you from somewhere?". This is a clear confirmation that within the social zone eye contact is only sanctioned between acquaintances, and not between strangers.

ours. Friends interact at a closer distance than strangers, and high-status people are addressed at a greater distance than low-status people. A strength of the anthropological approach is that it explicitly looks at the sometimes interesting cultural differences in distancing behaviour. In Middle-eastern cultures, for example, interpersonal distances tend to be much closer. It is said that Arabs like to use several modalities in their personal interactions, including a sense of smell, hence they stand uncomfortably close to each other by our standards. These differences illustrate quite nicely how finely balanced our expectations of 'normal' interactive behaviour are. Breaking an apparently minor rule by standing a few centimetres too close to a partner may be sufficient to make interaction uncomfortable, and possibly render a person a social outcast in a culture in which greater interpersonal distance is expected.

There are intriguing differences in the use of space even within the same cultural group. Despite the relatively open and homogeneous interpersonal norms in the United States, research has shown that distancing behaviour is related to both race and social class. On the basis of collecting and studying photographs of children interacting on school playgrounds, Aiello and Jones (1971; Jones and Aiello, 1973) reported that black children tend to stand closer to people than white children, and that working-class children also tend to stand closer to each other than do middle-class children (see Activity 9.5).

ACTIVITY 9.5
The Consequences of Standing Too Close

Social psychologists have demonstrated the importance of spacing behaviour by intentionally breaking the implicit rules we follow. In one experiment, the investigator simply moved closer to his conversation partner than the rules allow. Using this procedure, he managed to move the person several times around the room where the conversation took place, as his partner kept 'backing away' to restore what he/she considered a comfortable conversational distance. You may repeat this experiment yourself to demonstrate the importance of distancing rules in social interaction. Simply find a large and relatively empty space (such as a theatre lobby or the beach), and a partner who will not take offence. Then systematically adopt a conversational distance just a few centimetres closer than usual, and observe the reactions! Chances are your partner will soon back away to restore a comfortable distance. If you then repeat your move, you will probably be able to move this person around at will, given enough time!

A more experimental analysis of spatial behaviour was undertaken by Sommer, who in his book *Personal Space: the Behavioural Basis of Design* looked at how man-made environments are used in interpersonal communication (see also Chapter 16). A good example of this approach is the way people prefer different seating positions around a table, depending on the kind of social interaction they are engaged in. We seem to have an inbuilt sense of preference for certain seating positions when in a restaurant, when working together, or competing with somebody. Figure 9.2 shows the results of this study. Larger physical environments, such as airport waiting rooms, churches, magistrates' courts and coffee houses impose similar restrictions on interaction possibilities by their very layout. A formal social process, such as a mass or a court hearing leaves its imprint on the physical design of the rooms where it is enacted.

SEATING ARRANGEMENT	CONDITIONS			
	CONVER-SATION	COOPERA-TION	CO-ACTION	COMPE-TITION
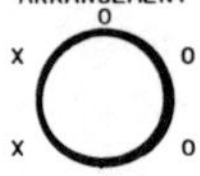	63	83	13	12
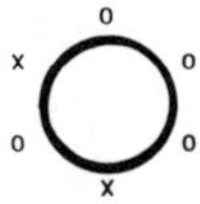	17	7	36	25
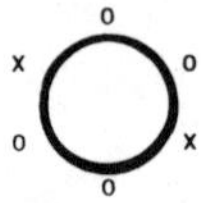	20	10	52	63
TOTAL:	100	100	100	100
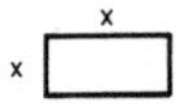	42	19	3	7
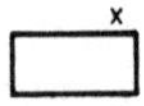	46	25	3	41
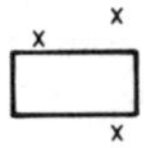	1	5	43	20
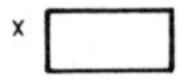	0	0	3	5
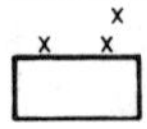	11	51	7	8
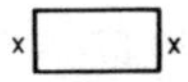	0	0	41	18
TOTAL:	100	100	100	100

FIGURE 9.2 Social interaction and seating preferences. Percentage of people choosing various seating arrangements around a rectangular and a round table, depending on the nature of the interaction. (After Sommer, 1965, p. 343-345).

A casual visitor to an empty church or an empty courtroom could quite well reconstruct from their physical layout the social events enacted in these settings. Less structured physical environments, such as street corners, shops, offices or theatres, also have a strong influence on the interactive behaviours which may be enacted within them. Indeed one could analyse the behaviour possibilities of a whole town in terms of the fluctuating availability of these various behaviour settings, as Barker (1968) and others have demonstrated. Nonverbal behaviours, in turn, partly derive their meanings from the behaviour settings in which they occur, as the study by Forgas and Brown (in Chapter 4) demonstrated.

Territoriality

Apart from the dynamic, readily changeable nonverbal dimensions of space and distance, we also have more enduring claims on physical areas. *Territoriality* is one of the most universal features of the social systems of animals. Human beings rarely display the same life-long attachment to territories as do animals, but a more subtle relationship to physical areas nevertheless exists. Goffman (1963) suggested that instead of permanent territorial possessions, humans usually claim temporary jurisdiction over certain areas. Another classification of territories was suggested by Altman (1975) who distinguished between 'primary' territories (such as our homes), 'secondary' territories (for example, a shared office), and 'public' territories.

There are many examples of how people express their claims to territory. Holidaymakers in camping grounds, where the dangers of trespassing are high, display many and varied forms of decorating and temporary fencing, defining and defending their tiny 'secondary' territories as distinct from the surrounding 'public' territory. Weekend gardeners spend inordinate amounts of time working on their allotments, and making their tiny gardens identifiably different from those of their neighbours. Office workers often become attached to their rooms and desks, and I must admit that I became quite upset upon hearing the news that I had been allocated another office in my absence, while doing work at an overseas university.

Our houses and flats are also primary territories which serve to project our chosen values and identity, and thus function as very important sources of nonverbal information about their occupiers. The way academics, bureaucrats or doctors arrange and organise their offices again serves a similar territorial function. By the very arrangement of our desks, we can signal an attitude towards those entering our office. By positioning furniture in appropriate ways we can subdivide the room into clearly recognised 'public' (in front of the desk), and 'private' (behind the desk) sub-areas. Several studies have shown that an occupier's personality can be fairly accurately guessed simply by looking at photos of that person's office, living room or college bedroom.

Apart from such enduring territories, there are many other public areas, such as library desks, street benches or restaurant tables which we occupy for only short periods of time. People reserve such transient territories using symbolic territorial markers, such as personal objects or a newspaper. The effectiveness of such territorial markers in keeping out 'invaders' is directly proportional to their personal character, and inversely proportional to the pressure for space. Researchers in university libraries deposited personal (half-eaten lunch) or impersonal (an open book) objects at unoccupied desks in busy or quiet periods.

Some examples of territorial markers. Public territories such as library desks may be most effectively reserved by using highly personal (for example, a half-eaten sandwich) rather than impersonal (for example, a book) objects.

ACTIVITY 9.6
The Role of Territorial Markers

You may demonstrate the relative effectiveness of various territorial markers by finding an area where people usually claim such territories (such as an airport lounge, a railway waiting room, a library or a park bench), and then leave either very personal (piece of clothing, bag, half-eaten lunch, etc.) or impersonal (newspaper, book, etc.) markers behind. You can also manipulate the pressure for territory, by making your experiment both in quiet and in peak-hour periods. Note how often your 'marked' territory is invaded, and how long it takes for such an invasion to take place under varying circumstances.

Invasion of territory (occupation of the reserved desk) was observed more frequently when the marker was impersonal, and the demand for space great. There is a moral in this — if you wish to make sure that no-one will take your place in a situation where competition for space is great, use *very* personal territorial markers (see Activity 9.6)!

Touching or physical contact

Touching is one of the most important nonverbal signals in early life: parents and infants communicate a great deal by touch. In most Western cultures, however, touching between adults is rigidly regulated by complicated cultural conventions. Who can be touched, where, how, when and by whom is quite clearly specified. Jourard (1966) asked 300 young American adults of both sexes to indicate which areas of their bodies are accessible for touching by various other categories of people (for example, mother, father, same-sex friend, other-sex friend). A summary of their responses showed that there was strong agreement about acceptable forms of touching. These results are summarised in Figure 9.3. Other cultures may have such 'touching maps' which are very different from ours. For example, in many Buddhist societies it is strongly prohibited to touch any part of another person's head, which is seen as the seat of the soul.

In our culture, light touching usually signals intimacy and interest, and leads to a slight arousal reaction in the person being touched. It is interesting to note that touching may result in more positive attitudes even when the person is not aware that he has been touched. In one of the unobtrusive studies in this field, students in a library were randomly touched by the librarian when she handed them books (Fisher, Rytting and Heslin, 1976). Students were later approached and asked a number of questions. Those females who were touched reported more positive attitudes towards the library, the assistant and themselves. Males however were not affected by touching. There is other evidence suggesting that males and females react differently to an identical touch. Females who were touched by a nurse in a hospital just before undergoing surgery responded with less anxiety and lower blood-pressure, while with males exactly the opposite reaction was observed (Whitcher and Fisher, 1979).

Most commonly, touching occurs in a ritualistic form. Heslin and Boss (1980) observed touching between travellers and people seeing them off at an airport. They found that almost 60 per cent of the people engaged in some sort of touching in this setting. Males initiated touching with females more often than the other way around, and older people initiated touching more often than younger people. Touching may also function to signal superiority and dominance. Submissive or inferior individuals are more physically accessible, 'touchable', than dominant individuals. Children, the handicapped, servants or subordinates are usually more open to such non-reciprocal touching. The 'politics of touching' (Henley, 1977) operates between members of the two sexes as well as between status groups and classes. Men usually initiate touching women in public, and certain physical contact gestures between the sexes serve to express 'ownership rights' as much as to indicate affection and involvement (for example, hand on the partner's hip, and so on). Just as was the case with the variation in personal address forms studied by

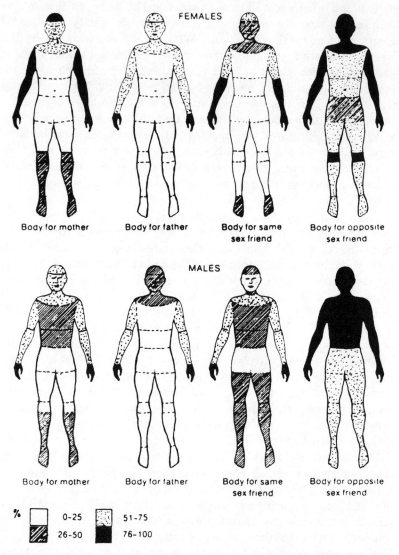

FIGURE 9.3 The rules of touching. Areas of the body which are touchable by mother, father, same-sex friend and opposite sex friend, for males and for females. (After Jourard, 1966, p.229).

Roger Brown (Chapter 7, Figure 7.1), it seems that touching may serve to communicate messages which may be categorised in terms of a status and an intimacy dimension.

The rules of touching. Who can be touched, where, when, how, by whom and in what situation is very rigidly regulated in most cultures.

The way we sound: paralinguistic cues

As we have seen earlier, in a conversation the verbal content of what is said represents only a small part of the total message. Much can be expressed with our voices apart from the words we pronounce. What we say is the verbal message, how we say it is part of the paralinguistic message. Broadly defined, all vocal cues which are not verbal may be regarded as paralinguistic cues. Some paralinguistic messages are very closely related to the words being spoken: timing, pitch, rhythm, loudness and tempo of speech are not verbal, but are intimately linked to the verbal content. Other vocal cues, such as accent, personal voice quality, tone or loudness may be more enduring personal characteristics of the speaker, not related to any particular verbal message. There is also a whole range of other vocalisations which are capable of communicating a message all by themselves: crying, yawning, laughing, whistling, or loudly exhaling are examples of such paralinguistic messages.

In order to study how we use the vocal cues accompanying language in social interaction, it is necessary to separate the verbal meaning of a sentence from the underlying vocal quality. This can be achieved by electronic filtering, which makes the words incomprehensible but retains the vocal quality, or by simply asking subjects to recite meaningless words in various tones. Davitz and Davitz (1959) used this technique, asking eight subjects to express ten different feelings in their voice (such as anxiety, anger, jealousy, etc.) while reciting the alphabet. Thirty judges listened to this material, trying to identify the feelings expressed. Results showed (Table 9.2) that some emotions, such as anger, nervousness, sadness or happiness were much easier to recognise from voice quality than others, such as love, jealousy and pride. Other studies (cf. Davitz, 1964) confirm that vocal cues are very effective in communicating certain kinds of emotional information. It is an interesting question whether these vocal cues are culturally as universal as was the case with facial expressions of emotion (see Darwin, and Ekman, in Chapter 8). We do not yet have a final answer to this question.

Exactly what is it about our voices which communicates a particular emotion? In order to answer this question, it is necessary to construct sound sequences with experimentally manipulated vocal characteristics. Scherer (1974) used a synthetiser to imitate the intonation contours of a short sentence, manipulating five characteristics of the tonal sequence (pitch variation, pitch level, amplitude variation, amplitude level and tempo). Ten subjects were asked to listen to these tonal sequences, rate them on a number of scales, and try to identify which emotion was communicated. Results suggested that pitch variation and tempo were particularly important sources of information. Generally, slow tempo and little pitch variation indicated negative, unpleasant emotions (sadness, anger, boredom, disgust, fear) and fast tempo and high pitch variation signalled positive emotions (pleasantness, activity, surprise). A more detailed summary of these findings is given in Table 9.3. Modern computers allow for more refined analyses. In Klaus Scherer's laboratory at the University of Giessen, spoken sentences are converted into digital data so that the vocal parameters of this record can be changed at will, and the manipulated sentences are then re-converted into synthetised speech (Scherer, 1985).

TABLE 9.2

THE RECOGNISABILITY OF DIFFERENT EMOTIONS FROM VOICE (THE NUMBERS INDICATE THE TOTAL NUMBER RECOGNISED OUT OF A POSSIBLE TOTAL OF 240, I.E. 30 RATERS EACH HEARING 8 SPEAKERS)

Feelings expressed	Number of correct identifications
anger	156
fear	60
happiness	104
jealousy	59
love	60
nervousness	130
pride	50
sadness	118
satisfaction	74
sympathy	93

After Davitz and Davitz, 1959

The global impression we gain from somebody's voice may also depend on the particular combination of several of these characteristics in everyday speech. Ostwald (1963) used a speech spectograph to analyse the voice patterns of mental patients as well as normal subjects. He found four distinct kinds of voice types using this method: (a) the sharp voice, querulous, childish and excited, found in some neurotic patients; (b) the flat voice, typical of some depressed and dependent patients; (c) the hollow voice, found in some debilitated or brain damaged patients, and (d) the extroverted, confident booming voice often found in well adjusted, healthy people.

TABLE 9.3
THE EFFECTS OF VARIOUS ACOUSTIC VARIABLES ON THE
PERCEPTION OF EMOTIONS

Acoustic variable	Quality	Perceived as
amplitude	moderate	pleasantness, activity, happiness
variation	extreme	fear
pitch variation	moderate	anger, boredom, disgust, fear
	extreme	pleasantness, activity, happiness, surprise
pitch contour	down	pleasantness, boredom, sadness
	up	potency, anger, fear, surprise
pitch level	low	pleasantness, boredom, sadness
	high	activity, potency, anger, fear, surprise
tempo	slow	boredom, disgust, sadness
	fast	pleasantness, activity, potency, anger, fear, happiness, surprise
duration (shape)	round	potency, boredom, disgust, fear, sadness
	sharp	pleasantness, activity, happiness, surprise
filtration (lack of overtones)	low	sadness, pleasantness, boredom, happiness
	moderate	potency, activity
	extreme	anger, disgust, fear, surprise
	atonal	disgust
tonality	tonal-minor	anger
	tonal-major	pleasantness, happiness
rhythm	not rhythmic	boredom
	rhythmic	activity, fear, surprise

After Scherer, 1974, p. 109

Voice is a particularly effective signal for communicating arousal and anxiety. We have all had experiences of listening to people whose voices immediately reveal their excitement. In extreme cases, severe communication anxiety may lead to various speech disturbances, including stuttering (Bergmann and Forgas, 1985). Vocal cues can also be used for detecting deception, and some studies report that tone of voice is indeed a better source of detecting deception than the face (Zuckerman et al. 1982). Some psychologists believe that spectographic analysis of voice patterns could be used as a reliable lie detector method, a claim not yet unequivocally supported by scientific evidence.

Such elusive cues as voice quality may be very important for people who rely on verbal communication a great deal, such as medical practitioners. Milmoe and his colleagues (1967) used an ingenious technique to look at this possibility. The doctors they studied worked at an alcoholic referral clinic, and one of their tasks was to convince clients to volunteer for treatment. Milmoe found that the voice quality of the doctors was a significant predictor of their success in referring patients for treatment. Of course, this evidence may not indicate a causal link between voice quality and referral success. It could be, for example, that doctors with a pleasant and sympathetic personality have both a more pleasant voice, and more success in referring patients.

Not all paralinguistic cues are limited to the communication of attitudes and emotions. Many other aspects of how we speak say a great deal about us. A person's accent, for example, may communicate ethnic background, social status or level of education (Giles, 1970). Perceptions of accents also depend on the sex of the speaker, and the particular situational context. Accented English may be more acceptable in Australia in informal, friendly, than formal, official situations (Gallois and Callan, 1985). Many other aspects of vocal communication also depend on the particular situation. I once shared a room in England with a colleague who for purposes of everyday conversation used a broad London cockney accent, signalling his working-class background and left-wing political orientation. When he had to talk to journalists, reporters or book publishers, his pronunciation changed dramatically: he used a high class 'Oxford' accent, as if to signify his status as a professional and an academic. Many studies show that the same verbal message may have very different acceptance and persuasive power, depending on whether it is spoken in a working-class or an upper-class accent. Many professional groups develop particular speaking styles in accordance with their roles. Doctors, lawyers, actors and clergymen tend to have such role-defined voice patterns.

Communicating with our bodies: body language
When we interact with other people, we communicate with our whole body. As Ekman showed, the information conveyed by subtle

movements of our arms or legs may be sufficient to inform an observer when we are not telling the truth. Of all nonverbal channels of communication, perhaps 'body language' has received the greatest popular attention. Many rather superficial books have appeared on the subject, promising their readers unsuspected insights into the motives and intentions of others and themselves. The use of body language is, of course, a great deal more complicated than such volumes suggest. Although most normal adults have little difficulty in sending and receiving such messages, many interaction problems have to do with breakdowns in bodily communication. This is also a major area for social skills training and therapy (Chapter 16).

Scientists have used several approaches to study bodily communication. One possibility is to think of such communication as similar to language, constituted of smaller basic units of movement, which are combined into larger 'statements' using the rules of something like a grammar of movement. Ray Birdwhistell, an anthropologist, is one of the pioneers of this quasi-linguistic approach to studying bodily communication. In his research, he sought to identify and categorise basic units of body movement, or 'kinemes', which are combined into more complex bodily displays conveying a message, or 'kinemorphs'. This anthropological strategy is based on the minute analysis of short recorded sequences of interaction. The transcription and detailed analysis of *everything* that happens in a short five-minute interview, or an 18-second sequence in which a cigarette is offered and lit can take years of work for a whole team of researchers (Birdwhistell, 1952; 1970).

Such detailed analyses revealed some interesting facts about body language. For example, the flow of bodily movements and gestures was found to be finely coordinated between the partners in an interaction. This 'interactional synchrony' was originally described by Condon and Ogston (1967), and later elaborated on by Kendon (1970) and others. The existence of such synchrony is more surprising than it first appears. The listener does not simply *react* to cues emitted by the speaker in a conversation, but actively anticipates them, so that their coordinated movement patterns are performed simultaneously.

A similar coordination of bodily signals was described by Scheflen, who observed the interaction patterns between people participating in psychiatric interviews. He noticed that the ebb and flow of gestures and postural changes was intimately related to the personal intentions and strategies of the participants. During an interaction, apparently irrelevant behaviours, such as 'preening' (adjusting ties, hair, clothes, etc.), leg-crossing and so on were performed at critical junctions to express interest and involvement with particular others. Scheflen called such behaviours 'quasi-courting' sequences. Such quasi-courting is often used to reject or incorporate particular others in an interaction, and to regulate and maintain a sufficient degree of involvement in the interaction. Scheflen (1974, p. 193) suggests that quasi-courting may be defined 'as a set of system-maintaining devices that is used when the insufficiency in sociability or attentiveness is due to some inhibition', a common enough occurrence not only in a psychiatric interview, but also in many everyday encounters.

Patterns of body movement are also closely related to a person's mental health. Fisch, Frey and Hirsbrunner (1983) carefully analysed the movement patterns of 13 people first when they were suffering from severe depression, and after they had fully recovered from the illness. They found that after recovery, "patients spent more time in motion, displayed a more complex pattern of movement, and initiated and terminated movement activity more rapidly than when they were depressed" (p. 316). It seems then that body movements have a complex, subtle and as yet not fully understood role to play in our social encounters.

Gender and body language

The use of bodily communication is also closely related to gender. Males and females have very different movement repertoires. A confusion of gender identity is often accompanied by a confusion of the movement repertoire as well. Some homosexuals communicate their divergent gender identity through the adoption of the movement patterns of the opposite sex. When a male displays feminine movements such as rolling the hip, a mincing walk and delicate hand gestures this is usually taken as a sign of homosexuality.

ACTIVITY 9.7

Male and Female Body Language

To better appreciate how significantly males and females differ in their use of body movement, you may carry out the following simple project.

1. Observe carefully the way ten members of your own sex, and ten members of the opposite sex (a) walk, (b) position their legs while sitting, (c) use their hands while talking, (d) position their torso when sitting, and (e) hold their heads relative to their body.

2. Try to enact the observed movement patterns of the opposite sex in front of a mirror. How does it feel?

3. Try to enact the movement patterns of the opposite sex when having a conversation with a good friend. How does it feel? Does your friend show any reaction?

Some popular writers, such as Desmond Morris, speculated that the differences between the sexes in body movement may have arisen to compensate for the relative lack of secondary gender characteristics in the human species. In other words, because the human male and female look very similar to each other (at least when compared with sexual differences in many other species), we use different movement patterns to signal our gender identity. Interesting as this idea may be, there is not enough empirical evidence to substantiate it to date (see Activity 9.7).

Gestures

Gestures constitute a very special category of bodily movements. Perhaps the most remarkable thing about gestures is that they are strongly culture dependent. A Frenchman, an Italian or an Englishman know and use significantly differing gesture repertoires (see also Activity 8.2). Even a simple observation of a conversation between, for example, two Italians, will demonstrate the existence of such differences. Some of our gestures have independent, clearly defined meanings (for example, the V-sign for victory, raised shoulders for puzzlement and incomprehension, etc.). Such gestures are sometimes called emblems. Many other gestures have no meaning of their own, but simply accompany some other verbal and nonverbal communication (for example, the way lecturers use their hands to emphasise or illustrate their verbal message). Such gestures which merely support some other message were called illustrators by Ekman and Friesen (1975).

To date, most research has concentrated on emblems, or the kind of gestures which have fixed meanings. Desmond Morris and his co-workers (Morris, Marsh, Collett and O'Shaugnessy, 1981) thought that the way such gestures are used follows cultural, linguistic and ethnic boundaries. That is, the kind of gestures which are used and understood in southern Italy, for example, would not be known to Germans. The assumption was that the distribution of gestures follows certain geographical and ethnic boundaries. They selected a small sample of 'critical' gestures, and asked people in a variety of places in Europe to interpret them. The study was apparently successful: distinct geographical boundaries were found for the use of various gesture repertoires.

Conclusions

In these last two chapters we have looked at some of the general characteristics of nonverbal communication, and tried to survey the most important nonverbal signals we use in everyday life. Although language and verbal communication are perhaps naturally the focus of our attention when we speak about social interactions, nonverbal signals can be just as important, and sometimes more important than language in communicating with others. Nonverbal signals are particularly powerful in communicating attitudes, emotions and liking, messages which are often difficult or cumbersome to express verbally. To the extent that social interaction mainly involves the continuous ebb and flow of positive and negative affective reactions (Zajonc, 1980), nonverbal messages are perhaps the most important carriers of this information.

The various nonverbal communication channels discussed in this chapter are typically used in a coordinated fashion. Gaze, spacing, gestures and facial expression support and reinforce each other in actual encounters. An important question in studying nonverbal messages is: why do individuals differ in their ability to send and receive them? In Chapter 16 we shall look at the general question of social skills. Before that, we shall consider another important aspect of interpersonal communication: how do people use communication to create particular impressions?

10. Presenting the right image: impression management

10.

PRESENTING THE RIGHT IMAGE: IMPRESSION MANAGEMENT

So far we have discussed interpersonal communication as if it simply consisted of sending and receiving messages. In reality, the process is much more complex. To know what the different verbal and nonverbal signals mean, and to know how, when, where and with whom to use them is, of course, extremely important. But interpersonal communication does not begin when a message is sent. We do a great deal of strategic thinking, planning and evaluation before choosing a particular message to be transmitted. Much of our communication is designed to achieve something, often simply to create a positive, desirable impression about ourselves.

Impression management is a term used to describe the totality of our plans, ideas, motivations and skills which influence our communications with others. This planned, strategic aspect of communication is of course very important. To use a market-place metaphor, we advertise, window-dress and promote ourselves so as to receive the greatest exchange value from our interactions with others. If our impression management strategies are successful, and others come to think positively of us, this in turn improves our self-concept and self-esteem. You may remember our analysis in Chapter 1 of the interactive environment modern, large-scale societies provide for their members. In a social milieu where we have to interact with many people quite superficially, the ability to quickly and easily create a positive impression is very important. In smaller, more intensive face-to-face communities, such as a mediaeval village, a small work community or a primitive tribe, impression management is less important, since the real qualities of people are more likely to be revealed during prolonged interaction.

Creating the right impression is particularly important for people whose encounters with others are mostly brief and superficial, such as politicians or salesmen. Alexander Haig, one time U.S. Secretary of State in the Reagan Administration, comments in his memoirs on the importance of television and image management in political life as

179

follows: "To a significant degree, the television camera has driven the natural, the heart-felt out of our national life. The rule used to be 'What am I saying?'. Now it is 'How do I appear?' " (in *Time*, 2 April 1984, p.32). Of course, politicians are not the only ones who need to create the right impression to be successful. To a lesser extent, everybody faces the same task in large-scale societies where our interactions with others are frequently brief and superficial. It is no coincidence then that it is precisely in our age that books such as Dale Carnegie's *How to win Friends and Influence People* can become major bestsellers.

The term impression management itself has negative connotations for some people. It sounds as if one is trying to replace honest, straightforward interaction with manipulative, dishonest practices. This is not necessarily the way social psychologists understand impression managament. We start from the premise that all social interaction is by definition influenced by the actors' plans and motivations. It is the very essence of human social life that we have certain ideas about ourselves, our interaction partners and the world we live in, which we try to bring to expression in our interactions with others. Impression managament is thus not synonymous with dishonest interaction. Rather, it refers to the basic human tendency to imagine, plan and regulate our social behaviours so that the impression we present will express our view of ourselves and others.

The dramaturgical model

Erving Goffman was one of the more influential social scientists to recognise the strategic, goal-oriented nature of interpersonal communication. Goffman used a sociological method, consisting of the description and critical analysis of everyday encounters. He developed a theory of social interaction processes, the so-called 'dramaturgical' model. The basic idea underlying Goffman's theory is that role playing in general, and the metaphor of the theatre in particular, provide a best approximation to what people try to achieve in their everyday interactions. We are engaged, as are professional actors, in the business of trying to enact particular roles, attempting to create a public perception of ourselves which is in accordance with our wishes. We prepare for our performances backstage the same way as actors do (in our bathroom and in front of our wardrobe mirror), select our costumes for the day with no less care, and try to convince our audience (friends, strangers or lovers) with our performances so that they accept our offered self-presentations as real.

The terminology provided by the theatre is also appropriate for analysing everyday interactions. As is the case in the theatre, our presentations may be successful or unsuccessful. We use selected scripts, as well as backgrounds or stages for our performances. Choosing an office decor, furniture, or a lounge suite for our living room are activities similar to stagecraft: we seek to create a stage for our social life which projects and defines a particular view of ourselves. We also use a mask or 'face' to project ourselves in public. Goffman defined 'face' as the positive social value a person effectively claims for himself. Face is a projected image of the self, defined in terms of approved social attributes (Goffman, 1959). Dress, manner, accent and vocabulary can all be part of a 'face' we present to the world.

To fail in our performances, to lose face is not only a source of embarrassment, but also threatens our sense of predictability and order in our social relations. When people act 'out of role', we no longer know what to expect, how to predict or cope with the situation. The resulting tension often leads to a cooperative effort to 'cover up', to help to re-establish the usual and predictable system of roles. After incidents involving embarrassment and 'loss of face', the nervous laughter, feeble joke or painful silence warn us that social order has broken down. There is usually a cooperative effort to restore that order, using tactics such as pretending that nothing has happened.

Strategic role playing as described by Goffman is an all-pervasive feature of social life: "The process of mutually sustaining a definition of the situation in face-to-face interaction is socially organised through rules of relevance or irrelevance...it is to these flimsy rules, not the unshaking character of the external world, that we owe our unshaking sense of realities...To be awkward or unkempt, to talk or move wrongly, is to be a dangerous giant, a destroyer of worlds" (Goffman, 1963, p. 81).

The good impression manager
Although we are all engaged in playing roles as a means of impression management, we are not all equally good at it. What does it take to be a good actor, to be a successful impression manager? We all know people who never lose their self-confidence, are always cheerful and sociable — but are they good impression managers? Not necessarily. Sometimes, losing face, not knowing what to do or losing your temper may be the most appropriate impression management strategies. Just like a skilled actor on the stage, a good impression manager must have a clear idea about what the audience expects, have a critical understanding of how judgments are made, and must be sensitive to the requirements of various social situations he finds himself in.

Curiously, concern with how to manipulate others in order to accumulate power and social standing is by no means a new phenomenon. The Renaissance scholar Machiavelli (1469-1527) in his classic sixteenth century work, *The Prince*, provides detailed advice on how to go about developing the strategic skills required. Christie and Geis (1970) reached back to Machiavelli's notions to construct a scale which would discriminate between good and bad impression managers.

Their questionnaire contains items such as 'The best way to handle people is to tell them what they want to hear', 'Anyone who completely trusts another is asking for trouble' and 'People who talk about abstract problems usually don't know what they are talking about' (!). Extensive empirical research with this scale showed that middle class urban males in management or person-oriented jobs, such as administration or counselling score higher on this scale than others. But there is no relationship between Machiavellism and intelligence, education or political preference.

The Machiavellism scale was also validated in a number of realistic situations, for example where high and low scorers were asked to engage in competitive bargaining. In one study, high, medium and low Machiavellians had to divide up $10.00 among themselves. High scorers got an average of $5.57, medium scorers $3.14 and low scorers only $1.29! In another study, males scoring high on Macchiavellism were more successful in convincing a female to go to a party with them by communicating deference, attachment and need for help to their prospective partners. A crucial aspect of Machiavellism is cool intellectual detachment from the situation confronting a person, and lack of emotional involvement.

Machiavellians are also more willing to employ devious tactics such as lying or cheating, if this leads to success and the chances of detection are low. In one study, high and low scorers were given the task of distracting a person allegedly taking a test, without appearing to do so. High Machiavellians produced a startling series of events, such as whistling, pencil tapping, dissecting a ball point pen and 'accidentally' knocking over a table, followed by loud and profound apologies. Such manipulative skills are manifest quite early. A version of the

'Santa, you are so clever!' Machiavellianism shows early! One of the characteristics of Machiavellians is that they change their interaction strategies depending on their partners and the situation, and their communications are strategically controlled.

Machiavellism questionnaire can assess this trait in children. In a startling study by Braginsky (1970), ten-year-old children were asked to persuade other children to eat bitter-tasting cookies (soaked in quinine), allegedly as part of a market research exercise. The children were offered 5 cents for each cookie they got another child to eat. High Machiavellian children managed to get others to eat an average of 6.46 cookies, against only 2.79 cookies by low Machiavellians. In addition, observers of these interactions rated the Machiavellian children as more honest, effective, innocent and comfortable than the low Machiavellians.

Which image to present?
It is implied by the term impression management that we have some freedom to choose which particular self-image we want to convey in a given situation. To a dominant, boastful person we may wish to appear more assertive and confident, and we may try to present a quieter, modest image if our interaction partner is also a humble, unassuming person (Gergen and Wishnow, 1965). Most commonly, we choose a performance which will match the image our partner presents. We also try to fit in with the situation and what our partners expect us to be like. Even when discussing deeply involving political attitudes, people were found to adjust their opinions about such salient issues as the Vietnam War to fit in with the expected attitudes of the audience (Newtson and Czerlinsky, 1974). As we shall see later, there are good reasons to follow such a strategy: people tend to like those who are similar to them. It certainly seems to make sense to appear similar, particularly in the early stages of a relationship.

Whether we will attempt such opinion matching to create a good impression largely depends on how much we value our partner, and the potential possibilities of the relationship. In one study, Princeton women undergraduates were found to match the opinions of a prospective dating partner on issues such as women's roles, but only if the date was described as a desirable, tall, older unattached Princeton student (a 'valued' partner). When the person was described as a younger, small, non-Princeton student with a girlfriend, no opinion matching was found (Zanna and Pack, 1975). In this study, the potential partner was either valued or simply neutral. What happens if we positively dislike somebody, who happens to express ideas and opinions similar to ours? Studies have shown that in such situations, people tend to select a self-presentation strategy which will distance them from the disliked partner. If necessary, we are ready to change our existing attitudes and opinions just to distance ourselves from that person (Cooper and Jones, 1969).

Such image management strategies are quite common in everyday life. To a considerable extent, we select our images to match those we like and esteem, and contrast with those we dislike. This must be a constant danger to advertisers who use well-known public figures, such as politicians or actors, to recommend their products. Potential consumers who dislike the public promoters may easily come to dislike the espoused products as well, simply to distance themselves from the person promoting them. The danger to the public personalities selling their good name to promote products may be even greater: consumers may come to dislike them simply to distance themselves from the advertisers and the product!

Image and self-image
We have suggested above that people have considerable freedom to change the images they present to others. Yet it is also a common belief that we only have one true self-image. It should therefore follow that the various images we present to others are somehow false, often contrary to our 'true' selves. What exactly is the relationship between the images we present to others, and our 'real' self-image?

It would be a mistake to believe that our self-image is somehow separate from our various presented images, a solid unchanging entity amidst all the fluctuation of our interactions with others. The two concepts are much more intricately interrelated, as symbolic interactionists such as George Herbert Mead and Charles Horton Cooley so clearly realised. Our view of ourselves is not independent of what others think of us, but the product of it. It is in the course of everyday social interaction that we 'try on' various public self-images, and the most successful of these will eventually become part of our enduring view of ourselves. As Mead (1934) argued, "the self...is essentially a social structure, and it arises in social experience" (p. 140). To put it in another way, the self is not some sort of a mysterious individual category. It is our representation of how other people see us, the internalised equivalent of their reactions. Impression management is thus not only a process to influence how others think about us, but ultimately, it will also determine how we think about ourselves! In a real sense then, we become what other people think we are!

The interdependence between our successful 'public' images and our 'private' self-image was nicely illustrated in a study by Jones, Gergen and Davis (1962). These authors asked their subjects to present the most flattering image possible of themselves to an interviewer who was in fact a confederate of the experimenter. The interviewers were instructed to accept and reinforce the positive self-presentations of half the subjects, but reject and invalidate the self-presentations of the other half. Afterwards, all subjects were asked to what extent they thought that their self-presentations in fact matched their 'true' self-image. Subjects whose self-presentations were accepted by the interviewer came to believe their performance much more, claiming that they were really just being themselves. Those who failed tended to distance themselves from the image they unsuccessfully presented.

More recently, Fazio et al. (1981) found that people's self-perceptions can even be influenced by the kind of questions they are asked in an interview. In this study, people were selectively asked for information which would describe them either as an extrovert, or an introvert. Following the interviews, people tended to see themselves in a light consistent with the direction of the interview questions!

There is even some interesting evidence suggesting that primates may also possess a rudimentary self-concept, which can only develop if the animals are exposed to intensive social interaction. In animals as in humans, self-concept is based on the ability to recognise themselves as distinct individuals. In one study, researchers placed mirrors in the cages of chimpanzees, and noted that after a few days the apes ceased to react to their mirror image as if it was another ape, and used the mirror instead to clean, groom and observe themselves. However, only apes who were reared in regular social interaction with others were able to do this: apes reared in isolation had no notion of themselves as independent individuals, and never learnt that the mirror image was a reflection of themselves. Not having known others of their species, they had no 'concept' of themselves as distinct individuals.

It seems thus that it is necessary to engage in social interaction in order to develop a notion of ourselves as unique individuals. In humans, the quality of that self-image is largely determined by how others see us, that is, the way we appear to be distinct and different from others. Several studies have tried to explicitly test the interdependence of self-concept and judgments by others. Most commonly, subjects are asked to rate themselves on scales such as intelligence, self-confidence, physical attractiveness and likeableness, and also to estimate how others would rate them on these traits. Typically, ratings by friends and acquaintances are also obtained. It is generally found that individuals who rate themselves high on a particular trait also believe that others would rate them high, and in fact they do receive such high ratings. Studies of this kind thus suggest a strong interdependence between self-concept and how others see us.

Sometimes our self-concept can undergo fairly rapid reassessment, as a result of changes in the situation. Morse and Gergen (1970) suggested that our self-evaluations are strongly influenced by the behaviour of others in a similar situation, who will be our 'reference group' for assessing ourselves. Their experiment provides a good illustration of these processes. Individual subjects completed a self-assessment questionnaire, allegedly as part of an interview for a part-time job. After completing this first questionnaire, a second applicant was shown into the room. This person was in fact a collaborator of the experimenter, and had either very desirable qualities (wearing a neat business suit, carrying an attaché case containing books on science and philosophy, prepared for the test with sharpened pencils, and so on) or very undesirable qualities (dirty, worn clothes, no socks, disoriented, unprepared for the test).

After the arrival of the second 'candidate', subjects completed another questionnaire which also measured their self-esteem. When the partner was 'undesirable', the subjects' own self-esteem significantly increased relative to the first questionnaire. However, exactly the opposite happened when the partner had highly desirable qualities. The study suggests that our self-concept may change quite drastically even within a single hour, depending on the information we obtain about others in a similar situation.

Self-concept is then not the kind of deep-seated, strong, and enduring image of ourselves it is sometimes thought to be. It is a profoundly social creation, the product of how other people see us, which in turn is strongly influenced by our impression management skills. We are quite capable of feeling intelligent or dull, good-looking or plain, self-confident or shy within the course of a single day, depending on where we find ourselves, and on how other people react to us.

Self-awareness and self-monitoring

The image we wish to present of ourselves in social interaction is thus a joint product of the requirements of the social situation, and our self-concept, which was itself generated in past interactions with others. Not all people are equally sensitive to these requirements, and the same person may be more aware of his/her self-presentation in some situations than in others.

Duval and Wicklund (see Chapter 6) suggested that a state of objective self-awareness exists when a person's attention is focussed inward on himself, that is, when we become the *object* of our own attention. Objective self-awareness may be induced in a person by directing attention to the self, using objects such as mirrors, cameras or tape-recorders for this purpose. We are all familiar with situations when momentarily we become the focus of our own attention, looking in a mirror, posing for a photograph or talking into a tape recorder. At such times, we are particularly aware of how we look or sound, and of what others might think of our performances. Research shows that in such situations of heightened objective self-awareness, people become more concerned with how their actions might look to others, tend to follow social rules and norms more closely, and their interactions become more controlled and 'strategic'.

There are also enduring individual differences in how much we are aware of ourselves, the way others see us, and the requirements of various social situations. Some people are able to carefully monitor their social performances, while others are quite ineffective in monitoring themselves. Snyder (1974) defined the self-monitoring individual as "one who, out of a concern for social appropriateness, is particularly sensitive to the expression and self-presentation of others in social situations and uses these cues as guidelines for monitoring his own self-presentations'' (p. 528). Snyder developed a scale consisting of 25 items which measures self-monitoring ability in individuals. You may try your hand on some items similar to those used by Snyder in Activity 10.1.

People who score highly on this scale are better able to change their behaviours to fit in with a situation, are better in communicating emotions even when they do not feel particularly emotional, and are better at monitoring and assessing how other people react to their performances. A study by Snyder and Monson (1975) provides a nice illustration of self-monitoring. Subjects who participated in a discussion group were told that they would be videotaped, and that the tape would be played back to (a) the same group, or (b) to other students only. High self-monitoring subjects varied their behaviour depending on who the prospective audience was. When it was their own discussion group, they appeared likeable and agreeable, characteristics likely to be valued by a group. When the expected audience was other students, they appeared independent, autonomous and non-conformist, characteristics which they thought other students would value. Low self-monitoring individuals behaved similarly in both situations, showing moderate levels of independence and conformity irrespective of the expected audience. Self-monitoring ability thus enables an individual to manage impressions by changing his/her behaviour to fit in with the perceived requirements of different audiences.

The need for consistency in impression management
From the discussion above, it would appear that the good impression manager would have to be a chameleon-like character, somebody who can manipulate his self-presentation strategies almost at will, to fit in with every situation. While such strategies may be quite successful with people we meet once, or with whom we interact only superficially, in any enduring relationship the consistency of our self-presentation is extremely important. We cannot appear generous one day, and stingy the next, friendly today and unfriendly tomorrow. Once we have established a 'public persona' accepted by others, there is a strong tendency to remain consistent and live up to that image.

Several studies suggest that the need to appear consistent is a very important factor in impression management. Many direct sales techniques capitalise on people's perceived need for consistency. Freedman and Fraser (1966) suggested that once a person is persuaded to comply with a small, reasonable request, the need to appear consistent will induce him to comply with a large and unreasonable request later. They labelled this the 'foot-in-the-door' effect, for obvious reasons. Their study supported these expectations. As a small request, students asked Californian housewives to sign a petition, or put a small sign in

ACTIVITY 10.1
How Much Do You Monitor Yourself?

The statements below describe possible personal reactions to a variety of situations. Please read each statement carefully, and decide how much it applies to you. Be as honest as possible — there are no right or wrong answers!

	Tick under one of these two columns	
	True or mostly true for me	Untrue or mostly untrue for me
1. I can appear friendly to people I do not really like.	—	—
2. I usually let other people be the centre of attention at parties.	—	—
3. I often behave differently depending on the kind of people I am with.	—	—
4. I am not very good at imitating the behaviour of other people.	—	—
5. If I am uncertain about how to behave, I take my cues from others.	—	—
6. I find it hard to make other people like me.	—	—
7. I would probably make a good actor.	—	—
8. I do not change my opinions in order to please another person.	—	—
9. Even if I am not enjoying myself in the company of people, I usually pretend that I am happy.	—	—
10. I am not very good at changing my behaviour to suit different situations.	—	—

Continued on facing page

You can score your answers by adding up all the 'untrue' answers you gave to even numbered questions, and 'true' answers you gave to uneven numbered questions. The closer your score to 10, the more likely that you are a high self-monitoring person. In Snyder's study, people who are particularly good at monitoring their behaviours and adapting them to the requirements of the situation, such as professional actors, scored particularly high on a similar instrument. Remember — this is not a properly constructed psychological scale, but simply an illustration of the kinds of items which are relevant to self-monitoring, so you should not place too much emphasis on your scores!

their windows about issues such as safe driving or keeping the country beautiful. A few weeks later, the same housewives were again approached, together with a second control group of housewives not previously contacted. This time, they were asked to comply with a 'large' request, asking them to place a large billboard supporting the same issues in their front yard. Significantly more of the housewives who had previously agreed to the small request complied.

The importance of consistency in impression management. Inconsistency of our self-presentations inevitably leads to loss of face, loss of credibility and even looking ridiculous. The need to project a consistent image is so important to many people that they can be readily manipulated to do things they would otherwise avoid doing, simply to appear consistent.

The technique is, of course, well known to door-to-door salesmen who often work on the premise that once they have induced you to be helpful to them in some small way (for example, by giving them a glass of water), it is more likely that you will also help them in a major way (for example, by buying an encyclopaedia from them). A related sales technique also capitalises on a person's need to project a consistent impression. The method is often used by car salesmen, and was called the 'low-ball' technique by Cialdini, Cacioppo, Bassett and Miller (1978). According to this method, potential customers are persuaded to make a purchasing decision at a special, low price offered to them. At the last moment, they are informed that 'the boss didn't approve such a low price as we would be losing money on it', and a new, often substantially higher price is offered. In order to remain consistent with their initial decision to buy, people frequently complete the purchase at the new, higher price.

The need to project a 'good' image may be exploited by salespersons in other ways as well. After a large and unreasonable request (say, for money, donations) has been refused, there is often a tendency for people to give in to subsequent small and more reasonable requests in order not to appear 'mean' (Cialdini et al. 1975). This is the other side of the 'foot-in-the-door effect', also called the 'door-in-the-face' effect: the target complies in order to make up for a prior refusal forced on him by a manipulative salesman. In all these examples, a person's behaviour is guided by the perceived need to project a positive image consistent with a previously presented impression, even if this entails substantial costs. Everyday life, of course, offers many such examples of curious impression management strategies. People often go to great lengths in order to save face, to appear serious, consistent and predictable.

The art of flattery: ingratiation
A common form of impression management is when a person seeks to obtain favours or positive evaluation from a specific other person by ingratiation. The term 'ingratiation' is often used in a pejorative sense, describing dishonest and untruthful tactics to influence others. In reality, ingratiation need not be deceitful, and most people use techniques of ingratiation at some time or another in their lives. Jones, who extensively studied this question, broadly defined ingratiation as "comprising those episodes of social behaviour that are designed to increase the attractiveness of the actor to the target" (1964, p. 2). By this criterion, ingratiation must be a very common occurrence indeed! According to Jones, there are four major strategies that ingratiators commonly use. These are (1) complimentary other enhancement, or simply flattery, (2) conformity in opinion, judgment and behaviour, (3) direct self-enhancement in self-presentation, and (4) rendering of favours.

Ingratiation is usually a very complex interpersonal task, since it is precisely in situations where a positive impression is useful that the audience is most likely to be on the lookout for ingratiation strategies. To overcome such scepticism, ingratiators develop complex and subtle tactics (Tedeschi, 1981). Instead of consistently flattering a superior, it might be more credible to offer constructive criticism on some minor points, and praise on the more important issues. Although it is important for the ingratiator to be seen to be acting honestly, this is not always essential. Flattery can work quite well when the praised characteristics are the ones the other person feels most insecure about. People are strongly motivated to accept positive information about themselves at face value, even if the motives of the communicator are doubtful.

The particular ingratiation strategy chosen also depends on the relative status and power of the partners. Jones, Gergen and Davis (1962) asked pairs of Navy cadets — some of equal status and some of unequal status — to be ingratiating (try to be as compatible as possible) or non-ingratiating (try to be as honest as possible) towards each other. The written messages exchanged were later analysed for various ingratiation strategies. Lower status subjects (cadet freshmen) used flattery or other-enhancement as their favourite ingratiation strategy, while higher status cadets (seniors) preferred positive self-presentation and opinion conformity about Navy matters as their strategies. It seems, then, that

---

ACTIVITY 10.2
Status and Ingratiation

Observe at least two examples of interactions between the following categories of people:

1. Two casual acquaintances of equal status (for example, housewives having a chat in the supermarket, people chatting on the bus).

2. Two casual acquaintances of unequal status (for example, manager and employee in a store).

3. Two friends or relatives of equal status (spouses, colleagues, etc.)

4. Two friends or relatives of unequal status (father and son, elder brother and younger brother, etc.).

Note the messages exchanged, and try to analyse each communication in terms of the presence or absence of the four ingratiation strategies described by Jones. Are there any differences between the interactions as a function of the relative status and intimacy of the partners?

ingratiation may be just as common in high status as in low status individuals, although the preferred ingratiation strategies may well depend on the social status of the person (see Acitivity 10.2).

Why do people use ingratiation? Contrary to common belief, ingratiation is not only used when people have some specific objective to achieve. Even without a direct interest, we tend to try to present a positive image of ourselves, and try to be accepted and well thought of by others. The very fact of being approved of is in itself reinforcing, without any further expected advantages. When ingratiation has a specific objective, Jones suggested that our motivations may be classified as follows: (a) acquisition, or the hope of tangible gain, such as promotion or salary increase; (b) protection against danger and harm from the other (such as a volatile boss or a vindictive relative); and finally, and perhaps most commonly; (c) the need to be liked. This last motivation is by far the most common in everyday life, although there are considerable differences between people in the extent to which they need such positive evaluation from others, as we shall see below.

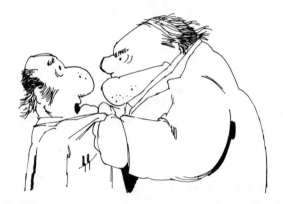

'I am really grateful for your very kind and helpful critical comments, sir!' One of the reasons for ingratiation is to protect the communicator from harm. Often it doesn't particularly matter whether the communication is truthful, since people are strongly motivated to believe flattery about those characteristics they feel most insecure about.

The need for approval

People differ greatly in how much they want or treasure the approval of others. Those who have a high need for approval will presumably use impression management strategies more extensively (although not necessarily with greater success) to obtain it than people who have a low need. Crowne and Marlowe (1964) designed a scale, called the Social Desirability Scale, to measure this characteristic. The scale consists of two kinds of items. The first kind describes desirable attitudes and behaviours which hardly anyone in fact lives up to, for example 'I never tell a lie' or 'Before voting, I thoroughly investigate the qualifications of all candidates'. The second kind of item describes undesirable characteristics which are nevertheless very common in most people, for example 'I sometimes get angry and resentful when I don't get my way'. People who give affirmative answers to the first kind of items, and negative answers for the second kind of items have a high need for approval — they try very hard to present themselves in a positive light, even when the probability of their answers being truthful is rather low.

However, people with a high need for approval are not necessarily good impression managers. They tend to be quiet and conforming in groups, and they rarely initiate social interaction with others for fear of being rejected. As Schlenker (1980) summarises the evidence, "the composite picture of the high-need-for-approval individual is of someone who badly wants to be liked, yet lacks the confidence, assertiveness and skill to make the most of social situations'' (p. 79). An acute perception of the requirements of various social situations is indeed a very important pre-requisite for successful impression management, as we have seen above. We shall now turn to considering the factors involved in the accurate perception of various social episodes.

Perceptions of everyday interaction episodes

In the course of this chapter we repeatedly found that impression management very much depends on a person's ability to correctly interpret the requirements of various social situations. The episodes we participate in as part of our daily interactions have a major influence on our behaviours, perceptions and impression management strategies, as well as our mood (Stone and Neal, 1984). The time has now come to look more closely at the nature of various social situations, and how people perceive and think about such occasions.

Most of our everyday interactions with others involving impression management take place within the frameworks of well established, regular interaction routines, or 'social episodes'. You may have noticed that this term also has its roots in theatrical terminology. We could have used the concept of 'scenes' with equal plausibility. Both terms imply that our interactions almost always follow a predictable course, as if governed by an agreed-on 'script' (another theatrical term!). It is not too difficult to find examples of such recurring interaction episodes: shopping with your spouse on a Saturday morning, having morning coffee with colleagues in the office, going to a restaurant with friends or chatting with an acquaintance while queuing for a bus are common examples of such everyday encounters. It is quite surprising that in fact almost all of our daily interactions with others fit into a limited number of such recurring routines (see Activity 10.3).

Researchers found that most people can adequately summarise their daily interaction routines in terms of about 15 to 30 such recurring episodes (Pervin, 1976; Forgas, 1976; 1982). To know what the requirements of each episode are is essential for successful interaction and impression management. The gestures and nonverbal cues we use at a football match are totally inappropriate at a dinner party, and we use language and gaze differently when discussing a problem with a superior at work from the way we use the same signals when having a chat at home. To be skilful in social interaction and impression management means not only knowing how to use verbal and nonverbal communication, but also knowing exactly what sort of behaviours different episodes call for.

Our expectations and definitions of social episodes are built up in the course of our everyday interactions. As Mead (1934) suggested, it is the unique capacity of human beings to symbolise and abstract their experiences which allows them to create consistent representations of

---

ACTIVITY 10.3
Collecting Interaction Episodes

This activity will make you familiar with some of the simple techniques which may be used to study how people think about social episodes. First, write down on a series of cards all the social encounters (involving at least one other person) you participated in during the past two days. For each encounter, note all relevant details such as time, location, partner(s), activities, duration, etc. When you have finished, expand your list by writing down on additional cards all those social encounters which occur fairly regularly in your life, but which did not happen to occur during the past two days.

How many episodes could you list? Do you feel that your list adequately reflects your range of social activities?

Next, create 'piles' of cards on the table, by trying to sort your episodes into groups in terms of how similar you think they are to each other, as you see them. You may use any criteria you like in deciding whether two episodes are similar or not. Keep sorting your episodes until you are quite happy that all episodes within the same group are indeed more similar to each other in some way than they are to any episodes in other groups.

How many episode categories did you create? What sorts of characteristics did you use in creating your groups? Did you sort your episodes mainly in terms of how you felt about the interactions (for example, good — bad, self-confident — shy, etc.), or did you rely on their objective characteristics (for example, episodes at home, episodes in public places)?

themselves and their social environment. In every interaction we engage in, we base our behaviours on our accumulated previous experience in similar episodes, and these abstract expectations in turn will be confirmed or revised as a result of the interaction itself. To put it differently, we learn about the rules of episodes while participating in them, and once learnt, the same rules are used to guide our behaviours in other, similar encounters. The question arises: is it at all possible to study such elusive representations about social encounters?

Most prior research has found that people have difficulty identifying more than about 30 such episodes, and that they tend to discriminate between them very much in terms of how they feel about an encounter. The objective characteristics of the episodes seemed to play relatively little role in such judgments.

Empirical research on social episodes
In the past several years, psychologists have devoted more and more attention to research on social situations. We may define a social episode as a typical and recurring unit of social interaction within a defined sub-cultural milieu, of which members of that subculture have a clear and consensually shared cognitive representation (Forgas, 1976). The first step in studying such social episodes is to collect a sample of typical encounters. This may be accomplished by interviewing people, or by a diary method, asking people to write down all their social encounters over a period of time. The number of episodes commonly reported is quite manageable, as we have seen above. In the next step, we may ask people to look at these episodes again, and rate them for similarity or other characteristics, just as you did in the previous activity. These judgments may then be analysed using techniques such as multidimensional scaling (MDS), which produces a spatial 'map', showing how the episodes differ from each other as people see them. As an illustration of such an episode 'map', Figure 10.1 will show you how members of an academic group generally thought of their social encounters (Forgas, 1978).

Using these techniques, the episodes of many different groups of people (American, Australian, Swedish and British students, housewives, academics and sports players) have been studied to date (Battistich and Thomson, 1980; Forgas, 1979, 1982; Pervin, 1976). Results typically show that people's episode representations are based on how they feel about such encounters: anxiety or self-confidence, intimacy, involvement, pleasantness and formality are the main characteristics differentiating between episodes. Such perceptions also depend on the norms and values of the person's subculture: housewives and students may see the same episodes very differently (Forgas, 1979), and students from different cultures (e.g. Hong Kong Chinese and Australians) were found to think about identical aspects of student life

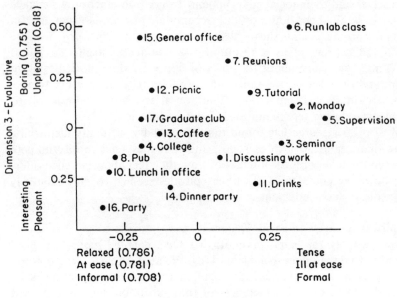

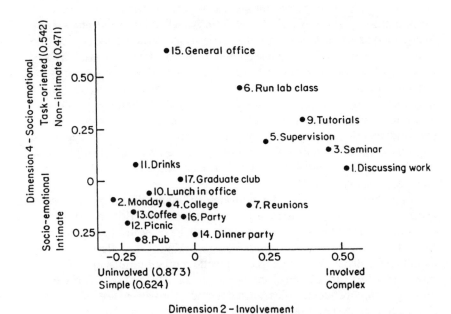

FIGURE 10.1 The social episodes of an academic group. This is how members of this academic group, consisting of faculty members, research students and other staff (see Figure 11.2), perceived their regular interaction episodes. (After Forgas, 1978, p.444).

in very different terms (Forgas and Bond, 1985). Indeed, knowing how to behave in a strange culture largely depends on learning about the typical episodes enacted in that milieu (Triandis, 1972). Culture training programmes often rely on a single interaction unit, or episode, as the most effective way to demonstrate typical cross-cultural differences in behaviour.

Individual differences are also important in episode representations. Persons who are anxious, introverted and have low social skills tend to have a much more simplistic view of the same episodes than do people who are skilled, confident and extroverted (Forgas, 1983). Social anxiety dominated the episode perception strategy of a group of socially unskilled students, while their highly skilled colleagues made much finer distinctions between episodes, relying on several perceptual dimensions (Figure 10.2). It seems that social skill and successful impression management partly depend on how accurately a person can discriminate between different episodes. A person's social status also influences episode perceptions. In one academic group studied (see Figure 10.1), faculty members, staff and research students perceived the same episodes in terms of very different characteristics. Involvement was a most important characteristic of interactions for faculty members; socio-emotional versus task orientation was a major episode dimension for research students; and anxiety was the single most important aspect of episodes for other staff. It seems, then, that each of us possesses a unique mental 'episode repertoire' which tells us how to react to and behave in the common interaction situations which occur in our

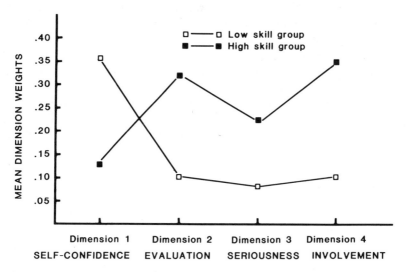

FIGURE 10.2 Social skill and episode perceptions. Unskilled subjects perceived episodes only in terms of their effects on their self-confidence, while skilled subjects relied on several other dimensions. (After Forgas, 1983).

environment. Our culture, subculture and reference group as well as our personal background and history are all related to such episode representations.

The cues which define an interaction episode
How do we know when a particular episode is to be enacted? What are the cues which alert us to a specific kind of encounter? Several kinds of information are important here. The first one is the physical environment, or behaviour setting, where the interaction occurs. Psychologists such as Barker (1968) found that it is possible to adequately describe the complete interaction repertoire of a small town simply by analysing all the physical behaviour settings which are available to people to interact in at various times. A street corner, a theatre lobby, a restaurant or a public service office are behaviour settings which exert a very strong influence on the kind of interactions which may normally be enacted within their confines. A second important source of information defining an episode is the relationship between the partners. You may behave very differently towards the same person depending on whether he is your relative, or if you expect the relationship to progress rather than terminate after the encounter. Studies have shown that we also have a very clear idea about the various kinds of relationship scenarios available in our culture (see Chapter 13), and that we use this information to define and code our interactions.

Knowing the requirements of the interaction episode, and having an accurate cognitive representation of the appropriate and accepted sequence of behaviours is thus an important requirement for successful interpersonal communication and impression management. People who are socially skilled and are high on self-monitoring also have a more refined and sensitive view of interaction episodes (cf. Forgas, 1983; Snyder and Monson, 1975). Research on the characteristics of social episodes is an active area today. Since so much of skilled social behaviour depends on the accurate perception of the requirements of the situation, becoming aware of the range and variety of the social situations surrounding us could be an important step towards increasing our own social competence.

Conclusions
We have seen in this chapter that social interaction, the sending and receiving of verbal and nonverbal messages, involves far more than simple communication skills. Interaction amongst human beings is always strategic interaction, in the sense that we seek to satisfy our expectations, goals and plans in interacting with each other. Impression management is the generic term we used to describe all aspects of this strategic process. We have seen that the impressions we make on others will not only influence their behaviours towards us, but ultimately will

also determine how we come to see ourselves. To be sensitive to the requirements of various situations, to be consistent in our self-presentations, and to have a good assessment of our own behaviours are essential prerequisites for skilled impression management. Once a person has mastered these skills, he/she will be much more effective in initiating and establishing rewarding social relationships with other people. We shall look at the psychological processes involved in relationship development in the next chapter.

11. Human sociability: affiliation and attraction

11.

HUMAN SOCIABILITY:
AFFILIATION AND ATTRACTION

Up to this point we have discussed the basic components of social interaction: how we perceive and interpret other people, and how we use verbal and nonverbal messages and impression management strategies to communicate with each other. It is now time to turn to a very important third aspect of social interaction: the development of affiliation and attraction between people, and the emergence of personal relationships. Social interaction and relationship development are closely interrelated. When we interact with others, our behaviours usually express a level of attraction and intimacy which seems appropriate to the existing relationship between us and and our partners. You may remember that this was the basis for Argyle and Dean's intimacy-equilibrium theory, discussed in Chapter 9. Conversely, as a result of every interaction, the original level of relatedness and intimacy between the partners is either confirmed, degraded or upgraded, depending on the outcome of that particular encounter. Episodes of social interaction are thus both the antecedent and the consequence of affiliation and attraction between people.

Psychologists studying interpersonal relationships typically ask such questions as: Why do people generally seek each other's company? What attracts one person to another? What sorts of people will become friends? Under what circumstances will a casual romantic relationship develop into marriage? Why do relationships sometimes fail to progress? These are the sorts of questions which have also been of interest to philosophers, writers, poets and artists since antiquity. Much of our cultural heritage consists of works which were stimulated by intense affiliative emotions such as love, friendship, comradeship or kinship. In this chapter we shall look at some of the basic characteristics of human sociability. In the next chapter, we shall continue this theme by discussing the way social relationships develop and progress.

201

Social psychology and the study of relationships

The central role affiliative relationships play in our lives was perhaps the main reason why social psychologists were reluctant, until recently, to subject these highly personal and involving experiences to cold scientific scrutiny. Many people still believe that personal relationships constitute a sacred and inviolable part of our lives, which should not be exposed to objective analysis which could possibly destroy their mystique. Even in recent years, some politicians have severely criticised social psychological research on romantic love. The US Senator William Proxmire argued just a few years ago "I believe that 200 million Americans want to leave some things in life a mystery, and right at the top of things we don't want to know is why a man falls in love with a woman and vice versa".

This feeling of suspicion about scientific research on human relationships is shared by many people. I don't think these worries are justified. It is unlikely that we will know everything about human relationships in the near future, so there is plenty of scope left for mystery and romanticism. On the other hand, the number of people who have serious difficulties with interpersonal relationships is steadily growing in Western societies. Philip Zimbardo, who has made an extensive study of social isolation and shyness, found this to be a major problem not just in the United States, but in many other countries as well. You may recall the discussion in Chapter 1 outlining some of the possible historical reasons for the growing isolation of many people in modern industrial societies. In order to be able to help, we must use scientific methods to study relationships. There are still large gaps in our knowledge about this topic, but research on relationships has nevertheless succeeded in discovering some interesting facts about how and why people are attracted to each other.

Are human beings inherently social?

We must begin by asking a fundamental question: is it really necessary to have intimate social relationships? Could people not live just as well, and perhaps better, alone, without the company of others? The answer seems to be clearly 'no'. It is sometimes said that Homo sapiens is an inherently gregarious species, and there appears to be a lot of truth in that assertion. We seem to seek and enjoy each others' company, our personal relationships play an inordinately important role in our lives, and the capacity for cooperative group activity has probably had a lot to do with our evolutionary success as a species.

We spend most of our lives in the company of others. Latane and Bidwell (1977) simply observed people on a university campus, and found that about 60 per cent of the individuals they saw were in the company of others. Women were much more likely to be in company than men, suggesting that in public places at least women show more affiliative behaviours than men. We can get a more accurate idea about the proportion of time we spend with others by recording all our interactions in a diary. Deaux (1978) used this technique, and found that her subjects spent only about 25 per cent of their waking time alone. The rest of the time was divided as follows: 12 per cent with a member of the opposite sex, 15 per cent with a member of the same sex, 17 per cent with a group of people of the same sex, and 30 per cent with a mixed-sex group. However, not everybody shares this pattern.

There are, of course, large differences in sociability between people (Activity 11.1). Swap and Rubin (1983) recently suggested that interpersonal orientation may be defined as the extent to which a person is "interested in and reactive to other people" (p. 208). Interpersonal orientation is almost like a personality trait, and can be reliably measured using a standard psychological scale according to these authors. As one of my colleagues observed, it is paradoxical that social psychologists and other academics seem to be a major exception to the almost universal pattern of sociability: we seem to spend most of our time alone, reading, writing or sitting in front of a computer screen, as I am doing at the moment of writing this sentence!

ACTIVITY 11.1
How Sociable Are You?

Are you a gregarious person? How important are social contacts in your life? How much of *your* waking time do you think is spent in other people's company? First, write down on a piece of paper your estimate of what percentage of your waking hours you spend (a) alone, (b) in the company of a member of the opposite sex, (c) in the company of a member of the same sex, (d) in a same-sex group, (e) in a mixed group.

You can examine how well your estimates correspond to reality by using a procedure similar to Deaux's (1978). Keep a diary for a few days, recording your activities in every 15 minute period, noting what you are doing, where and with whom. You can later add up the amount of time you spent with various kinds of people. You can also use your diary record to analyse your activities in terms of location (where?) and in terms of activity type (work, leisure, etc.). This simple technique should almost certainly reveal some quite interesting facts about the actual patterns of your social encounters, which may turn out to be quite different from your previous estimates!

The consequences of isolation

What happens when people are forced for some reason to abandon their usual round of social contacts, and live in isolation from others? Occasionally, information is obtained about human infants who were reared by animals and grew up without any contact with other human beings. Such individuals usually manifest serious symptoms of retardation which are irreversible however meticulously they are cared for later. Of course, it is never possible to say in such cases whether retardation was not possibly due to some prior birth defect, and thus the reason for, rather than the consequence of being abandoned by human society.

We can get a more reliable picture about the consequences of isolation by studying the reactions of normal, healthy individuals who for some reason experienced long-term isolation. There are many historical and literary accounts of shipwrecked sailors occasionally enduring several years alone. Their reports are uniformly negative. Despite abundant food and shelter, the absence of other human beings soon becomes a source of suffering and depression. Other psychological symptoms, such as hallucinations and the tendency to talk aloud to oneself, or to animals, is also a common reaction to prolonged isolation.

Experimental studies give us additional information about the consequences of isolation. Schachter (1959) paid volunteer male students $20.00 per day (worth much more then than nowadays!) to stay in

'It's kind of you to think of me, Miss Pomerenky, but I don't really think I could handle pussy's pregnancy!!' A common reaction to isolation is to seek the company of other living things, such as animals, who are then endowed with almost human qualities.

complete social isolation in windowless but artificially lit rooms. The subjects received food at regular meal times, but were not allowed to see anybody, read, listen to radio or watch television. The five subjects reacted very differently to isolation: one could only stand it for 20 minutes, another remained for eight days, and the rest stayed for about two days, reporting either no effects, or growing uneasiness.

It seems that there are very large individual differences in how well people tolerate isolation, and the amount of social contact and stimulation they need. Psychologists such as Hebb (1955) and Eysenck and Eysenck (1969) suggest that individuals differ in their basic level of arousal, and as a result, the optimum level of stimulation they need from others. Eysenck suggested that different underlying levels of arousal, determined by biological and genetic factors, also account for such major personality differences as extroversion-introversion and neuroticism. Such theories seem to imply that sociability is related to basic patterns of personality as well as the genetic and physiological make-up of a person. Although this is an exciting theory, and one of the very few which attempts to link social behaviour to biological variables, the questions posed by Eysenck's model have not yet been satisfactorily resolved in the psychological literature.

Temporary social isolation also has some other interesting consequences. During periods of deprivation from social contact people usually become very open to new experiences and influences, and vivid dreams, images and sometimes hallucinations may be experienced (Suedfeld, 1974). At least some of the 'visions' and 'visitations' reported by people living in extreme social isolation because of religious principles, such as hermits or monks, may also be due to such hallucinations. Isolation also makes a person very open to outside influences. Isolation was part of the brainwashing procedure used to influence American prisoners' attitudes during the Korean War, and shorter periods of isolation have been used for such therapeutic purposes as persuading people to give up smoking. These methods capitalise on the fact that communications during and after social isolation have a much greater impact than otherwise. It seems then that we all need social contacts with our fellow human beings to maintain normal psychological adjustment, although there are large individual differences in exactly how much contact is 'optimal' for each of us. Deprivation from social contact is upsetting, and leaves most people disoriented and easy to influence.

Loneliness

Most of us have experienced some episodes of loneliness in our lives. These are times when we long for human companionship, for some joint activity with others, for a sign of acceptance and liking. The experience of loneliness is a very hard one to define, since people have differing needs and expectations of social contact. Whereas one person may feel lonely even with dozens of friends, others may be perfectly happy with having just a single other person for a companion. By publishing a questionnaire about loneliness in newspapers, Rubinstein and Shaver (1979) obtained detailed information about this experience from some 25 000 people in the USA. Having parents who divorced was found to

---

ACTIVITY 11.2
A Measure of Loneliness

Loneliness is hard to define objectively. Researchers typically use self-report scales, similar to this one, in studying loneliness. To complete this scale, read each of the questions below carefully, and answer as honestly as you can, by circling one of the numbers as follows:

1 this is definitely not true for me
2 this is probably not true for me
3 I am not sure
4 this is probably true for me
5 this is definitely true for me

1. I often feel very much alone..............	1	2	3	4	5
2. I find it hard to make friends.............	1	2	3	4	5
3. I often do things by myself	1	2	3	4	5
4. I often wait for people to call or write ...	1	2	3	4	5
5. I find it hard to meet people.............	1	2	3	4	5
6. I am frequently excluded by people......	1	2	3	4	5
7. I wish I knew more people to do things with...	1	2	3	4	5
8. I think people don't really understand me..	1	2	3	4	5
9. I do not have an attractive personality ..	1	2	3	4	5

You can score your answers simply by adding up the numbers you circled for each of the questions. The closer the number to 45, the more likely that you are indeed a person who has experienced loneliness. The above scale is not in fact a proper standardised instrument, but it resembles in form and content the loneliness scales often used by researchers.

be a major antecedent in the life histories of lonely people, as if they suffered from the fact that their parents apparently rejected them.

Different kinds of loneliness were reported, including such forms as (1) *desperation* (being helpless, afraid and desperate), (2) *impatient boredom* (wishing to be elswhere, being bored and uneasy), (3) *depression* (feeling isolated, melancholy and sad), and (4) *self-depreciation* (feeling unattractive, insecure and stupid). How people react to loneliness largely depends on the explanations they have for it. You may remember that attribution theorists classified such explanations in terms of the location (internal-external) and stability (stable-unstable) of the causes given (see also Chapter 5). Lonely people who gave internal-stable explanations for their loneliness (for example, looks, personality) were most resigned and depressed. Those who thought lack of effort on their part (internal-unstable) was the cause of their loneliness were least upset and most optimistic about a change. Unstable-external causes (for example, I am lonely because I have just moved to a new area) gave much hope for change, while stable-external causes (for example, people are intentionally excluding me) often lead to hostility.

Those who are lonely most of the time may paradoxically withdraw even from occasional social contacts when they become available, and for a very good reason. "Loneliness seems aggravated by social interaction and the following isolation" (Schultz and Moore, 1984, p.67). In other words, lonely persons are less willing to take a risk with occasional encounters, as these make the pain of enduring loneliness worse, rather than better.

The personality trait most commonly associated with reports of loneliness is shyness: shy people are afraid of human contact, particularly if it is with an authority figure, or is of an emotionally threatening nature. Zimbardo (1977) found that almost 80 per cent of people are, or have been, shy at some time in their lives. Shyness can be overcome through careful training, although in some circumstances

Why am I so lonely? The experience of loneliness is highly subjective, and reactions to loneliness also largely depend on the explanations people find for their predicaments.

being shy may be a desirable characteristic. By withdrawing from human contact, shy people have more time to think about and understand others, and are less likely to act in an aggressive or offensive manner towards their partners. As you can see, getting just the right amount of human contact is not an easy task. We shall next look at some of the reasons for the need for sociability.

The reasons for sociability
Why exactly do human beings seek each other's company so persistently? What do we get out of being with others? There are several psychological explanations for human sociability. According to some theorists, the company of others is in itself rewarding and reinforcing. It may be that as a consequence of our evolutionary history, we have come to see other people more as sources of positive experiences rather than negative ones. This 'learning experience' is eventually generalised to all potential social contacts.

It is suggested by other theories that companionship with others is necessary for us to be able to evaluate ourselves. According to this view, human beings use a process of *social comparison* (Festinger, 1954) to assess themselves relative to others when other objective criteria are absent. Without the company of other people, we would have difficulty in evaluating ourselves, and therefore in forming a consistent self-image. We have already seen in the previous chapter that self-concept is largely a social creation, built up as a result of interactions with people and the feedback we receive from our partners. Yet another explanation of sociability — social exchange theory — suggests that we seek the company of people because we can obtain greater rewards and satisfaction by cooperating with others than through being alone. Interaction is thus the necessary means by which we achieve our ends, and is therefore rewarding.

Just being with others also helps to reduce stress, and people who are anxious or worried about something often seek out the company of others. Schachter (1959) demonstrated this tendency in an interesting experiment. Female students were told that they would be receiving some electric shocks as part of an experiment. Some subjects were told that the shocks would be painless, almost like a tickle. The rest of the subjects were informed that the shocks would be quite painful, but would not cause any permanent damage. The subjects were then told that there would be a few minutes delay while the equipment was being set up, and they were asked whether they would prefer to wait in a waiting room by themselves, or wished to join some other people in a different room.

Schachter expected that the women who were made anxious by expecting painful shocks would have a stronger preference for company while waiting. Of the 32 anxious subjects, 20 chose to wait with others. Of the 30 low-anxiety subjects, only 10 did so, suggesting that the company of others is sought particularly when people feel anxious or stressed about something. In a follow-up study, the anxious subjects were given a further choice of either waiting with people who also expected painful shocks, or people who were not even participating in the experiment. Most subjects chose to wait with somebody in the same predicament as themselves. In other words, the company of people in a situation similar to ours is particularly effective in reducing anxiety: apparently, 'misery prefers miserable company'! However, whether the presence of other people can make us feel better also depends on the specific situation. When people were anxious because they expected to participate in an embarrassing (rather than painful) experiment, most of them preferred to wait alone (Sarnoff and Zimbardo, 1961).

Affiliation and attraction

The need to be with people, the motivation to socialise, is almost universal, as we have seen above. But we do not simply spend our time with anybody randomly. Our social contacts are usually selected from a much larger pool of potentially available partners. Exactly how do we make such choices? What determines whether we will establish a relationship with a person or not? Out of the hundreds or even thousands of potentially available people in our university class, our workplace, our neighbourhood or our club, how do we decide on the few individuals with whom we shall have a closer acquaintance? There are several variables which are important here. Perhaps most surprising is the fact that at the very early stages of a relationship, we really do not decide who to spend time with, we do not select our partners consciously. The variables which determine our potential range of superficial acquaintances are largely external to us, and we rarely even become aware of them.

The first obvious, but much neglected factors in acquaintanceship are simply space and time: we must be at the same place at the same time in order to become aware of a potential partner. Surprising as it seems, this simple and obvious fact represents perhaps the greatest single restriction on our social contacts. Of the millions of people living, we shall only ever encounter a very small percentage in our lives. Of those whom we do encounter, only an even smaller fraction will ever be close enough for long enough for us even to become aware of them. This small group is the potential source of all our future acquaintances and friends. Several intriguing studies show the importance of spatial proximity on friendship formation.

In a well-known field study, Festinger, Schachter and Back (1950) were interested in the role physical proximity plays in the development of relationships. Would the mere fact that people live near and have a greater opportunity to bump into each other predispose them to friendship? These researchers analysed the developing friendship patterns between new residents at a housing project at the Massachusetts Institute of Technology. They expected that "where people moving into the area have few or no previous contacts in the community, friendships are likely to develop on the basis of brief and passive contacts made going to and from home or walking about the neighbourhood. These brief meetings, if they are frequent enough, may develop into nodding acquaintanceships, then into speaking relations and eventually, if psychological factors are right, into friendships" (p. 34).

The study generally supported these expectations: the smaller the physical distance between two flats, the greater the probability that the residents would develop a friendly relationship. When residents were asked to list their best friends, next-door neighbours were mentioned 41 per cent of the time, those living two doors away were mentioned 22 per cent of the time, and people three doors away were mentioned as friends by only 10 per cent of the subjects in this study. We shall see later that similar chance occurrences, such as who you happen to sit next to at your first lecture, or who happens to occupy the neighbouring desk, work bench or office may influence your personal friendships for years to come (see Activity 11.3).

Of course Festinger's results mean simply that physical proximity facilitates attraction, but does not necessarily cause it. Indeed, quite often enforced close proximity has exactly the opposite effect. People in crowded apartment houses are often friendlier with distant residents than with their immediate neighbours, as a precaution against possible invasions of their privacy. However, when people are new to an area and their social contacts are restricted, those who happen to be near them

---

ACTIVITY 11.3
Space and Friendship

You may carry out a small project yourself checking on the validity of Festinger, Schachter and Back's findings. Prepare a small sketch of the physical layout of your immediate living environment (building, street, etc.). Mark on that map all the individuals (a) whom you know by sight only but have never spoken to, (b) with whom you have a superficial, nodding relationship only, (c) whom you occasionally talk to, and (d) whom you would call your friends. Is there any relationship between spatial proximity and your relationship with any of these groups? If you find no links between proximity and friendship, can you think of any particular characteristics of your situation which could explain this?

constitute the most obvious pool from which their future friends will be selected. During the three years I spent living at a graduate apartment block at Oxford, which was not unlike the estate studied by Festinger and his colleagues, it was certainly my impression that people who lived near each other or shared the same staircase became friends more often than did more remote neighbours.

Physical nearness often leads to attraction because it increases the likelihood of brief contacts. It is a remarkable fact that simple, brief exposure to another person is often a sufficient cause in itself for increased attraction (see Activity 11.4). The most likely explanation of this often-found effect is that repeated exposure to a person increases our familiarity, and we are more attracted to familiar people and objects than to unfamiliar ones (Zajonc, 1970). I have often become aware of this fact while marking students' examination papers. When the class is

---

ACTIVITY 11.4
Familiarity and Liking

Are people really more attracted to another person simply because that person looks familiar? To test this hypothesis, you need to get hold of a number of identically shaped photographs of different people. Newspaper pictures showing portraits of football team members, cabinets, graduating classes, etc. are a good source. Cut out these pictures to obtain a set of similar sized photos. Pick out about half the pictures from the set randomly, and make a note of your selection. Show these selected photos to your subjects, and get them to look at each photo briefly, for example by asking the subject to guess the age of each person.

One or two days later, when your subjects have certainly forgotten the individual photos they have seen, present them with the complete set. This time, ask them to rate each photo in terms of how attractive they think the person is. You can use a seven-point scale like this:

I find the person in this photo very attractive	1 2 3 4 5 6 7	I find the person in this photo very unattractive

Average the judgments you obtained for both sets of photos. You should find that even though people are unlikely to remember whether they saw a particular picture before or not, they will find familiar pictures (the half set they already saw) on the whole more attractive than unfamiliar ones.

large, and consists of many unknown people, I automatically have a more positive attitude and expectation when I encounter a name which is familiar. Being a social psychologist, I try of course to make sure that this does not affect my marking!

Sometimes, attraction may be facilitated by completely unforeseen factors. We will probably be more attracted to a person whom we meet at a pleasant, relaxing place when we feel happy and contented, than we would when meeting that same person in an unpleasant, noisy environment. Staats and Staats (1958) proposed that we may come to inadvertently associate people with positive or negative qualities using principles of classical conditioning. In their experiment, subjects saw names (for example, Brian, Tom, Bill, etc.) at the same time as either pleasant (for example, happy) or unpleasant (for example, bitter, ugly) words were spoken. Later, subjects were asked to rate the names they saw. Those names which happened to be associated with pleasant words previously were rated as more pleasant than names which were associated with unpleasant words. Following a similar principle, the situation and context in real-life encounters may become associated in our minds with the presumed qualities of people, influencing our attraction towards those individuals.

Towards a definition of liking: attraction as an attitude
Up to this point we have talked about attraction and relationships as if the meaning of these terms was clear to everybody. But what exactly does it mean to like, and to be liked? Can we really assume that various kinds of attraction, such as being popular in a classroom, being in love, being approved of at a job interview or being sought out by a colleague at a party are based on similar processes? In everyday life, we use words such as 'liking' or 'attraction' in a great variety of situations. Is it not the case that different situations and different relationships are associated with different processes of attraction? Most social psychologists believe that despite the underlying differences, most kinds of interpersonal attraction follow basically similar rules. The most generally accepted definition of interpersonal attraction asserts that attraction is simply the existence of positive attitudes towards another person.

The notion of *attitude* is one of the central concepts in social psychology. It is a complex construct, referring to the fact that all people have certain enduring inclinations, predispositions, feelings, beliefs and knowledge about the persons and objects they come across. You may remember that we have already come across the concept of attitudes in discussing Bem's self-perception theory in Chapter 6. According to a widely accepted model, an attitude may be subdivided into three basic components: (a) a cognitive component, or the knowledge and beliefs we have about the attitude object; (b) an affective component, or the feelings and emotions we have about the object; and (c) a conative component, or the behaviour intentions or plans we have about an object (Berscheid and Walster, 1969; Rubin, 1973). Following this pattern, attraction also consists of these three sets of interrelated components: beliefs about, feelings towards, and behaviours with the other person. By defining attraction as the existence of a positive attitude towards another person we have a sufficiently general term to cover all the various situations in which attraction occurs. Defining attraction as an attitude also allows us to measure it using any of the many different methods used for attitude measurement.

Measuring attraction

Many of the earliest research projects on social relationships were generally limited to attempts at empirically measuring the extent to which people were positively inclined towards each other. The social distance scale developed by Bogardus (1925) is among the first such empirical instruments measuring attitudes towards others. In this instrument, respondents are asked to indicate how closely they would be prepared to be involved with various kinds of people, along seven steps ranging from very close (would admit that person to close kinship by marriage), through intermediate (would admit that person to employment in my occupation), all the way to complete rejection (would exclude that person from my country). You will note that this scale measures behaviour intentions, rather than feelings (the affective component), or beliefs (the cognitive component) about a person. According to this 1925 study using the social distance scale, Canadians and the English were allowed the 'closest' relationship, and Negroes, Japanese and Turks were kept at the greatest social distance by white American subjects. The technique has been extensively used in stereotype research, as well as in studying interpersonal relationships.

A more sensitive method for analysing interpersonal affiliations was developed by Moreno (1934). At that time, interest in group processes was very keen, and Moreno's method, called *sociometry*, was capable of objectively representing the whole structure of positive and negative links which existed between members of a small group. The principle used by Moreno was strikingly simple. Every member of a small group is simply asked to write down on a piece of paper the names of their most (and sometimes least) preferred person (or persons) in the group. This information is then used to draw up a *sociogram*, in effect a map of the group, where each individual and the recorded preference links between individuals are shown (Figure 11.1). Looking at such a map enables us to simultaneously get a very good impression about the social structure of the group as a whole, and the personal affiliations of every member individually.

We may also use this map to characterise types of individuals in terms of their relationships. Sociocentres are those members of a group who

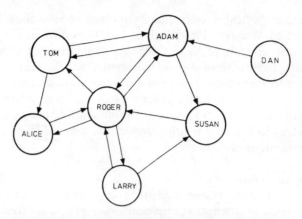

FIGURE 11.1 The sociogram of an imaginary group. The circles represent group members, and the arrows indicate preference choices. In this group, Roger is a 'sociocentre' and Dan is an 'isolate'.

are chosen by a great many others, and isolates are individuals who are rarely chosen by others. In the figure above, Roger may be called a sociocentre, and Dan an isolate. The sociometric method has been extensively used in group research, and the method is still popular today. Teachers, for example, may use it to obtain a working model of the personal relationships within their classrooms. Sociograms can also be useful in highlighting various sub-groups or 'cliques' within a larger group. If you happen to have cooperative colleagues at your work place, you can obtain the necessary information and draw up a sociogram yourself. If you do so, make sure that you treat the data confidentially: it can sometimes be painful and embarrassing for people if their position in a group is openly revealed. Nobody likes to be an isolate, and isolates are not always responsible for their predicament!

More recently, the sociometric technique has been further developed by using sophisticated statistical techniques such as multidimensional scaling (MDS) to convert preference ratings into a multidimensional geometric map of the group (Jones and Young, 1972). In a recent study, we used this method (Forgas, 1978) to construct a model of the affiliative relationships within an academic group. Members were full-time faculty, graduate research students and other staff (see Figure 11.2). In such a model, the distance between any two individual group members in the figure is proportional to the perceived similarity between them, and the dimensions of the 'group space' indicate which personal characteristics were most important in differentiating between members. You will see in Figure 11.2 that status was quite an important aspect of perceived group structure, even among this group of supposedly openminded academics!

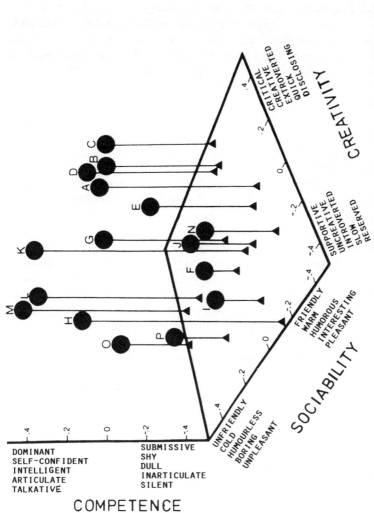

FIGURE 11.2 The structure of an academic group. The figure shows the perceived structure of this 15-member academic group, based on the multidimensional scaling (MDS) analysis of their judgments of each other. Position in the group is determined by a member's location along the sociability, creativity and competence dimensions. A-E faculty members; F-M research students; N-P other staff (for the episode perceptions of the same group, see Figure 10.1). (After Forgas, 1978)

Apart from measures of attraction such as the social distance scale and the sociometric methods mentioned above, there are a number of other methods to measure attraction as an attitude. We may also ask people to complete adjective checklists describing their attitude towards another person, we may use bipolar scales or semantic differential scales or even open-ended interview methods. Most measures of attraction, in fact, try to assess the affective component of this attitude. Indirect measures, analysing the behavioural component, may also be used to assess attraction. The frequency or intensity of nonverbal behaviours, such as the amount of eye gaze, talking, or smiling at a person, and the kind of gestures, proximity, and body orientation observed are also indicative of attraction (see Chapter 9).

Another possibility is to measure attraction through the physiological arousal which often accompanies such evaluative reactions. Heart rate, breathing rate, or galvanic skin response can be measured in the presence of a partner to assess attraction. An interesting related measure of attraction was developed by Hess (1975), who found that arousal is reliably associated with the dilation of a person's pupils. You may recall the study mentioned in Chapter 9, where subjects were shown nude pictures of males and females. They were found to react with pupil dilation, indicating attraction, to images of the opposite sex but not their own sex (see Table 9.1). The process was reversed for homosexuals, who reacted to same-sex pictures with pupil dilation. However, such physiological measures are cumbersome and are not very often used in research on attraction. Paper-and-pencil methods enquiring about feelings towards a target person are most frequently employed.

The two varieties of attraction: liking and admiration
In existing empirical studies, researchers most frequently measured attraction using a series of bipolar Likert-type scales on which the target person is to be rated. The two most commonly used scale types measure (a) a person's likeability, and (b) competence or desirability as a potential work partner. Analyses of attractiveness ratings usually show that these two are quite independent reactions to people. We may like somebody because of their endearing social qualities (friendliness, pleasantness, popularity, and so on), or we may admire and respect them because of their competence and task performance (judged on scales such as intelligence, competence, efficiency and hard work).

In a way, it appears that liking and respect are two quite distinct aspects of positive attitudes towards another person. We may like somebody without admiring him/her, and we may admire a person without liking him/her. There may, of course, be other, more distinct aspects of attraction. Rubin (1973) suggested, for example, that liking and romantic love are characterised by very different features (see Chapter 12). But most researchers are content to define attraction as a general positive attitude, and measure it using simple bipolar scales tapping one or both of the two basic components of this attitude, liking and admiration.

Theories of attraction

Now that we have some idea about the nature and importance of human sociability, we may turn to describing in more detail some of the theories psychologists use to explain the consequences of this almost universal need for affiliation and attraction. Perhaps the oldest idea is that people seek each other's company because of an inbuilt drive, the affiliation motive. According to this view, being with others is in itself satisfying. It is sometimes suggested that this 'affiliation drive' is an evolutionary characteristic — part of our genetic heritage which explains the success of our species. This is, of course, also a circular explanation — by stating that affiliation is a drive, we do not get very much closer to understanding exactly how it works.

Reward, exchange and attraction

Learning theories provide an alternative explanation. The reinforcement-affect theory of Byrne and Clore (1970) states that we are attracted to those people who in the past provided us with positive reinforcements or rewards. When a person does something or says something that makes us feel good, we 'learn' to make an association between that happy feeling and the person who caused it. In the future, we will be attracted to that person. This very simple theory of attraction is based on an even older principle, the concept of reward, and the notion of hedonism as a basic component of human nature. This ancient view assumes that human behaviour is largely explainable as a quest to seek pleasure and avoid pain. The learning theoretical concept of reinforcement is based on this hedonistic principle and its use to explain interpersonal attraction is thus little more than an application of the theory of hedonism (see Chapter 1).

Exchange theory represents a further development of the basic learning theoretical model. It takes into account the specific costs and benefits obtained in a relationship by both partners. This is an explicitly economical view of human relationships. Each person is assumed to be motivated to obtain 'profit' from his/her relationships with others, that is, an excess of rewards over costs. In functioning relationships, both partners must by definition gain such a profit, otherwise the relationship would terminate once a partner incurs greater costs than benefits.

Commercial as this view may seem, it represents quite a good approximation to at least some of the most widely used practices in personal relationships. In many societies, both ancient and modern, the 'reward value' of a partner was quite explicitly assessed by families on the basis of widely accepted ideas of partnership value. Just a brief look at 'personal' advertisements in any newspaper will give you a clear idea of the major assets in the interpersonal marketplace today: good looks, youth, money, preference for travel and adventure, education, etc. Not so long ago, specialist 'matchmakers' were engaged to perform the delicate task of weighing up and matching a potential bride's beauty, dowry and social status with the family background, habits, money and looks of a suitable bridegroom.

This exchange principle is still with us today, if in a less institutionalised form: "indeed, it may be argued that the transition from the arranged marriage has brought the bargaining attitude to the love relation more explicitly, for previously families bargained, but now everyone must haggle for himself" (Willard Waller, 1970, p. 182). It has become more difficult nowadays to assess personal assets, hence the many books providing guidance on personal relationships, one of them revealingly entitled *The Interpersonal Marketplace: An Investor's Guide* (quoted in Rubin, 1973, p. 67).

We are usually inclined to assume that in every relationship such personal assets must have been well matched. When you see an extremely attractive young woman with an elderly and not particularly endearing man, you tend to automatically infer that despite appearances, a mutually beneficial exchange must have taken place. Perhaps the aged husband is extremely rich, possibly he has a brilliant intellect which is appreciated by his young wife, or perhaps he rendered some important service in the past. When Jacqueline Kennedy married Aristotle Onassis, most people had little difficulty in seeing that a fair exchange had occurred: the partners provided each other with interpersonal resources which were mutually valued. Studies have shown that personal assets such as physical beauty have an enduring effect, and even reflect on the

Is this a fair match? In most interpersonal relationships we assume that a fair and equitable match must have taken place, sometimes despite appearances. A common exchange in heterosexual relationships is youth and physical attractiveness on the part of the female against the resources and sometimes personal qualities of an older and less physically attractive male.

perceived standing of the partner. A man seen with an attractive woman is often more positively evaluated than when seen without such company (see study by Sigall and Landy, Chapter 12).

Cognitive balance theories

Cognitive balance theory provides another explanation for affiliation and attraction. According to this view, we tend to choose as partners those people who help us to maintain our consistent and balanced view of the world. Thus, people who think like us, have attitudes similar to ours, and behave like us are preferred as friends, since they confirm our view of the world. Fritz Heider and later Newcomb (1961) were the major exponents of the cognitive balance principle. They suggested that the relationship between three basic elements, the person (P), the other (O) and the attitude object (X) can be jointly analysed in terms of a limited number of triangular relationships.

For example, if I (the person, P) like John, my friend (the other, O), and we both approve of nationalised medicine (the attitude object, X), the relationship is *balanced* and stable. If however, I (P) like John (O) but he disapproves of nationalised medicine while I support it, a cognitive *imbalance* occurs which can only be resolved if either John or I change our minds about X, or if I change my mind about John (O)! My attraction towards John is thus clearly dependent on the number and kind of such triangular cognitive units we are involved in.

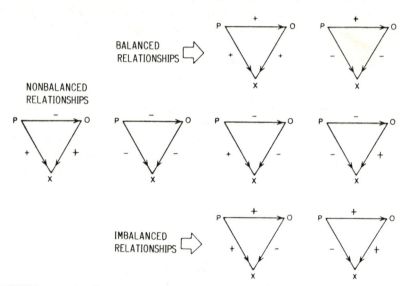

FIGURE 11.3 An illustration of the balance model. P = person, O = other and X = attitude object. Arrows indicate the direction, and signs the value of each attitude. If P has positive attitudes towards O, the relationship may be balanced or imbalanced, depending on their attitudes towards X. If P dislikes O, the relationship is nonbalanced. (After Newcomb, 1961, p. 9).

If, on the other hand, I don't much care about John, it will be of little interest to me whether he shares my attitudes: the relationship may remain *nonbalanced*, without any further consequences (Figure 11.3). My only possible preference in non-balanced relationships would be for some misfortune, such as punishment to befall the disliked other (Eiser, 1980). Newcomb (1968) and later Feather (1964; 1971) developed Heider's cognitive balance model further, specifying the kind of balanced, imbalanced and nonbalanced relationships which can exist between the various elements (Figure 11.3). As you can see, this simple idea can be quite effective in explaining the various possible links between P, O and X!

There is considerable support for such a cognitive balance principle operating in relationships. In a classic study which exerted much influence on subsequent research on relationships, Theodore Newcomb (1961) investigated the 'acquaintance process'. Newcomb was interested in whether the similarity of personal attitudes, values and opinions would indeed be related to friendship choices, as balance theory predicts. His subjects were a group of male students, all strangers to each other, who took up residence in a student housing unit at the same time. Their attitudes, values and feelings towards other students in the unit were assessed before moving in, and several times during the term of their residence. Results showed that similarity of attitudes and values before moving in was a very good predictor of who would become friends with whom in the long run. Also, residents who liked each other tended to agree in their evaluations of other residents, suggesting that their similar attitudes towards third parties also constituted a factor in the development of their friendships.

This study was among the first to provide evidence that attitude similarity is a significant factor in the development of relationships, confirming predictions derived from balance theory. The idea that 'similarities attract each other' remains one of the most important principles of relationship development (see next chapter as well). But cognitive balance theory also has some more far-reaching implications. Would it be the case, for example, that we will like a person for no better reason than that he happens to be an enemy of one of our enemies (for example, Eiser, 1980)?

The balance formulation predicts such an outcome. Aronson and Cope (1968) tried to evaluate this possibility in an experiment, where subjects were either harshly or pleasantly treated by an experimenter, and later 'overheard' the experimenter himself receiving either a severe dressing-down or praise from his own superior. This superior in turn later approached the subjects, asking them for help with some telephone calls. More subjects volunteered to make more phone calls on behalf of the superior when he was overheard being nasty to the original experimenter the subjects had reason to dislike. Subjects were less willing to help when the superior was heard to be nice to their enemy! Curious as it may seem, these subjects seemed to be better disposed to somebody whom they had observed being nasty rather than pleasant, simply because he happened to have been nasty to one of their 'enemies'!

My enemy's enemy is my friend. One of the predictions of balance theories is that we should like those who cause harm to our enemies, even in the absence of other endearing qualities. This is indeed what the research by Aronson and Cope (see text) found.

Conclusions

These theories and studies illustrate quite nicely the development of research on interpersonal relationships in social psychology. Our first concern in this chapter was simply to explain the origins and character of the universal human need for social relationships. Later, we discussed the way 'attraction' may be defined, and surveyed the various empirical measures commonly used to assess attraction. We also had an opportunity to summarise some early research in this field. These early studies were predominantly carried out in natural settings (housing estates, student dormitories) and looked at real life relationships. With the emergence of various theories of interpersonal relationships, and the growing interest in relationships in the 1960s and 1970s, the research methods employed also changed. Instead of field studies, laboratory experiments became dominant, and more sophisticated techniques for studying attraction have been developed. As a result, we now have a far better idea about the various stages involved in a relationship than used to be the case. In the next chapter we shall look in more detail at research which seeks to evaluate the many factors which influence the development of attraction and relationships.

12. The development of personal relationships

12.
THE DEVELOPMENT OF PERSONAL RELATIONSHIPS

As a result of spending so much of our time in the company of others throughout our lives, we come to establish a very large number of relationships of differing duration and intensity. The pleasant chatting acquaintanceship with the grocer at the corner, the formal, polite relationship with one of our colleagues, the long-standing, hidden enmity towards our mother-in-law or the intense, deep friendship rooted in a shared childhood are all relationships which had a beginning, developed according to certain patterns, and eventually reached a steady equilibrium. Many of our other relationships failed to progress satisfactorily, and all that remain of them now are faded memories. We all have many such terminated relationships in our past. Why did that friendship at school, or the romantic relationship that started so promisingly, never develop as we expected at the time?

What sorts of things influence the progress (or failure) of personal relationships? Although every relationship we have is, of course, different from every other, can we identify general rules in their development? More precisely, what sort of factors play a role at different stages in the progression of a relationship? In this chapter we shall try to summarise the results of research on the variables affecting relationship development. Before we begin discussing these separate factors, we must first develop a general model of how relationships change.

A model of relationship development
As relationships progress, many things change: liking, intensity, trust, predictability, interdependence, to name but a few. But perhaps the most important universal characteristic of human relationships is the degree of involvement between the partners. Levinger and Snoek (1972) suggested that involvement is the single most important feature of a relationship, and they used this characteristic as the basis for their model of relationship development. We shall also rely on their simple but very

useful model as the background to our discussion of the factors affecting the progression of relationships.

Levinger and Snoek's (1972) model is based on the assumption that all relationships move between two theoretical extremes of relatedness between two people, ranging from no contact at all, to perfect mutuality or identity between the partners. Several stages along this continuum may be identified (see left-hand side of Figure 12.1): (a) zero contact, (b) unilateral awareness (when only one partner is aware of the other without actual interaction), (c) surface contact (involving superficial, impersonal interaction) and (d) mutuality (when some degree of real, in-depth interaction takes place). We shall briefly look at the characteristics of each of these stages below.

Level 1 relationships: the stage of unilateral awareness
This type of relationship involves only a bare minimum of contact between the partners, consisting simply of the one-sided awareness by one person of another, without any actual interaction. By far the majority of our social relationships are of this type: most people we 'know' only from a distance. The people sitting next to you in the bus, passers-by on a street, your favourite actor in the popular TV soap opera, the pretty woman wearing a striking dress just walking past your window: these are all level 1 relationships in terms of Levinger and Snoek's (1972) model. We perceive a person, react in one way or another (with approval, liking or disapproval), and usually pass on without ever exchanging a word.

Occasionally, such unilateral, level 1 relationships may nevertheless evolve into deep and involving experiences. Common examples are the relationship between a fan and a popstar, or the distant admirer and the famous actress. (John Hinckley, who attempted to assassinate President Reagan, claimed that his love for a screen actress and his wish to become famous and thus meet her were the reasons for his act.) But most commonly, level 1 relationships are brief, superficial and rarely lead to more intensive involvement. Despite the fact that level 1 relationships are usually minimal, they form the basis from which all our more involved relationships develop. What helped them to develop further? What influences how we react to people we only see briefly and superficially? We shall seek answers to these questions later in this chapter.

It is perhaps suprising that despite their superficiality, level 1 relationships have been among the most frequently studied ones in social psychology during the past decade or so. The reason for this is that level 1 relationships are extremely easy to create and manipulate in a laboratory. All we have to do is to show subjects some manipulated pictures, films, videotapes or descriptions of other people, and ask them how much (or little) they like such a person. This strategy has the

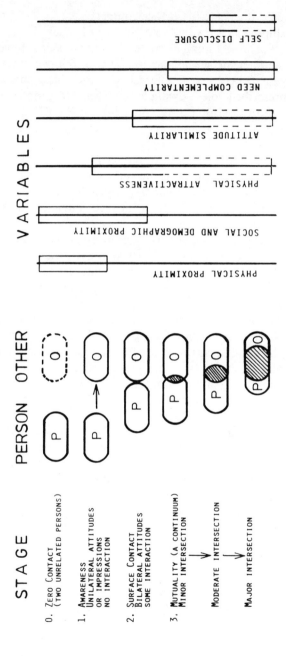

FIGURE 12.1 A model of relationship development. The left-hand side shows the stages in relationship development with increasing levels of involvement, the right-hand side illustrates the most important variables determining progress at each stage. (After Levinger and Snoek, 1972, p. 102).

advantage that it allows researchers to accurately control the various factors which may influence liking.

Level 2 relationships: the stage of surface contact

Of those relationships which involve some degree of actual interaction with others, by far the largest number are level 2 relationships. Levinger and Snoek (1972) defined surface contact as a relationship with minimal personal involvement, where people interact with each other mainly in terms of strictly prescribed roles. Examples of level 2 relationships are encounters with shop assistants, receptionists, box office clerks, insurance representatives or car salesmen. We tend to see these people not as distinct individuals in their own right, but as performers of certain prescribed roles, and our relation to them is also impersonal. Of course, other relationships may also remain at the surface contact level. If you come to see your aunt as just an 'aunt' and never develop a degree of involvement with her, this too could be a surface contact relationship even if it lasted for 25 years.

At such a surface level, the characteristics of a person which are likely to determine whether the relationship will progress further are largely directly observable surface characteristics. Features of the roles performed, dress, physical attractiveness, verbal and nonverbal signals such as eye contact, smiling, gestures and personal mannerisms have a major influence on how we react to such surface contacts. Because so many surface contact relationships take place within the commercial sphere, people performing these roles are often specially trained to elicit the most favourable response possible from clients and customers. Waitresses, telephonists, receptionists and sales clerks are often taught to use very positive verbal and nonverbal signals as part of their job.

Natural good looks, or physical attractiveness has a particularly important influence on surface contact relationships. In one controlled study, physical attractiveness was found to be the single best predictor of how much each person liked his/her assigned partner at a computer-matched dance, even after the couples had spent several hours together (Walster, Aronson, Abrahams and Rothman, 1966). Apart from good looks, none of the numerous other psychological tests given to participants was a good predictor of how much the partners would be attracted to each other. We shall discuss the role of physical attractiveness in relationships in more detail later.

Level 3 relationships: the stage of mutuality

In everyday language, we usually only really call level 3 relationships a 'relationship'. It is only at this level that some degree of real personal involvement and intimacy exists between the partners. In level 3 relationships, we see our partner as a unique individual, we understand and appreciate his/her private, subjective view of the world. There is an emotional, cognitive and behavioural mutuality: to a greater or lesser extent, the partners feel the same, think the same and act the same. Relationships develop to this level due to factors such as self-disclosure, similarity of attitudes and values, complementarity of personal needs and mutually valued personal characteristics. A particularly interesting aspect of developing mutuality is the emotional involvement between people. We still know very little about how the initial intensity of a first love, for example, develops into the later more even, deeper but perhaps less intense emotions typical of shared married life. Romantic relationships are also a special category of level 3 relationships which we shall consider in more detail in the next chapter.

In summary, Levinger and Snoek's (1972) model gives us a simple but very useful way of thinking about various human relationships. We shall refer back to this model in the rest of this chapter as we discuss the many factors which influence the progression of relationships along the continuum of involvement defined by Levinger and Snoek (1972) (see right-hand side of Figure 12.1). As we shall see, different factors come into play as a relationship progresses through the stages of unilateral awareness, surface contact and finally mutuality. To some extent, we may think about this process as if relationships were passing through a series of 'filters' as they develop, with different characteristics becoming critical at each stage of development. Try to keep this model in mind as we proceed to discuss each of these characteristics individually in the rest of the chapter.

The importance of establishing contact: physical proximity

Perhaps the most critical selection factor in our relationships is physical proximity. This is the variable which largely determines which of the

Another kind of love? The early intense emotional commitment may often give way to more even, but also cooler feelings in enduring heterosexual relationships such as marriage.

many people around us we will become aware of, who will transcend the boundary between level 0 (no relationship) to level 1 (unilateral awareness). Following the study of friendship formation on a housing estate by Festinger, Schachter and Back, described in the previous chapter, many other researchers have shown that being close in space is an important factor in relationships. Perhaps a study by Segal (1974) is the best illustration of this principle. In this investigation, newly arrived trainees at a police academy were allocated to classrooms and dormitories in strict alphabetical order. In other words, the closer two people were to each other in the alphabet, the nearer they sat to each other in the classroom, and the closer they were to each other in the dormitories. Six months later, each trainee was asked to nominate his closest friend in the academy. On the average, the best friend nominated was only 4.5 letters removed in the alphabet, confirming that spatial proximity had a major effect on the emerging friendship choices (see Figure 12.2 for results).

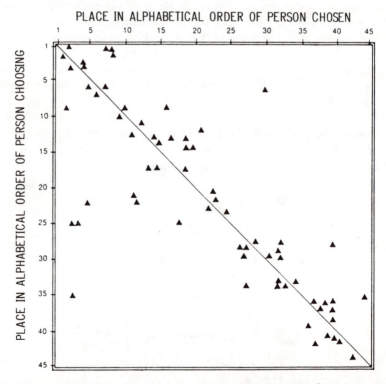

FIGURE 12.2 The effects of physical proximity on friendship. Spatial proximity between these police cadets was determined by allocation to classrooms and dormitories in strict alphabetical order. As the figure shows, they ended up choosing as friends people who were near to them in the alphabet, and thus in the classrooms and dormitories as well. (After Segal, 1974).

Social and demographic similarity

Of course, not everybody in our close physical environment becomes our friend. A second factor, social and demographic similarity, also plays an important filtering role in influencing whether unilateral awareness and surface contact develop between people. We are more likely to come across, and take notice of, people whose background, religion, occupation, status or financial position is similar to our own. Once we become aware of such people our relationship will be more likely to progress to at least surface contact level, than with people who come from different social and demographic backgrounds. It is a statistical fact that most friendships, marriages or romances involve people from extremely similar backgrounds. In a now classic study of a small town in the United States, 'Elmstown', Hollingshead and Redlich (1958) found that marriages, friendships, cliques, and school groupings were largely made up of people who came from very similar social and demographic backgrounds.

The importance of looking good: physical attractiveness

Physical attractiveness plays a major role in influencing whether a relationship will progress from no contact to level 1 (unilateral awareness), and from unilateral awareness to level 2 (surface contact). The visible characteristics of a person, foremost among them looks, are the basis on which people usually decide whether to engage in any interaction with others they become aware of. Just think, for a moment, of how important physical attractiveness can be in determining which of several girls boys will ask to dance, which of the many guests at a cocktail party you will seek out to talk to, or which of several idle shop assistants you will approach with a purchase! The way these people look is the major influence on such choices; not being chosen, by definition, also means an end to relationship development at the unilateral awareness stage.

What exactly does it mean to be physically attractive? Beauty is still largely in the eye of the beholder. There are no fixed scientific criteria which define attractiveness, and what is considered attractive today may not be so tomorrow. A brief glimpse at paintings from different ages will convince you that ideas of feminine beauty, for example, have undergone major changes throughout the centuries. Every age has its own ideas about what is considered attractive, and our own standards of physical attractiveness also change throughout our lives.

Beauty is indeed an elusive quality: even a minor change in facial expression can influence ratings of attractiveness (Mueser et al. 1984). Judgments of beauty also depend on our immediate basis for comparison: a female student was rated as less attractive than otherwise, immediately after her male raters watched 'Charlie's Angels', a TV show featuring very attractive women (Kenrick and Gutierres, 1980). The crucial thing about standards of attractiveness is that they are shared by people of a certain age, class, status, or geographic region. All those party to such standards know that looking 'good' is extremely important, and have no difficulty in evaluating each other's physical appearance.

Certain periods in our lives, such as adolescence, are marked by an almost obsessive concern with physical appearance. I can still remember the almost cosmic importance having the right hairstyle and clothes used to play in my adolescent years, and the amount of time boys and girls would spend in the restrooms during dances to work on keeping their appearance just right. Despite the obvious importance of looks in social life, psychologists were once again relatively late in studying this field. Research only began in earnest towards the late sixties, and by 1974 a voluminous literature on physical attractiveness existed. As recently as 1969, Aronson speculated about the reasons for this long neglect of physical attractiveness as follows: "It is difficult to be certain why the effects of physical attractiveness have not been studied more systematically. It may be that at some levels, we would hate to find evidence indicating that beautiful women are better liked than homely women — somehow this seems undemocratic" (1969, p. 160).

Although there are limits as to how much people can do about the way they look, researchers found exactly what Aronson suspected: that physical attractiveness plays a major role in how people are evaluated. Dion, Berscheid and Walster (1972) decided to find out "if a physical attractiveness stereotype exists, and if so, to investigate the content of the stereotype along several dimensions" (p. 72). The procedure was simple and typical of many later studies. Subjects were shown photographs of people who were previously classified as physically attractive, unattractive or average-looking, and were asked to rate them on a

TABLE 12.1
THE EFFECTS OF A PERSON'S PHYSICAL ATTRACTIVENESS ON PERCEPTIONS OF OTHER CHARACTERISTICS

Rated characteristics	Physical appearance of target*		
	Unattractive	Average	Attractive
Social desirability of personality	56.31	62.42	65.39
Occupational status	1.70	2.02	2.25
Marital competence	.37	.71	1.70
Parental competence	3.91	4.55	3.54
Social and professional happiness	5.28	6.34	6.37
Total happiness	8.83	11.60	11.60
Likelihood of marriage	1.52	1.82	2.17

*Higher numbers correspond to more positive judgments

After Dion, Berscheid and Walster, 1972, p. 288

number of different scales. Good-looking people were rated as better on almost every dimension except parental competence (see Table 12.1). Attractive people were thought to have better personalities, to be more happy and competent, to be more likely to marry — but average-looking people were thought to be the more competent parents. (One wonders why parenthood in particular was thought to be unrelated to good looks. Perhaps because handsome people find it easier to engage in alternative relationships?) These judgments are in themselves quite surprising, if you consider that the judges in fact knew absolutely nothing about the people they saw except how they looked! Their judgments obviously said something quite important about their own expectations and implicit personality theories, in which physical attractiveness clearly played a major role (see Chapter 4).

Physical attractiveness has many other advantages as well. Good-looking people often get preferential treatment in a variety of areas. Landy and Sigall (1974) found that the same essay will be evaluated more positively by men when the writer is presented as an attractive rather than a plain-looking woman (Table 12.2). It seems that we believe that 'what is beautiful is also good' (Dion et al. 1972). Good-looking people are also held less responsible for a transgression than unattractive people. Dion (1972) found that a transgression committed by an unattractive child was judged as more serious and more likely to occur again than the same transgression when committed by an attractive child (see also Activity 4.1). Efran (1974) asked students to play the role of a university court, and make decisions about other students charged with misconduct, such as cheating in an exam. The jurors were less likely to believe the charges, and awarded less severe sentences, when the defendant was good-looking.

TABLE 12.2
THE EFFECTS OF A FEMALE'S PHYSICAL ATTRACTIVENESS ON MALE
JUDGES' RATINGS OF AN ESSAY WRITTEN BY HER*

	Actual quality of the essay	Physical attractiveness of the writer			
		Attractive	Control	Unattractive	Total
Ratings of essay quality	Good essay	6.7	6.6	5.9	6.4
	Poor essay	5.2	4.7	2.7	4.2
	Total	6.0	5.5	4.3	
Ratings of writer's overall ability	Good essay	6.4	6.3	6.0	6.2
	Poor essay	5.7	4.7	3.4	4.6
	Total	6.5	5.6	4.7	

*Higher numbers indicate more positive evaluations on a scale 1 to 10
After Landy and Sigall, 1974, p. 302

However, there are some clear limits to the 'beautiful is good' assumption. When a person is seen to be using his/her good looks to get away with something, the judges are particularly severe on physically attractive people. Sigall and Ostrove (1975) found that an attractive person was given a more severe punishment when she used her attractiveness to commit a crime (swindle). However, the same person was treated more leniently than others when the crime, although serious, (burglary) was unrelated to her attractiveness. (See Table 12.3.) It even appears that a smile may have the same effect as attractiveness: smiling students were rated more favourably and given less severe punishments after a transgression than the same people when not smiling, in a recent study by Forgas, O'Connor and Morris (1983) (Table 12.4).

Why do people believe so strongly that good looks are associated with better personal characteristics? One possible explanation is that good looks create a 'halo effect', a phenomenon already discussed in Chapter 4. Could it also be that physically attractive people are *in fact* more competent and skilled? Is there a kernel of truth in the common belief

TABLE 12.3
THE EFFECTS OF A FEMALE'S PHYSICAL ATTRACTIVENESS ON
SENTENCES FOR CRIMES IN WHICH ATTRACTIVENESS DID (SWINDLE)
OR DID NOT (BURGLARY) PLAY A ROLE

Offence	Mean sentence preferred (in years) for		
	Attractive target	Unattractive target	Control target
Swindle	5.45	4.35	4.35
Burglary	2.80	5.20	5.10

After Sigall and Ostrove, 1975, p. 412

TABLE 12.4
THE EFFECTS OF FACIAL EXPRESSION ON RESPONSIBILITY
ATTRIBUTION AND THE EVALUATION OF A PERSON WHO
COMMITTED A TRANSGRESSION

Facial expression	Average judgments*	
	Responsibility attribution	Evaluation
Smiling	1.83	1.04
Not smiling	.715	– .60

*Higher numbers correspond to less responsibility attributed, and more positive evaluation

After Forgas, O'Connor and Morris, 1983

that what is beautiful is also good? Goldman and Lewis (1977) asked exactly this question. In their study, students who were previously rated for physical attractiveness had to talk to somebody of the opposite sex without actually seeing their partner (through a telephone). Each student was asked after the conversation to rate their (unseen) partner for likeability, anxiety, social skill, and to say how much they wanted to meet that person.

Surprisingly, results showed that better-looking people were indeed rated as more skilful and likeable than less attractive students by their partners, even without any visual contact. These results suggest that there may after all be something in the common bias towards attractive people. Although they may not be born superior, it could well be that good-looking people have better and more rewarding interactions with others from early childhood. As a result they may grow up to be more competent and likeable adults.

Birds of a feather flock together: attitude similarity and attraction
Once a relationship is established at at least the surface contact stage (level 2), there is scope for more personal, internal characteristics to come into play in influencing the development of that link. Perhaps the most important such influence in the early stages of a relationship is attitude similarity. Aristotle was already well aware of this tendency when he wrote: "they are friends who have come to regard the same things as good...who are friends of the same people...We like those who resemble us and are engaged in the same pursuits...(who) desire the same things as we" (1932, pp. 103-105). The field study by Newcomb, described in the last chapter, illustrates the link between attitudes and liking quite convincingly: students who held similar attitudes before moving into a housing unit were more likely to become friends later. The common saying that 'birds of a feather flock together' thus apparently has some foundation in reality.

Following Newcomb's field study, the influence of similar attitudes on liking has been also extensively studied in the social psychology laboratory. In a typical experiment, the subject's own attitudes are assessed on a separate occasion some time (often weeks) before he/she arrives for the experimental session. Subjects are then given to read manipulated information about another person who is presented as having either similar or dissimilar attitudes to themselves. Finally, they are asked to indicate how much they like that individual. Byrne has done an extensive series of investigations on this topic (Byrne, 1971), and has consistently found that the proportion of similar attitudes between a subject and a target person was strongly related to liking. This relationship holds across a variety of population groups and cultures, and is so powerful that it can even be expressed in a mathematical formula, as shown in Figure 12.3 (Byrne and Nelson, 1965).

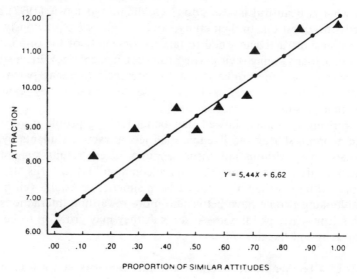

FIGURE 12.3 The link between attitude similarity and attraction. The proportion of shared attitudes is directly related to the attraction between people, as the above formula illustrates. (After Byrne and Nelson, 1965, p. 661)

In studies of this kind, the subject never actually meets the person he has to rate. In Levinger and Snoek's (1972) terms, the relationship is merely at the unilateral awareness level, with no prospect of face-to-face contact. The question arises: how far can we generalise from findings in such superficial relationships to what happens in the much more involved relationships which occur in real life? For example, would attitude similarity still predict attraction when the partners meet under extremely demanding and stressful circumstances? Griffitt and Veitch (1974) tried to test this possibility. They studied the developing patterns of attraction between 13 male volunteer subjects who were confined together for ten days in a simulated fall-out shelter. They were exposed to very stressful conditions, such as crowded, uncomfortable quarters, high temperature and humidity, and limited diet. Under such demanding conditions, one would expect that much more basic personal characteristics than attitude similarity would determine who was attracted to whom.

Quite surprisingly, the initial similarity of attitudes between the 13 volunteers as assessed on a 44 item questionnaire before they first met each other was, in fact, a very good predictor of friendship choices at the end of the simulation (see Figure 12.4). To see whether the similarity-attraction relationship is as strong as Byrne (1971) suggested, other researchers also turned to investigating real-life relationships. Kandel (1978) collected extensive information using a questionnaire from more than 1800 young people between the ages of 13 and 18. When she analysed the attitudes and values of subjects and their best friends, she found that they were again strongly related. Having similar attitudes and values is apparently an important part of a developing relationship.

But why exactly is attitude similarity so important in the progression of a relationship from level 2 to level 3? There are several possibilities. In terms of the cognitive balance theory of Heider (discussed in the previous chapter), we may simply like to see our own views and beliefs confirmed by others. According to learning theoretical formulations, those who think as we do are more likely to make us feel good, to give us positive reinforcement which we soon come to associate with such people. Just imagine a situation when you first meet somebody, and begin to talk about various topics. Most of the topics are in fact relevant to personal attitudes (attitudes towards joint acquaintances, life styles,

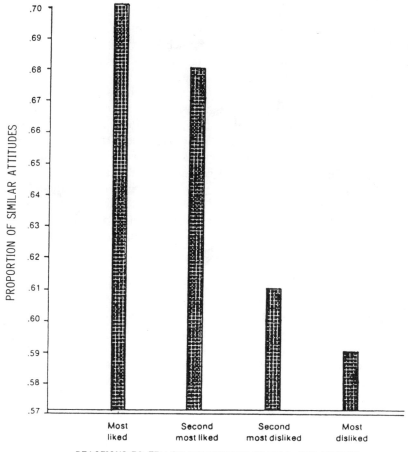

REACTIONS TO FELLOW VOLUNTEERS IN FALL-OUT SHELTER

FIGURE 12.4 Attitude similarity and attraction. Even after several days of demanding interaction in a simulated fall-out shelter, attitude similarity remained a very good predictor of friendship choices. (After Griffitt and Veitch, 1974, p. 170)

religion, food, drink, and so on). It is fairly obvious that the more a person agrees with you the more you will be attracted to him/her. It seems that this initial attraction may endure even in more involved relationships, as the study by Griffitt and Veitch showed.

Of course, it is not unimportant *which* of your attitudes are shared by your partner. In the study by Kandel (1978) mentioned above, friends were more likely to have similar attitudes towards drug use than towards their parents or their teachers. Would attitudes towards religion or sexual behaviour, for example, have equal importance in influencing attraction by males and females? Touhey (1972) looked at this possibility in a computer dating study, in which couples were assigned to each other so that they were either similar or dissimilar on attitudes towards either religion or sexuality. After a period of interaction, each person was asked how much they were attracted towards their partner. In general, couples whose attitudes were similar liked each other more than couples with dissimilar attitudes. But for women, attitudes towards religion played a much more important role than attitudes towards sexuality, and exactly the opposite was the case for men.

What is particularly intriguing is that attitude similarity predicts liking even in much more developed relationships, where people meet under prolonged and stressful circumstances, as in the Griffitt and Veitch (1974) study, or over a long time period of several months, as in the Newcomb study. Perhaps the relationship between attitude similarity and attraction endures simply because we rarely embark on a more intimate relationship with someone who has very different attitudes from the start. In other words, the requirement of attitude similarity acts as something like a filter at the early stages of a relationship. Few relationships develop without first clearing this hurdle, so it is not really surprising that longer or intense relationships are still predictable on the basis of early attitude similarity.

Of course, it is also possible that once a relationship is established, the partners come to develop an even greater degree of attitude similarity by influencing each other. Byrne and Blaylock (1963) found that married couples had reasonably similar attitudes, but believed that their partner's attitude was in fact much more similar to their own than in reality. Even if not actually influencing attitude similarity, a long-term relationship seems at least to predispose people to believe that their attitudes are more similar now than they were before.

Complementarity of needs
Research on attitude similarity thus by and large confirmed the popular belief that similarities attract each other. But there is an equally common contradictory belief that people who have dissimilar, complementary characteristics will be most attracted to each other in a close relationship — the 'opposites attract' principle. Which of these beliefs is really true?

We all know of couples or strong friendships where the very dissimilarity of the partners seems to be the main cohesive force in the relationship. In such a relationship people seem to complement each other.

The complementarity hypothesis was first developed by Winch (1958) who suggested that in finding a marriage partner, people may tend to select a mate who will satisfy their needs and complement their own inclinations. Extroverted and introverted, submissive and dominant, dependent and nurturing people may be attracted to each other as a means of satisfying their complementary needs. It is also possible that complementarity only develops as a relationship becomes established. In the course of living together, people may establish a 'modus vivendi' which capitalises on their differing personalities.

How can we reconcile the apparent conflict between the similarity and complementarity hypotheses? In an interesting longitudinal field study, Kerckhoff and Davis (1962) tried to accomplish just this. They recruited a large group of 'seriously attached' couples as their subjects, and assessed them on a large number of personality and attitude measures. Couples were also asked to indicate how satisfied they were with their relationship. Subjects were again contacted about six months later, and asked to indicate how their relationship had developed in the intervening period. Kerckhoff and Davis found that for those couples who had known each other for only a short period (less than 18 months) at the beginning of the study, attitude similarity was the best predictor of progress in the relationship. However, for couples who already had a long history (more than 18 months) at the beginning of the study, complementarity of personal needs was more important.

How can we explain these apparently conflicting results? Kerckhoff and Davis suggested a so-called 'filtering hypothesis' for relationship development. In the very first stages, superficial characteristics such as similar social and demographic backgrounds, spatial proximity and physical attractiveness are important in relationship development. Later, similar attitudes play a major role in deepening the bond between the couple. Only much later, with growing involvement, do complementary personal needs come to play a central role. The filtering hypothesis has a lot of intuitive appeal, and fits in very nicely with the kind of relationship development model proposed by Levinger and Snoek (1972). Unfortunately, it is very difficult to obtain hard evidence for such a filtering process, since it requires investigators to follow relationships over a long period of time.

Such longitudinal studies are rare and often problematic. Levinger, Senn and Jorgensen (1970) tried to replicate the results of Kerckhoff and Davis, but without success. They found that the best predictor of relationship success was the degree of reported involvement between the partners at the beginning of the study, and the extent to which they engaged in shared activities. Nevertheless, it is almost certain that the various factors influencing relationship development differ in importance at different times in a relationship. The exact sequence of these influences in a particular relationship probably depends on factors such as the partners' expectations (see next chapter) and the type of relationship.

Competence and attraction

Not surprisingly, most of us are more attracted towards people who are competent, intelligent and successful than to those who are incompetent, unintelligent and unsuccessful. Furthermore, this preference remains strong even when the observer or judge does not in any way benefit from the competence of a future partner. It seems as if intelligence and competence have the same sort of halo effects associated with them as physical attractiveness. Of course, it is possible to have too much of a good thing. People who are extremely competent are not necessarily endearing, and their ability may be seen as threatening, leading to dislike. In fact, our liking for such super-competent people may *increase* after they have made a mistake or committed a blunder, since this makes them more human (and more like ourselves?).

There are some interesting examples for such processes. Aronson (1976) noted the paradox that Kennedy's popularity actually increased after a major blunder, the Bay of Pigs fiasco. "Kennedy was young, handsome, bright, witty, charming and athletic; he was a voracious reader, a master political strategist, a war hero... he had a beautiful wife... two cute kids ... and a talented, close-knit family. Some evidence of fallibility (like being responsible for a major blunder) could have served to make him more human in the public eye, and hence, more

The effects of a blunder on attraction. Committing a minor blunder by a highly competent person can make that individual more attractive. Major blunders by less competent people usually have very different consequences!

likeable" (Aronson, 1976, p. 224). Aronson, Willerman and Floyd (1966) tried to examine this process under more controlled laboratory conditions. Their subjects were asked to rate for attractiveness candidates seeking to represent the university in a competition. There were two manipulations. One candidate was shown to have superior competence and ability, answering 92 per cent of the questions correctly, and the other was of average ability, giving only 30 per cent correct answers. In addition, half the subjects in each condition learned that the candidate committed a minor blunder by spilling coffee over himself.

Results showed that, in accordance with expectations, the more able candidate was generally liked more. But how did the minor blunder (spilling coffee) influence the attractiveness of the candidates? Paradoxically, the superior candidate was liked even more after the coffee-spilling incident, while the average candidate was evaluated more negatively after the blunder (see Table 12.5). In the absence of other information, it seems that we like competent people, and like them even more if they display the universal human ability to make mistakes!

TABLE 12.5
THE EFFECTS OF COMMITTING A BLUNDER ON LIKING FOR A
SUPERIOR AND AN INFERIOR CANDIDATE

	Mean attraction scores: (higher scores indicate greater liking)	
	Blunder	No blunder
Superior ability candidate	30.1	20.8
Average ability candidate	−2.5	17.8

After Aronson, Willerman and Floyd, 1966

Self-esteem and attraction
Attraction and self-esteem are also closely related. Being liked by other people provides one of the most important sources of positive self-evaluations, and during periods of self-doubt and low self-esteem, we particularly value and appreciate positive relations with others. Walster (1965) demonstrated this connection in an ingenious experiment. Her female subjects were approached by a good-looking male confederate of the experimenter while waiting for the experiment, who indicated that he was attracted to them, and asked them for a date. During the actual experiment, the female subjects were either made to feel good about themselves or bad about themselves, by being given positive or negative feedback about their performance on some tests. At the end of the experiment, among other things, they were asked how much they liked the man they had encountered in the waiting room. Those who were made insecure by negative feedback on their tests liked the young man much more than those women whose self-esteem had been increased.

Our level of self-esteem also plays a role in decisions about the kind of people we seek out as partners. When you feel 'low' and insecure, it can be particularly devastating to be rejected, so it is a wise strategy to play it safe, and approach partners likely to react positively. Kiesler and Baral (1970) found that males whose self-esteem had been 'boosted' made romantic overtures to a highly attractive rather than an unattractive female. Male subjects whose self-esteem had been deflated in contrast preferred an unattractive rather than an attractive female partner, with whom their chances of success were presumed to be higher. Liking from others thus seems most valuable and likely to be reciprocated when our self-esteem is low, and we are likely to select our partners with this very much in mind.

Positive personal characteristics and attraction
Apart from personal characteristics such as competence or self-esteem, discussed above, a whole range of other personal attributes may influence how much we like a person. By and large, we reward 'good' characteristics with liking, and 'bad' characteristics with dislike. What sorts of characteristics are thought to be likeable or dislikeable can be fairly easily established, simply by asking a large number of people to give us their judgments of the 'likeability' of various personal features. Norman Anderson (see Chapter 4) did just this, calculating a mean likeableness value for each of 555 personal characteristics (see also Chapter 5 on impression formation). There are great individual differences in the estimation of how likeable characteristics are. Honesty and truthfulness are generally highly valued, but individuals may well select different characteristics as being on the top of their private 'likeableness' lists (see Activity 12.1).

ACTIVITY 12.1
What is Likeable?

Write down on a piece of paper the five characteristics which in your opinion are most likeable, and the five characteristics which you think are most dislikeable in other people. You may find it interesting to compare your judgments with Anderson's list (extract shown in Chapter 4, Table 4.3). Anderson collected the average likeability ratings of 555 different personal characteristics.

Reciprocity and attraction
The almost universal tendency to prefer balanced relationships to imbalanced ones is also a strong influence on attraction. When we learn

that somebody likes us, our automatic reaction is to be also positively inclined towards that person. In turn, showing liking for somebody is one of the best ways to ensure that they will like us in return. In one study, members of a discussion group were informed that certain other members liked them. When given a chance to form smaller groups, people showed reciprocal liking by preferring to work with those who liked them (Secord and Backman, 1964). Of course reciprocity works both ways. We not only like those who like us, but also dislike those who dislike us. The tendency to reciprocate attraction is so strong that many commercial enterprises try to capitalise on it. By training employees to express superficial signs of liking towards their clients (for example, smiles, gaze and positive verbal messages), it is more likely that clients will reciprocate, and come to see the organisation in a more positive light.

Gain and loss effects in relationships
Such automatic reactions of reciprocity are most characteristic of fairly superficial, level 1 (unilateral awareness) or level 2 (surface contact) relationships. Once a relationship becomes somewhat more established, the evaluations we receive from our partners and our attraction towards them is likely to depend on factors other than reciprocity, and may undergo major fluctuations, sometimes over brief periods of time. An interesting question is how such changes in liking from others influence our attraction towards them. Do we like somebody who always had, and continues to have, a positive attitude towards us, more than a person who only came to like us after an initially negative reaction? According to simple reinforcement theory, we should like the first person more, since we have received more positive reinforcement from him/her over the time involved. But things are not quite so simple. Often, we place greater value on positive affect from somebody who started out disliking us, and conversely, we dislike more a person who was once our friend than somebody with whom we never had a good relationship.

Such changes in the attraction level of a relationship were labelled gain-loss effects by Aronson. It is possible to evaluate the gain-loss hypothesis experimentally, by giving subjects personal evaluations in various sequence orders. Aronson and Linder (1965) in an ingenious experiment allowed subjects allegedly doing a learning task to 'overhear' evaluations of themselves by their partner, who was in fact a confederate of the experimenter. These evaluations were either always positive or always negative, or positive followed by negative (loss condition), or negative followed by positive (gain condition). Afterwards, subjects were asked to indicate how much they liked their partners. Results showed that people were more attracted to a partner who gave positive evaluations only later (gain condition) than to a consistently positive evaluator, and disliked their partner in the 'loss' condition (positive followed by negative) more than a consistently negative partner (Table 12.6).

Such gain-loss effects may be quite common in everyday life. Sometimes, changes in nonverbal expressions alone are sufficient to elicit such paradoxical reactions. In a study by Clore, Wiggins and Itkin (1975), subjects watched a videotape in which attraction was signalled nonverbally. A cold-warm sequence of nonverbal reactions was rated as expressing more attraction than a consistently warm performance. However, both of these studies looked at gain-loss effects in shortlived, level 1 or level 2 relationships. What sort of role do these effects play in long-term relationships, such as marriages or friendships? Aronson (1976) speculated that in most typical marriages, attraction is by far the highest at the early romantic stages of the relationship, and these positive sentiments often decline in the later stages. This common 'loss' pattern may lead to a disproportionate decrease in attraction, which in turn may account for some marriage break-ups (see Chapter 13).

TABLE 12.6
GAIN AND LOSS EFFECTS ON ATTRACTION

Relationship history	Measure of Liking*
Negative followed by positive reactions	7.67
Positive followed by positive reactions	6.42
Negative followed by negative reactions	2.52
Positive followed by negative reactions	.87

*The higher the numbers, the greater the liking

After Aronson and Linder, 1965, p. 163

Self-disclosure

Once a relationship develops to the stage of surface contact or mutuality, one of the more important driving forces in its further development is the amount of self-disclosure the partners undertake. Telling your partner about yourself, and finding out about him/her is a powerful method for deepening a relationship. But self-disclosure is a more complicated process than it first appears. Who can disclose what to whom at which stage of a relationship is governed by finely tuned rules and expectations. Research on self-disclosure was pioneered by Jourard, who constructed the Jourard Self-Disclosure Questionnaire. This questionnaire consists of 60 personal conversation topics, and subjects are typically asked to select in which order they would feel comfortable talking about different topics with different sorts of potential partners.

Using this method, Jourard showed that in most people's minds there exists a clear hierarchy of 'disclosability'. Certain topics, largely to do with the weather, public issues, tastes, interests, attitudes, work, etc. are quite readily disclosed. Other topics, to do with financial matters, our bodies, personality or sexuality are usually not disclosed unless the relationship is already highly intimate. There are also important sex differences in who discloses to whom. Women disclose most to their mothers, followed by female friends, male friends and then fathers, in that order, whereas men disclose most to their mothers, male friends, fathers and only then women friends. The amount disclosed also varies with the liking between two people.

The ability to disclose about ourselves is very important for normal adjustment, according to Jourard. It is through self-disclosure that we obtain the kind of supportive, intimate social contacts without which life would be intolerable. The empirical finding that males tend to disclose much less than females may point to a major cause of stress and illness in males. "The time is not far off when it will be possible to demonstrate with adequately controlled experiments the nature and degree of correlation between level and amount of self-disclosure, proneness to illness, and/or death at an early stage" speculated Jourard (1964, p. 48).

Jourard also suggested that self-disclosure plays a particularly important role in relationship development: "once contact has been made between two persons, they proceed to 'uncover' themselves one to the other at a mutually regulated pace. It is generally true that intimate self-disclosure begets intimate self-disclosure, while impersonality begets impersonality" (Jourard, 1971, p. 17). Even more, self-disclosure may be the prime means by which surface contact relationships can be transformed into mutuality. It is through intimate self-disclosure that "strangers performing roles in relation to each other transmute their relationship to one that is more 'personal' where increased closeness is tolerated if not welcomed" (Jourard, 1971 p. 140). It seems now well established that for any given relationship, there exists a tolerated and expected 'optimum' level of self-disclosure. Gradual, slow increases in this level, if mutual, will help to deepen and develop the relationship.

Major and non-reciprocal increases in self-disclosure, however, could have the opposite effect. Rubin (1973) reports an experiment looking at the effects of low, medium and high levels of self-disclosure on attraction in a surface contact relationship. His subjects were passengers who were waiting in an airport lounge. These people were approached by the experimenters, and asked to make judgments about a person on the basis of how his handwriting looked on a piece of paper. In fact, the handwriting was always the same, but the content of the script was different. Sometimes it contained low, sometimes medium, and sometimes highly intimate self-disclosing information. Results showed that the high self-disclosing individual was not necessarily judged as the most attractive. In fact, medium levels of self-disclosure resulted in greater liking than either very high, or very low self-disclosure.

We repeated this experiment a few years ago, using tape recordings rather than written messages as the stimuli. Subjects were asked to rate a person on the basis of his/her voice quality on a tape recording. In fact, the voice was always the same, but the content of what was said was again varied to range from low disclosure (for example, talking about the weather) to high disclosure (for example, talking about personal sexual problems) topics. Our results were essentially identical to those of Rubin. Medium-disclosing targets were liked more than either too high or too low-disclosing targets. It seems then that we make an almost automatic evaluation of what constitutes acceptable self-disclosure in a particular relationship. Too little is just as negatively evaluated as too much. Presumably, somebody who discloses very intimate information too soon is avoided because we think that he/she is either maladjusted, or expects similar high levels of intimacy from us which we may not yet be ready for. Both of these alternatives mean that the high discloser is threatening, and is disliked as such.

Since in a normal relationship the regulated, gradual development of self-disclosure intimacy is very important, the question arises: how do we manage the complex task of negotiating and coordinating our self-disclosure strategies with our partners? Davis (1976) proposed that there are three alternative possibilities: (a) partners may compete for disclosure control, a situation likely to arise when investment in the relationship is large; (b) they may cooperate in jointly determining their desired level of intimacy after explicitly discussing it; (c) one of the partners may adopt the role of 'manager' of the relationship, initiating gradually increasing levels of self-disclosure. In a study of these alternative processes, Davis (1976) found that in the absence of any other instructions, subjects tend to adopt the third strategy. One of the partners tends to assume responsibility for proposing topics of increasing intimacy. The other partner tacitly accepts this arrangement. When partners are encouraged to explicitly discuss the issue of intimacy, the second, democratic strategy in self-disclosure is most often adopted.

Self-disclosure is thus one of the most important determinants of relationship development, particularly in the achievement of increasing levels of mutuality. Cultural norms play a major role in regulating the

Too much of a good thing? Self-disclosure begets self-disclosure, and can be a major force in helping a relationship to develop. Too much or inappropriately intimate self-disclosure has the opposite effect, making the partner wary and defensive.

level and extent of self-disclosure between various categories of partners. Sexual and demographic differences as well as the need for reciprocity also exert an important influence on who can disclose what to whom. The self-disclosure process must be implicitly managed by one of the partners, or by both of them jointly. Perhaps most importantly, the ability to disclose intimate information about ourselves seems to be a psychological necessity, a prerequisite for healthy mental adjustment.

Summary and conclusions
In this chapter we discussed some of the most important stages and influences on the development of a relationship. Following the model proposed by Levinger and Snoek (1972), we may think about relationships as characterised by a particular level of involvement and intimacy between the two hypothetical extremes of no contact at all or complete mutuality. As a relationship slowly develops from unilateral awareness through surface contact to increasing degrees of mutuality, the variables influencing this progression also slowly change (Figure 12.1). Most of the factors we discussed here have a critical influence on relationship development at a particular stage only, although they may continue to play a role in relationship maintenance at other stages.

Social and demographic similarity, for example, are critical in enabling unilateral awareness and surface contact to occur — but even in a highly involved relationship, having a similar background will continue to play a facilitating role. Similarly, physical attractiveness is most important in helping unilateral awareness to turn into surface contact. Yet even in marriages of many years standing, the physical attractiveness of the partners often continues to play an important role in the maintenance of the relationship. As Sigall and Landy (1973) showed, a male seen with a highly attractive female will be evaluated more positively than the same person without attractive company. Attitude similarity, need complementarity, competence, positive personal characteristics and self-disclosure will become more and more important as a relationship progresses from surface contact to increasing levels of mutuality.

As we have seen, relationship development involves a sequence of complex interactions, where partners gradually come to know and get involved with each other. Following Kerckhoff and Davis (1962), we may compare this process to a multi-stage filter. At each stage, the relationship may fail to clear the hurdle and cease to develop. But after each filter, there is another even more demanding one to clear. Eventually we reach a level in a relationship when long-term, permanent commitment becomes a feature of our contacts. Such intimate relationships, be they with a lover, a spouse or a best friend play a very special role in our lives. We shall discuss some of the characteristics of intimate relationships in the next chapter.

13. Intimate relationships

13.

INTIMATE RELATIONSHIPS

Intimate relationships with other people are perhaps the most involving experiences in our lives. To fall in love, to have good friends, to get on well with our parents, children and siblings are exceedingly important for all of us. To have good relationships with others is considered by most people as more essential for their happiness than almost anything else in their lives. This is also substantiated by empirical research. Campbell, Converse and Rodgers (1976) surveyed people about how important various things were to them. They found that financial and work achievement were less important to most of their respondents than having good friends and a happy marriage and family life.

There is also considerable evidence suggesting that the absence of such supporting intimate relationships may have serious consequences for individuals. Statistics prepared by the American Council of Life Insurance (1978) strikingly indicate that lonely or unattached people are much more likely to suffer from health problems such as strokes, tuberculosis, cancer, alcoholism and accidents, and have higher mortality and suicide rates than people who are married and live in a network of intimate relationships. The ending of an intimate relationship, for example through divorce or the death of a parent, friend or spouse is one of the most stressful life experiences we can have. In this chapter we shall look at some of the characteristics of intimate relationships, beginning with one that is of particular importance to most of us: romantic love.

Romantic love
In the previous two chapters we considered interpersonal attraction and the development of relationships in very general terms, without differentiating between the many different types of relationships people have. We argued that the common characteristic of most valued relationships is the existence of a positive attitude, liking, respect or regard towards the partner. But some of our relationships go much

247

further: they involve far more intense emotions. It is now time to take a closer look at a very special kind of relationship which in many ways differs from all others: romantic love. Romantic relationships are among the most formative, intense and memorable of human experiences. However, the subjective experience of love is exceedingly difficult to measure. As a consequence, social psychologists have been far more interested in studying the social and psychological factors which influence the origins and development of love rather than the nature of the experience itself.

Liking and loving

We have already seen in Chapter 11 that there are several different ways of measuring interpersonal liking. The question arises, do these techniques also measure love? Rubin (1973) suggested that loving and liking should be thought of as "moderately correlated, but nevertheless distinct dimensions of one person's attitude towards another person"

ACTIVITY 13.1
Loving and Liking

Please indicate how well each of the following statements reflects your real feelings towards your (a) current, or most recent romantic partner, and (b) your best friend. Use a seven point scale for each judgment, where 1 = I don't agree with statement at all, and 7 = I completely agree with this statement.

	My best friend	My romantic partner
	Name	Name. . . . .
1. If he/she were unhappy, it would be my duty to cheer him/her up.	. . .	. . .
2. I think that he/she is very well-balanced.	. . .	. . .
3. I feel that I can tell him/her about everything that happens to me.	. . .	. . .
4. I think he/she would do very well in a responsible job.	. . .	. . .

---

5. There is almost nothing I
   wouldn't do for him/her.   . . .   . . .

6. I believe he/she is an
   unusually mature person.   . . .   . . .

7. I often feel possessive
   toward him/her.   . . .   . . .

8. His/her judgments are
   usually correct.   . . .   . . .

9. I would feel very depressed
   if I could not be with
   him/her.   . . .   . . .

10. I think that I am quite
    similar to him/her.   . . .   . . .

11. I find it easy to forgive
    him/her for almost
    anything.   . . .   . . .

12. He/she is a very intelligent
    person.   . . .   . . .

Now you can analyse your scores by adding up your replies separately for even and uneven numbered questions, and for your best friend and your romantic partner separately. Write these numbers in the following spaces below:

Total of answers to uneven
questions (1,3,5,7,9,11)   . . .   . . .

Total of answers to even
questions (2,4,6,8,10,12)   . . .   . . .

In fact, the uneven numbered questions are very similar to items in Rubin's (1973) love scale, and the even numbered questions to items in his liking scale, designed to discriminate between these two kinds of relationships. Accordingly, you should get a higher score on the love scale (uneven questions) for your romantic partner, and the liking scale (even questions) for your best friend. At least this is what Rubin found with a large group of subjects. After reading the section below, you may want to have another careful look at each of the questions to get a better idea of what sorts of characteristics best differentiate between liking and loving.

After Rubin, 1973

The importance of being married. Satisfactory long-term intimate relationships, such as marriage and friendship, are more important to most people than almost anything else in their lives.

(p. 215). Rubin undertook to develop an attitude scale which would measure love as distinct from liking. He began by collecting a large number of items relevant to romantic relationships, which he organised into a 'love scale'. He suggested that love has three characteristics which distinguish it form mere liking: (a) *caring*, or concern with the other person's happiness and well-being; (b) *attachment*, or the need to be with and be cared for by the person; and (c) *intimacy*. Liking in contrast is more often characterised by (a) *positive evaluation* and high regard and respect for the partner, and (b) the assumption that the partner is *similar* to ourselves.

Rubin (1973) gave both the 'love scale' and the 'liking scale' to numerous dating couples, asking them to indicate how they felt about their romantic partner as well as their best friend on both scales. As expected, romantic partners were rated higher on the love scale, and best friends on the liking scale, suggesting that Rubin's scales indeed discriminate between these two kinds of close relationships. Other studies showed that scores on the love scale better predicted the expectation that a couple would marry than scores on the liking scale. Scores on the love scale were also associated with observable behavioural differences. In one study, Rubin observed couples from behind a one-way mirror while they allegedly waited for an experiment to begin. Those couples who scored high on the love scale showed greater nonverbal interest in each other, and gazed at each other more frequently, than couples who scored relatively low on the love scale.

Another feature of romantic love is that it has a sexual component which is missing from mere liking relationships. Dermer and Pyszczynski (1978) were interested to see whether sexual arousal influenced ratings more on the love scale than on the liking scale. Their male subjects were asked to rate their girlfriends on both the love scale and the liking scale, after being sexually aroused by reading a description of the sexual fantasies and behaviour of a female student. Sexual arousal led to an increase in the men's romantic attraction towards their partners, as measured by the love scale, but not their liking reactions, as measured by the liking scale.

Exclusivity is also an important component of romantic love not usually associated with mere liking. This sometimes means that an intensive romantic relationship may come to dominate a person's social life, to the detriment of other kinds of relationships. In a recent study, Milardo et al. (1983) found that couples in the later, more involved stages of courtship "interact with fewer people, less often, and for shorter periods of time" (p. 964) than do less involved couples. Interestingly, the stability of many romantic relationships seems less dependent on equity than is the case with other relationships. The relative gains and losses that partners derive from their romantic liason may continue to be inequitable for prolonged periods of time (Lujansky and Mikula, 1983).

Romantic attraction thus seems to be an identifiably different kind of attraction from liking. But romantic love itself is not an unchanging feeling. We all know from experience that our feelings towards a romantic partner may fluctuate, and the initial highly intense, emotional experience with time becomes a more even, and perhaps deeper feeling of attachment. Walster and Walster (1978) suggested exactly such a distinction between two types of love: passionate love and companionate love. Passionate love is intense and absorbing, while companionate love is a more balanced, affectionate emotion often typical of enduring romantic relationships. In both kinds of love, however, emotional

Liking and loving are not the same! Romantic love is a very different kind of attraction from mere liking. It is characterised by emotional intensity, caring, attachment, involvement, exclusivity and intimacy, while liking is more likely to involve esteem, positive evaluation and similarity between the partners.

reactions are very important, and require an explanation which goes beyond our conventional definition of liking as a simple attitude.

Theories of romantic love

Romantic love seems to be an emotion which is quite distinct from other forms of interpersonal attraction. If love is an emotion, however, it is likely that it is influenced by exactly the same kinds of processes as other emotions. In Chapter 6 on self-attribution we discussed Schachter and Singer's two-factor theory of emotions. According to this model, emotions consist of two components: physiological arousal, and a cognitive label we attach to that arousal, interpreting it as a particular emotion in the light of the available information at the time. Applying the same idea to romantic love, we may expect that love also consists of these two separate components: arousal and cognitive labelling.

In other words, 'being in love' is not a basic form of human experience. We must 'learn' to identify the cues which make it appropriate to label our emotional arousal 'love'. Such cues are, for example, in our culture the existence and availability of a single heterosexual partner who is not available to others (exclusivity). What can be labelled love also depends on our surrounding culture. At other places and at other times, the dominant definition of what constitutes love may have been very different. At first it may be hard to accept such a labelling theory, since most of us like to believe that the experience of love is a unique, readily identifiable feeling. We simply 'know' when we are in love without needing to search for appropriate cues to interpret our arousal as Schachter and Singer proposed.

Based on Schachter and Singer's ideas, Berscheid and Walster (1974) proposed a theory of romantic love using the same self-attribution framework. They defined love as also consisting of two components, (a) arousal, and (b) appropriate cues indicating to the person that the arousal may be labelled 'love'. The model implies that the stronger the physiological arousal a person experiences, *whatever its source*, the more he/she would feel in 'love', if the surrounding cues are right. In other words, any arousal state can lead to an increase in romantic feelings, as long as we attribute the arousal to a romantic source. Several experimenters tried to create situations in which arousal caused by some external factor was matched by situational cues indicating the appropriateness of the 'love' label.

Dutton and Aron (1974) used such a procedure. Male subjects were interviewed by either an attractive woman (love label appropriate) or another man (love label inappropriate) in an arousing situation (after walking across a swaying suspension bridge) or a non-arousing situation (walking across a stable bridge). Results confirmed Berscheid and Walster's (1974) theory: subjects were more attracted to the woman when they encountered her in the arousing situation, whereas feelings towards the male partner were not influenced by arousal. In a second study, Dutton and Aron (1974) found that male subjects who were aroused by the expectation of an electric shock were also more attracted to a female confederate than subjects who did not receive the arousal manipulation. However, these studies are not entirely conclusive. Since in both situations arousal was caused by fear or anxiety, the female partner may have been liked more because her presence was rewarding and reduced anxiety, rather than because of any real attraction.

More recently, White, Fishbein and Rutstein (1981) reported two experiments suggesting that misattribution of arousal can indeed facilitate romantic experiences. In the first study, arousal was manipulated through a neutral procedure, exercise. Male subjects who were either aroused or non-aroused by prior physical exercise saw a videotape of a female student they expected to meet later, who looked and behaved either in an attractive, or a non-attractive way. In the attractive condition, she said that "she was looking forward to meeting people in general, and the subject in particular, and that she had no current boyfriend." She wore form-fitting attractive clothes, and had her face and hair made up. In the unattractive condition, "she wore loose-fitting, unattractive clothes; had the sniffles; covered her head with a scarf...and gave a generally dull delivery" (p.57). Subjects were then asked to rate the female they saw in terms of (a) general personality traits, (b) how much they liked her, and (c) how romantically attracted they were to her. Aroused subjects were more attracted to the attractive female, and less attracted to the unattractive female, than were subjects who were not aroused (see Table 13.1).

TABLE 13.1
THE EFFECTS OF AROUSAL ON ROMANTIC ATTRACTION TOWARDS AN ATTRACTIVE OR AN UNATTRACTIVE FEMALE

Condition	Reactions to the female*		
	Judgments of personality traits	Liking scores	Romantic attraction scores
Highly attractive female			
— aroused subjects	98.15	28.54	32.38
— non-aroused subjects	86.63	25.13	26.06
Unattractive female			
— aroused subjects	58.69	12.62	9.38
— non-aroused subjects	68.50	17.42	15.08

*The higher the score the more favourable the response.
After White, Fishbein and Ruttstein, 1981, p. 59

This study shows not only that arousal can lead to romantic attraction if the target is appropriate, but also the opposite: unattractive targets are judged much more negatively by aroused than unaroused people! It appears that aroused subjects probably misattributed their arousal as romantic attraction when the female target was attractive, and as repulsion or dislike when the target was unattractive. A second study by White et al. (1981), using positive (humorous) or negative (gory) videotapes as arousal manipulation also confirmed these findings. Of course, these experiments are pretty far removed from the involvement and complexity of everyday romantic relationships. The plausibility of the two-factor theory of romantic love largely depends on specifying the conditions necessary for genuine misattribution of arousal to occur. This probably requires the study of real-life relationships. There is some evidence from such studies that misattribution of arousal can indeed facilitate romantic love, as we shall see in the next section.

Frustration and attraction: the Romeo and Juliet effect
One of the most frequent sources of arousal in everyday life is frustration. When lovers find that there are obstacles in their way, that financial, religious or parental pressures are at work against their relationship, the reaction is often increased love and attachment. Indeed, many classic works of Western art and literature illustrate this principle. The story of Romeo and Juliet is perhaps the best known example. In terms of Berscheid and Walster's (1974) theory, it may be that the arousal such frustrations cause is reinterpreted as increased romantic involvement by the partners.

The effects of external obstacles on the intensity of a romantic relationship were investigated by Driscoll, Davis and Lipetz (1972). These authors asked 91 married couples, and 49 dating couples to complete a number of scales, measuring romantic love, trust, companionship and the degree of parental interference. For the couples already married, there was no relationship between parental interference and love, but for the unmarried couples, those reporting parental interference also expressed stronger romantic attachment. In a later follow-up study, Driscoll and his colleagues also found that changes in parental interference were correlated with changes in romantic attachment, clearly supporting the existence of a 'Romeo and Juliet effect'.

Perhaps we should note here that in the case of the couples studied by Driscoll et al., a period of negative reactions from parents had already been successfully resisted by the time of the study. Undoubtedly many promising relationships are never allowed to take sufficiently deep root for such a Romeo and Juliet effect to occur. Perhaps we may coin the term 'Montague and Capulet effect' to describe those external influences on a romantic relationship which succeed in breaking it up before really strong ties are established. But once such an initial onslaught is survived, it seems likely that externally caused frustrations strengthen instead of weaken a romantic involvement.

Towards a general model of intimate relationships
Romantic love is just one form of close involvement between people, although perhaps the most intense one. Many other close relationships play dominant roles in our lives: friendships, maternal and paternal love, and so on. How can we best describe the characteristic differences between different kinds of close relationships? You may remember that the model of relationship development proposed by Levinger and Snoek (Chapter 12) had relatively little to say about how relationships progress once the stage of mutuality is reached. In a more recent paper, Levinger (1980) himself raised the question: "How can we measure gradations of mutual interdependence? What are the suitable indicators of high versus low P-O (person-other) intersection?" (p.514). He suggested that close relationships are by and large characterised by three distinct qualities: "moments of intense affection, broad areas of behavioural interdependence, and long-term enduringness" (p.512).

There is indeed some empirical evidence that supports this view. Rands and Levinger (1979) asked their subjects to rate the probabilities of different behaviours occurring between couples who differed both in closeness and sex composition. Their judgments suggested that they discriminated between different kinds of relationships in terms of two major attributes: affective interdependence, and behavioural interdependence. In other words, the closer the relationship, the greater the number and range of joint behavioural activities, and the greater the emotional involvement and interdependence between the couple. Sexual composition also plays a role: male couples are rated as less affectively interdependent than female or heterosexual couples. Increasing mutuality does not only mean growing positive feelings, however: mutual criticism and periodic hostility are also an important part of becoming intimate. As couples come to negotiate and define their mutual needs and activities conflict is sometimes inevitable (Huston and Burgess, 1979). The give-and-take of intimate relationships has often been analysed in terms of exchange theory (see Chapter 11), a model which assumes that the costs and benefits associated with various moves have a determining influence on the progress of a relationship (Kelley, 1979).

Taking several of these processes into consideration, Levinger (1980) proposed a five-stage model of long-term relationships, summarised by the ABCDE mnemonic. Phase A "refers to *attraction* at an early stage in a relationship. B pertains to the *building* of a relationship. C denotes a period of *continuation*, the midstage of a developed relationship. This may take several forms, such as (a) continuing growth to a satisfying interdependence, (b) a congenial but bland coexistence, or (c) an unstable, fluctuating relationship. D means the *decline* or deterioration of a relationship. Finally, E is the *ending*; it signifies breakup through death or some other form of separation" (p.521).

Figure 13.1 gives a hypothetical illustration of some possible developmental paths for long-term relationships. It must be noted that the 'involvement' shown in Figure 13.1 on the vertical axis by definition only reflects the perspective of one of the partners. There are likely to be large differences in involvement between the partners, particularly in the 'building' and 'deterioration' stages of a relationship. In terms of this model, most of the research we discussed in the previous chapter concerns the attraction and building phases. We know far less about the continuation, deterioration and ending of relationships. At every phase of relationship progression, we are also influenced by the common habits and definitions of our culture which finds expression in relationship 'scripts'.

Cultural influences on relationship 'scripts'
Romantic relationships, as well as other intimate relationships, may be classified into various distinct categories. Up to this point, we have paid little attention to differences between unique relationship types. Yet it is quite clear that different relationship categories such as a 'one night stand', an 'engagement for several years', a 'platonic relationship with an older partner' or a 'marriage of 20 years' represent very different expectations and scenarios. In every culture, there exists a finite number of commonly recognised relationship scenarios. When we meet a new person for the first time, we quickly develop a definition of the probable course of the relationship. We do this on the basis of our relationship repertoire, the available range of relationship types with which we are familiar. Such relationship definitions are usually shared by members of our culture. One of the most interesting tasks in relationship research is to develop classifications of relationship types, and to study how such expectations influence the actual development of a relationship.

In their review of the literature, Huston and Levinger (1978) noted that "there exists no comprehensive classification of relationships, a problem that is beginning to be recognised" (p. 116). While most of the early studies such as Moreno's sociometric research, Newcomb's work on the acquaintance process and Festinger's housing study, looked at natural, real-life relationships, the majority of the experimental research in the past few decades has involved the study of one-sided impressions or superficial encounters between strangers in the laboratory. In a survey of attraction research between 1972-1976, Huston and Levinger (1978) found that more than two-thirds of published studies looked at level 1 or level 2 relationships only. Of the remaining one-third, most studies analysed same-sex friendship or dating and marriage. Other kinds of

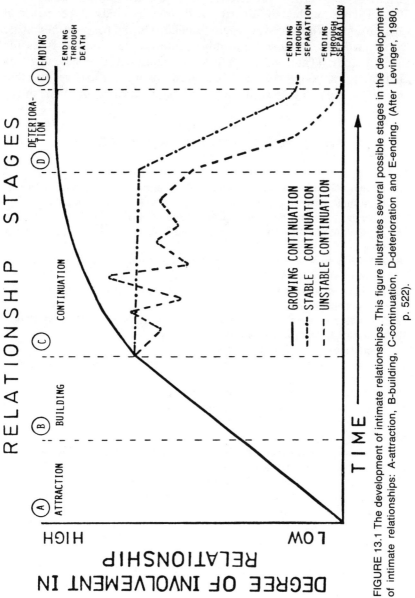

FIGURE 13.1 The development of intimate relationships. This figure illustrates several possible stages in the development of intimate relationships: A-attraction, B-building, C-continuation, D-deterioration and E-ending. (After Levinger, 1980, p. 522).

relationships, such as platonic love, extramarital affairs, parent-child relationships, or cross-sex friendships are relatively rarely studied.

It is thus important to understand how various relationship types differ from each other. In a recent study, we asked (Forgas and Dobosz, 1980) a large number of subjects to list all the kinds of heterosexual relationships with which they were familiar. On the basis of these lists, we selected the 25 most frequently mentioned relationship types for further study (Table 13.2). We were interested in what sorts of characteristics people use to distinguish between these relationship categories. We prepared cards each bearing the description of one of the

TABLE 13.2
LIST OF 25 COMMON RELATIONSHIP SCRIPTS

1. Verbal and physical flirting at a party, without follow-up.
2. A boy/girlfriend living together for a period after several months of dating.
3. A de facto relationship between two previously married people.
4. A young marriage after an unwanted pregnancy.
5. A permanent, but non-sexual relationship between two young religious people.
6. A "going steady" relationship maintained mainly to impress peers.
7. A long-lasting, close platonic relationship.
8. A steady relationship where each person goes out with other members of the opposite sex.
9. Widowers re-married in middle-age, after several years of living alone.
10. A one night sexual encounter.
11. A marriage of twenty-five years.
12. A mainly physical relationship with an older and more experienced person.
13. A school affair between teacher and pupil.
14. Brief, fluctuating relationships among members of a permanent social group.
15. A young marriage after a long, involved courtship.
16. A relationship in which only one of the partners is deeply involved.
17. Having an affair with a married person.
18. A short, mainly sexual affair between two students.
19. An irregular, occasional dating relationship for mutual entertainment between two young people.
20. The continuation of a once personal relationship by letters and phone calls from overseas.
21. A short, emotional holiday affair.
22. A long, involved "going steady" relationship at school.
23. "Love at first sight", followed by engagement, after a brief but intensive relationship.
24. A short, mutual first love.
25. The recommencement of an old relationship, that didn't work out before.

After Forgas and Dobosz, 1980, p. 293

25 relationships, and asked a further group of 129 subjects to sort these relationship types into smaller groups on the basis of how similar they thought they were. This sorting procedure resulted in a number of groups for each subject, each containing relationship types thought to be similar. We analysed these judgments using a multidimensional scaling procedure, a technique which explores the underlying representations subjects used in deciding which relationships were similar. We found that this sample of 25 heterosexual relationships (see Table 13.2) were best described in terms of three major characteristics: (a) how socially desirable and balanced a relationship was, (b) how much love and commitment existed between the partners, and (c) whether the relationship was sexual or not (see Figure 13.2 for results).

Research of this kind allows us to measure exactly how relationship scenarios such as marriage, platonic love, superficial dating or an

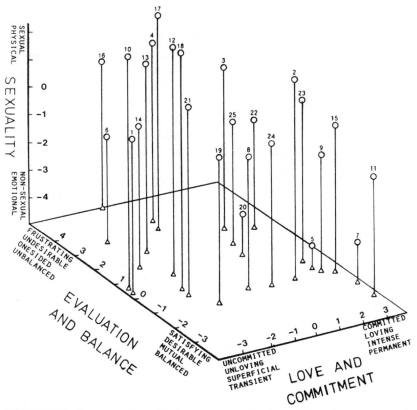

FIGURE 13.2 The perception of heterosexual relationships. This is how a group of students differentiated between the 25 relationship types described in Table 13.2. The three dimensions, evaluation and balance, love and commitment, and sexuality are basic characteristics of heterosexual relationships. (After Forgas and Dobosz, 1980, p. 295).

extramarital affair are seen to differ from each other. This is important to know if we want to study the role of such perceptions in the development of relationships. There is some evidence for example that in relationships involving a great deal of adjustment and transition, such as engagement, the partners' prior perceptions and expectations play a considerable role in the progress or downfall of the relationship (Morris, 1983). People also choose their interactions with each other in terms of their perceptions of various relationship types. Argyle and Furnham (1982) found that the situations and activities preferred were significantly influenced by the type of relationship between the partners.

Cultural scripts and individual perceptions are particularly important in relationships, such as engagement, which involve a great deal of change and adaptation. The common perception of the engagement relationship is that of a blissful period when the partners are very much in love and have mainly positive experiences and expectations about their future life together. The reality can be very different. Engagement is a period of great change for most couples, when they are confronted perhaps for the first time with the numerous minor and major problems which are likely to arise when living with another person. It is a time for facing reality, recognising the difficult as well as as the pleasing aspects of the partner's personality and habits, a time of preparing for the assumption of shared responsibilities. Research has shown that the partners' initial perceptions and expectations of the engagement relationship have a strong influence on their later success. Those who begin by regarding engagement as a happy, unproblematic period have much greater difficulty later than couples with a more realistic set of expectations. Research on the characteristics of how relationships are perceived can help us to understand the role such perceptions and expectations play in the later success of a relationship (Morris, 1983).

Conflict in close relationships
We have seen throughout the previous discussion that intimate relationships are not necessarily synonymous with blissful emotional and behavioural involvement. Intimacy often has to be gained through the resolution of conflicts to the mutual satisfaction of the partners. It makes a great deal of difference how couples go about dealing with conflict. A recent survey of married couples identified three conflict-resolution strategies: simply avoiding the conflict, resolution through attacking the partner, or resolution through compromise. Only the last of these strategies was positively correlated with marital satisfaction, while the first two were negatively correlated (Levinger, 1980). In a related study of the same issue, Falbo and Peplau (1980) identified 13 power strategies commonly used in intimate relationships. These included strategies such as asking, bargaining, showing positive or negative affect, persuasion, withdrawal, and so on. These 13 strategies

were seen by experts as differing in terms of two features: their directness (direct/indirect) and whether they involved one or both partners (unilateral/bilateral) (see Activity 13.2).

**ACTIVITY 13.2
How Do You Get Your Way?**

How do *you* get your way with other people? What are your preferred power strategies in dealing with conflict in different kinds of intimate relationships? Try to complete the following few questions:

1. Recall your last disagreement with your current/most recent romantic partner. What sort of strategy did you use in trying to get your way?
2. Recall your most recent disagreement with a person in authority (boss, parent, etc.). Again, try to remember the strategy you used in dealing with the situation.
3. Now think about the last time you were in conflict with a younger or subordinate person. How did you deal with it?

You will probably find that you, like most people, have a relatively broad range of power strategies at your disposal. You select the most appropriate one depending on the requirements of the situation. Try to classify your power strategies in terms of Falbo and Peplau's two dimensions, directness and laterality. When did you use direct rather than indirect, and when unilateral rather than bilateral strategies? This may also be a good opportunity to reflect on the success of your strategies. Could you have done better in these conflict situations by using some other strategy?

Dealing with dissatisfaction

Few intimate relationships follow the 'ideal', top curve shown in Figure 13.1. The average marriage, for example, is almost certain to involve some minor or major decline in marital satisfaction over time (Blood and Blood, 1978). Within an exchange theoretical framework, such decline may be caused by a perceived increase in costs and decrease in rewards that the partner(s) derive from the relationship. According to Levinger (1980), it is particularly during the early, formative and late, declining stages that partners are very concerned with the rewards and costs of a relationship. The cost of foregone alternatives forms an important part of the relationship 'equation'. Recurring concern about the 'fairness' of the exchange that forms the basis of all relationships is a potential danger signal.

Whether a deteriorating relationship will actually be terminated largely depends on the availability of alternative partners. People often persevere with unsatisfactory relationships if they see no preferable alternatives on the horizon. Marital break-up is most commonly precipitated by the availability of alternative sexual relationships to one or both of the partners (Jaffe and Kanter, 1976). Rarely do people choose loneliness as an alternative to an unsatisfactory marriage. In general, declining satisfaction in an intimate relationship may lead to one of four possible reactions: 1. *Exit* — formally leaving the relationship; 2. *Voice* — discussing problems, seeking outside help, trying to change; 3. *Loyalty* — waiting and hoping for improvement; and 4. *Neglect* — ignoring the partner and problems, criticising partner, 'just letting things fall apart' (Rusbult, Zambrodt and Gunn, 1982). These four reactions can again be classified in terms of two dimensions: constructiveness (voice and loyalty are constructive, exit and neglect are destructive), and activity (exit and voice are active, loyalty and neglect are passive).

Which of these four responses is chosen as a reaction to dissatisfaction largely depends on three factors: (a) the degree of satisfaction with the relationship prior to the emergence of problems, (b) the magnitude of the person's investment of resources in the relationship (for example, time spent together, shared property, etc.), and (c) the quality of the best available alternative (Rusbult et al. 1982, p. 1230). The links between these prior variables, and the preferred reactions to dissatisfaction in 'real' relationships were empirically established by Rusbult et al. (1982), who asked their subjects to describe their past reactions to declining romantic relationships. Results showed that high prior satisfaction and large investment in the relationship predisposed people to react with

The terminating female. Exit is one way to deal with dissatisfaction in a relationship, which tends to be chosen when prior satisfaction and investment in the relationship is small, and there is an alternative relationship available. Research shows that romantic relationships terminated by the female partner are less likely to continue as casual friendships.

voice and loyalty, while choosing exit or neglect were correlated with the availability of alternative relationships (Table 13.3).

TABLE 13.3
DISSATISFACTION IN ROMANTIC RELATIONSHIPS: CORRELATIONS BETWEEN PREDICTOR VARIABLES AND REACTIONS TO DISSATISFACTION

Predictor variable	Reactions to dissatisfaction with			
	Exit	Voice	Loyalty	Neglect
Prior satisfaction	−.48**	.56**	.49**	−.45**
Investment size	−.27**	.59**	.38**	−.38**
Alternative relationship	.54**	−.14	−.48**	.19

**p<.001

After Rusbult et al., 1982, p. 1239

Termination of intimate relationships
Irrespective of how a person decides to deal with dissatisfaction, relationships are sometimes beyond repair. It is increasingly common in contemporary societies that deep and involving relationships are terminated by causes other than the death of one of the partners. 'Till death us do part' is no longer a valid maxim for modern marriages: in the US it is estimated that about 40 per cent of recent marriages will end in divorce. Perhaps inevitably, the greater the individual freedom people enjoy, the less likely it is that their close relationships will survive intact. We discussed in general terms the social and cultural changes which have occurred in the Western world since the French Revolution and the advent of its individualistic, rational philosophy in Chapter 1. Freedom, individualism and mobility are not always reconcilable with close relationships, which are by definition restrictive, since they imply both longevity and commitment.

Modern societies of course encourage freedom and mobility, and offer many alternative relationship types. Not only marriages, but also close friendships and traditional family relationships are under strain. The kind of intense, committed friendships which lasted from primary school to the grave, or the kind of parent-child relationship which was based on decades of shared family life are increasingly rare today. As a result, it is more and more common for close relationships to be terminated by choice. As regards romantic relationships, Hill, Rubin and Peplau (1976) found that of the 231 student couples they studied, 103 (45 per cent) had broken up two years later. Break-ups were most likely to occur at times when critical changes in the partners' life-routine were taking place. The beginning or the end of the university term were 'popular' times, particularly if the breaking up was initiated by the less involved partner. Most break-ups were not mutual but initiated by one of the partners, who was more likely to be the woman than the man. Interestingly, if the break-up was started by the man, the couple were more likely to remain casual friends afterwards than in cases where the break-up was initiated by the woman.

Marital break-ups represent a more serious social problem, since they affect not only individuals but whole families. Children in particular can be adversely affected by the dissolution of a marriage, although precise data are difficult to come by. The negative consequences are not always obvious, and psychological damage is much more difficult to assess than physical or material damage. We seem to know far more about why relationships develop than about the reasons for their demise. Considering that the termination of intimate relationships is an increasingly common phenomenon in our society, there is clearly a need for more research to be devoted to this issue.

The terminating male. Relationships terminated by the male partner often continue as casual friendships.

Summary and conclusions

In this chapter we looked at close relationships which involved a greater or lesser degree of mutuality between the partners. We saw that behavioural and affective interdependence and longevity are essential features of intimate relationships. Romantic love and heterosexual relationships in particular are among the most intensive, and perhaps also the most common intimate relationships for most people. This was also reflected in our discussion, in which we devoted most attention to such heterosexual relationships. Scientific explanations of romantic love, based on the two-factor theory of emotions by Schachter and Singer, offer a challenging view of romantic love which not all researchers as yet agree on. We also saw that conflict and conflict resolution are essential components even of very successful relationships: progress in intimate relationships is the result of a continuing process of accomodation, adjustment and negotiation between the partners.

Social interaction within the framework of intimate relationships has special qualities. Exchange theorists have attempted to analyse these processes in terms of the exchange of costs and rewards, for the ultimate benefit of both partners. Apart from intimate relationships, membership in larger groups provides us with another special kind of interaction setting. The characteristics of interpersonal influence and group interaction processes will be considered in the next two chapters.

14. Social influence: conformity, obedience and leadership

14.

SOCIAL INFLUENCE: CONFORMITY, OBEDIENCE AND LEADERSHIP

Every interaction between people involves the exercise of some degree of social influence. Even the most superficial encounter leaves its mark, however minor, on the participants. Strictly speaking, every opinion we utter, every request we make, and every behaviour we undertake towards another person will in one way or another influence that person. There are, of course, many more powerful forms of social influence, which mainly occur in larger groups. We have so far concentrated on interactions between two people at a time, or dyadic interactions. But not all our interactions occur in pairwise relationships. Frequently, we interact with several people at the same time. Time budget studies (for example, the research by Deaux referred to in Chapter 11), show that a significant proportion of the time we spend with others is in fact spent in the company of several people simultaneously. At such times we function as members of more or less enduring social *groups*.

There are some important differences between interacting with just one person, and interacting with a whole group. Groups, if only by virtue of their number, can exert a far greater influence on individuals than a single partner can. Correspondingly, skilful interaction in a group can be far more difficult and demanding for an individual than interaction with a single partner. Of course, not all forms of social influence are specific to groups. While conformity, compliance, social facilitation or leadership are examples of group-based influence processes, other kinds of social influence, such as obedience, are not specific to groups. In this chapter we shall consider social psychological research on social influence, particularly as it occurs in groups. In the next chapter we shall continue this theme by discussing the specific features of interaction in groups.

The effects of the mere presence of others on behaviour
To really understand the important role others can play in influencing our behaviours, we must start our discussion by looking at the simplest possible case: how does the mere presence of other people, without any

social interaction, influence us? Psychologists noticed as early as the end of the last century that people perform a variety of individual tasks better when other people are present than they are able to do when alone. These effects occur whether others are simply observing the actor (audience effects), or are themselves engaged in a similar individual activity (coaction effects). Triplett (1897) found, for example, that individuals were able to wind fishing reels faster when doing it in the company of others than when they did it alone. Travis (1925) reported that the simple presence of an audience improved the performance of subjects on a pursuit rotor task (following a point on a revolving disk) well beyond their best scores when doing the same task alone.

In a more systematic study of this phenomenon, Allport (1924) asked subjects to perform a number of different tasks, ranging from the simple (crossing out letters in a text) to the complex (writing refutations of logical arguments). Subjects were asked to do this while alone in a room, or while sharing the room with five other people. Output was better on almost all tasks when there were five people together. Psychologists came to call this a 'social facilitation' effect. However, the improvement in the presence of others was not universal. The quality of the arguments presented on the last, most complex task in fact declined in the presence of others. We shall return to this paradox later.

Just how universal is this so-called 'social facilitation' effect? Several investigators looked at animal rather than human groups to see if social facilitation occurs in other species as well. Chen (1937) placed ants alone, in pairs, or in groups of three in a milkbottle filled with sand, and carefully measured the amount of sand excavated in each condition as the insects set about digging their nests. Ants in groups started nest building much sooner, and excavated more material per individual than did the same insects when working alone. Social facilitation has been demonstrated in several other species as well, such as goldfish learning to swim in a maze (Welty, 1934) or rats, who were found to copulate with greater frequency when there were two other pairs in their cage (Larsson, 1956).

But not all experiments showed social facilitation effects. We have already seen that the quality of performance in Allport's study (1924) declined in the presence of others when a new, complex task (mental reasoning) was to be performed. Dashiell (1930) also found that more mistakes were made in a complex multiplication task when there was an audience, and Pessin (1932) reported that the presence of an audience interfered with performance on a memory task. Similar patterns of 'social inhibition' were also reported with some animals: finches and parakeets were found to perform certain tasks better when alone than in the company of others.

How can we make sense of these contradictory findings? When does being in a group help individual performance, and when does it hinder

An illustration of social facilitation. Performance usually improves when two or more people are simultaneously engaged in the same well-learnt individual task (co-action effects).

it? Robert Zajonc (1965) carefully surveyed all the available evidence, and came up with a surprising result: the presence of others always improved performance when the task was simple, or very well rehearsed. Performance declined when the task was new and complex. Zajonc (1965) suggested that these disparate results may be reconciled if we assume that the presence of others is always a source of arousal and increased drive and motivation.

When the task is well-known (high in the organism's response hierarchy), this increased motivation invariably results in improved performance. When the task is new and little-known (low in the response hierarchy), the increased drive level interferes with, rather than facilitates learning and performance. This theory may be easily evaluated if we directly manipulate the difficulty of the task to be performed. Hunt and Hillery (1973) did just this. They asked human subjects to learn an easy or a difficult maze, and to do this either alone or in the company of others. Subjects performed best when doing a difficult maze alone, or when doing an easy maze in the company of other people.

TABLE 14.1
SOCIAL FACILITATION AND INHIBITION: NUMBER OF ERRORS MADE WHILE LEARNING AN EASY OR A DIFFICULT TASK ALONE OR WITH AN AUDIENCE

	Alone	With audience
Easy task	44.67	36.19
Difficult task	184.91	220.33

After Hunt and Hillery, 1973, p. 566

Zajonc's (1965) arousal theory is not the only possible explanation of social facilitation effects, particularly in humans. His theory seems to ignore the fact that human beings react to the presence of others not only unconsciously, in the form of autonomous arousal, but also consciously, using their ability to interpret and differentiate between different situations. Cottrell (1972) suggested that the mere presence of others induces arousal at least partly because we learn to expect some form of evaluation, and subsequent reward or punishment when being observed by others. "It is these anticipations, elicited by the presence of others, that increase the individual's drive level" (p. 227). When other people are physically present, but are unable to evaluate our performance (for example, because they are not looking at us or are blindfolded), a weaker social facilitation effect usually occurs (Innes and Young, 1975).

Markus (1978) designed an interesting unobtrusive experiment in which the separate influence of arousal and evaluation anxiety were nicely demonstrated. Subjects had to perform an easy, well-known task (put on their own clothes), or a difficult, novel task (put on new, unfamiliar clothes), while they were alone, or in the company of others, who were either able to observe their performances, or were not able to do so. Results showed that the presence of others who could 'evaluate' the actor most improved the familiar task, and most interfered with the unusual task. Presence of others who could not evaluate the person had similar, but weaker effects.

As we have seen above, even the simple presence of others may have a strong, and perhaps unsuspected influence on our behaviours. This influence can be very important in many everyday settings. All those who

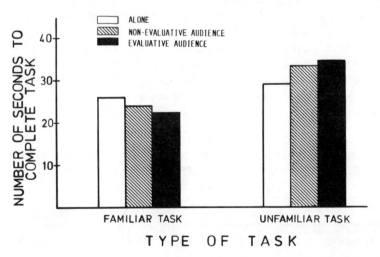

FIGURE 14.1 Social facilitation and inhibition. A familiar task is performed faster, and a new, unfamiliar task more slowly in the presence of others, particularly if the audience is able to evaluate the performance. (After Markus, 1978).

have to perform tasks in front of, or together with, others are subject to such social facilitation and inhibition processes. Actors, singers or competitive sportsmen are particulary subject to such effects. In realistic situations, however, arousal is not likely to be an automatic, uncontrollable reaction to the presence of others. Among other things, the extent of arousal also depends on how threatening or novel the situation, and how well subjects can monitor or 'keep an eye' on the others present. Many studies show that "the conditions for which social monitoring is not possible are those conditions for which the mere presence of others affects task performance" (Guerin and Innes, 1982, p.7).

In one recent study, we looked at the effects an audience has on people engaging in a competitive game, squash (Forgas et al. 1980). Our subjects were unsuspecting squash players at the university courts. By counting their correct and incorrect shots, we designated each pair as 'expert' or 'novice', and we used similar objective measures to determine the superior and inferior player within each pair. Our audience manipulation

---

ACTIVITY 14.1
Social Facilitation

Social facilitation and inhibition are very common occurrences in everyday life. If you have some willing subjects, you might demonstrate these effects yourself. First, you have to design a task which is either simple and well-known to the subjects, or difficult and new to them. You could use a series of simple and difficult mazes, for example. You can manipulate social influences by leaving your subject to do the task alone in a room, or by acting as an audience, observing his/her performance. Finally, you can manipulate the evaluative potential of the audience by either directly looking at and assessing your subject's performance, or turning away and not looking at what he/she is doing. You can expect the same pattern of findings as reported by Markus in her experiment: greatest facilitation/inhibition with the 'looking' audience, and similar, but weaker effects with the 'not looking' audience.

You could also use unobtrusive methods, for example by observing and recording the performances of squash or tennis players while they are, or are not being watched by others. The patterns of social facilitation and inhibition in such cooperative games can be quite complex, as the study by Forgas et al. (1980) showed.

was fairly simple: several observers ostentatiously appeared on the squash court gallery for a designated period of time, and they recorded the performance of the players during this period. We then compared their performance with a similar period of play without visible observers.

The results were quite interesting, and somewhat different from what we expected. The main effect of the audience was that the two players within each pair coordinated their shots better than previously. As a result, superior members of a pair became somewhat worse, and inferior members somewhat better when being observed. The game also became much 'smoother', with fewer interruptions, as if the pair were attempting to present cooperatively the best possible 'face' to the observers. These results suggest that audience effects can indeed be very much dependent on such complex factors as our ability to monitor the observers (Guerin and Innes, 1982) as well as our subtle self-presentation strategies in a given situation (Bond, 1982).

Social loafing and bystander apathy
When others are not simply passive observers or co-actors, but are engaged in the same cooperative activity as we are, their influence on performance can be far more complicated. For one thing, shared activity may often mean that individual performance cannot be objectively assessed. Under these conditions, people sometimes engage in what Latane et al. (1979) called 'social loafing'. The term refers to the fact that individuals will tend to put less effort into their work when they know that individual contribution to a group task cannot be reliably established. One explanation for this reaction is the diffusion of responsibility for collective performance among many individuals. Since many group members are jointly responsible for the outcome, personal motivation and responsibility suffer.

The same kind of process can also be observed in situations in which voluntary help to another person is required. Latane and Darley (1970) studied the probability of bystander intervention in reaction to accidents or emergencies in public places such as on the street, in metro cars, in offices, and so on. They found that in all of these situations, the larger the size of the group of bystanders able to help, the less likely that any one individual will volunteer to help. This is, of course, not the result of any conscious attempt at social influence by anyone. Each bystander believes in the necessity of helping, but assumes that somebody else will do so. The larger the group, the easier it is to assume that another person will do whatever is necessary and the greater the potential cost of getting involved in a messy and possibly embarrassing situation. This is an example of a very subtle kind of group influence, brought about by the automatic diffusion of responsibility for an act in a larger social unit.

If the simple presence of others can have such a profound influence on behaviour, it seems clear that actual interaction will further enhance this effect. In 'real' groups of course, people do not just share each other's company, but interact with, and directly influence other group members. Social facilitation and inhibition effects, social loafing and bystander apathy are examples of the most basic kinds of social influence processes. We shall next look at conformity — one of the more powerful and direct forms of group influence.

Conformity

One of the most puzzling things about social life is the fact that large numbers of people who are basically all very different as individuals nevertheless manage to successfully live together in groups, communities and societies. How is this possible? What forces people to give up some of their unique, individual desires and habits for the sake of participating in larger social units or groupings? It appears that the ability to conform and to accept the often almost arbitrary conventions of the social groups we belong to is the very foundation of interacting with people. Every human group, be it a neighbourhood association, a work team, a university or a whole society, can only exist because its members conform to certain norms. All groups tend to develop their own unwritten (and often written) rules of behaviour which individual members are expected to follow. How is such conformity possible? What are the processes which force us to behave like others? These are the issues that conformity research addresses.

Perhaps the most basic fact about conformity is that groups of people will tend to develop shared, consensual ways of behaving and seeing the world almost automatically, even when there are absolutely no objective reasons for doing so. Sherif (1935) demonstrated this tendency using an ingenious procedure. He capitalised on the common perceptual illusion that in a completely dark room, a stationary light source will appear to move about erratically (the so-called autokinetic effect). Subjects when asked to estimate the movement of such a light source, usually offer widely different judgments, ranging from a few centimetres to a metre or more.

Sherif introduced a social component into this inherently ambiguous situation. He asked people to make their estimates in the presence of others, who of course first gave quite different judgments. After a number of trials, subjects tended to revise their own estimates to be more similar to those of the others, and judgments eventually converged towards a single shared 'group norm'. This experiment represents an almost pure form of conformity. In the absence of reliable information, we seem to follow others, as if we had an automatic tendency to agree with what other people think.

Once such a group norm was established, subjects freely adopted it. In later individual tests their estimates continued to reflect the earlier group consensus. Would people persevere even with a completely artificial group norm? Jacobs and Campbell (1961) established such an artificial norm by including one 'confederate' in the group who consistently gave much higher estimates than usual (15-18 inches, instead of the 'norm' of 3.5 inches). They then kept replacing group members one at a time, until every position in the group had been exchanged several times over. They found that groups persevered with the artificial norm for up to six generations of newcomers! It seems that groups are very conservative, maintaining their norms and routines even after the initial reasons for adopting them have long since disappeared.

What would happen if the judgments concern not an ambiguous stimulus, but a clearly visible target? Would we still go along with others when their judgments are obviously mistaken? Most people would probably answer "No" to this question. Asch (1951) investigated exactly this possibility, and came up with some very unexpected results. He asked his subjects to make some simple judgments about the lengths of lines which were clearly visible. For example, subjects had to decide which of three lines was the same length as a fourth, target line. The task was extremely simple to answer, and everybody could give a correct answer when asked individually.

Asch, however, was interested in group influences, and designed the situation in such a way that several people (all confederates of the experimenter) gave their judgments before the last person (the only 'real' subject) was asked to judge the lines. On the first few trials the confederates gave the obviously correct answer, and so did the real subject. Soon, however, the confederates started to give unanimously incorrect answers. What would you as a subject do in such a situation? You have only two alternatives: defy the group and give what you believe to be the right answer, or go along with the group and give a clearly incorrect answer? Surprisingly, about 35 per cent of the time subjects chose the second alternative. They conformed to the norm established by the group, even when it was clearly incorrect.

Asch also looked at some of the specific variables which influence conformity. For example, is it true that the larger the group, the greater the conformity? Interestingly, this was not the case: a group of three or four people generated almost as much conformity as a much larger group. But in some real life situations, different results were found. Milgram studied conformity in an everyday setting, on a busy New York street. His confederates were instructed to gaze intently at the sixth floor window of an office building. When only one person was looking up, conformity was low: only 4 per cent of passersby followed suit. With five people looking, conformity increased to 16 per cent, with ten people it was 22 per cent, and with 15 people it reached 40 per cent. In other words, increases in group size further increased conformity. However, the conformity pressures in the Asch and Milgram experiments were of a very different kind, as we shall see shortly.

Another factor influencing conformity, according to Asch, is the presence or absence of supporters. When there is at least one other person dissenting from the incorrect group judgments, Asch found that conformity also decreased dramatically. Subjects were now no longer alone, and apparently felt much less constrained about 'standing up' to the group.

Following Asch's unexpected findings, many other psychologists became interested in studying conformity. Crutchfield (1955) designed an apparatus where subjects no longer sat facing a group, but were informed about the alleged choices of other group members on an electronic console while sitting alone in a booth. Even in this much reduced 'group' situation, the assumed opinions of others (in fact now provided by the experimenter manipulating the console) still carried a great deal of weight. Subjects could be made to endorse almost absurd statements (such as 'the average life expectancy of males in the USA is 25 years', or 'men are on the average 8 to 9 inches taller than women') simply by learning that all other group members thought this was true.

The extent of conformity also depends on the particular culture from which the subjects come. Milgram (1961) compared the degree to which French and Norwegian subjects were prepared to conform to a group in judging the duration of acoustic tones. The French, coming from a heterogeneous and individualsitic culture conformed much less than did the Norwegians, who came from a homogenous culture where community spirit and uniformity are treasured. Shouval et al. (1975) present an even more interesting example of cultural differences. They found that among children now living in Israel, those brought up in the Soviet Union showed far greater conformity than children born in Israel. The reasons are easy to find. While in the Soviet Union childhood is a time for learning the discipline and obedience required for living in a totalitarian society, in Israel childhood is seen very differently, as a time for mischief and adventure, and the assertion of individuality. It appears that Israelis remain 'rugged individualists' in adult life as well. In a study of conformity to queuing at bus stops in Jerusalem, Mann (1977) found that it took a queue of six to eight people to induce a majority of newcomers to join the end of the queue. It seems that "bus queues are not a well-ingrained custom in Jerusalem" (Mann, 1977, p. 441), while this form of public conformity is very highly developed in some other cultures, such as Britain.

Varieties of conformity

What is really going on in these various conformity situations? Why do apparently normal people, who know the correct answers perfectly well when asked individually, give a patently wrong answer, just because others before them have done so? These studies demonstrate most clearly the very powerful forces of conformity operating on all of us. We all seem to feel a deep necessity to be like other people, think like other people and be accepted by other people. However, there are also considerable differences between the kinds of conformity induced in these different experiments.

In the Sherif study, subjects presumably really came to believe that the other person's judgments were in fact more accurate than their own. They did not simply conform to be accepted, while maintaining a different private view — they almost certainly changed their private view as well as a result of the information they received. The Asch situation is very different. Subjects here publicly complied with a majority position, without changing their private opinions. When asked alone, they would once again revert to giving the correct answers. We may thus distinguish between true conformity and public compliance as the two basic forms of yielding to group pressures.

What are the means a group has at its disposal to exert such pressures on an individual? Deutsch and Gerard (1955) suggested that conformity pressures may be roughly classified into two types: *informational* influence, and *normative* influence. Informational influence occurs when the group provides new knowledge, arguments or information to the individual which succeeds in altering his/her views or behaviour. Milgram's 'staring crowd' study is a good example of almost pure informational influence. Normative influence is quite different: the individual is not offered any new knowledge, but conforms because he/she wishes to be accepted by the group, as in the Asch situation. And groups go to a great deal of trouble to establish consensus amongst their members, as we shall presently see.

In a more naturalistic study on group processes, Schachter (1951) created discussion groups to consider a variety of topical issues. Unbeknown to the participants, he 'planted' two of his assistants in each group, one of whom was expressing a consistently deviant, non-conformist view, while the other started as a non-conformist but slowly changed his opinions to agree with that of the group. Group members devoted a great deal of time and effort to influencing the two deviant members to adopt the group position. These efforts intensified further when one of the deviants showed signs of changing (as he was 'programmed' to do). When it finally became clear that the second deviant would remain non-conformist, communications towards him stopped: in effect, the group ceased to regard him as one of its members, and he was no longer considered eligible for any role within the group. We may look at this process as an efficient system of self-preservation on the part of the group. To function as a social unit, a group must create a degree of consensus, and it is willing to expend a great deal of effort to achieve this. If all efforts fail, all that remains is for the non-conforming member to be rejected and ignored, thus ensuring the survival of the group.

Social contagion

To act and think as others do seems to be a basic human tendency. However, people do not simply yield to the informational and normative pressures of a group: sometimes just being in the company of a group is enough to change behaviour. The automatic yielding to group influences was first described by the French sociologist and physician Le Bon, who suggested that, just like a contagious disease, emotionalism, aggression and violence can spread through a crowd with similar speed. Social contagion is not limited to crowds or aggressive behaviour. There are many well-documented cases, for example, of mysterious illnesses 'spreading' by social contagion: the 'sufferers' imitate the symptoms of others, without knowing about it. Recently, several girls in a Palestinian school on the Israeli-occupied West Bank fell victim to a mysterious disease, allegedly caused by Israelis. The international investigating committee found no evidence of any illness-causing agent, and the girls recovered in a few days. Such hysterical contagion is a relatively common occurrence in other countries as well.

Sometimes, the contagion effect can have dangerous consequences. For example, suicides tend to increase after publicity about the suicide of a famous person (Phillips, 1979). Social contagion also plays a role in many other group phenomena, such as the spreading of new styles of fashion, novel political views, or new styles of behaviour. In each case, publicity about the preferences or opinions of leading groups and individuals generates broadly based voluntary conformity. The above examples illustrate 'unintended' social influence processes, when people do as others because of an internal inclination, rather than any intentional attempt to pressure or persuade them. Both conformity and social contagion effects have an important role to play in making cooperative social life possible.

Obedience

Conformity represents perhaps the major form of indirect social influence exerted by groups on individuals. But there are other kinds of more direct influence, no less intriguing in their implications. Obedience to direct commands or instructions is the next major category of influence we shall consider. Obedience, or doing as we are told, seems on first consideration somehow objectionable — it implies the giving up of our individual freedom of action, and the acceptance of somebody else's instructions as the controlling force on our behaviour. Most of us like to think of ourselves as autonomous agents, not simply obedient followers of commands from others. Just how great a role does obedience play in our lives?

Most Western cultures place a major value on individual freedom of action and responsibility, and consequently regard obedience as undesirable in some way (see Chapter 1). Yet almost all social organisations and groupings rely on explicit obedience relationships for at least part of their efficiency. The army, the police and the fire brigade are only the most obvious examples of organisations in which obedience plays a central role. Almost all other social organisations, such as hospitals, the public service, local administration and even universities possess explicit authority structures in which obedience to instructions from superiors is expected and freely (or indeed, sometimes grudgingly!) given by subordinates. In the British university system, heads of departments are formally responsible for the teaching and research in their schools, and in principle may instruct academic staff to carry out any task relevant to these objectives. This is not all that different from obedience to leaders in the army or in industry.

Obedience in the laboratory
Psychological experiments themselves are among the most frequently studied examples of almost blind obedience. Subjects in an experiment will accept almost any command or instruction from the experimenter, and carry it out to the best of their ability. It is indeed difficult to find the limits of such blind obedience. Some researchers attempted to create a task which would be so absurd and meaningless that no subject would persevere with it. In one memorable study, the experimenter gave subjects large piles of papers with mathematical problems on them, and asked them (a) to solve the problems, and (b) after finishing with each page, to throw it in a wastepaperbasket before starting on the next page. Instead of refusing, subjects continued this futile work for hours, until they were stopped by the experimenter. The extreme compliance of experimental subjects is also a source of great methodological problems: since subjects will do almost anything to 'please' an experimenter, it is necessary to keep the real purpose of an experiment hidden from them, so that they do not 'fake' the results they believe the experimenter desires (see also Chapter 16).

In most of these examples, obedience is limited to well-defined authority relations, and no illegitimate or immoral behaviours are demanded. What would happen if we tried to command subjects to behave aggressively towards an innocent person, to inflict severe pain and suffering, and possibly even endanger life? Naturally, they would refuse, we would like to think. Unfortunately, this is far from certain, as a very well-known study by Milgram (1963) showed.

Subjects in this alleged 'learning' experiment were told that they would have to teach another subject (in fact, a confederate of the experimenter) to learn some word pairs. The 'learner' sat in an adjoining room, and was wired up to electrodes. Subjects were told that every time the 'learner' made a mistake, they were to punish him by administering an electric shock of increasing magnitude. An impressive looking shock-generator was provided for the purpose, with a series of buttons corresponding to shock levels from 15 volts to 450 volts. The higher voltages were labelled 'danger' and 'extreme danger'. Subjects were themselves given a quite painful shock described by the experimenter as 'very mild', to give them an idea of the magnitude of the punishment they were administering.

As the experiment progressed, the 'learner' inevitably made some mistakes, and the subject was required to deliver increasingly painful and dangerous shocks. Soon, the learner was heard crying out with severe pain in the neighbouring room, pounding the wall, begging to be let out, and finally, at extreme shock levels he fell completely silent. What would you have done if you were a subject in this experiment? Milgram found, to his great surprise, that only about 12.5 per cent of the subjects refused to administer what appeared to be deadly electric shocks, and about 65 per cent of subjects went all the way to 450 volts! (See Figure 14.2). This was a truly unexpected finding. These subjects were normal, well-adjusted Americans, with no record of antisocial behaviour, yet they were willing to be obedient to the extent of inflicting pain and injury on another human being. How can we explain such behaviour?

Variables influencing obedience
There are several factors which influence obedience. Perhaps most importantly, subjects may have felt that they were not personally responsible for their action, since it all happened under the experimenter's authority, who was after all a qualified academic in a respectable university. To control for this possibility, Milgram repeated the experiment away from the university, in a seedy downtown office without any obvious claim to academic respectability. Results were almost identical. A second factor may be the proximity between the subject and the 'learner'. Since the subject was only indirectly confronted by the suffering of the 'learner', perhaps this made it easier for him to be obedient.

In follow-up studies, Milgram did include variations of proximity between the learner and the subject: they were placed in the same room, and in one condition, the subject was required to actually press the learner's hands down on the electrodes. Milgram found that with increasing proximity between the subject and the victim, obedience predictably decreased from 65 per cent to 49 per cent. This finding has some important real-life implications. It is apparently much easier to inflict great suffering when the victims are far removed. In a war, bomber pilots are much less likely to be confronted with the consequences of their actions than are the soldiers involved in the immediate battle. Politicians and other decisionmakers are of course even further removed from the human results of their decisions, which may perhaps help to explain their occasional lack of concern for the consequences.

The proximity of the experimenter giving the orders was also a significant factor. When he was removed from the vicinity of the subject, by giving orders through an intercom system, or on a recorded tape, obedience again decreased, to about 45 per cent. But throughout all conditions, the belief in the experimenter's ultimate responsibility was a major factor in securing obedience. Since he showed no visible disturbance when hearing the cries of the suffering 'learner', subjects could have remained obedient because they were confused about what was really going on (Mixon, 1972).

You may know that after the Second World War, Nazi war criminals at the Nuremberg trials used a similar justification for their horrific actions: they were only carrying out orders. The responsibility lay with those who gave the orders. Just how acceptable is this justification? In the Milgram experiment, subjects could have simply walked out without any repercussions. Indeed, there is evidence that German soldiers during the Nazi period could have acted similarly. There are very few records of prosecution of individuals refusing to participate in atrocities against civilian populations. Yet most of the time, we seem to underestimate our own freedom of action, and take the easy way out by disclaiming all responsibility for our actions carried out under orders. The inclination to obey authority is a very strong influence indeed on human behaviour.

To what extent would people be prepared to give dangerous shocks when there are no explicit commands? Milgram (1964) also looked at this possibility, using an identical procedure, but allowing subjects to decide the most appropriate shock level at each stage. Less than 5 per cent of the subjects chose to deliver dangerous shocks under these circumstances. Could we say then that the direct, accepted authority of the

To be near you is to obey! Obedience is particularly high when the person who gives the commands is in the immediate proximity of the subject.

experimenter is the main factor forcing subjects to behave in this way? Not entirely. Simple group pressure from fellow subjects was almost as effective in influencing subjects to deliver lethal shocks as direct commands from the experimenter.

In a further modification of the procedure, Milgram (1964) asked groups of three subjects to suggest the most appropriate shock level. The lowest proposal would automatically be accepted. In fact, two of the 'subjects' were really confederates of the experimenter, and proposed increasing the shock levels at every trial. Under these conditions, the sole 'real' subject could have ensured that the minimum 15 volt shock was used every time, but only àt the cost of going against the opinion of the others. Instead, almost 70 per cent of the subjects went along with group pressure and delivered shocks of 150 volts, although only about 20 per cent continued all the way to 450 volts. It seems then that simple group pressure from two people was quite sufficient to induce conformity in many subjects, without any direct backup from the experimenter.

The behaviour of others need not necessarily be an influence for the worse. When two members of three-subject groups (again, confederates of the experimenter) refused to continue with the experiment after dangerous shock levels were reached, more than 90 per cent of the 'real' subjects also defied the experimenter at some point (Figure 14.2), and refused to employ maximum shock levels (Milgram, 1965). Taken

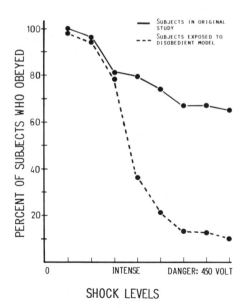

SHOCK LEVELS

FIGURE 14.2 Obedience to authority. About 65 per cent of subjects obeyed an experimenter and delivered 450 volt electric shocks to an innocent victim (top line). When two others refused to go along beyond 'intense' shock levels, obedience markedly decreased (bottom line). (After Milgram, 1974).

together, these findings provide a dramatic illustration of the powerful effects of obedience. We do not have to look to such extreme examples, however. Frequently, people seem to be content enough to do as they are told, if the costs are not too great. In one study, strangers on a bus were simply ordered by an apparently healthy young male to yield their seats to him. Very few refused. Interaction in groups is often characterised by the exercise of such more or less direct social influence strategies, either in the form of obedience, or through conformity pressures.

Leadership
Obeying somebody implies the acceptance of that person's superior authority and *leadership*. What exactly do we mean when we say that a person is a good leader? Do we refer to that individual's special personal qualities, the power conferred on him by a job or his unique ability to influence people? Leadership is a very important aspect of social life, and interaction within a leadership context represents special problems both for the leader and the followers. Leadership is also of great importance in the economic sphere. Most human organisations rely on leaders to motivate workers and to organise production processes in a way which will satisfy the organisation's goals. In this section we shall briefly consider some characteristics of leadership.

Perhaps the earliest, and, to this day, most appealing theory of leadership emphasises the special personal qualities of leaders. Throughout history, there are many examples of leaders who possessed unique personal characteristics which helped them to obtain the loyalty and obedience of others. The trouble is that many different personal features may facilitate leadership, depending on the circumstances: is it

---

ACTIVITY 14.2
Qualities of Leadership

Try to think of five individuals well known to you whom you would consider to be good 'leaders'. Write their names on a piece of paper. Next, try to think of the three most important personal characteristics of each of the five people which make them good leaders, in your opinion. Write these characteristics on that piece of paper as well. As you read on in this section, refer back to your descriptions to see to what extent your personal theory of leadership, as revealed in these choices, coincides with the results of social psychological research.

empathy or ruthlessness, intelligence or demagoguery, openness or secretiveness, selfishness or generosity which will serve a leader best?

There are examples of almost any combination of personal characteristics amongst known 'leaders'. Churchill and Stalin, De Gaulle and Hitler, Gandhi and Mao were all 'leaders' with very different individual personalities. There seems to be no single quality of 'leadership' shared by this small group, and it is even less likely that historians will identify unique leadership traits amongst the many 'great men' of history. Psychologists attempting to identify the critical traits of a leader fared no better. Despite considerable effort, they failed to isolate a specific list of characteristics which would universally distinguish leaders from non-leaders.

We are thus forced to accept the conclusion that optimal leader characteristics very much depend on the particular situation the leader is facing. Almost anybody can become a 'good' leader, given the right circumstances. Churchill was less than successful as a politician in peacetime, but the situation created by the outbreak of war suited his talents ideally. Similarly, Hitler's rise was closely tied to the aftermath of the Depression. According to this situationist view, the processes of social influence operating in leadership are not all one-way. A leader is not simply there to influence the group, but the group, and the problems facing it, in turn select, and later shape and influence the appropriate leader. In unstructured groups in particular, a potential leader has to accumulate a certain amount of respect and standing, often by first displaying conformity, before he/she can credibly seek to influence others. Hollander called this process the accumulation of *idiosyncracy credit* — the acquisition of sufficient respect and standing through conformity which allows a person to be creative and non-conformist later on.

Different leaders often have very different leadership styles. In one early study, Lewin, Lippitt and White (1939) compared the effectiveness of democratic, autocratic and laissez-faire leadership on the performance and satisfaction of groups. They found that democratic leaders, using a consultative style, achieved both higher productivity and satisfaction in these experimental groups. However, it is far from certain that democratic leaders would enjoy the same advantage in other cultures and under different circumstances.

Much depends on the source of the leader's power. French and Raven (1959) developed a highly influential analysis of the varieties of social power leaders (and others) may use. Power may be derived from our ability to punish (*coercive* power) or to reward (*reward* power) others, from our special skill, expertise or knowledge (*expert* power), from the authority and legitimacy of the position we occupy (*legitimate* power), and finally, from the attractiveness of our ideas or personality which influences others to refer to us and identify with us (*referent* power). The kind of power a leader has will obviously influence his/her ability to function effectively. What sorts of power did the leaders you nominated in Activity 14.2 have?

Other social psychologists went a step further in specifying the exact characteristics of situations which will call for particular kinds of leaders. Fred Fiedler (1967) developed what is called the contingency model of leadership, which assumes that effective leadership is the result of the combination of particular leader personality traits and situational characteristics. According to Fiedler, leaders mainly differ along a dimension of task orientation versus person orientation. Some leaders concentrate on task performance even at the expense of good personal relations, while others are more interested in maintaining a warm, cohesive atmosphere than in task completion. These leader characteristics can be empirically assessed using a simple questionnaire. This asks each leader to describe the person they would least like to work with, their least preferred coworker (LPC). Task-oriented leaders give a more negative evaluation than socially-oriented leaders of such inefficient performers.

The situation confronting the leader was analysed by Fiedler in terms of its overall favourability. This depends on factors (in decreasing order of importance) such as (a) the existence of good or bad relations between the leader and the group, (b) the structure and clarity of the task to be performed, and (c) the leader's power over group members. Directive, task-oriented leaders function best in highly favourable, or highly unfavourable situations; non-directive, socially-oriented leaders perform best when the situation is of intermediate difficulty. Figure 14.3 provides a summary illustration of Fiedler's model.

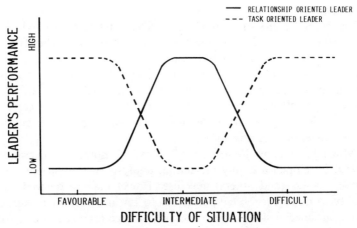

FIGURE 14.3 A situational model of leadership. Task-oriented leaders perform best when the situation is either highly favourable, or very difficult; relationship-oriented leaders do best when the situation is of intermediate difficulty. (After Fiedler, 1967).

Numerous empirical studies were carried out by Fiedler and others to test this theory in groups such as army teams, production units and so on. The model has been criticised, however, on the grounds that the measure of leader style through the LPC scale is unreliable, and that situational features other than those considered by Fiedler also play an important role in determining optimal leadership style (for example, whether the power of a leader is accepted as legitimate or not). Appointed leaders, for example, often have less legitimacy and power than leaders elected and accepted by the group (French and Raven, 1959).

As Fiedler as well as others realised, effective leadership involves two often incompatible functions: to keep group members happy, satisfied and friendly with each other, and to ensure that the group performs its tasks as effectively as possible. The first kind of leader is called a socio-emotional leader, and the second kind of leader a task leader. Often two different individuals will perform these two tasks within the same group. While one person coordinates and enforces task performance, the other 'leader' helps members to solve personal conflicts, release tension and obtain satisfaction from their membership. If you now go back to the five leaders you nominated in the previous activity, can you identify who is a task leader, who is a socio-emotional leader, and who can carry out both of these functions effectively?

There are leaders and leaders. Relationship-oriented leaders are not very good at handling difficult leadership situations. Task-oriented leaders do best when the situation is either very difficult (their concentration on the task at hand is essential), or very favourable (interpersonal relationships are already good, and they do not need to improve things in that respect). This is the major conclusion of Fiedler's leadership model.

Conclusions

Interpersonal influence is an essential part of the social interaction process. However slightly, we cannot help influencing each other even in the course of the most superficial interaction. In this chapter we discussed some of the most common forms of social influence that individuals and groups can exert on each other in the course of interaction. At the most basic level, the mere presence of other people may cause arousal, and either an improvement or a decrease in performance. Conformity and compliance are processes which commonly occur when groups attempt to influence their members to behave in ways acceptable to the group. Most of us are very sensitive to such group demands and expectations, and in most situations readily conform to them. This almost universal human tendency is the very foundation on which all higher-level social organisations rely for their effectiveness.

Social influence processes are not limited to groups, however. Individuals issuing direct requests or commands are capable of influencing others and most people have a strong tendency to obey such orders. As Milgram showed, even when the commands are immoral or objectionable, many people obey them as long as they can disclaim personal responsibility for the consequences of their actions. Finally, we looked at a very special question in interpersonal influence processes: what are the factors which determine effective leadership? All of these various kinds of influence are readily observable in the course of our daily interactions with others. In the next chapter, we shall look at some of the specific interaction processes which take place within groups.

15. Interaction in groups

15.

INTERACTION IN GROUPS

We looked at some of the basic processes of interpersonal influence in the previous chapter. In this chapter we shall expand our discussion further by considering some of the general features which characterise social interaction within groups. All of us belong to numerous social groups, which may be small or large, involving or casual, and may or may not involve direct contact between the members. Your family, workplace, neighbourhood, club or school are all in a sense 'groups' of which you are a member. Since we are mainly concerned with interaction processes in this volume, those groups which are based on immediate face-to-face interactions will be of prime interest to us. By and large, we may classify the groups people belong to into two kinds: small, intimate groups characterised by frequent interactions and personal involvement, and larger, formal groups in which relationships between members are regulated through more formal and impersonal rules or contractual processes.

Toennies, a German sociologist writing at the end of the last century, described these two kinds of groups respectively as communities (Gemeinschaft) and associations (Gesellschaft). Communities are warm, involving face-to-face groups with a great deal of cohesion, conformity and control, while associations are less involved and more formal and impersonal groups. These two types of groups, of course, provide very different interaction environments for their members. Charles Cooley (1902) used the terms 'primary groups' and 'secondary groups' to refer to these two basic forms of human social units.

You may remember that in the introduction to this volume, I suggested that the historical breakdown and disappearance of primary group relationships, and the growing importance of impersonal secondary group relationships may have a lot to do with the fact that social interaction represents a problem for more and more people. The evolution of modern industrial societies freed people from the bondage of community based village life, making social and geographic mobility possible. As a result, 'primary group' relationships decreased. The emergence of impersonal secondary groups as the main scenes for our social interactions is thus a fairly recent development. Indeed, most of the people with whom we have intimate relationships belong to no single group, but are scattered both geographically and socially. Social scientists call this a 'network' pattern of relationships. Despite the apparently declining importance of primary groups, interaction in face-to-face groups remains one of the most complex and involving social experiences people have. We shall deal with some of the most important features of interaction in a group below.

Measuring group interactions

Perhaps the first hallmark of direct interaction within a primary group is the enormous complexity of what is going on. Even in groups of as few as three or four members, it is very difficult for an observer to keep track of all the interaction processes which take place, let alone analyse and interpret them adequately (see Activity 15.1).

ACTIVITY 15.1
Observing Group Interaction

To appreciate the full complexity of group interaction processes, try to carry out a small observation project yourself. Select a small group of three or four members in a public setting (street, pub, etc.), and try to observe accurately for a period of ten minutes everything that happens within this group of people. Do not forget to pay attention to both verbal and nonverbal messages (see Chapters 9 and 10). Try to note your observations on a piece of paper for further analysis. You may refer to these notes later as you read this chapter.

The difficulty of accurately observing and describing group interactions has occupied social psychologists for some time. At the most basic level, we may simply record the proportion of time each individual group member spends in a particular activity, for example, speaking, listening, fidgeting, looking away, etc. Even such a simple observation system can tell us quite a lot about a group. The amount of time spent speaking, for example, is likely to be a good indicator of a group member's relative dominance and leadership position within a group. Can you identify such a dominant person on the basis of speaking time in the group you observed? Of course, those talking most are not necessarily the most popular. In fact, the second-most talkative member was found to be the most popular in some studies!

Of course, such elementary interaction measures do not give us very detailed information. Apart from knowing how much a person speaks, we may be interested in recording what he/she said, if it was positive or negative, and so on. The great problem in such analyses is to design a scoring scheme in advance, so that we know what we are looking for when observing a group. Bales (1950) designed a widely used method for the continuous observation of interactions, called 'interaction process analysis'. He proposed that the success of a group depends on two factors: how well it can solve the tasks facing it (task function), and how well it can keep its members satisfied with the group (integrative, or socio-emotional function).

In his scoring system, 12 interactive 'moves', falling into four basic categories, can be identified: socio-emotional—positive (showing solidarity or agreement), task related—attempted solutions (e.g. give suggestions or opinions), task related—questions (ask for opinion or orientation) and socio-emotional—negative (disagree and show antagonism) (see Table 15.1 for details). In the usual procedure, at least one rater is assigned to observe and score each group member's behaviour. The method has been used in a variety of settings, and has been found to be a reliable and useful way of analysing group interactions.

Stages of group formation
How do previously isolated individuals become a 'group'? Studies showed that in groups which emerge naturally, there is a fairly standard sequence of interaction patterns. The process of becoming acquainted with a group of strangers and forming a new social unit, a group, out of what has been a collection of individuals, places special strains on most people's interactive skills. Tuckman (1965) and others suggested that there may be four common phases which groups have to pass through before they are firmly established. We can label these stages as follows: forming, storming, norming, and performing.

Forming involves becoming acquainted with each other, and the task facing the group. *Storming* is a crucial stage when conflicts and individual differences come to the surface, and competition for status and particular roles emerges. *Norming* is the stage when these conflicts are resolved through the creation and acceptance of shared group norms, attitudes and role definitions. Finally, the *performing* stage implies that a stable pattern of personal relationships and task functions has been established which allows the group to get on with its normal functions. Just think back to the last time you had occasion to participate in such a newly forming group — can you identify these four phases? A few years ago I spent some time teaching at Open University summer schools in Britain, where students had to form such groups in order to participate in a simulation exercise where they pretended to function as the cabinets

TABLE 15.1
A SYSTEM FOR ANALYSING GROUP INTERACTION: BALES'
INTERACTION PROCESS ANALYSIS

a. SOCIAL-EMOTIONAL MOVES
   Positive reactions   1. Shows solidarity, raises others'
                            status, gives help and reward _____
                         2. Shows tension release; jokes, laughs,
                            and shows satisfaction _____
                         3. Agrees, showing passive acceptance;
                            understands, concurs, and complies _____

b. TASK-RELATED MOVES
   Attempted answers   4. Gives suggestion and direction,
                            implying autonomy for others _____
                         5. Gives opinion, evaluation, and
                            analysis; expresses feelings and
                            wishes _____
                         6. Gives orientation and information;
                            repeats, clarifies, and confirms _____

c. TASK-RELATED MOVES
   Questions   7. Asks for orientation, information,   abcdef
                            repetition, and confirmation _____
                         8. Asks for opinion, evaluation, analysis,
                            and expression of feeling _____
                         9. Asks for suggestion, direction, and
                            possible ways of action _____

d. SOCIAL-EMOTIONAL MOVES
   Negative reactions 10. Disagrees, showing passive reaction
                            and formality; withholds help _____
                        11. Shows tension and asks for help;
                            withdraws from field _____
                        12. Shows antagonism, deflates others'
                            status and defends or asserts self _____

   a = problems of orientation
   b = problems of evaluation
   c = problems of control
   d = problems of decision
   e = problems of tension management
   f = problems of integration

After Bales, 1950

of various countries. In over 60 such groups I observed, the above stages of group formation were clearly identifiable.

These four stages in group interaction also show that even negative behaviours, for example showing hostility and competition in the storming stage, play a useful role in group formation. If such conflicts are not expressed and resolved early on, the group is unlikely to reach higher stages of development and function effectively. The end result of this group formation process is a social unit whose members share certain norms. As Newcomb suggested, for social psychological purposes the distinctive thing about a group is that its members share norms about something. The establishment of specialised roles (for example, the 'leader', the 'joker', the 'programme organiser', etc.) and a fairly stable group structure are essential for the future success of a group.

Group structure

An inevitable consequence of the group formation process described above is that members come to occupy reasonably stable and predictable positions within the group, and vis-à-vis each other. These various positions may be described in terms of their status, the specific roles to be performed, their rank, or the cliques or subgroups to which members may belong. Once a group is established, much of what happens later in its daily interactions is predictable on the basis of the already existing group structure. You may recall that in Chapter 11 we described a method for analysing group structures developed by Moreno, called sociometry. This method consists of charting the various preference choices made by group members about each other (see Chapter 11 for an example). The resulting sociogram (for example, Figure 11.1) in essence gives us a 'map' of the existing network of personal relationships in the group.

Beyond this informal group structure based on friendship choices, in more formalised groups (such as work teams, university seminar groups, etc.) structure may also be determined by other criteria, such as skill, competence, expertise and so on. In organisations such as factories or offices the formal structure may even be explicitly planned and displayed on organisational charts. In a production unit, for example, group structure may depend on the requirements of the flow of the production process, or the chain of command imposed by management. In a seminar group, intellectual ability, past courses completed or verbal ability may influence a group member's position in the group structure.

In an American academic group studied by Jones and Young (see Chapter 11), consisting of faculty, staff and graduate students, a member's position in the group structure was dependent on three characteristics: his intellectual ability, his sociability, and political orientation (left-wing—right-wing). In a similar study which looked at a British academic unit, we found a very similar group structure (see Figure 11.2 for a model of this group structure). These studies illustrate that a person's position in a group's structure depends on a combination of formal and informal factors: being extroverted, friendly and sociable may be just as important as task-relevant characteristics, such as being intelligent and competent. In the group you observed in Activity 15.1, could you make any guesses about the overall structure and the position of individual members? What determined structure, and how were status and position displayed?

Some are more equal than others. Every group tends to develop its own hierarchy and structure, which also determines the interaction patterns and communication channels within the group. High-status members interact more, and are more central in the communication structure. A member's status and position in the group may be displayed using a variety of signals such as dress, nonverbal displays or various other insignia.

Communication channels

An important consequence of the establishment of a stable group structure is the channelling of communications. In every group, information is distributed unequally: not all members get to find out about everything at the same time. Members who are close to each other in the formal or informal group structure communicate more easily and frequently than more distant or isolated members. Communication is a real source of power in most groups: knowing what is happening, being able to contribute to and influence the group's actions is essential for a satisfying membership. Social psychologists have studied extensively the consequences of more or less open group communication systems on group performance and satisfaction. Leavitt (1951) is one of the pioneers of this research.

In Leavitt's (1951) study, five-member groups had the task of finding out which symbol out of the several they were each given was shared by all of them. This problem requires communication between all members. Leavitt regulated who could send messages to whom by creating various physical barriers between group members, making more or less open or closed communication networks (see Figure 15.1).

Results generally showed that highly centralised networks in which all information had to be channelled through one 'leader', such as the wheel below, were more efficient in solving the problem, but resulted in members being more dissatisfied with the group. More open and diffuse communicative systems on the other hand were far more satisfying to group members, although sometimes less efficient. Individual satisfaction with the group was thus directly related to a member's access to communication channels. In a related study, Shaw (1954) also manipulated the amount of information group members had, giving some people a lot of information, and others only very little.

Under these conditions, the 'circle' pattern was both most efficient and most satisfying, resulting in the relatively easy diffusion of information. In general, the more access a person had to information, either directly provided, or in the form of access to communication channels, the more positively he/she felt about the group. Furthermore, people who possess information are more likely to assume leadership roles, and be seen by others as leaders. Information is thus an important resource in group interaction, and access to it partly depends on the existing group structure.

The structure of a group influences other things as well, apart from access to information. Groups often go out of their way to give tangible expression to structural differences between members, as if to signal and reinforce their personal hierarchies for all the world to see. The arrangement of the desks in an office, the size of offices allocated to lecturers, senior lecturers and professors in an academic department, the preferred seating positions around a luncheon table (see Figure 9.2) are all things which express group structure and hierarchy. Sommer, whose work on the use of space we discussed in Chapter 9, found that group leaders preferred to sit in the dominant end position around a rectangular table (see Activity 15.2).

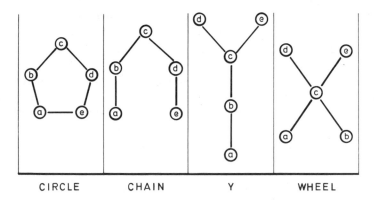

CIRCLE   CHAIN   Y   WHEEL

FIGURE 15.1 Communication networks. These communication networks in five-member groups differ in the degree of centrality; the wheel is the most centralised, and the circle is the least centralised. (After Leavitt, 1951).

ACTIVITY 15.2
Symbols of Status and Position in Groups

Try to think of the various groups of which you are a member. Select five groups which differ from each other in formality. For example, a formal group may be your work team, your university class, your school class and so on, while an informal group would be a group of friends, acquaintances or family. For each of these five groups, note the ways in which group structure, and the status or position of individual members is expressed through observable symbols (for example, dress, seating position, communication patterns or access to information). These are differences of which we are not usually conscious. If you observe your selected groups for some time, you are bound to discover many unusual facts about their status structure, interaction rituals and the way power is shared and allocated.

Group cohesion and reference groups

Not all group members have an equal interest in, and commitment to their group, and not every group is able to satisfy the wishes and aspirations of its members. Group cohesion may be broadly defined as the extent to which members of a group are committed to shared norms and objectives, and have positive sentiments about each other and their group. Those positive feelings may have a major influence on a group's performance. Studies of soldiers in battle have repeatedly shown that people fight and risk their lives not because of their belief in the ultimate purposes of the war, but because of their commitment to, and solidarity with, their immediate combat unit (Stouffer et al. 1949). Being in a group under extremely stressful and dangerous conditions gives group members a sense of emotional security and commitment.

In a curious way, we seem to have particularly high regard for and commitment to groups for which we have made sacrifices, and which were hard to join. In an interesting study, Aronson and Mills (1959) showed that subjects who had to undergo a difficult initiation to join a group liked the group more than subjects who were accepted without any problems. Presumably, similar processes operate in cohesive military units: having undergone strenuous initial training, and having experienced combat together, soldiers value their group far more than is common in civilian life. This process is consciously used in some instances to foster a strong group spirit and cohesion. The gruelling training an elite unit, such as the US Marine Corps, gives to its recruits might serve to increase their attraction to the group, instead of reducing it, as one might well expect.

Cohesiveness also influences interaction processes within a group. Cohesive groups are less tolerant of deviant behaviours, and exert stronger pressures towards conformity (Festinger, 1950). Cohesiveness and conformity are two sides of the same coin: the price of deriving satisfaction and a positive sense of identity from our group memberships is to subjugate our individual wishes and conform to group norms. In practice, this is often much less of an imposition than you would think. Once a group is established and its norms clear, members identify with those expectations relatively easily and no longer see them as restrictive impositions. In this way, the values and norms of the groups we belong to become our own values and norms, internalised as part of our own positive sense of self and identity. Several studies have shown that joining a group quickly results in a change of personal values and attitudes to conform with group standards (see Activity 15.2).

A classic study of this kind was carried out by Newcomb (1943). He was interested in the changes which would take place as students from middle-class, conservative homes joined an institution (Bennington College) known for its liberal attitudes. As expected, joining this new group resulted in a re-orientation of attitudes, and students soon came to adopt the liberal college as their reference group. The term 'reference group' itself means that our own values, and ultimately identity, are often 'borrowed' from the groups we belong to. Newcomb did a follow-up study of the Bennington students 25 years later, and found that many ex-students continued to identify with the liberal values of the college even after this lengthy period. They usually achieved this by continuing to select friends and group memberships which were consistent with the

A hard club to join! The more difficult, painful or embarrassing it is to become a member of a group, the more loyalty and devotion successful joiners will show towards that group.

ACTIVITY 15.3
Who Are You?

Your task in this activity is deceptively simple: take a blank sheet of paper, and write down 20 statements each of which is an answer to the question 'Who am I?'. Do not read any further until you have completed this task!

This procedure, the so-called 20 statements test, used to be a favourite research tool of symbolic interactionist researchers. We are interested in your answers for a slightly different reason here. Most people, when asked to define their own social identity as is done in the 20 statements test, rely surprisingly heavily on their various group memberships. It seems that we all define ourselves, to a large extent, through the various groups we belong to.

Describing yourself, for example, in terms such as being white, Australian, male, university graduate, public servant, resident in Sydney, and so on are essentially group definitions. These characteristics define your identity as different from non-white, female, non-graduate non-Australian, non-public servants. Why do we choose such categories instead of any of thousands of others? By and large, self-definitions reflect those group memberships which we perceive as positive and valuable, and which distinguish us from other groups. How many of the 20 answers you gave describe your group affiliations? As you read on, the important role of various group memberships in supporting a person's social identity should become even clearer.

---

values they acquired at the college. You may recall that attitude similarity is in any case one of the most important antecedents of friendship formation (Chapter 12)!

Membership in cohesive groups also has some practical consequences. The more strongly a person identifies with a group, the more likely that his/her individual behaviour can be changed through group processes. The use of group dynamics to create change was developed by Kurt Lewin (1947) during and after the Second World War, when the necessity to influence people's behaviour in accordance with wartime and post-war requirements was particularly acute. Principles of group identification were used in the planning of various advertising and propaganda campaigns to influence, for example, people's dietary habits. Campaigns to promote the consumption of orange juice, or meat substitutes used such approaches. Lewin's work laid the foundations of most of the later applied work on group dynamics, and many advertisers still use similar techniques without necessarily realising it.

Group decisionmaking and 'groupthink'
However, strong group cohesiveness is not always an asset. When a group is faced with the task of making decisions on the basis of complex and often controversial information, it is an advantage if group members feel free to argue strongly for competing positions. This is usually not readily tolerated in highly cohesive groups. Janis (1972) coined the term 'groupthink' to describe the position when a highly cohesive group, usually under the influence of a strong and dynamic leader, insulates itself from the realities of the surrounding situation by considering only one aspect of a complex problem. The group usually feels secure and optimistic about its ability, and members come to believe that whatever doubts they may have are less important than supporting the group.

Groupthink may lead to disastrous decisions. A frequently quoted example is the decision by President Kennedy and his closest advisers to embark on the Bay of Pigs invasion of Cuba, against readily available evidence suggesting the difficulty of the task. Groupthink may occur in many business or informal groups as well. Whenever strong group cohesion prohibits the expression of relevant dissenting opinions there is a danger of unrealistic decisions being made.

Groupthink is, of course, only an extreme case of suboptimal performance by groups. Since cohesion, conformity and even emotional attachment are essential aspects of almost every group, the danger of mistaken decisions due to such normative pressures is always present. In their authoritative review, Janis and Mann (1977) consider the extensive evidence available about group decisionmaking processes, and suggest several 'rational' problem-solving strategies to improve group performance in this field.

These include techniques for the rational analysis of the decision alternatives, such as the preparation of 'balance sheets', showing both the positive and the negative aspects of all relevant alternatives. In long-established groups, it is sound practice to challenge established decisions from time to time, suggest Janis and Mann (1977). Another technique is to role-play decision consequences, in effect, asking members to imagine how they would act *after* a particular decision has been made. This helps to clarify all the possible consequences of a decision. Outsiders observing and commenting on the group's decisionmaking performance may provide another valuable source of improvement in decisionmaking performance.

Group contagion and deindividuation
Another commonly noted effect of group membership is that individuals tend to feel less direct, personal responsibility for their actions than they

do if they act alone. In a sense, a group will 'hide' us as individuals. As a result, in collaboration with others we may be willing to carry out acts which we would not be prepared to perform alone (see also Chapter 14). Since the last century, many writers have noted this facilitating effect of groups. French sociologists such as Le Bon and Tarde described the behaviour of mobs and crowds as contrary to normal human rationality and ethics. Members of a crowd were thought to be 'swept away' by the emotionalism of the group, their reason temporarily suspended. And indeed, being in a group often gives people a sense of self-confidence and assertiveness which they may otherwise lack.

Apart from these emotional influences, being in a group also means that we are simply less distinct and visible as individuals. Our usual sense of individual identity may be temporarily replaced by a sense of group identity and our actions may no longer be subject to individual control. The less identifiable people are as individuals, the more likely that such a 'deindividuation' will be experienced. The wearing of uniforms and sunglasses by police, hoods by members of the Ku Klux Klan or uniform jackets and regalia by members of motorcycle gangs or football fans all facilitate a sense of deindividuation and group identity.

Zimbardo (1970) showed that by making individuals less identifiable as individuals, the probability of aggressive acts is also increased. In this experiment, female subjects were given an opportunity to give electric shocks to another girl. Some of the subjects were dressed in an oversize,

---

ACTIVITY 15.4
Observing Crowd Behaviour

Do people behave differently in a crowd from the way they would if they were alone? If so, is their behaviour really less rational and more emotional? You may get some insight into questions such as these by carefully observing crowds, for example, at a demonstration, or a sports event. Try to note the frequency of various forms of behaviours performed by such crowds, and the incidence of collective as against individual acts (for example, chanting and coordinated movements). Try to pay particular attention to behaviours which would not normally be acceptable if performed by an individual alone. You should have little difficulty in finding examples of socially undesirable behaviours which the same people would probably not engage in without the facilitating influence of deindividuation that a crowd provides.

loose lab coat and wore a hood over their heads, making them unidentifiable as persons. The other group of subjects was given name tags to make them readily identifiable. The 'deindividuated' group gave almost twice as many electric shocks as the others. Being anonymous seems to lift the usual constraints on individual behaviour which apply in everyday life. Group membership is often one of the ways of achieving such anonymity.

Sometimes such 'deindividuation' may lead to bizarre kinds of behaviours. There are many reports of so-called 'suicide baiting', when groups of people cheer and encourage a potential suicide victim to jump and take his own life. Leon Mann (1981) investigated numerous accounts of such suicide-baiting incidents. He found that conditions which favoured deindividuation, such as large crowds, darkness, and a prolonged episode were also predominantly associated with suicide baiting. It is precisely under these conditions that people have a chance to be influenced by a group atmosphere, to lose their sense of individual identity and responsibility and do something which as individuals they would probably hesitate to do: to urge another person to kill himself.

Inter-group conflict and cooperation
Being a member of a group can contribute to our sense of positive self-worth and identity only to the extent that our group is seen as different from, and better than, similar other groups. This was one of the points demonstrated by Activity 15.3. Accordingly, people seem to have a strong tendency to overvalue their own groups and undervalue others. Whenever two groups are in competition, the consequence is an exaggerated perception of the differences between the groups. In a now classic field study, Sherif et al. (1961) looked at various features of inter-group competition and conflict. Their subjects were children participating in a summer camp. When rewards were dependent on competitive group performance, intense competition between groups of children was the result. The experimenters then tried to eliminate competition using several techniques. The most successful method was to make collective rewards (for example, seeing a movie) dependent on the performance of a task which could only be completed by cooperation between the groups.

The tendency to overvalue our own group, and devalue others may be a very important source of prejudice and discrimination in the real world. In an intriguing series of experiments, Henri Tajfel and his colleagues (Tajfel, 1978; Tajfel and Forgas, 1981; Turner, 1975) showed that even belonging to an extremely superficial and short-lived group is sufficient for many people to discriminate against outgroup members.

In the typical experiment, subjects who do not know each other are allocated to a group according to completely arbitrary criteria (for example, the throw of a die). Later, they are asked to divide rewards (for example, money) between two other people about whom they again know nothing except that one is a member of their own 'group' and the other of the second 'group'. Surprisingly, even this almost meaningless 'group membership' is apparently sufficient for most people to practise discrimination against the outgroup. Often, a strategy is adopted which maximises the differences between in-group and out-group members, even at the cost of obtaining the maximum benefit for the in-group. For example, if people have the choice of either giving $8.00 to their own group and $7.00 to the other group, or $6.00 to their own group and $2.00 to the other group, they often choose the second alternative.

Tajfel suggests that discrimination against other groups is an almost automatic process characteristic of all human beings. It is as if we were 'programmed' to believe that our own group is better than similar others. Such instant biases in favour of 'our' group account for many forms of prejudice and discrimination. It is enough to know that I am in group 'a' and you are in group 'b' for me to assume that group 'a' is superior, and act accordingly. We do this because being in a 'superior' group gives us a positive sense of identity. People are thus naturally interested in making the differences between their groups and others seem as great as possible.

The polarising effects of groups
We have already seen above that in some circumstances, groups tend to make less than ideal decisions. In a highly cohesive group, 'groupthink' may take over, resulting in the biased evaluation of the available evidence. Yet groups are frequently used as decisionmaking instruments in our society. The more important a decision, the more likely it is that it will be entrusted to a group rather than a single individual. Juries, interviewing panels, cabinets, committees and boards of companies all operate on the assumption that groups are better at decisionmaking than individuals. The widespread use of groups as decisionmaking instruments probably has a lot to do with the democratic ideology of Western societies. Groups are not only more representative, but are also believed to be less likely to make extreme or unreasonable decisions. We have discussed previously the strong conformity processes operating in groups, which are likely to eliminate deviant or extreme individual opinions (for example, the work by Sherif, Asch, Schachter, etc. covered in Chapter 14).

The assumption that groups are less extreme than individuals is, however, not always justified. Considerable evidence suggests that in some circumstances at least, groups may be more extreme, and take greater risks than their individual members would. Several studies found that in decisions about acceptable levels of risk, groups tend to opt for riskier alternatives than individuals: they generate a so-called 'risky shift'. In the typical experiment, individuals are presented with everyday dilemmas, and asked at what level of risk they would be prepared to opt for the risky choice. For example, an engineer with a stable but low-paying job is offered a better-paying job with a risky new company — should he take the job if the chances of success are 1 in 10, 2 in 10, and so on? Later, the same individuals are assigned to groups, and are asked to go through the same problems again, this time making a joint consensus decision as a group. Surprisingly, groups consistently opt for greater acceptable risk levels than do individuals on most problems of this kind (Kogan and Wallach, 1964).

How can we explain this bizarre effect? Isn't it true that groups generate caution and conformity by 'suppressing' extreme opinions and behaviours? Why then this group-induced shift towards risk? There may be several factors at play here. One possible explanation is that *diffusion of responsibility* for a decision occurs in a group. Since no single individual has to carry the whole responsibility for the risky decision, everybody feels inclined to be a little more daring. Another possible explanation has to do with *leadership*. It may be that the most 'risky' or extreme individual group members also turn out to be the most persuasive leaders, so that the group will come to accept their extreme positions. Some research at least suggests that people who have more extreme positions also have more confidence in their judgments.

Yet another explanation is that in a society such as ours in which risk taking is generally seen as a positive *value*, members of a group may try to outdo each other in riskiness, something which would not occur if they were making the decisions as individuals (Brown, 1965). Moscovici and Zavalloni (1969) suggested another explanation: as a result of group discussion, individuals come to be more personally *involved* in the issue. As a result, their confidence in the correctness of their positions, and the strength of their identification with those views increases. The result is that they argue for, and willingly accept more extreme positions than they initially held.

After some years of research on this so-called 'risky shift' phenomenon, some psychologists began to ask whether groups are also more extreme on other, non-risk related decision tasks (Moscovici and Zavalloni, 1969). There is now strong evidence suggesting the generality of the extremity shift: group decisions on issues such as attitudes, values, person perception judgments, and judgments about group stereotypes were all found to be more extreme than exactly the same judgments when made by individuals. In one of our studies (Forgas, 1977) subjects were shown videotaped interviews with nine different people, and were asked to form impressions about these people first alone, and later as a group. Once again, we found that group judgments were more extreme. In a follow-up study (Forgas, 1981) subjects were asked to decide whether a student caught cheating at an exam was responsible, and how he/she ought to be punished. Groups were more extreme in their responsibility attribution judgments and tended to give more severe punishments than did individuals. These shifts are usually quite small, but statistically significant.

Given the widespread use of decisionmaking groups in everyday life, what conclusions can we draw from these results? Could it be that groups such as juries or interviewing panels indeed have a tendency to make unreasonably extreme judgments? Fortunately, the problem is less serious than would at first appear. For a group shift to occur it is also necessary that a completely free, unrestricted and informal discussion between group members takes place, allowing a high degree of personal involvement by members (Moscovici and Zavalloni, 1969). This is, by and large, not the procedure used in formal decisionmaking groups. Formal groups tend to follow strict procedural rules, have to obey time limits and are subject to the authority of formal leaders or chairmen. Under these conditions, the group shift is less likely to occur, or indeed, the opposite, cautious shift might take place.

Studies which explicitly manipulated the formality of the group discussion (cf. Moscovici and Zavalloni, 1969; Forgas, 1977; 1983) report that group opinions are likely to become more extreme than individual opinions only in informal groups. It seems then that groups of friends, neighbours or work colleagues engaged in free and unrestrained discussion are far more likely to be a source of polarised attitudes and opinions than official decisionmaking groups. Indeed, this seems to be the common experience of most of us. We seem to be far more concerned about being discussed informally by a group of neighbours or acquaintances, than about being discussed by a formal group. In conclusion, the group shift effect is more likely to contribute to biased opinions in the private sphere than in the formal, public sphere. To use the terminology introduced earlier, primary groups are more likely to produce extreme opinion shifts than are secondary groups.

Training groups and encounter groups

Interaction in groups can be a very satisfying, yet demanding experience. Perhaps the most important thing about group behaviour is the unusual intensity of the interaction. Whereas in a dyadic relationship it might take years before a stage of great emotional involvement and mutuality is reached (see Chapters 12 and 13), even quite shortlived and superficial groups are capable of generating a great deal of emotional intensity and involvement. Just think of the way people behave on a football ground when their team scores, or interact with a large group of people they otherwise hardly know in the pub. Being 'in' a group and part 'of' a group are among the most intense and involving interaction experiences we can have. No wonder then, that 'instant' groups are often used for therapeutic or manipulative purposes. Lewin was among the first to use 'training groups' (T-groups) as forums for bringing about personal and social changes. In this original form, group discussion was simply used to bring about new perceptions and attitudes in members.

In recent times, the use of groups as agencies of change has proliferated. Many week-end programmes, often promoted by commercial, self-improvement organisations, employ extreme forms of group pressure to make people 'confess' to their personal and interpersonal shortcomings, in the hope of bringing about an improvement. There is little reliable evidence for lasting beneficial change from such experiences, although most participants do report some improvement. Of course, it is not easy to determine whether the group experience really changed them, or simply influenced them to describe themselves more positively. Such intensive group sessions can also be dangerous, since the powerful forces of conformity and obedience may be brought to bear on possibly disturbed individuals who are also separated from their usual sources of social support. There are numerous cases of psychological breakdowns being precipitated by unscrupulous group training programmes.

In writing about such commercial encounter groups, we must not forget the financial aspect of the experience. A person who has possibly paid several hundred dollars to spend a weekend being shouted at and abused is not likely to admit that it was a waste of time and money. As the study by Aronson and Mills (1959) so clearly showed, the higher the entrance price to a group, and the more doubtful the experience, the more likely that people will feel motivated to defend their participation, and react with a strong commitment to the group. It is perhaps for this reason that the cost of such group programmes is often out of all proportion to the economic cost of providing the 'service'.

What's the attraction? Many fringe groups as well as encounter groups may not be intrinsically enjoyable, and indeed, can be very threatening. People's commitment to such activities often increases in direct proportion to the difficulty of the experience.

Despite such reservations, training groups have a very important role to play as agencies of change. In psychotherapy, group meetings can play a major role in establishing and reinforcing adaptive behaviours. In business, groups are often used to improve morale, teach new skills, or increase loyalty and cohesiveness within the company. Many other encounter groups can provide exciting, revealing and entertaining experiences which would otherwise be inaccessible. It seems to me that the value of such group experiences is almost certainly likely to be inversely related to the financial cost. The more expensive the group experience, the more likely that you are dealing with an exploitative commercial programme where psychological principles are likely to come second.

Conclusions

Many of our daily interactions take place within groups. Groups may differ in size, formality, cohesiveness or structure. Groups can only function as social units as long as their members believe that membership is desirable and valuable. In real-life groups, the balancing of the cohesive-integrative functions and the task-performance functions may be a difficult task, often handled by leaders specialising in these two aspects of group life. Membership in a group is an important source of our sense of identity: people often define themselves in terms of the groups they belong to. Because of the close links between a positive sense of identity and group membership, people tend to overvalue their own groups and undervalue others.

Most of the groups we belong to also exert considerable influence on us, not only by enforcing outright conformity, but also by more subtle means. Social contagion, or the automatic following of behaviours in the group can lead to outrageous actions we may not otherwise contemplate. The suicide-baiting described by Mann is a relevant example. In certain circumstances, interacting with a group can lead to more extreme opinions and judgments. Highly cohesive groups in particular are subject to the 'groupthink' phenomenon, the wishful collective perception of reality as being the way we would like it to be, instead of the way it is.

Groups are extremely well suited to generating a great deal of emotional involvement. Some of the most powerful positive as well as negative experiences in our lives are likely to be associated with groups. Being accepted and valued in a group can be just as exciting and joyful as rejection and criticism from a whole group is devastating. Totalitarian societies, such as the Soviet Union, have learnt to use this principle extensively to instil conformity and obedience. Children from the first year in school are encouraged to engage in 'approved' praise, denunciation and criticism of each other publicly in the classroom, so that the weight of the whole group can be brought to bear on a possibly deviant individual. Encounter groups provide us with another example of the emotional potential of group interactions. Groups represent perhaps the most complex and demanding milieus for our interactions. Having reached this stage, it is time for us to consider some general issues related to social interaction, such as the role of the environment in our encounters, the principles and uses of social skills training, and some methodological issues of interaction research. This will be the task of the next, and final chapter.

16. The ecological, methodological and applied aspects of social interaction

16.

THE ECOLOGICAL, METHODOLOGICAL AND APPLIED ASPECTS OF SOCIAL INTERACTION

We have covered much of the psychology of interpersonal behaviour, from person perception, through communication and the building of relationships, to social influence and interaction processes in groups. In this final chapter we shall consider several themes which are not strictly speaking part of the psychology of social interaction, but are closely related to it. The first such theme concerns the ecology of social interaction: every encounter takes place within some physical environment which often has a determining influence on interpersonal behaviours. We will look at the links between environment and social behaviour in the first part of the chapter.

Secondly, we will consider some of the methodological issues and problems involved in research on interaction processes. You have now had a chance to read about a great many research studies, as well as to carry out several small activities yourself illustrating the research techniques used. The time has arrived to say a few words about the research methods of social psychologists which have yielded such knowledge as we have about interpersonal behaviours. In the final section of the chapter we will discuss the applications of research on interaction processes in the clinical diagnosis and therapy of interactional difficulties. Social Skills Training (SST) is the common summary term used to describe this form of training. We will outline some of the assumptions and procedures of SST before concluding this chapter, and the book.

The ecology of social interaction
Most of our discussion so far has centred on the psychological and the cultural determinants of interaction processes. However, there is another very important influence on our interactions which is often ignored: the physical environment in which it occurs. All human interaction is by definition situated interaction, in the sense that it takes place within the confines of certain physical places. Yet people are often oblivious to the

impact of the physical environment on their encounters. We have already seen some examples of such influences in earlier chapters. The physical background of an interaction has a major influence on how social behaviours are perceived and interpreted (Forgas and Brown, in Chapter 4), and physical variables, such as furniture arrangements and office layout in turn can be seen as an extension of the nonverbal communication of the person occupying these spaces (Chapter 9).

Our reactions to the environment in general, and the space around us in particular, are often unconscious and automatic (see Chapter 9 on the use of space). To take an example, males and females differ in their preferred spatial arrangements. Females like to sit side-by-side with a friend, and males like to sit face-to-face. Both sexes get more upset if their 'favoured' partner location is invaded by a stranger, for example, on a bus, or in a library (Fisher and Byrne, 1975). Observations of male and female students in a library confirmed that they 'structured' their physical environments differently depending on such preferences. Males built barriers out of books, clothing and other items in front of them, foreclosing the invasion of their favourite partner's spot, and females did the same beside themselves, effectively defending their preferred side-by-side position. These are just a few examples suggesting the close

---

ACTIVITY 16.1
The Effects of the Environment

This activity has a very simple objective: to raise your environmental consciousness! Wherever you are at the moment of reading this section, stop for a second, and make yourself concentrate on various aspects of the physical environment you are in. If inside, look around the room, notice its shape, size, colours, lighting, furniture, floor covering, and so on. If outside, concentrate on the setting, the light, the noises, and the smells around you. How do they affect you? Is your environment optimal for the activity you are engaging in (reading)? Does it help or hinder you? How do you feel about this environment? Does it make you tense or relaxed, happy or unhappy, alert or sleepy? What features of this environment could you change easily, and which are unchangeable? Since we spend most of our lives in environments which are 'given', we often take our surroundings for granted, rarely noticing their features and possibilities. Social interaction, perhaps even more than other human activities, is environment sensitive: where we are and what goes on around us influence our social behaviour in profound ways.

interdependence between environment and social behaviour, a link that we shall explore in more detail below (see Activity 16.1).

Static aspects of the environment

Roger Barker (see also Chapter 10) was one of the pioneers of the ecological study of social interaction. He found that there is a unique association between certain behaviour settings (for example, restaurant, street corner, lift, bedroom, store, etc.) and certain interactions (for example, eating, talking, shopping, etc.), which almost suggests that behaviour settings define what can be enacted within their confines. Exhaustive lists of such behaviour settings, for example in a small town, also inform us about the behaviour possibilities available to residents.

Architects need to be particularly aware of the physical determinants of social behaviour. How many apartments open on the same corridor or staircase? Are there public areas available for informal use? How much privacy is available? These are all environmental factors which influence a person's well being and satisfaction with his/her living space. The study by Festinger, Schachter and Back (Chapter 11) provided a nice illustration of how the physical layout of a housing estate can influence the emergence of a network of friends.

A much quoted example of an architecturally successful, but socially disastrous housing development was the Pruitt-Igoe estate in Pittsburgh in the US. Although the physical amenity provided by the estate was excellent, it was designed in a way which made informal social contact between the residents, and the emergence of a sense of community and shared responsibility, extremely difficult (Yancey, 1972). There were no places where residents could meet, and the fact that most inhabitants came from the most underprivileged social strata did not help matters. The whole estate, over 40 eleven-storey houses, eventually had to be demolished as the only solution to the insurmountable social problems it created.

All other man-made spaces can have similarly important, although less extreme consequences. The layout of an apartment, a hospital ward, a student dormitory, an office or a factory by definition influences the social lives of those using these spaces (Canter and Stringer, 1976). Certain spaces and furniture arrangements facilitate social interaction, while others have the opposite effect. The first kind has often been called a 'sociopetal' space, pulling people together, and the latter 'sociofugal', driving people apart. Many public places, such as waiting rooms or lobbies, are supposed to foster interaction, but are organised in ways which make even casual conversation almost impossible.

Environments often have more subtle influences, influencing our moods, perceptions and feelings. Schwarz (1984; Schwarz and Clore, 1983) showed that even the quality of the room a person occupies for a very short time (for example, a small, bare, depressing experimental room with flickering lights versus a comfortable, well-lit room) had a noticeable effect on that person's ratings of life satisfaction. Subjects in the unpleasant room reported much lower general life satisfaction than subjects in the pleasant room! Similarly, the perceived accessibility and attitude of a public servant receiving clients while seated around a coffee table, standing behind a counter, or sitting behind a desk behind closed doors is very different indeed. In Germany, it is usual for public service offices to be located behind closed doors. When invited to enter such an office after politely knocking, a client is forced by such a physical arrangement to symbolically see him/herself as a temporary trespasser in the official's private domain. The interaction between the two people will of course be strongly coloured by the nature of the physical layout.

Similar environmental influences on behaviour were observed by Baum and Valins (1977) studying student dormitories. The common layout of student rooms, opening from a long corridor, created a lot of enforced interaction, and lack of privacy when compared to other designs, such as 'short corridors' or 'flats'. Interestingly, the physical layout of the dormitories affected students' lives not only inside, but also outside that setting. Baum and Valins (1977) observed these students while they waited for an experiment. 'Long corridor' students behaved more antisocially, and guarded their privacy more than did other students. It is indeed surprising to find that aspects of the physical environment in which we live can actually influence our social behaviours in profound ways, without most of us realising it!

Selecting the right environment has a lot to do with being happy!

However, the link between environment and social interaction is by no means a direct one. What matters most is how we perceive and cognitively represent our surroundings. The same office space which may be considered inadequate, depressing and unsuitable for serious work by an American or a European official or academic may be regarded as luxurious and exuding status in some Third World countries. Our satisfaction with the environment thus depends on subtle processes of social comparison: how do our surroundings compare with the surroundings of comparable others? We feel happy or unhappy, satisfied or dissatisfied with a physical environment in the light of what is available, what we have had before, and what other people in similar circumstances (our reference group) have today. There are also major cultural differences in people's reactions to space. A Chinese visitor out of his country for the first time had difficulty in believing that the spacious and sunny double garage of one of my colleagues in Sydney was not in fact used for human habitation.

Nor do we see our environment in objective terms. Considerable research on so-called 'cognitive maps' (Lynch, 1960) showed that people's knowledge and internal representations of their physical surroundings reflect their own particular behaviour patterns, habits and uses rather than real characteristics of the environment. Activity 16.2

ACTIVITY 16.2
Cognitive Maps

The idea underlying cognitive mapping is quite straightforward. You should ask several people, all familiar with a given city or neighbourhood area, to draw you a map showing all the important features and landmarks of that environment. You will find that the maps will differ markedly, depending on who draws them, what sort of activities they perform within the map's area, where they are located within that space, etc. There will be some agreement about major landmarks, but there will also be large empty spots, showing territories which are unknown, or unimportant to the subjects. Philip Pearce has done considerable research on the cognitive maps of tourists (Pearce, 1982), and shown that tourists' cognitive maps of the cities they visit largely reflect their own interests and activities, rather than the real features of the towns. For example, tourists who stayed in a youth hostel in Oxford, England, and had to follow a particular route to reach the city centre had an entirely different cognitive map from tourists staying in other lodgings, or residents.

should give you some insight into the various factors influencing people's cognitive maps of their living environments.

Dynamic environmental factors: noise, light and temperature

Our interactive environment does not just consist of bricks and mortar. Noise, light, temperature and other fast-changing 'dynamic' environmental factors play an equally important role. Noise has a subtle but debilitating effect on many aspects of human performance, including interaction processes (Glass and Singer, 1972). In an interesting study, Mathews and Canon (1975) found that the powerful noise from a nearby lawnmower was sufficient to stop most people from volunteering to help a student who dropped a pile of books. While up to 80 per cent helped without the noise, helping decreased to 10-15 per cent when the noise was present.

Not all sound is noise. Pleasant sounds, such as music, can have a positive influence on our interactions. Some studies found that the quality of the background music could significantly influence how much a person was liked. In the presence of liked music (in this case, rock) liking for the partner was considerably greater than without music, or in the presence of disliked music (contemporary atonal music!) (see Figure 16.1).

Light (or the absence of it) can have similarly powerful effects. Most of our social life takes place in well-lit environments, and most of the norms, rules and roles we conform to are such 'daylight' norms. What happens when the light goes out? Gergen, Gergen and Barton (1973)

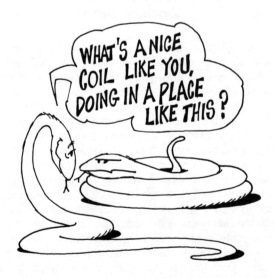

You — here? The environment can have a major effect on the way we perceive others, and react to them.

carried out a surprisingly simple study: they simply asked their subjects to spend some time in a completely dark room with several other, unknown people. Their social interactions turned out to be very different from the behaviour of subjects who underwent the same experience, but in a well-lit room. The dark-room subjects reached a high level of intimacy relatively quickly. They readily discussed important topics with their unseen partners, and up to 90 per cent of them also engaged in some form of physical contact, frequently of an explicitly sexual nature.

Why would darkness by itself influence social interactions so profoundly? It seems that being anonymous and invisible helped people to lose some of their daylight inhibitions, and made them more prepared to seek out and find intimate human contacts. Although the situation is similar to those created in the various deindividuation experiments (see Chapter 15), the reactions are very different: instead of increased aggression, people reacted with expressions of love and intimacy. What is remarkable about these studies is that apparently powerful social norms and expectations can be so readily dissolved through something as simple as turning out the lights!

Another environmental factor influencing social behaviours is the weather. When it was too hot or too humid, people were more likely to express negative feelings, and liked a stranger less than under normal circumstances (Griffitt, 1970). There are some suggestions that

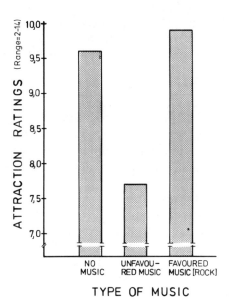

TYPE OF MUSIC

FIGURE 16.1 The effects of music on attraction. In the presence of liked music (in this case, rock) people were more attracted to a partner than without music, or with disliked music (a contemporary atonal piece). (After May and Hamilton, 1977).

unpleasant weather, such as extreme heat, may facilitate expressions of aggression and violence on a large scale (cf. Anderson and Anderson, 1984). Lynchings and other violence often take place in the hot summer months, and Baron and Ramsberger (1978) indeed found that in the US at least, there was some link between weather and riots. Violence was most likely to occur in moderately hot temperatures (about 80-90° F), but decreased again with extremely high temperatures. These authors suggest that extremely high temperatures force people to seek relief and escape — in fact, such conditions are too unpleasant even for engaging in violence!

Crowding versus privacy

One of the most important environmental factors influencing social interaction is the sheer number of people available for contact within a defined spatial area. As we saw in Chapter 12, spatial proximity is a major determinant of our future relationships. However, having too many people in too small a space can result in the psychological perception of crowding. There are large differences between people in what they consider crowding, depending on their basis for comparison. A person from a small town of 500 inhabitants may find Sydney impossibly crowded; Sydneysiders visiting New York often find that city intolerably full of people, and New Yorkers visiting Hong Kong often react the same way.

Reactions to crowding in humans can vary from arousal to alleged pathological reactions. However, since people living in crowded conditions usually also suffer from a number of other handicaps, such as low income, low education, and poor quality housing, negative reactions cannot be proven to be due to crowding. When these other factors are controlled, crowding seems to have no negative consequences. In animals, extreme reactions to crowding are easier to establish. Calhoun (1962) simply allowed a colony of 48 rats to multiply in a given space, and observed the reactions to the increased population density. Infanticide, increased fighting, homosexuality, disturbed maternal behaviour and even physical abnormalities were some of the consequences.

Human reactions to too much or too little social contact are much more elastic. Much depends on subjective expectations. Altman (1975) suggested that the amount of social contact desired fluctuates across people, across situations and even during different times of the same day. People use so-called 'privacy regulation mechanisms', including manipulations of their own physical environments, to keep their social contacts at a desired level. One of my colleagues at one time had a notice hanging on his door reading 'Please do not disturb, I believe I am on to something big in my research', a rather grandiose, but effective privacy regulator.

Privacy is in fact a rather complex notion. The word is used in at least four different senses: the freedom to choose physical *solitude* from others, the freedom to have undisturbed *intimacy* between self and selected others (as in a family or between lovers), the freedom to remain *anonymous* among others, and the freedom to be *reserved* in withholding information about ourselves (Westin, 1970). Only the first two kinds of privacy involve the control of physical spaces, and are influenced by crowding. Perceptions of privacy, like perceptions of crowding, are highly variable. Many records of living conditions of even 100 years ago indicate that having one's own room, let alone one's own bed, was an undreamt of luxury for most people. In many peasant cultures, whole extended families lived from generation to generation within the same single room. Our contemporary notions of necessary living space are thus relatively recent, reflecting Western cultural values rather than inherent human needs.

Both the static and the dynamic aspects of the physical environment thus play a major role in social interaction. An awareness of this interdependence between human beings and their surroundings, particularly by those responsible for creating our physical environments such as architects and planners, is extremely important. Paying more attention to the environment/interaction link can also be important for all of us in improving our interaction skills. To a considerable extent, we can select, create, or at least modify the environments for our interactions. Such 'stagecraft', and a general sensitivity to the features of interaction settings are important aspects of skilled social interaction. We shall next look at some of the methodological aspects of research on social interaction, before turning to the question of social skills training and therapy.

Research methods for studying social interaction
Throughout this book, you have been reading about empirical studies on various problems associated with social interaction. We have not said much about the characteristics of research techniques used in this field until now. The reason is that it is probably easier to appreciate the differences between methods after you have already become quite familiar with a wide range of studies.

Social psychology, perhaps more than any other branch of psychology, is a multi-method science. The variety of issues studied by social psychologists is reflected in the variety of techniques they use. Whereas in physiological psychology, or learning research, the experimental methodology is more or less mandatory, in social psychology perhaps the most important decision a researcher faces is the selection of the most suitable methodology to fit a problem. As you progressed through this book, you probably noticed how many different ways researchers usually found to address quite similar issues.

Observation, interviews, surveys, field experiments, laboratory experiments, questionnaire studies or unobtrusive studies have all been used to study problems of interpersonal attraction, for example. What are the characteristics of these different methods? What are their advantages and disadvantages? These few paragraphs will try to give you some insight into these questions.

The research process: creative and critical phases
All scientific research is concerned about the establishment of empirical laws and regularities, which usually take the form "if (a,b,c) is the case, then (x,y,z) happens". Note that empirical laws are neither absolute, nor eternally true: they are simply summary statements describing our current state of knowledge, based on observation, in a particular field. The role of the researcher is to carry out systematic and repeated observations which will yield empirical laws. Theorists such as Louis Guttmann developed whole methodological schemes, called facet theory, to help researchers remain logical and systematic in their endeavours. In order to establish empirical laws, scientists must first have some idea about what they are looking for (a hypothesis or an expectation), and must then be able to collect relevant evidence to evaluate the validity of their expectations.

These two phases of research, hypothesis generation and hypothesis testing, were respectively called the creative, and the critical phases (cf. McGuire, 1973). We still know relatively little about the creative phase. Why do researchers ask the questions they ask? Where do their expectations and intuitions which guide their observations come from? Sometimes, the answer is simple. Previous empirical studies, or existing theories give us a rich base from which to derive further ideas and hypotheses. Occasionally, simple observations of everyday events may suggest to a scientist underlying regularities, which may be formalised in hypotheses. And sometimes, the process is almost mysterious. How did Einstein chance on the theory of relativity? Why did Archimedes first think of the regularities associated with bodies submerged in water while having a bath, and not the millions of bathers who surely experienced the same sensations before him? In social psychology, hypotheses most often originate in prior research, and quite frequently, they are derived from simple observations of everyday social behaviour.

Once a hypothesis or expectation is formulated, it is the researcher's task to carefully evaluate it against observable evidence. This is the second, critical phase of research. Our methods are far more developed in this phase than in the creative phase. However, the empirical confirmation of a hypothesis is never final, nor does it result in universal laws. There is always the possibility of new, as yet unknown relationships being discovered which will make the prior observation outdated. Indeed, as Karl Popper so convincingly argued, logically it is never possible to conclusively verify a hypothesis, however often it is confirmed. Yet it is possible to disprove a hypothesis by finding a single instance when it does not apply! Any number of repeated verifications still does not secure us against the possibility of a single instance of future falsification. (If you are interested in the philosophical and logical underpinnings of scientific methodology, Magee's (1979) book on Popper is an extremely readable and stimulating introduction). What are the major methods of the critical phase of research? We shall now turn to this question.

Some research techniques

Empirical laws, or statements of observed connections between prior conditions and observed consequences, can be established through a very wide range of techniques. We shall only have space to cover some of them here. One possibility is the inspection and analysis of *historical data* and records. If you wish to know whether there was indeed a link between summer heatwaves and riots in the southern US between 1900 and 1970, all the information is already available in meteorological records, and in police records or newspapers. All you have to do is collect this material, and you can evaluate whether your hunch (or more formally, hypothesis) was correct. This is exactly what several researchers have done (cf. Anderson and Anderson, 1984).

If the data are not already available, you will have to collect them yourself. The simplest way is by *observation*, as many of the previous Activities (for example, Activity 1.3) required you to do. You can make your observation more reliable and accurate by deciding in advance what it is that you are looking for, for example by drawing up a list of observational categories. This is called *structured observation*, and the method developed by Bales (Table 15.1) to analyse group interactions is an excellent example of such a technique. Occasionally, you know in advance that some important event is about to occur, and you observe with the intention of evaluating people's reactions to it. This is called a *natural experiment*: nature provides you with the 'manipulation', and you simply record how your 'subjects' react to it!

Sometimes, you are mainly interested in a person's own explanation or verbal reaction to something which would be very difficult to observe in natural circumstances (for example, how often he fights with his wife, or what he thinks about the current prime minister). There are many highly specialised ways of studying such verbal responses. These include *interviews*, which may again be open and unstructured, or structured, when you have a specific set of prepared questions, and perhaps even prepared response alternatives. There are very many standardised questionnaires, rating scales, inventories and so on which a subject can complete himself. These are often called *paper and pencil* methods, for obvious reasons.

Another class of research methods involves some pre-planned interference by the researchers designed to elicit a particular reaction. When the subjects are not aware of the fact that they are being manipulated and observed, this is an *unobtrusive experiment*. The study by Ellsworth et al. (Chapter 9), who stared at drivers at a red light and then recorded how fast they crossed the intersection once the lights turned to green, is such an unobtrusive study. It has the great advantage that subjects, since they do not even know that they are subjects, behave as they do in everyday life.

The laboratory experiment
For the greatest amount of control, and the most reliable kind of observations, researchers use *laboratory experiments*. In this technique, subjects are brought to the laboratory, where the experimenter has carefully set up some manipulation, and where he/she can observe the subjects' reactions under highly controlled conditions. The self-attribution study by Valins (Chapter 6) is an example of such a method: male subjects were given false feedback about their heartrates through earphones while looking at certain nude female pictures, and this was found to influence their preferences for those pictures later. Obviously, this kind of manipulation could only be carried out under highly controlled circumstances. The studies by Asch on conformity, or Milgram on obedience (Chapter 14) are further examples of this method. The laboratory experiment has the major advantage that it allows a researcher to most clearly establish links between antecedent and subsequent events, in the absence of any other uncontrolled influences.

Laboratory experiments maximise internal validity: within the limited confines of a particular set of manipulations, one can be certain that a predicted connection exists or does not exist. It is sometimes claimed that experiments are unique in allowing researchers to prove causal connections. However, causality is no more than the human attribution of underlying regularity to repeatedly observed event sequences, as philosophers such as Hume and Berkeley recognised a long time ago. In this sense experiments are not all that different from other kinds of empirical observations. In social psychology, laboratory experiments also have a number of critical shortcomings. The main problem is that once the purpose of the experiment is known to a subject, this knowledge in itself could change his behaviour in dramatic ways. If you participated in a conformity experiment such as the one designed by Asch (Chapter 14), would you still conform if you knew that it was conformity that was being studied? And if you knew that Milgram was really studying obedience and not 'learning', would you have obeyed him as a subject?

Experimenters have to invent clever cover stories to hide the real purpose of their studies from subjects. The result is often something like a competition in stagecraft. The experimenter tries to set up the situation in such a way that the subject cannot guess the real purpose of the study, and the subject does his best to do well in whatever he perceives as being required of him.

There are many methodological problems: if the cover story works, the subject is concentrating on something other than the real purpose of the experiment, and may behave unnaturally. If he guesses the purpose of the study, there is a strong motivation to be a 'good' subject, and behave as the experimenter expects him to behave. In other words, he accedes to the implicit demands of the situation and the experimenter, hence the label *demand characteristics* to describe this source of biases. Despite its problems, the laboratory experiment remains one of the most important research tools in social psychology, as the work surveyed in this book clearly illustrates. However, there are many new techniques now becoming available which may provide a suitable alternative to laboratory research in some cases (for example, Ginsburg, 1979).

The ethics of research
There is also a host of *ethical issues* associated with social psychological research, which are not unique to the laboratory experiment. Under what conditions is it legitimate to invade other people's privacy, for example, by observing them, interviewing them or sending them questionnaire surveys? When is it acceptable to cause discomfort to subjects? The stared-at drivers in the Ellsworth et al. study clearly felt some minor discomfort through this manipulation. Can it be justified? In many experiments, subjects are lied to about the real purpose of the investigation, since the experiment would be pointless if the subjects knew exactly what is expected of them. Is it ethically acceptable to lie to subjects? In many studies, the discomfort subjects experience can be considerable. Milgram's subjects in the obedience experiment were clearly upset about being asked to give what appeared to be deadly electric shocks to another person, and later even more upset about the knowledge that they obeyed!

As with most ethical problems, there are no hard and fast answers to these questions. Ethical standards are often a matter of opinion. Scientific bodies, such as the American Psychological Association, or the Australian Psychological Society draw up their own ethical guidelines, and most universities have ethics committees which approve or reject research projects. In general, an experimenter is responsible for his/her handling of subjects, and is expected to cause no physical or psychological damage, safeguard the subjects' privacy, be as truthful as is consistent with the aims of the study, and make every effort to de-brief subjects after the completion of the research.

We can do little more here than give you the briefest of outlines of the methods used by social psychologists to study interaction processes. You may want to spend some time thinking about the advantages and disadvantages of these various research procedures (see, for example, Ginsburg, 1979). If you completed some of the Activities suggested throughout the book, you must by now have an understanding of a range of research methods. It is now time to consider one last aspect of the study of interaction processes: how can the knowledge we gained be applied to help people?

Interaction as a skill

We saw that the ability to successfully interact with people involves a great many complex tasks: person perception, impression formation, attributions, verbal and non-verbal communication, impression management, the building of relationships, and interacting in groups. What is the common link between these various processes? I think we may best think about social interaction as involving a variety of interrelated *skills* which we all learn from childhood through adolescence and even as adults. Being skilled and competent in these fields is a prerequisite of all social life.

Of course, there are very great differences between individuals in how skilled they are in each of these areas. Many people who engage in social interaction professionally must possess an additional range of skills appropriate for their speciality. Teachers, doctors, lawyers, nurses and salesmen must be skilled in interacting with others in general, and also know the special interactive requirements of their respective fields. For example, the ability to put people at ease and elicit intimate self-disclosure (to be an 'opener') is an important skill for people working in the helping professions (Miller et al. 1983).

Looking at interaction as a skill has several advantages. First of all, it will help us to de-mystify the processes people use to get on with each other. The term 'skill' implies that everybody must have learnt these various competencies at some time or other, and those who are presently doing less well than others can be helped to further improve their interactive skills through additional learning experiences. The term Social Skills Therapy (SST) is commonly applied to training programmes which set out to teach such interactive skills (Trower, Bryant and Argyle, 1978).

The nature of social skills deficiencies

Lack of social skills is, of course, not at all unusual. We all know people who have difficulty in person perception or in communicating with others, and who find it difficult to establish rewarding social relationships or interact successfully in large groups. How can one define and diagnose lack of social skills? Unfortunately, there are no objective criteria for establishing exactly what constitutes skilled social performance. Different cultures, different groups and even different individuals have widely varying notions about what they consider acceptably skilled social behaviour. At this everyday level, social skill is very much a subjective phenomenon. A person must be dissatisfied with his/her social interactions and relationships before we may speak of a social skill deficit.

There are, of course, far more extreme cases of social inadequacy which can be diagnosed more empirically. Many forms of psychological disturbance are also associated with a lack of social skills. People who have been hospitalised for a variety of neurotic or psychotic illnesses frequently also display major social skills deficits. It is now becoming increasingly common for patients, before release from psychiatric institutions, to be given some form of social skills therapy, mainly focusing on everyday 'living skills' (Goldstein, Sprafkin and Gershaw, 1976).

There is general agreement among researchers that social skills deficits have a behavioural as well as a cognitive and an affective component. Not knowing how to perform the various behaviours which make up skilled social performance, such as sending or receiving nonverbal signals, may be one aspect of skill deficit. Often, however, people have the required behavioural skills, but lack the cognitive and perceptual sensitivity to identify the right context or the right situation in which certain behaviours should be performed. We discussed such episode perception strategies in Chapter 10, and also saw that people with low social skills have deficits in this area. Yet another aspect of skill deficit is affective. Frequently, people experience such high levels of anxiety and arousal in otherwise innocuous social situations that their interactive behaviours are seriously impaired.

The diagnosis of social skills deficits can be accomplished by several alternative methods. There are numerous standardised psychological scales available for the assessment of social anxiety and various forms of social inadequacy (Hersen and Bellack, 1977). A common problem with such scales is that scores may not necessarily correspond to a person's actual social behaviours. The second diagnostic method relies on direct behavioural observation. For example, clients may be requested to participate in a variety of interactions, often of a stressful and demanding character, and their social behaviours are then recorded and analysed (cf. Trower et al. 1978). A third, complementary diagnostic technique is located somewhere between the first two: clients are asked to report their behavioural problems on some kind of a self-report questionnaire. Finally, physiological measurements of arousal and anxiety may also be used in the diagnosis of social skill deficits.

What is considered inadequate behaviour also very much depends on the surrounding culture. In the highly mobile, extroverted, verbally expressive and individualistic interaction milieu characteristic of many behaviour settings in the US, assertiveness is a particularly important skill. Assertiveness training, a variety of the general social skills approach, is designed to teach people who are shy, withdrawn or submissive to stand up for themselves (Bower and Bower, 1979). In the different cultural milieu of Britain, for example, far more emphasis is placed in social skills training on interpersonal sensitivity, being a rewarding partner, and the use of nonverbal signals (Trower et al. 1978).

Social skills training and therapy

The model of social skills most commonly accepted today emphasises the role of social learning principles in skill training (Goldstein et al. 1976; Eisler and Frederiksen, 1980). In other words, clients are taught new skills using processes such as modelling, imitation, social reinforcement and transfer learning. A few words may be in order about each of these techniques. *Modelling* and *imitation* simply mean that the trainer, or others (sometimes on videotape) present the behaviours to be learned to the trainee. He is then requested to role-play the performance, imitating the models he just observed. Social *reinforcement* in the form of praise, or encouragement is used to reward correct performance, and if the training takes place in a group, social pressure may also be used to shape the trainee's behaviour. *Transfer learning* is the process whereby the client learns to transfer the new skills acquired in the training group to his/her normal interactive routine. This is often accomplished with the help of 'homework': a client is told to perform a certain number of the newly learned skills in his daily interactions, at home, at work or in the pub.

What sorts of skills can be taught by social skills therapy? By and large, varieties of social skills training may be oriented towards (a) teaching general interactive skills (Trower et al. 1978); (b) remedial teaching of skills of community living, for example, to psychiatric patients about to be released (cf. Goldstein et al. 1976), and (c) teaching specialised interaction skills for professional groups such as teachers, nurses, etc. In the training programme developed by Trower et al. (1978), interactive skills such as listening, speaking, communicating and perceiving emotions, and using and perceiving nonverbal signals such as eye contact, body language and the use of space are taught.

Surprising as it may sound, even such very basic skills as how to listen may require careful training. In a recent study, Miller et al. (1983) found that there are large differences between people in how well they can listen, and help others to 'open up' to them. Showing interest, reinforcing the speaker, asking the right questions, using the correct amount of eye contact may all be part of 'skilled listening'. Such training programmes are largely based on the empirical research on interaction processes we dealt with in this book. In order to teach a person how to use the correct amount of eye contact while speaking or listening, for example, the therapist must rely on the results of research on nonverbal behaviour we discussed in Chapter 9.

Numerous other techniques may be used to facilitate SST, many of them taken from the techniques of theatrical performances. A common method for increasing interpersonal sensitivity is to take the role of the other: clients may be requested to play their partner's role for a while, to make them sensitive to how their performance may look to another (Argyle, 1980). Videotape recordings are also often used to confront a client with inadequacies in his earlier performances, and to create a sense of self-monitoring and objective self-awareness (see also Chapter 10). This technique is also suitable for sensitising clients to other shortcomings, for example inadequate self-presentation strategies, or not being rewarding enough to their partners.

In you are interested in the details of social skills training, you should look at any of the books referred to here, such as Trower et al. (1978), Goldstein et al. (1976) or Eisler and Frederiksen (1980). Many community health centres, as well as psychological and psychiatric practitioners and clinics, provide social skills training, often to people who only experience minor difficulties in some specific areas of their lives. The important point is that research on social interaction is not simply a scientific enterprise for its own sake. It has definite practical uses in helping people to better understand their own, and others' social behaviours.

The skill of listening. Even such apparently 'passive' activities as listening to another person require considerable skill. The judicious use of many nonverbal signals is necessary to help a person keep talking. People in the helping professions need to be particularly adept at this skill.

Some concluding comments

Let us look back on the material covered in this book. We began by discussing some of the reasons for the growing interest in studying social interaction processes in Chapter 1. Historical developments since the

French Revolution, and the emergence of industrialised mass societies have had a lot to do with the fact that social interaction, and our relationships with other people have become increasingly complex and problematic. Instead of the taken-for-granted community of a primary group, we must now live amongst a society of strangers. Our friends and acquaintances are usually widely scattered, often fulfilling only highly specialised and limited roles in our lives. The ability to smoothly interact with strangers is also a working skill of growing importance for many people, as the tertiary 'service' industries employ an increasing proportion of the population in most Western countries. Social psychological research on 'people skills' will thus continue to gain in importance.

We considered several aspects of social interaction processes in this volume. Problems of accuracy in social perception, the impression formation process, and ways of making attributions about others and ourselves was the first major topic area discussed (Chapters 2 to 6). It is such aspects of person perception which determine our interactive behaviour in everyday encounters. Next, we looked at the process of interpersonal communication: the use of language, the characteristics and variety of nonverbal messages, and the use of impression management strategies (Chapters 7 to 10). As social interaction largely consists of the regulated exchange of messages, it is communication which lies at the heart of research on interpersonal behaviour.

The development of personal relationships is an inevitable consequence of social interaction. We discussed the nature of human sociability, the factors influencing the development and deterioration of personal relationships, and the special features of intimate relationships in this section (Chapters 11 to 13). The next section dealt with the nature and characteristics of social influence processes, and the way people interact with each other in groups (Chapters 14 and 15). This last chapter has sought to integrate these topics, and discussed the universal role physical environments play in social interaction, the methodology of social psychological research, and the concept of social skills.

Throughout the discussion, the close interdependence between cultural influences and individual behaviour was emphasised. Interactive skills by definition reflect the specific requirements of the surrounding culture. Knowing the shared person prototypes, interaction 'scripts' or relationship scenarios practised in our immediate cultural milieu is an essential prerequisite for effective social interaction. It is in the course of everyday encounters that such shared representations originate, and are maintained or modified. The study of social interaction processes is also the key to understanding how our self-concept and self-esteem are a reflection of the way people react to us in our daily interactions. The recently developed field of social cognition deals with many of these issues, as we have seen throughout the book.

Of course, the material presented here has been, by definition, selective. The field is constantly changing, and as new research findings emerge, others become obsolete. The study of how human beings interact with each other is one of the most exciting topics in psychology. Both its attraction, and its difficulty lie in the fact that its subject matter is of immediate interest to all of us. I hope that reading this book has provided you with additional insights into the psychology of social interaction processes, and has aroused your interest to read further in this intriguing field.

REFERENCES

CHAPTER 1

Allport, F.H. *Social Psychology*. Boston: Houghton-Mifflin, 1924.

Allport, G.W. The historical background of modern social psychology. In: G. Lindzey & E. Aronson (Eds) *The Handbook of Social Psychology*. (Vol. 1), Reading, Mass.: Addison-Wesley, 1968.

Bochner, S. (Ed.) *Cultures in Contact*. Oxford: Pergamon Press, 1981.

Cooley, C.H. *Human Nature and the Social Order*. New York: Scribner, 1902.

Darwin, C. *The Expression of Emotions in Man and Animals*. New York: Appleton, 1890.

Dawkins, R. *The Selfish Gene*. New York: Oxford University Press, 1976.

Farr, R. The social origins of the human mind. In: J.P. Forgas (Ed.) *Social Cognition: Perspectives on Everyday Understanding*. London: Academic Press, 1981.

Forgas, J.P. (Ed.) *Social Cognition: Perspectives on Everyday Understanding*. London: Academic Press, 1981.

McDougall, W. *Introduction to Social Psychology*. London: Methuen, 1908.

Mead, G.H. *Mind, Self and Society*. Chicago: University Press, 1934.

Ross, E.A. *Social Psychology*. New York: Macmillan, 1908.

Stone, G.P. & Farberman, H.E. *Social Psychology Through Symbolic Interaction*. Waltham, Mass.: Ginn-Blaisdell, 1970.

Verplanck, W.S. The control of the content of conversation: reinforcement of statements of opinion. *Journal of Abnormal and Social Psychology*, 1955, 51, 668-676.

Zimbardo, P.G. Shyness and the stresses of the human connection. In: L. Goldberger & S. Breznitz *Handbook of Stress: Theoretical and Clinical Aspects*. New York: Free Press, 1982.

CHAPTER 2

Bower, G.H. Affect and cognition. *Philosophical Transactions of the Royal Society*, London, 1983.

Brigham, J.C. & Barkowitz, P. Do they all look alike? *Journal of Applied Social Psychology*, 1978, 8, 306-318.

Buckhout, R. Figueroa, D. & Hoff, E. Eyewitness identification. Report No. CR-11, Center for Responsive Psychology, Brooklyn College, Brooklyn, 1974.

Clark, M. & Isen, A. Toward understanding the relationship between feeling states and social behaviour. In: A. Hastorf & A. Isen (Eds) *Cognitive Social Psychology*. New York: Elsevier, 1981.

Clark, M. Milberg, S. & Erber, R. Effects of arousal on judgments of others' emotions. *Journal of Personality and Social Psychology*, 1984, 46, 551-560.

Cline, V.B. Interpersonal perception. In: B.A. Maher (Ed.) *Progress in experimental personality research*. Vol. 1. New York: Academic Press, 1964.

Cline, V.B. & Richards, J.M. Jr. Accuracy of interpersonal perception — a general trait? *Journal of Abnormal and Social Psychology*, 1960, 60, 1-7.

Cronbach, L. J. Processes affecting scores on 'understanding others' and 'assumed similarity'. *Psychological Bulletin*, 1955, 52, 177-193.

Crow, W.J. The effect of training upon accuracy and variability in interpersonal perception. *Journal of Abnormal and Social Psychology*, 1957, 55, 355-359.

Ekman, P., Sorenson, E.R. & Friesen, W.V. Pan-cultural elements in facial displays of emotions. *Science*, 1969, 164, 86-88.

Forgas, J.P. Argyle, M.A. & Ginsburg, G.P. Social episodes and person perception: the fluctuating structure of an academic group. *Journal of Social Psychology*, 1979, 109, 207-222.

Forgas, J.P. Bower, G.H. & Krantz, S. The effects of mood on perceptions of interactive behaviours. *Journal of Experimental Social Psychology*, 1984 (in press).

Gage, N.L. Judging interests from expressive behaviour. *Psychological Monographs*, 1952, 66, 18 (whole No. 350).

Izard, C.E. *The Face of Emotion*. New York: Appleton-Century-Crofts, 1971.

Kassin, S.M. Deposition testimony and the surrogate witness. *Personality and Social Psychology Bulletin*, 1983, 9, 281-288.

Katz, D. & Braly, K.W. Racial stereotypes of one hundred college students. *Journal of Abnormal and Social Psychology*, 1933, 28, 280-290.

Landis, C. Studies of emotional reactions 2. General behaviour and facial expression. *Journal of Comparative Psychology*, 1924, 4, 447-509.

Loftus, E. *Eyewitness Testimony*. Cambridge: Harvard University Press, 1979.

Langman, B. & Cockburn, A. Sirhan's gun. *Harper's*, January 1975, 250, 16-27.

Schiffenbauer, A. Effect of observers emotional state on judgments of the emotional state of others. *Journal of Personality and Social Psychology*, 1974, 30, 31-35.

Sherman, M. The differentiation of emotional responses in infants. *Journal of Comparative Psychology*, 1927, 7, 265-284.

Schwarz, N. Mood and information processing. Paper given at the Congress of the European Association of Social Psychologists, Tilburg, Holland, 1984.

Taft, R. The ability to judge people. *Psychological Bulletin*, 1955, 52, 1-23.

Taft, R. Ethnic stereotypes, attitudes and familiarity: Australia. *Journal of Social Psychology*, 1959, 49, 177-186.

Vernon, P.E. Some characteristics of the good judge of personality. *Journal of Social Psychology*, 1933, 4, 42-58.

CHAPTER 3

Bartlett, F.C. *Remembering*. Cambridge: Cambridge University Press, 1932.

Bellezza, F.S. & Bower, G.H. Person stereotypes and memory for people. *Journal of Personality and Social Psychology*, 1982, 11, 1-23.

Bond, M. & Forgas, J.P. Linking person perception to behaviour intention across cultures. *Journal of Cross-Cultural Psychology*, 1984 (in press).

Bruner, J.S. Social psychology and perception. In: E.E. Maccoby, T.M. Newcomb & E.L. Hartley (Eds) *Readings in Social Psychology*. New York: Holt, Rinehart & Winston, 1958.

Bruner, J.S. & Tagiuri, R. Person perception. In: Lindzey, G. (Ed.) *Handbook of Social Psychology*. Vol. 2. Reading, Mass.: Addison-Wesley, 1954.

Cantor, N. & Mischel, W. Prototypicality and personality: effects on free recall and personality impressions. *Journal of Research in Personality*, 1979, 13, 187-205.

Dornbusch, S.M. Hastorf, A.H. Richardson, S.A. Muzzy, R.E. & Vreeland, R.S. The perceiver and the perceived: their relative influence on the categories of interpersonal cognition. *Journal of Personality and Social Psychology*, 1965, 1, 434-440.

Forgas, J.P. The effects of prototypicality and cultural salience on perceptions of people. *Journal of Research in Personality*, 1983, 17, 153-173.

Hastie, R. & Kumar, P.A. Person memory: personality traits as organising principles in memory for behaviours. *Journal of Personality and Social Psychology*, 1979, 37, 25-38.

Hastie, R. Ostrom, T.M. Ebbesen, E.B. Wyer, R.S.Jr. Hamilton, D.L. & Carlston, D.E. (Eds) *Person Memory: The Cognitive Basis of Social Perception*. Hillsdale, N.J.: Erlbaum, 1980.

Jones, E.E. & Nisbett, R.E. *The Actor and the Observer*. Morristown, N.J.: General Learning Press, 1971.

Kelly, G.A. *The Psychology of Personal Constructs*. New York: Norton, 1955.

Norman, W.T. Toward an adequate taxonomy of personality attributes. *Journal of Abnormal and Social Psychology*, 1963, 66, 574-583.

Passini, F.T. & Norman, W.T. A universal conception of personality structure? *Journal of Personality and Social Psychology*, 1966, 4, 44-49.

Rosenberg, S. & Jones, R.A. A method for investigating a person's implicit theory of personality: Theodore Dreiser's view of people. *Journal of Personality and Social Psychology*, 1972, 22, 372-386.

Rosenberg, S. Nelson, C. & Vivekenanthan, P.S. A multidimensional approach to the study of personality impressions. *Journal of Personality and Social Psychology*, 1968, 9, 283-294.

Rosenberg, S. & Sedlak, A. Structural representations of implicit personality theory. In: L. Berkowitz (Ed.) *Advances in Experimental Social Psychology*, Vol. 6. New York: Academic Press, 1972.

Snyder, M. & Campbell, B. Testing hypotheses about other people: the role of the hypothesis. *Personality and Social Psychology Bulletin*, 1980, 6, 421-426.

Snyder, M. & Uranowitz, S. Reconstructing the past: some cognitive consequences of person perception. *Journal of Personality and Social Psychology*, 1978, 36, 941-950.

Snyder, M. & White, P. Testing hypotheses about other people: strategies of verification and falsification. *Personality and Social Psychology Bulletin,* 1981, 7, 39-43.

Tajfel, H. & Forgas, J.P. Social categorisation: Cognition, values and groups. In: J.P. Forgas (Ed.) *Social Cognition: Perspectives on Everyday Understanding,* London: Academic Press, 1981.

CHAPTER 4

Anderson, N.H. Averaging vs. adding as a stimulus-combination rule in impression formation. *Journal of Experimental Psychology,* 1965, 70, 394-400.

Anderson, N.H. Averaging model analysis of set size effects in impression formation. *Journal of Experimental Psychology,* 1967, 75, 158-165.

Anderson, N.H. Likeableness ratings of 555 personality trait words. *Journal of Personality and Social Psychology,* 1968, 9, 272-279.

Anderson, N.H. Cognitive algebra: integration theory applied to social attribution. *Advances in Experimental Social Psychology,* 1974, 7, 1-101.

Asch, S. Forming impressions of personality. *Journal of Abnormal and Social Psychology,* 1946, 41, 258-290.

Dion, K.K. Berscheid, E. & Walster, E. What is beautiful is good. *Journal of Personality and Social Psychology,* 1972, 24, 285-290.

Fishbein, M. & Hunter, R. Summation versus balance in attitude organisation and change. *Journal of Abnormal and Social Psychology,* 1964, 69, 505-510.

Forgas, J.P. *Social Episodes: The Study of Interaction Routines.* London: Academic Press, 1979.

Forgas, J.P. & Brown, L.B. Environmental and behavioural cues in the perception of social encounters. *American Journal of Psychology,* 1977, 90, 635-644.

Forgas, J.P. O'Connor, K. & Morris, S. Smile and punishment: the effects of facial expression on responsibility attribution by groups and individuals. *Personality and Social Psychology Bulletin,* 1983, 9, 587-596.

Hamilton, D.L. & Zanna, M.P. Context effects in impression formation processes for evaluation changes and connotative meaning. *Journal of Personality and Social Psychology,* 1974, 29, 649-654.

Harari, H. & McDavid, J.W. Name stereotypes and teachers' expectations. *Journal of Educational Psychology,* 1973, 65, 222-225.

Hendrick, C. & Constantini, A.F. Effects of varying trait inconsistency and response requirements on the primacy effect in impression formation. *Journal of Personality and Social Psychology,* 1970, 15, 158-164.

Jones, E.E. Rock, L. Shaver, K.G. Goethals, G.R. & Ward, L.M. Patterns of performance and ability attribution: an unexpected primacy effect. *Journal of Personality and Social Psychology,* 1968, 10, 317-341.

Kelley, H.H. The warm-cold variable in first impressions of persons. *Journal of Personality,* 1950, 18, 431-439.

Luchins, A.S. Experimental attempts to minimize the impact of first impressions. In: C. Hovland (Ed.) *The Order of Presentation in Persuasion.* New Haven: Yale University Press, 1957.

Mueser, K.T. Grau, B.W. Sussmann, S. & Rosen, A. You are only as pretty as you feel: facial expression as a determinant of physical attractiveness. *Journal of Personality and Social Psychology*, 1984, 46, 469-478.

Owen, J. Bower, G.H. & Black, J.B. The soap opera effect in story recall. *Memory and Cognition*, 1979, 3, 185-191.

Razran, G. Ethnic dislikes and stereotypes: a laboratory study. *Journal of Abnormal and Social Psychology*, 1950, 45, 7-27.

Riskey, D.R. & Birnbaum, M.H. Compensatory effects in moral judgment: two rights don't make up for a wrong. *Journal of Experimental Psychology*, 1974, 103, 171-173.

Rosenthal, R. & Jakobson, L. *Pygmalion in the Classroom*. New York: Holt, 1968.

Sisson, M. Social class and nonverbal behaviour. D101 Course Notes, The Open University, 1978.

Suedfeld, P. Bochner, S. & Matas, C. Petitioners attire and petition signing by peace demonstrators: a field experiment. *Journal of Applied Social Psychology*, 1971, 1, 23-31.

Wilson, P.R. The perceptual distortion of height as a function of ascribed academic status. *Journal of Social Psychology*, 1968, 74, 97-102.

CHAPTER 5

Antaki, C. *The Psychology of Ordinary Explanations of Social Behaviour.* London: Academic Press, 1981.

Bassili, J.N. Temporal and spatial contingencies in the perception of social events. *Journal of Personality and Social Psychology*, 1976, 33, 680-685.

Borgida, E. & Nisbett, E.E. The differential impact of abstract vs. concrete information on decisions. *Journal of Applied Social Psychology*, 1977, 7, 258-271.

Cialdini, R.B. Braver, S.L. & Lewis, S.K. Attributional bias and the easily persuaded other. *Journal of Personality and Social Psychology*, 1974, 30, 631-637.

Falbo, T. & Beck, R.C. Naive psychology and the attributional model of achievement. *Journal of Personality*, 1979, 47, 185-195.

Feather, N. Positive and negative reactions to male and female success and failure in relation to the perceived status and sex-typed appropriateness of occupation. *Journal of Personality and Social Psychology*, 1975, 31, 536-548.

Feather, N.T. & Simon, J.G. Reactions to male and female success and failure in sex-linked occupations. *Journal of Personality and Social Psychology*, 1975, 31, 20-31.

Feldman, N.S. Higgins, E.T. Karlovac, M. & Ruble, D.N. Use of consensus information in causal attributions as a function of temporal presentation and availability of direct information. *Journal of Personality and Social Psychology*, 1976, 34, 694-698.

Forgas, J.P. Morris, S. & Furnham, A. Lay explanations of wealth: attributions for economic success. *Journal of Applied Social Psychology*, 1982, 12, 381-397.

Furnham, A. Attributions for affluence. *Journal of Personality and Individual Differences*, 1983, 4, 31-40.

Gurwitz, S.B. & Panciera, L. Attributions of freedom by actors and observers. *Journal of Personality and Social Psychology*, 1975, 32, 531-539.

Harre, R. Social psychology as rhetoric. In: J.P. Forgas (Ed.) *Social Cognition*. London: Academic Press, 1981.

Hastie, R. Causes and effects in causal attributions. *Journal of Personality and Social Psychology*, 1984, 46, 44-56.

Heider, F. *The Psychology of Interpersonal Relations*. New York: Wiley, 1958.

Heider, F. & Simmel, M. An experimental study of apparent behaviour. *American Journal of Psychology*, 1944, 57, 243-249.

Hedrick-Smith, S. *The Russians*. Harmondsworth: Penguin, 1977.

Jones, E.E. & Davis, K.E. From acts to dispositions. In: L. Berkowitz (Ed.) *Advances in Experimental Social Psychology*, New York: Academic Press, 1965.

Jones, E.E. Davis, K.E. & Gergen, K.J. Role playing variations and their informational value for person perception. *Journal of Abnormal and Social Psychology*, 1961, 63, 302-310.

Jones, E.E. & Harris, V.A. The attribution of attitudes. *Journal of Experimental Social Psychology*, 1967, 3, 1-24.

Jones, E.E. & Nisbett, R.E. The actor and the observer: divergent perceptions of the causes of behaviour. In: E.E. Jones et al. (Eds) *Attribution: Perceiving the Causes of Behaviour*. Morristown, N.J.: General Learning Press, 1971.

Kahneman, D. & Tversky, A. On the psychology of prediction. *Psychological Review*, 1973, 80, 237-251.

Kelley, H.H. Attribution theory in social psychology. In: D. Levine (Ed.) *Nebraska Symposium on Motivation*, Lincoln: University of Nebraska Press, 1967.

Kelley, H.H. *Attribution in Social Interaction*. Morristown: General Learning Press, 1971.

Lalljee, M. A knowledge structure approach to explanations. Paper presented at the General Meeting of the European Association of Experimental Social Psychologists, Tilburg, Holland, 1984.

Lerner, M.J. Evaluation of performance as a function of performer's reward and attractiveness. *Journal of Personality and Social Psychology*, 1965, 3, 355-360.

McArthur, L. The how and the what of why: some determinants and consequences of causal attribution. *Journal of Personality and Social Psychology*, 1972, 22, 171-193.

McArthur, L. & Post, D.L. Figural emphasis and person perception. *Journal of Experimental Social Psychology*, 1977, 13, 520-536.

Nesdale, A. Effects of person and situation expectations on explanation seeking and causal attribution. *British Journal of Social Psychology*, 1983, 22, 93-99.

Piaget, J. *The Moral Judgement of the Child*. Glencoe: The Free Press, 1965.

Robinson, J. & McArthur, L.Z. Impact of salient vocal qualities on causal attributions for speakers behaviour. *Journal of Personality and Social Psychology*, 1982, 43, 236-247.

Ross, L. The intuitive psychologist and his shortcomings: distortions in the attribution process. In: L. Berkowitz (Ed.) *Advances in Experimental Social Psychology*, New York: Academic Press, 1977.

Schneider, D.S. & Miller, R.S. The effects of enthusiasm and quality of arguments on attitude attributions. *Journal of Personality*, 1975, 43, 693-708.

Semin, G. A gloss on attribution theory. *British Journal of Social and Clinical Psychology*, 1980, 19, 291-300.

Shaver, K.G. Defensive attribution: effects of severity and relevance on the responsibilities assigned for an accident. *Journal of Personality and Social Psychology*, 1970, 14, 101-113.

Shaver, K.G. *An Introduction to Attributional Processes*. Cambridge, Mass.: Winthrop, 1975.

Sigall, H. & Ostrove, N. Beautiful but dangerous: effects of offender attractiveness and nature of crime on juridic judgments. *Journal of Personality and Social Psychology*, 1975, 31, 410-414.

Storms, M.D. Videotape and the attribution process. *Journal of Personality and Social Psychology*, 1973, 27, 165-175.

Strickland, L.H. Surveillance and trust. *Journal of Personality*, 1958, 26, 200-215.

Taylor, S. & Fiske, S.T. Point of view and perceptions of causality. *Journal of Personality and Social Psychology*, 1975, 32, 439-445.

Thibaut, J.W. & Riecken, H.W. Some determinants and consequences of the perception of social causality. *Journal of Personality*, 1955, 24, 113-133.

Walster, E. The assignment of responsibility for an accident. *Journal of Personality and Social Psychology*, 1966, 5, 508-516.

Walster, E. Aronson, E. & Abrahams, D. On increasing the persuasiveness of a low-prestige communicator. *Journal of Experimental Social Psychology*, 1966, 2, 325-342.

Weiner, B. *Achievement Motivation and Attribution Theory*. Morristown, N.J.: General Learning Press, 1974.

West, S.G. Gunn, S.P. & Czernicky, P. Ubiquitous Watergate: an attributional analysis. *Journal of Personality and Social Psychology*, 1975, 32, 55-65.

Zuckerman, M. Attribution of success and failure revisited. *Journal of Personality*, 1979, 47, 288-305.

CHAPTER 6

Berglas, S. & Jones, E.E. Drug choice as a self-handicapping strategy in response to noncontingent success. *Journal of Personality and Social Psychology*, 1978, 36, 405-417.

Bem, D.J. Self perception theory. In: L. Berkowitz (Ed.) *Advances in Experimental Social Psychology*, New York: Academic Press, 1972.

Brehm, J.W. *Responses to Loss of Freedom: a Theory of Psychological Reactance*. Morristown, N.J.: General Learning Press, 1972.

Buss, A.R. Causes and reasons in attribution theory: a conceptual critique. *Journal of Personality and Social Psychology*, 1978, 36, 1311-1321.

Cotton, J. A review of research on Schachter's theory of emotion and the misattribution of arousal. *European Journal of Social Psychology*, 1981, 11, 365-397.

Deci, E.L. *Intrinsic Motivation*. New York: Plenum Press, 1975.

Dienstbier, R. & Munter, P. Cheating as a function of labelling of natural arousal. *Journal of Personality and Social Psychology*, 1971, 17, 208-213.

Duval, S. & Wicklund, R.A. *A Theory of Objective Self Awareness*. New York: Academic Press, 1972.

Duval, S. & Wicklund, R.A. Effects of objective self awareness on attribution of causality. *Journal of Experimental Social Psychology*, 1973, 9, 17-31.

Dweck, C.S. The role of expectations and attributions in the alleviation of learned helplessness. *Journal of Personality and Social Psychology*, 1975, 31, 674-685.

Festinger, L. & Carlsmith, J.M. Cognitive consequences of forced compliance. *Journal of Abnormal and Social Psychology*, 1959, 58, 201-211.

Greene, D. Sternberg, B. & Lepper, M.R. Overjustification in a token economy. *Journal of Personality and Social Psychology*, 1976, 34, 1219-1234.

James, W. What is emotion? *Mind*, 1884, 9, 188-205.

Jones, E.E. & Berglas, S. Control of attributions about the self through self-handicapping strategies: the appeal of alcohol and the role of underachievement. *Personality and Social Psychology Bulletin*, 1978, 4, 200-206.

Kolditz, T.A. & Arkin, R.M. An impression management interpretation of self handicapping strategies. *Journal of Personality and Social Psychology*, 1982, 43, 492-450.

Lepper, M.R. Greene,D. & Nisbett, R.E. Undermining children's intrinsic interest with extrinsic reward. *Journal of Personality and Social Psychology*, 1973, 28, 129-137.

Marshall, G.D. & Zimbardo, P.G. Affective consequences of inadequately explained emotional arousal. *Journal of Personality and Social Psychology*, 1979, 37, 970-988.

Maslach, C. Negative emotional biasing of unexpected arousal. *Journal of Personality and Social Psychology*, 1979, 37, 953-969.

Nisbett, R.E. & Schachter, S. Cognitive manipulation of pain. *Journal of Experimental Social Psychology*, 1966, 2, 227-236.

Nisbett, R.E. & Wilson, T.D. Telling more than we can know: verbal reports on mental processes. *Psychological Review*, 1977, 84, 231-159.

Schachter, S. & Singer, J.E. Cognitive and social psychological determinants of emotional state. *Psychological Review*, 1962, 69, 379-399.

Seligman, M. *Helplessness*. San Francisco: Freeman, 1975.

Storms, M.D. & Nisbett, R.E. Insomnia and the attribution process. *Journal of Personality and Social Psychology*, 1970, 16, 319-328.

Taylor, S.E. On inferring one's attitude from one's behaviour: some determining conditions. *Journal of Personality and Social Psychology*, 1975, 31, 126-131.

Valins, S. Cognitive effects of false heart-rate feedback. *Journal of Personality and Social Psychology*, 1966, 4, 400-408.

Valins, S. Persistent effects of information about internal reactions. In: H. London & R.A. Nisbett (Eds) *The Cognitive Alteration of Feeling States*. Chicago: Aldine, 1972.

White, P. A model of the layperson as pragmatist. *Personality and Social Psychology Bulletin*, 1984, 10, 333-349.

Wicklund, R. & Frey, D. Cognitive consistency: motivational vs non-motivational perspectives. In: J.P. Forgas (Ed.) *Social Cognition*. London: Academic Press, 1981.

Zillman, D. *Hostility and Aggression*. Hillsdale, N.J.: Erlbaum, 1978.

Zillman, D. Katcher, A.H. & Milarsky, B. Excitation transfer from physical exercise to subsequent aggressive behaviour. *Journal of Experimental Social Psychology*, 1972, 8, 247-259.

CHAPTER 7

Bavelas, J.B. A situational theory of disqualification: using language to 'leave the field'. In: J.P. Forgas (Ed.) *Language and Social Situations*. New York: Springer, 1985.

Bernstein, B.B. A socio-linguistic approach to social learning. In: F. Williams (Ed.) *Language and Poverty*. London: Markham, 1970.

Brown, R. *Social Psychology*. New York: Free Press, 1965.

Brown, R. & Gilman, A. The pronouns of power and solidarity. In: T. Sebeok (Ed.) *Style in Language*. Cambridge: Technology Press, 1960.

Brown, R. & Lenneberg, E.H. A study in language and cognition. *Journal of Abnormal and Social Psychology*, 1954, 49, 454-462.

Bruner, J.S. *Children's Talk*. New York: W.W. Norton, 1983.

Bruner, J.S. The role of interaction formats in language acquisition. In: J.P. Forgas (Ed.) *Language and Social Situations*. New York: Springer, 1985.

Bruner, J.S. & Sherwood, V. Thought, language and interaction in infancy. In: J.P. Forgas (Ed.) *Social Cognition: Perspectives on Everyday Understanding*. London: Academic Press, 1981.

Fishman, J. (Ed.) *Advances in the Sociology of Language*. The Hague: Mouton, 1971.

Forgas, J.P. (Ed.) *Language and Social Situations*. New York: Springer, 1985.

Forgas, J.P. The effects of prototypicality and cultural salience on perceptions of people. *Journal of Research in Personality*, 1983, 17, 153-173.

Friendly, M.L. & Glucksberg, S. On the description of sub-cultural lexicons. *Journal of Personality and Social Psychology*, 1970, 14, 550-565.

Gallois, C. & Callan, V. J. Situational influences on perceptions of accented speech. In: J. Forgas (Ed.) *Language and Social Situations*. New York: Springer, 1985.

Gardner, R.A. & Gardner, B.T. Teaching sign language to a chimpanzee. *Science*, 1969, 165, 664-672.

Garton, A. Children's language in collaborative and cooperative interactions. In: Proceedings, 2nd International Conference on Social Psychology and Language, University of Bristol, 1983.

Gibbs, R. Situational conventions and requests. In: J.P. Forgas (Ed.) *Language and Social Situations*. New York: Springer, 1984.

Grice, H.P. Logic and conversation. In: P. Cole & J.L. Morgan (Eds) *Syntax and Semantics*, Vol. 3. New York: Seminar Press, 1975.

Gumperz, J.J. & Hymes, D. (Eds) *The Ethnography of Communication*. New York: Holt, Rinehart & Winston, 1972.

Harre, R. Situational rhetoric and self-presentation. In: J.P. Forgas (Ed.) *Language and Social Situations*. New York: Springer, 1985.

Hedrick-Smith, J. *The Russians*. Harmondsworth: Penguin, 1977.

Hockett, C.F. The problem of universals in language. In: J.H. Greenberg (Ed.) *Universals of Language*. Cambridge: MIT Press, 1963.

Lenneberg, E.H. *Biological Foundations of Language*. London: Wiley, 1967.

Morris, C. *Signs, Language and Behaviour*. London: Prentice-Hall, 1946.

Pratt, C. Children's performance on a referential communication task: playing according to the rules of the game. In: Proceedings, 2nd International Conference on Social Psychology and Language, University of Bristol, 1983.

Premack, D. Language in chimpanzees. *Science*, 1971, 172, 808-822.

Rayfield, J.R. *The Languages of a Bilingual Community*. The Hague: Mouton, 1970.

Shipler, D. *Russia: Broken Idols, Solemn Dreams*. London: Macdonald, 1983.

Vygotsky, L.S. *Thought and Language*. Cambridge: MIT Press, 1962.

Wetzel, P. Ingroup-outgroup deixis: situational variation in the verbs of giving and receiving in Japanese. In J.P. Forgas (Ed.) *Language and Social Situations*. New York: Springer, 1985.

Whorf, B.L. *Language Thought and Reality*. Cambridge: MIT Press, 1956.

CHAPTER 8

Argyle, M. *Social Interaction*. London: Methuen, 1969.

Argyle, M. *The Psychology of Interpersonal Behaviour*. Harmondsworth: Penguin, 1972.

Argyle, M. Alkema, F. & Gilmour, R. The communication of friendly and hostile attitudes by verbal and nonverbal signals. *European Journal of Social Psychology*, 1971, 1, 385-402.

Argyle, M. Salter, V. Nicholson, H. Williams, M. & Burgess, P. The communication of inferior and superior attitudes by verbal and non-verbal signals. *British Journal of Social and Clinical Psychology*, 1970, 9, 222-231.

Darwin, C. *The Expression of Emotions in Man and Animals*. London: John Murray, 1872 (reproduced by the University of Chicago Press, 1965).

Ekman, P. (Ed.) *Darwin and Facial Expression: A Century of Research in Review*. New York: Academic Press, 1973.

Ekman, P. & Friesen, W.V. Nonverbal leakage and cues to deception. *Psychiatry*, 1969, 32, 88-106.

Ekman, P. & Friesen, W.V. Detecting deception from the body or face. *Journal of Personality and Social Psychology*, 1974, 29, 288-298.

Ekman, P. & Friesen, W.V. *Unmasking the Face*. Englewood Cliffs, N.J.: Prentice-Hall, 1975.

Ekman, P. Friesen, W.V. & Ellsworth, P.C. *Emotion in the Human Face*. New York: Pergamon Press, 1972.

Ekman, P. Levenson, R.W. & Friesen, W.V. Autonomic nervous system activity distinguishes among emotions. *Science*, 1983, 221, 1208-1210.

Forgas, J.P. (Ed.) *Language and Social Situations*. New York: Springer, 1985.

Kendon, A. Some functions of gaze direction in social interaction. *Acta Psychologica*, 1967, 26, 22-63.

Marsh, P. Rosser, E. & Harre, R. *The Rules of Disorder*. London: Routledge and Kegan Paul, 1978.

Mehrabrian, A. Some referents and measures of nonverbal behaviour. *Behavioural Research and Instrumentation*, 1969, 1, 201-207.

Mehrabrian, A. & Ferries, S.R. Inference of attitudes from nonverbal communication in two channels. *Journal of Consulting Psychology*, 1967, 31, 248-252.

Mehrabrian, A. & Weiner, M. Decoding inconsistent communications. *Journal of Personality and Social Psychology*, 1967, 6, 109-114.

Osgood, C.E. Suci, G.J. & Tannebaum, P.H. *The Measurement of Meaning*. Urbana: University of Illinois Press, 1957.

Schlossberg, H. The three dimensions of emotion. *Psychological Review*, 1954, 61, 81-88.

Walker, M. The role of nonverbal signals in coordinating speaking turns. Proceedings, 2nd International Congress on Language and Social Psychology, Bristol, 1983.

CHAPTER 9

Aiello, J.R. & Jones, S.E. Field study of the proxemic behaviour of young children in three subcultural groups. *Journal of Personality and Social Psychology*, 1971, 19, 351-356.

Altman, I. *The Environment and Social Behaviour*. Monterey: Brooks-Cole, 1975.

Argyle, M. & Dean, J. Eye-contact, distance and affiliation. *Sociometry*, 1965, 28, 289-304.

Argyle, M. & Ingham, R. Gaze, mutual gaze and proximity. *Semiotica*, 1972, 6, 32-49.

Barker, R.G. *Ecological Psychology*. Stanford: University Press, 1968.

Bergmann, G. & Forgas, J.P. Situational influences on speech dysfluency. In: J.P. Forgas (Ed.) *Language and Social Situations*. New York: Springer, 1985.

Birdwhistell, R. *Introduction to Kinesics*. Louisville: University of Louisville Press, 1952.

Birdwhistell, R. *Kinesics and Context*. Harmondsworth: Penguin, 1970.

Condon, W.S. & Ogston, W.D. A segmentation of behaviour. *Journal of Psychiatric Research*. 1967, 5, 221-235.

Davitz, J.R. *The Communication of Emotional Meaning*. New York: McGraw-Hill, 1964.

Davitz, J.R. & Davitz, L.J. The communication of feelings by content-free speech. *Journal of Communication*, 1959, 9, 6-13.

Ekman, P. & Friesen, W.V. *Unmasking the Face*. Englewood Cliffs, N.J.: Prentice-Hall, 1975.

Ellsworth, P.C. Carlsmith, J.M. & Henson, A. Staring as a stimulus to flight in animals: a series of field studies. *Journal of Personality and Social Psychology*, 1972, 21, 302-311.

Exline, R. Visual interaction: the glances of power and preference. In: S. Weitz (Ed.) *Nonverbal Communication*. New York: Oxford University Press, 1974.

Exline, R. & Yellin, A. Eye contact as a sign between man and monkey. 19th International Congress of Psychology, London, 1965.

Fisch, H.U. Frey, S. & Hirsbrunner, H.P. Analysing nonverbal behaviour in depression. *Journal of Abnormal Psychology*, 1983, 92, 307-318.

Fisher, J.D. Rytting, M. & Heslin, R. Hands touching hands: affective and evaluative effects of an interpersonal touch. *Sociometry*, 1976, 39, 416-421.

Gallois, C. & Callan, V. Situational influences on perceptions of accented speech. In: J.P. Forgas (Ed.) *Language and Social Situations*. New York: Springer, 1985.

Giles, H. Evaluative reactions to accents. *Education Review*, 1970, 22, 211-227.

Goffman, E. *Behaviour in Public Places*. Glencoe: The Free Press, 1963.

Hall, E.T. *The Hidden Dimension*. New York: Doubleday, 1966.

Henley, N.M. *Body Politics: Power, Sex and Nonverbal Communication*. Englewood Cliffs: Prentice-Hall, 1977.

Heslin, R. & Boss, D. Nonverbal intimacy in airport arrival and departure. *Personality and Social Psychology Bulletin*, 1980, 6, 248-252.

Hess, E.H. Attitude and pupil size. *Scientific American*, 1965, 212, 46-54.

Hess, E.H. *The Tell-tale Eye*. New York: Van Nostrand, 1975.

Jones, S.E. & Aiello, J.R. Proxemic behaviour of black and white first third and fifth grade children. *Journal of Personality and Social Psychology*, 1973, 25, 21-27.

Jourard, S.M. An exploratory study of body accessibility. *British Journal of Social and Clinical Psychology*. 1966, 5, 221-231.

Kendon, A. Movement coordination in social interaction: some examples considered. *Acta Psychologica*, 1970, 32, 1-25.

LaFrance, M. & Mayo, C. Racial differences in gaze behaviour during conversations. *Journal of Personality and Social Psychology*, 1976, 33, 547-552.

Milmoe, S. Rosenthal, R. Blane, M.T. Chafetz, M. & Wolf, I. The doctor's voice: postdictor of successful referral of alcoholic patients. *Journal of Abnormal Psychology*, 1967, 72, 78-84.

Morris, D. Marsh, P. Collett, P. O'Shaugnessy, M. *Gestures; Their Origins and Distribution*. London: Cape, 1979.

Ostwald, P.F. *Soundmaking*. Springfield, Ill.: Charles T. Thomas, 1963.

Scheflen, A.E. Quasi-courtship behaviour in psychotherapy. In: S. Weitz (Ed.) *Nonverbal Communication*. New York: Oxford University Press, 1974.

Scherer, K. Acoustic concomitants of emotional dimensions: judging affect from synthesised tone sequences. In: S. Weitz (Ed.) *Nonverbal Communication*. New York: Oxford University Press, 1974.

Scherer, K. Project on vocal communication. Unpublished, University of Giessen, 1985.

Sommer, R. Studies in personal space. *Sociometry*, 1959, 22, 247-260.

Sommer, R. *Personal Space: the Behavioural Basis of Design*. Englewood Cliffs, N.J.: Prentice-Hall, 1969.

Whitcher, S.J. & Fisher, J.D. Multidimensional reaction to therapeutic touch in a hospital setting. *Journal of Personality and Social Psychology*, 1979, 37, 87-96.

Zajonc, R.B. Feeling and thinking: Preferences need no inferences. *American Psychologist*, 1980, 2, 151-176.

Zuckerman, M. Amidon, M.D. Bishop, S.E. & Pomerantz, S.D. Face and voice in the communication of deception. *Journal of Personality and Social Psychology*, 1982, 43, 347-357.

Zuckerman, M. Miserandino, M. & Bernieri, F. Civil inattention exists: in elevators. *Personality and Social Psychology Bulletin*, 1983, 9, 578-587.

CHAPTER 10

Barker, R.G. *Ecological Psychology*. Stanford: University Press, 1968.

Battistich, V.A. & Thompson, E.G. Students' perceptions of the college milieu. *Personality and Social Psychology Bulletin*, 1980, 6, 74-82.

Braginsky, D. Machiavellianism and manipulative interpersonal behaviour in children. *Journal of Experimental Social Psychology*, 1970, 6, 77-99.

Christie, R. & Geis, F.L. (Eds) *Studies in Machiavellianism*. New York: Academic Press, 1970.

Cialdini, R.B. Vincent, J.E. Lewis, S.K. Catalan, J. Wheeler, D. & Darby, B.L. A reciprocal concession procedure for inducing compliance: the door-in-the-face technique. *Journal of Personality and Social Psychology*, 1975, 21, 206-215.

Cialdini, R.B. Cacciopo, J.T. Bassett, R. & Miller, J.A. Low-ball procedure for producing compliance: commitment then cost. *Journal of Personality and Social Psychology*, 1978, 36, 463-476.

Cooper, J. & Jones, E.E. Opinion divergence as a strategy to avoid being miscast. *Journal of Personality and Social Psychology*, 1969, 13, 13-40.

Crowne, D.P. & Marlowe, D. *The Approval Motive*. New York: Wiley, 1964.

Fazio, R.H. Effrein, E.A. & Falender, V.J. Self-perceptions following social interaction. *Journal of Personality and Social Psychology*, 1981, 41, 232-242.

Forgas, J. P. The perception of social episodes: Categorical and dimensional representations in two different social milieus. *Journal of Personality and Social Psychology*, 1976, 33, 199-209.

Forgas, J. P. Social episodes and social structure in an academic setting: The social environment of an intact group. *Journal of Experimental Social Psychology*, 1978, 14, 434-448.

Forgas, J. P. *Social Episodes: The Study of Interaction Routines*. London: Academic Press, 1979.

Forgas, J.P. Episode cognition: internal representations of interaction routines. In: L. Berkowitz (Ed.) *Advances in Experimental Social Psychology*, New York: Academic Press, 1982.

Forgas, J.P. Social skills and episode perception. *British Journal of Clinical Psychology*, 1983, 22, 195-207.

Forgas, J.P. & Bond, M. Cultural differences in episode perception between Australian and Chinese students. *Personality and Social Psychology Bulletin*, 1985.

Freedman, J.L. & Fraser, S.C. Compliance without pressure: the foot-in-the-door technique. *Journal of Personality and Social Psychology*, 1966, 4, 195-202.

Gergen, K.J. & Wishnow, B. Others' self-evaluations and interaction anticipation as determinants of self-presentation. *Journal of Personality and Social Psychology*, 1965, 2, 348-358.

Goffman, E. *The Presentation of Self in Everyday Life*. New York: Doubleday, 1959.

Goffman, E. *Behaviour in Public Places*. Glencoe: The Free Press, 1963.

Haig, A. Memoirs excerpted in *Time*, 2 April 1984.

Jones, E.E. *Ingratiation*. New York: Appleton-Century-Crofts, 1964.

Jones, E.E. Gergen, K.J. & Davis, K. Some reactions to being approved and disapproved of as a person. *Psychological Monographs,* 1962, whole of issue 76.

Mead, G. H. *Mind, Self and Society*, Chicago: University of Chicago Press, 1934.

Morse, S.J. & Gergen, K.J. Social comparison, self-consistency and the concept of self. *Journal of Personality and Social Psychology*, 1970, 16, 149-156.

Newtson, D. & Czerlinsky, T. Adjustment of attitude communications for contrast by extreme audiences. *Journal of Personality and Social Psychology*, 1974, 30, 829-837.

Pervin, L.A. A free response description approach to the study of person-situation interaction. *Journal of Personality and Social Psychology*, 1976, 34, 465-474.

Schlenker, B. *Impression Management*. Monterey: Brooks-Cole, 1980.

Snyder, M. Self-monitoring of expressive behaviour. *Journal of Personality and Social Psychology*, 1974, 30, 526-537.

Snyder, M. & Monson, T.C. Persons, situations and the control of social behaviour. *Journal of Personality and Social Psychology*, 1975, 32, 637-644.

Stone, J.A. & Neale, J.M. Effects of severe daily events on mood. *Journal of Personality and Social Psychology*, 1984, 46, 137-144.

Tedeschi, J.T. (Ed.) *Impression Management Theory and Social Research*. New York: Academic Press, 1981.

Triandis, H.C. *The Analysis of Subjective Culture*. New York: Wiley, 1972.

Zanna, M.P. & Pack, S.S. On the self-fulfilling nature of apparent sex differences in behaviour. *Journal of Experimental Social Psychology*, 1975, 11, 583-591.

CHAPTER 11

Aronson, E. & Cope, V. My enemy's enemy is my friend. *Journal of Personality and Social Psychology*, 1968, 8, 8-12

Berscheid, E. & Walster, E.H. *Interpersonal Attraction*. Reading: Mass.: Addison-Wesley, 1969.

Bogardus, E.S. Measuring social distance. *Journal of Applied Sociology*, 1925, 9, 299-308.

Byrne, D. & Clore, G.L. A reinforcement model of evaluative responses. *Personality: An International Journal*, 1970, 1, 103-128.

Deaux, K. Looking at behaviour. *Personality and Social Psychology Bulletin*, 1978, 4, 207-211.

Eiser, R. *Cognitive Social Psychology*. New York: McGraw-Hill, 1980.

Eysenck, H.J. & Eysenck, S.B.G. *Personality Structure and Measurement*. London: Routledge and Kegan Paul, 1969.

Feather, N.T. A structural balance model of communication effects. *Psychological Review*, 1964, 71, 291-313.

Feather, N.T. Organization and discrepance in cognitive structures. *Psychological Review*, 1971, 78, 355-379.

Festinger, L. A theory of social comparison processes. *Human Relations*, 1954, 7, 117-140.

Festinger, L. Schachter, S. & Back, K. *Social Pressures in Informal Groups: A Study of Human Factors in Housing*. New York: Harper, 1950.

Forgas, J.P. Social episodes and social structure in an academic setting: the social environment of an intact group. *Journal of Experimental Social Psychology*, 1978, 14, 434-448.

Hebb, D.O. Drives and the CNS. *Psychological Review*, 1955, 62, 243-254.

Hess, R.H. *The Tell-tale Eye*. New York: Van Nostrand, 1975.

Jones, L.E. & Young, F.W. Structure of a social environment: longitudinal individual differences scaling of an intact group. *Journal of Personality and Social Psychology*, 1972, 24, 108-121.

Latane, B. & Bidwell, L.D. Sex and affiliation in college cafeterias. *Personality and Social Psychology Bulletin*, 1977, 3, 571-574.

Moreno, A. *Who Shall Survive? A New Approach to the Problems of Human Interrelations*. Washington, D.C.: Nervous and Mental Diseases Publishing Co. 1934.

Newcomb, T.M. *The Acquaintance Process*. New York: Holt, Rinehart & Winston, 1961.

Newcomb, T.M. Interpersonal balance. In: R.P. Abelson (Ed.) *Theories of Cognitive Consistency: A Sourcebook*. Chicago: Rand, McNally, 1968.

Rubin, Z. *Liking and Loving: An Invitation to Social Psychology*, New York: Holt, Rinehart & Winston, 1973.

Rubinstein, C.M. Shaver, P. & Peplau, L.A. Loneliness. *Human Nature*, 1979, 1, 59-65.

Sarnoff, I. & Zimbardo, P.G. Anxiety, fear and social affiliation. *Journal of Abnormal and Social Psychology*, 1961, 62, 356-363.

Schachter, S. *The Psychology of Affiliation*. Stanford: University Press, 1959.

Schultz, N.R. & Moore, P.W. Loneliness: correlates, attributions and coping among older adults. *Personality and Social Psychology Bulletin*, 1984, 10, 67-77.

Staats, A.W. & Staats, C.K. Attitudes established by classical conditioning. *Journal of Abnormal and Social Psychology*, 1958, 57, 37-40.

Suedfeld, P. Social isolation: a case for interdisciplinary research. *Canadian Psychologist*, 1974, 15, 1-15.

Swap, W.C. & Rubin, J.Z. Measurement of interpersonal orientation. *Journal of Personality and Social Psychology*, 1983, 44, 208-219.

Waller, W. *On the Family, Education and War*. (Ed. by Goode, W. Furstenberg, F. & Mitchell, L.R.). Chicago: University Press, 1970.

Zajonc, R.B. Brainswash: familiarity breeds comfort. *Psychology Today*, 1970, February, 32-35 & 60-64.

Zimbardo, P.G. *Shyness*. New York: Jove, 1977.

CHAPTER 12

Aristotle. *The Rhetoric*. New York: Appleton, 1932.

Aronson, E. Some antecedents of interpersonal attraction. In: W.J.Arnold & D. Levine (Eds) *Nebraska Symposium of Motivation*. Lincoln: University of Nebraska Press, 1969.

Aronson, E. *The Social Animal*. San Francisco: Freeman, 1976.

Aronson, E. & Linder, D. Gain and loss of self-esteem as determinants of interpersonal attractiveness. *Journal of Experimental Social Psychology*, 1965, 1, 156-171.

Aronson, E. Willerman, B. & Floyd, J. The effects of a pratfall on increasing interpersonal attractiveness. *Psychonomic Science*, 1966, 4, 157-158.

Byrne, D. *The Attraction Paradigm*. New York: Academic Press, 1971.

Byrne, D. & Blaylock, B. Similarity and assumed similarity between husbands and wives. *Journal of Abnormal and Social Psychology*, 1963, 67, 636-640.

Byrne, D. & Nelson, D. Attraction as a linear proportion of positive reinforcement. *Journal of Personality and Social Psychology*, 1965, 1, 659-663.

Clore, G.L. Wiggins, N. & Itkin, S. Gain and loss in attraction: attributions from nonverbal behaviour. *Journal of Personality and Social Psychology*, 1975, 312, 706-712.

Davis, J.D. Self disclosure in an acquaintance exercise. *Journal of Personality and Social Psychology*, 1976, 33, 787-792.

Dion, K.K. Physical attractiveness and evaluations of children's transgressions. *Journal of Personality and Social Psychology*, 1972, 24, 1311-1322.

Dion, K.K. Berscheid, E. & Walster, E. What is beautiful is good. *Journal of Personality and Social Psychology*, 1972, 24, 285-290.

Efran, M.G. The effects of physical appearance on the judgment in a simulated jury task. *Journal of Research in Personality*, 1974, 8, 45-54.

Forgas, J.P. O'Connor, K. & Morris, S. Smile and punishment: the effects of facial expression on responsibility attributions by groups and individuals. *Personality and Social Psychology Bulletin*, 1983, 9, 587-596.

Goldman, W. & Lewis, P. Beautiful is good: evidence that the physically attractive are more socially skilful. *Journal of Experimental Social Psychology*, 1977, 13, 125-130.

Griffitt, W. & Veitch, R. Pre-acquaintance attitude similarity and attraction revisited: ten days in a fall-out shelter. *Sociometry*, 1974, 37, 163-173.

Hollingshead, A.B. & Redlich, F.C. *Social Class and Mental Illness*. New York: Wiley, 1958.

Jourard, S.M. *The Transparent Self*. New York: van Nostrand, 1964.

Jourard, S.M. *Self-disclosure: An Experimental Analysis of Transparent Self*. New York: Wiley, 1971.

Kandel, D.B. Similarity in real-life adolescent friendship pairs. *Journal of Personality and Social Psychology*, 1978, 36, 306-312.

Kenrick, D.T. & Gutierres, S.E. Contrast effects and judgments of physical attractiveness. *Journal of Personality and Social Psychology*, 1980, 38, 131-140.

Kerckhoff, A.C. & Davis, K.E. Value consensus and need complementarity in mate selection. *American Sociological Review*, 1962, 27, 295-303.

Kiesler, S. & Baral, R. The search for a romantic partner. In: K.J. Gergen & D. Marlowe (Eds) *Personality and Social Behaviour.* Reading: Addison-Wesley, 1970.

Landy, D. & Sigall, H. Beauty is talent: task evaluation as a function of the performer's physical attractiveness. *Journal of Personality and Social Psychology,* 1974, 29, 299-304.

Levinger, G. Senn, D.J. & Jorgensen, B.W. Progress towards permanence in courtship: a test of the Kerckhoff-Davis hypothesis. *Sociometry,* 1970, 33, 427-443.

Levinger, G. & Snoek, J.D. *Attraction in Relationships.* Morristown: General Learning Press, 1972.

Mueser, K.T. Grau, B.W. Sussman, S. & Rosen, A. You are only as pretty as you feel: facial expression as a determinant of physical attractiveness. *Journal of Personality and Social Psychology,* 1984, 46, 469-478.

Rubin, Z. *Liking & Loving.* New York: Holt, Rinehart & Winston, 1973.

Secord, P. & Backman, C. *Social Psychology.* New York: McGraw-Hill, 1964.

Segal, M.W. Alphabet and attraction: an unobtrusive measure of the effect of propinquity in a field setting. *Journal of Personality and Social Psychology,* 1974, 30, 654-657.

Sigall, H. & Landy, D. Radiating beauty: the effects of having a physically attractive partner on person perception. *Journal of Personality and Social Psychology,* 1973, 28, 218-224.

Sigall, H. & Ostrove, N. Beautiful but dangerous: effects of offender attractiveness and nature of crime on juridic judgments. *Journal of Personality and Social Psychology,* 1975, 31, 410-414.

Touhey, J.C. Comparison of two dimensions of attitude similarity on heterosexual attraction. *Journal of Personality and Social Psychology,* 1972, 23, 8-10.

Walster, E. The effect of self-esteem on romantic liking. *Journal of Experimental Social Psychology,* 1965, 1, 184-197.

Walster, E., Aronson, E. Abrahams, D. & Rothman, L. Importance of physical attractiveness on dating behaviour. *Journal of Personality and Social Psychology,* 1966, 4, 508-516.

Winch, R.F. *Mate Selection: A Study of Complementary Needs.* New York: Harper Bros. 1958.

CHAPTER 13

American Council of Life Assurance. *The Family Economist.* 5 February, 1978.

Argyle, M. & Furnham, A. The ecology of relationships: choice of situations as a function of relationship, *British Journal of Social Psychology,* 1982, 259-262.

Berscheid, E. & Walster, E. A little bit about love. In: T.L. Huston (Ed.) *Foundations of Interpersonal Attraction.* New York: Academic Press, 1974.

Blood, R.O. & Blood, M. *Marriage.* (3rd edn) New York: Free Press, 1978.

Campbell, A. Converse, P.E. & Rodgers, W.L. *The Quality of American Life*. New York: Russell Sage Foundation, 1976.

Dermer, M. & Pyszczynski, T.A. Effects of erotica upon upon men's loving and liking responses for women they love, *Journal of Personality and Social Psychology*, 1978, 36, 1302-1309.

Driscoll, R. Davis, K.E. & Lipitz, M.E. Parental interference and romantic love: the Romeo and Juliet effect. *Journal of Personality and Social Psychology*, 1972, 24, 1-10.

Dutton, D.G. & Aron, A.P. Some evidence for heightened sexual attraction under conditions of high anxiety. *Journal of Personality and Social Psychology*, 1974, 30, 510-517.

Falbo, T. & Peplau, L.A. Power strategies in intimate relationships. *Journal of Personality and Social Psychology*, 1980, 38, 618-628.

Forgas, J.P. & Dobosz, B. Dimensions of romantic involvement: towards a taxonomy of heterosexual relationships. *Social Psychology Quarterly*, 1980, 43, 290-300.

Hill, C.T. Rubin, Z. & Peplau, L.A. Breakups before marriage: the end of 103 affairs. *The Journal of Social Affairs*, 1976, 32, 147-167.

Huston, T.L. & Burgess, R.L. Social exchange in developing relationships: an overview. In: R.L. Burgess & T.L. Huston (Eds) *Social Exchange in Developing Relationships*. New York: Academic Press, 1979.

Huston, T.L. & Levinger, G. Interpersonal attraction and relationships. *Annual Review of Psychology*, 1978, 29, 115-156.

Jaffe, D.T. & Kanter, R.M. Couple strains in communal households: a four-factor model of the separation process. *Journal of Social Issues*, 1976, 32, 169-191.

Kelley, H.H. *Personal Relationships: Their Structures and Processes*. Hillsdale, N.J.: Erlbaum, 1979.

Levinger, G. Toward the analysis of close relationships. *Journal of Experimental Social Psychology*, 1980, 16, 510-544.

Lujansky, H. & Mikula, G. Can equity theory explain the quality and the stability of romantic relationships? *British Journal of Social Psychology*, 1983, 22, 101-112.

Milardo, R.M. Johnson, M.P. & Huston, T. Developing close relationships: changing patterns of interaction between pair members and social networks. *Journal of Personality and Social Psychology*, 1983, 44, 964-976.

Morris, S.L. Conflict and conflict resolution in engagement. Unpublished Master's Thesis, Macquarie University, Sydney, 1983.

Rands, M. & Levinger, G. Implicit theories of relationship: an intergenerational study. *Journal of Personality and Social Psychology*, 1979, 37, 645-661.

Rubin, Z. *Liking and Loving*. New York: Holt, Rinehart & Winston, 1973.

Rusbult, C.E., Zembrodt, I.M. & Gunn, L.K. Exit, voice, loyalty and neglect: responses to dissatisfaction in romantic involvements. *Journal of Personality and Social Psychology*, 1982, 43, 1230-1242.

Walster, E. & Walster, G.W. *A New Look at Love*. Reading, Mass.: Addison-Wesley, 1978.

White, G.L. Fishbein, S. & Rutstein, J. Passionate love and the misattribution of arousal. *Journal of Personality and Social Psychology*, 1981, 41, 56-62.

CHAPTER 14

Allport, F.H. *Social Psychology*. Cambridge, Mass.: Riverside Press, 1924.

Asch, S.E. The effect of group pressure upon modification and distortion of judgments. In: H. Guetzkow (Ed.) *Groups, Leadership and Men*. Pittsburgh: Carnegie press, 1951.

Bond, C.F. Social facilitation: a self-presentational view. *Journal of Personality and Social Psychology*, 1982, 42, 1042-1050.

Chen, S.C. Social modification of the activity of ants in nestbuilding. *Physiological Zoology*, 1937, 10, 420-436.

Cottrell, N.B. Social facilitation. In: C.G. McClintock (Ed.) *Experimental Social Psychology*. New York: Holt, Rinehart & Winston, 1972.

Crutchfield, R.S. Conformity and character. *American Psychologist*, 1955, 10, 191-198.

Dashiell, J.F. An experimental analysis of some group effects. *Journal of Abnormal and Social Psychology*, 1930, 25, 190-199.

Deutsch, M. & Gerard, H. A study of normative and informational influence upon individual judgment. *Journal of Abnormal and Social Psychology*, 1955, 51, 629-636.

Fiedler, F. *A Theory of Leadership Effectiveness*. New York: McGraw-Hill, 1967.

Forgas, J.P. Brennan, G. Howe, S. Kane, J.F. & Sweet, S. Audience effects on squash players' performance. *Journal of Social Psychology*, 1980, 111, 41-47.

French, J.R.P. & Raven, B.H. The bases of social power. In: D. Cartwright (Ed.) *Studies in Social Power*. Ann Arbor: University of Michigan Press, 1959.

Guerin, B. & Innes, J.M. Social facilitation and social monitoring: A new look at Zajonc's mere presence hypothesis. *British Journal of Social Psychology*, 1982, 21, 7-18.

Hunt, P.J. & Hillery, J.M. Social facilitation in a coaction setting. *Journal of Experimental Social Psychology*, 1973, 9, 563-571.

Innes, J.M. & Young, R.F. The effects of presence of audience, evaluation apprehension and objective self-awareness on learning. *Journal of Experimental Social Psychology*, 1975, 11, 35-42.

Jacobs, R.C. & Campbell, D.T. The perpetuation of an arbitrary tradition through several generations of laboratory microculture. *Journal of Abnormal and Social Psychology*, 1961, 62, 649-658.

Larsson, K. *Conditioning and Behaviour in the Male Albino Rat*. Stockholm: Almquist & Wiksells, 1956.

Latane, B. & Darley, J.M. *The Unresponsive Bystander: Why Doesn't He Help?*. New York: Appleton-Century-Crofts, 1970.

Latane, B. Williams, K. & Harkins, S. Many hands make light the work: the causes and consequences of social loafing. *Journal of Personality and Social Psychology*, 1979, 37, 822-832.

Leavitt, H.J. Some effects of certain communication patterns on group performance. *Journal of Abnormal Social Psychology*, 1951, 46, 38-50.

Lewin, K. Lippitt, R. & White, R.K. Patterns of aggressive behaviour in experimentally created social climates. *Journal of Social Psychology*, 1939, 10, 271-299.

Mann, L. The effect of stimulus queues on queue-joining behaviour. *Journal of Personality and Social Psychology*, 1977, 35, 437-442.

Markus, H. The effect of mere presence on social facilitation: an unobtrusive test. *Journal of Experimental Social Psychology*, 1978, 14, 389-397.

Milgram, S. Nationality and conformity. *Scientific American*, 1961, 205, 45-51.

Milgram, S. Behavioural study of obedience. *Journal of Abnormal and Social Psychology*, 1963, 67, 376.

Milgram, S. Group pressure and action against the person. *Journal of Abnormal and Social Psychology*, 1964, 69, 137-143.

Milgram, S. Some conditions of obedience and disobedience to authority. *Human Relations*, 1965, 18, 57-76.

Milgram, S. *Obedience to Authority*. New York: Harper & Row, 1974.

Mixon, D. Instead of deception. *Journal for the Theory of Social Behaviour*, 1972, 2, 145-177.

Pessin, J. The comparative effects of social and mechanical stimulation on memorizing. *American Journal of Psychology*, 1932, 45, 263-270.

Phillips, D.P. The influence of suggestion on suicide. *American Sociological Review*, 1974, 39, 340-354.

Schachter, S. Deviation, rejection and communication. *Journal of Abnormal and Social Psychology*, Stanford: University Press, 1951.

Sherif, M. A study of some social factors in perception. *Archives of Psychology*, 1935, 187.

Shouval, R. Venaki, S.K. Bronfenbrenner, U. Devereaux, E.C. & Kiely, E. Anomalous reactions to social pressure of Israeli and Soviet children raised in family versus collective settings. *Journal of Personality and Social Psychology*, 1975, 32, 477-489.

Travis, L.E. The effect of a small audience upon eye-hand coordination. *Journal of Abnormal and Social Psychology*, 1925, 20, 142-146.

Triplett, N. The dynamogenic factors in pacemaking and competition. *American Journal of Psychology*, 1897, 9, 507-533.

Welty, J.C. Experiments in group behaviour of fishes. *Physiological Zoology*, 1934, 7, 85-128.

Zajonc, R.B. Social facilitation. *Science*, 1965,149, 269-274.

CHAPTER 15

Aronson, E. & Mills, J. The effect of severity of initiation on liking for a group. *Journal of Abnormal and Social Psychology*, 1959, 59, 177-181.

Bales, R.F. *Interaction Process Analysis: A Method for the Study of Small Groups*. Reading, Mass.: Addison-Wesley, 1950.

Brown, R. *Social Psychology*. New York: The Free Press, 1965.

Cooley, C.H. *Human Nature and the Social Order*. New York: Scribner, 1902.

Festinger, L. Informal social communication. *Psychological Review*, 1950, 57, 271-292.

Forgas, J.P. Polarization and moderation of person perception judgments as a function of group interaction style. *European Journal of Social Psychology*, 1977, 7, 175-187.

Forgas, J.P. Responsibility attribution by groups and individuals: the effects of the interaction episode. *European Journal of Social Psychology*, 1981, 11, 87-99.

Janis, I. *Victims of Groupthink*. Boston: Houghton-Mifflin, 1972.

Janis, I. & Mann, L. *Decision Making: A Psychological Analysis of Conflict, Choice and Commitment*. New York: Free Press, 1977.

Kogan, N. & Wallach, M.A. *Risk-taking: A Study in Cognition and Personality*. New York: Holt, Rinehart & Winston, 1964.

Leavitt, H.J. Some effects of certain communication patterns on group performance. *Journal of Abnormal and Social Psychology*, 1951, 46, 38-50.

Lewin, K. Frontiers in group dynamics. *Human Relations*, 1947, 1, 5-41.

Mann, L. The baiting crowd in episodes of threatened suicide. *Journal of Personality and Social Psychology*, 1981, 41, 703-709.

Moscovici, S. & Zavalloni, M. The group as a polariser of attitudes. *Journal of Personality and Social Psychology*, 1969, 12, 125-135.

Newcomb, T. *Personality and Social Change*. New York: Dryden, 1943.

Shaw, M.E. Some effects of unequal distribution of information upon group performance in various communication nets. *Journal of Abnormal and Social Psychology*, 1954, 49, 547-553.

Sherif, M. Harvey, O.J. White, B.J. Hood, W.R. & Sherif, C.W. *Intergroup Cooperation and Competition: the Robbers Cave Experiment*. Norman, Okla.: University Book Exchange, 1961.

Stouffer, S.A. et al. *Studies in Social Psychology in World War II: The American Soldier, Combat and its Aftermath*. Princeton: University Press, 1949.

Tajfel, H. (Ed.) *Differentiation Between Social Groups*. London: Academic Press, 1978.

Tajfel, H. & Forgas, J.P. Social categorisations: cognitions, values and groups. In: J.P. Forgas (Ed.) *Social Cognition: Perspectives on Everyday Understanding*. London: Academic Press, 1981.

Tuckman, B. Developmental sequence in small groups. *Psychological Bulletin*, 1965, 63, 384-399.

Turner, J. Social comparison and ethnic identity. *European Journal of Social Psychology*, 1975, 5, 5-34.

Zimbardo, P.G. The human choice: individuation, reason and order versus deindividuation, impulse and chaos. In: W.J. Arnold & D. Levine (Eds) *Nebraska Symposium on Motivation 1969*, Lincoln: University of Nebraska Press, 1970.

CHAPTER 16

Anderson, C.A. & Anderson, D.C. Ambient temperature and violent crime. *Journal of Personality and Social Psychology*, 1984, 46, 91-98.

Altman, I. *The Environment and Social Behaviour*. Monterey, Calif.: Brooks-Cole, 1975.

Argyle, M. Interaction skills and social competence. In: P. Feldman & J. Orford (Eds) *The Social Psychology of Psychological Problems*. Chichester: Wiley, 1980.

Baron, R. A. & Ransberger, V.M. Ambient temperature and the occurrence of collective violence: the 'long hot summer' revisited. *Journal of Personality and Social Psychology*, 1978, 36, 351-360.

Baum, A. & Valins, S. *Architecture and Social Behaviour: Psychological Studies of Social Density*. Hillsdale: Erlbaum, 1977.

Bower, C. & Bower, G.H. *Assert Yourself*. Englewood Cliffs, N.J.: Prentice-Hall, 1979.

Calhoun, J.B. Population density and social pathology. *Scientific American*, 1962, 206, 139-148.

Canter, D. & Stringer, P. *Environmental Interaction*. New York: International Universities Press, 1976.

Eisler, R.M. Behavioural assessment of social skills. In: M. Hersen & A. Bellack (Eds) *Behavioural Assessment*. Oxford: Pergamon Press, 1976.

Eisler, M. & Frederiksen, L.W. *Perfecting Social Skills*. New York: Plenum, 1980.

Fisher, J.D. & Byrne, D. Too close for comfort: sex differences in response to invasions of personal space. *Journal of Personality and Social Psychology*, 1975, 32, 15-21.

Gergen, K.J. Gergan, M.M. & Barton, W. Deviance in the dark. *Psychology Today*, 1973, 7, 129-130.

Ginsburg, G.P. (Ed.) *Emerging Strategies in Social Psychology*. Chichester: Wiley, 1979.

Glass, D.C. & Singer, J.E. *Urban Stress*. New York: Academic Press, 1972.

Goldstein, A. Sprafkin, R.P. & Gershaw, N.J. *Skill Training for Community Living*. New York: Pergamon Press, 1976.

Griffitt, W. Environmental effects on interpersonal affective behaviour. *Journal of Personality and Social Psychology*, 1970, 15, 240-244.

Hersen, M. & Bellack, A.S. Assessment of social skills. In: A. Ciminero, K. Calhoun & H. Adams (Eds) *Handbook of Behavioural Assessment*. New York: Wiley, 1977.

Lynch, K. *The Image of the City*. Cambridge: M.I.T. Press, 1960.

May, J.L. & Hamilton, P.A. Females' evaluations of males as a function of affect arousing music. Paper presented at the Midwestern Psychological Association Meeting, Chicago, 1977.

McGuire, W.J. The yin and the yang of progress in social Psychology: seven koan. *Journal of Personality and Social Psychology*, 1973, 3, 124-134.

Mathews, K.E. & Cannon, L.K. Environmental noise level as a determinant of helping behaviour. *Journal of Personality and Social Psychology*, 1975, 32, 571-577.

Miller, L.C. Berg, J.H. & Archer, R.L. Openers: individuals who elicit self-disclosure. *Journal of Personality and Social Psychology*, 1983, 44, 1234-1244.

Pearce, P. *The Social Psychology of Tourist Behaviour*. Oxford: Pergamon Press, 1982.

Schwarz, N. Mood and information processing. Paper given at the Tilburg Meeting of the European Association of Social Psychologists, 1984.

Schwarz, N. & Clore, G. Mood, misattribution and judgments of well-being. *Journal of Personality and Social Psychology*, 1983, 45, 513-523.

Trower, P. Bryant, B. & Argyle, M. *Social Skills and Mental Health*. London: Methuen, 1978.

Westin, A. *Privacy and Freedom*. New York: Athenaeum, 1970.

Yancey, W.L. Architecture, interaction and social control: the case of a large-scale housing project. In: J.F. Wohlwill & D.H. Carson (Eds) *Environment and the Social Sciences*. Washington: A.P.A., 1972.

INDEX